OTHER TITLES OF INTEREST FROM ST. LUCIE PRESS

REASONABLE
ACCOMMODATION
Profitable Compliance with the
Americans with Disabilities Act

REASONABLE
ACCOMMODATION

Profitable Compliance with the
Americans with Disabilities Act

JAY W. SPECHLER, PH.D., P.E.

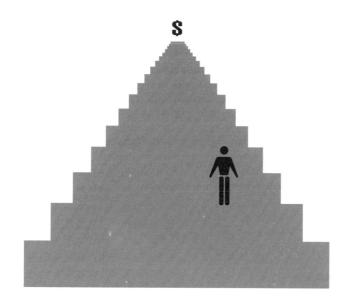

St. Lucie Press
Delray Beach, Florida

HD 7256
.U5
S64
1996X

Phone: (407) 274-9906
Fax: (407) 274-9927

S$\overset{t}{\text{L}}$

Published by
St. Lucie Press
100 E. Linton Blvd., Suite 403B
Delray Beach, FL 33483

Dedication

To my wife, Marilyn,
whose extraordinary skills as a psychotherapist
have helped so many people
cope successfully with their disabilities
and make the most of their lives.

Contents

Case Studies: Rehabilitation Organizations

Appendices

Index

Preface

This project was an eye-opener for me as an engineer and businessman working in the field of quality management. For years, I have researched and reported on the best practices in quality management. When I was asked to research the subject of the productivity of persons with disabilities in the workplace, I didn't know whether it would be greater than, equal to, or lower than that of persons without disabilities.

I decided that there was more than enough "bricks and mortar" information available on the Americans with Disabilities Act (ADA). What I would determine was whether or not business effectiveness and profitability could be maintained while employing people with disabilities. The answer is a resounding yes! In addition, an enormous amount of this research clearly demonstrates that companies can increase the bottom line by employing people with disabilities.

Reasonable Accommodation is designed as an aid to business managers in their efforts to initiate or enhance existing programs for cost-effective disability management and achieve the spirit of the ADA. The book will also serve to increase the understanding and cooperation between business and rehabilitation organizations. They have much to offer one another.

In preparing to write the book, I first surveyed over 300 companies in an effort to determine the productivity and quality performance of employees with disabilities. Three major sources were used: *Fortune* magazine's list of most admired companies, the list of America's best 100 companies to work for, and *The Economist* magazine's list of companies that provide the most value to their customers. On-site and telephone interviews were conducted to gather information on the experiences of companies employing persons with disabilities. I soon found a positive trend in the responses to this issue. Wherever I went, the answer was the same. In virtually every case, employees with disabilities were reported to be producing at levels equal to or beyond their non-disabled peers. Interestingly, for many types of disability, this would not have been the case just a few years ago. New technologies have enabled persons with disabilities to perform up to their innate potential.

Operating success requires more than combining the right people with the latest equipment. Additional keys to success are management leadership and strategy. The latter factor was thoroughly explored and the results are presented in the chapters of this book. I have incorporated these and other key factors in a model for successfully implementing the ADA presented in Chapter 2. The model is based on the successful strategies, practices, and processes found in the companies selected to be included in this book. These companies have achieved an exceptional level of success in employing persons with disabilities (success being measured by enhanced profitability and employee morale and community recognition for excellence).

Under the ADA, a company that employs 15 or more persons cannot discriminate against a qualified individual who has a disability or who is perceived to have the potential to become disabled. The ADA protects both employees and applicants with disabilities against discrimination in areas such as hiring, firing, discipline, assignments, compensation, and benefits. The ADA is not a guarantee of a job for a disabled person. It is a guarantee that persons with disabilities will be given an opportunity to demonstrate their ability to do a job.

Reasonable accommodation is a critical component of the ADA's assurance of non-discrimination. It is defined as any change in the work environment or in the way business is usually conducted that results in equal employment opportunity for an individual with a disability. Included in this book are numerous examples of reasonable accommodations for a full range of disabilities made in both manufacturing and service organizations. These examples demonstrate that most accommodations cost little or nothing. Those accommodations that cost between $1000 and $5000 (very few accommodations exceed these levels) have a very short payback period in terms of productivity and quality. In fact, many accommodations, such as job restructuring and equipment modifications, result in increased productivity for the non-disabled segment of the work force.

Employing the disabled has conclusively been demonstrated to be a win–win situation for employers and all their employees. Other stakeholders, including families of disabled persons, local communities, and taxpayers, also benefit.

My research in developing this book did reveal a significant disability management gap. Employers have not come to grips with the impact of AIDS in the workplace. Only a handful of companies have developed formal policies in this area. Very few companies have introduced awareness training programs to help their people deal with the fears and inaccurate information associated with working with fellow employees with AIDS. Companies that do not educate their managers on employer's legal responsibilities in this area are vulnerable to costly (and unnecessary) litigation and operating expense. I have, therefore, carefully researched the subject of AIDS in the workplace and included a full chapter that is must reading for every manager.

The company case studies contain many examples of training programs, policy statements, planning documents, job analysis formats, messages to employees, ADA implementation checklists, workplace assessments, ergonomic evaluations, and much more.

Rehabilitation agencies can offer considerable assistance to companies at little or no cost. Many of the chapters demonstrate the effectiveness of these liaisons and discuss the capabilities of rehabilitation organizations in training persons with disabilities in needed business skills, training businesspeople in disability management techniques, and providing on-site assistance to business in introducing persons with disabilities into the workplace. It is clear that many of the corporate success stories would not have happened without the guidance or participation of rehabilitation organizations. I have selected a group of exceptional rehabilitation organizations for inclusion in the book. They are representative of a broad spectrum of organizations that may be found throughout the United States.

Many technologies are available that greatly increase the productivity and quality performance of persons with disabilities. Digital Equipment Corporation and IBM have developed several leading-edge access technologies, and their stories are presented in Chapters 7 and 13, respectively. Other technologies that I have discovered are covered in Chapter 38.

Finally, the first chapter covers the role of the President's Committee on Employment of People with Disabilities, America's conscience for employing persons with disabilities. This organization is also a driving force in bringing the business community together on this subject. The committee is initiating new programs to involve many more businesses all over America. In my opinion, business organizations profit by being involved with the committee. The benchmarking opportunities alone are priceless. Having met with Richard Douglas, executive director of the committee, I can tell you that working with him is a most rewarding experience. His business background, government service at the state and federal levels, and unbounded energy make him the ideal executive to serve on the President's Committee.

Acknowledgments

My first point of contact with the companies and organizations I surveyed was the chief executive officer or president, who then assigned the project to the individual most closely associated with their disability management program. I offered each person the option of writing their case study with my guidance or having me write the case study based on an interview. The names of those who agreed to write their own stories appear on the first page of their respective chapters. The following individuals were generous in providing me with in-depth information and reviewing my work.

Alamo Rent A Car
Liz Clark

Bank of America
Terri Hanagan, Susan Portugal, Peter Magnani

Baylor Biomedical Services
Rex Moses

The Boeing Company and The International Association of Machinists and Aerospace Workers
Darsi Carico, Mike Earron

Commonwealth Edison
Julio Herrero, Lois Zebus

Digital Equipment Corporation
Michael Dodson, Ronald Gemma, Dr. Anthony J. Vitale

Florida Power & Light Company
Lance Craig, Robert Graham, Lynn Hayes, Ken Trueblood

General Electric Corporation
Phyllis Piano, Gerald Parks

Honeywell
J. Reed Welke, Dave Kringstad, Greg Heggberg, Henry Ryetzer, Kay Kramer

International Business Machines Corporation
Dennis O'Brien, Edward I. Shapanka, Robert B. Mahaffey

International Center for the Disabled (ICD)
Elyse M. Santucci

John Alden Life Insurance Company
Louyse Poirier, Carolyn Best

Marriott Foundation for People with Disabilities
Mark Donovan, Philip Magalong, Nancy N. Carolan

Marriott International, Inc.
Edward L. Sloan, Judi Hadfield, Janet Tully, Laura Davis

MEED Program
Stephanie T. Layton, Susan Burns Montie, Diane King

National Center for Disability Services
Lana Smart

National Leadership Coalition on AIDS
Jeff Monford

Philip Morris Companies, Inc.
Shirley Harrison, Ann Wasserman

  Philip Morris U.S.A.
  Brenda Racheau

  Miller Brewing
  Dave Brenner, Tice Nichols

  Kraft Foods, Inc.
  Chuck Reid, Gus Garcia, Alvin Cooper, Wayne Canty, Ann Bucher

Physical Ergonomics Rehabilitation Center of Dallas
James C. Brady

Physio-Control Corporation
Sandy Higgins, Brenda Draeser, Rick Karnofski, Dave Jay, LADrene Coyne

Reynolds Metals Company
J. Vernon Glenn

Texas Instruments
Cathy Allen, Debby Smelco

Trillium Employment Services
Trish Border

Union Pacific Technologies
Pat Rice, Jean Hanneke, Sandy Frazier, Ambose Maltagliati, Clarence DeGonia, Rosemary Calomese

UNUM Life Insurance Company of America
Cindy Berratta

Wausau Insurance Companies
Susan Burden Leonard, Francis Wickeham, Barbara Vosmak, Jean Matushak, Roger Lucas, Joe Calderaro

Wegmans Food Markets, Inc.
Jackie Fragassi, Rosemarie Becker

Others whose advice or effort were important to me are Elaine Abdo, Greg Balestrero, Mary O'Donnell, Larry Styron, Ray Noonan, and Johnson Edosomwan.

The Author

Jay W. Spechler, Ph.D., P.E., is President, Spechler Associates, located in Deerfield Beach, Florida. Prior to establishing his own consulting practice, he served as Director of Quality Assurance and Performance Engineering at American Express. His experience also includes working as Director of Management Services for Florida Power & Light Company, as an Internal Consulting Manager for Gulf & Western Industries, and as Director of Materials and Industrial Engineering for McCall's Printing Company.

He has conducted numerous seminars on the subjects of industrial engineering and total quality management for the American Management Association, the Japan Productivity Center in Tokyo, and other professional groups. He is an Adjunct Professor at the University of Miami and has also lectured at the University of Houston, the City College of New York, the University of Hawaii, Barry University, and Embry-Riddle Aeronautical University.

His innovative books, *Managing Quality in America's Most Admired Companies* and *When America Does It Right—Case Studies in Service Quality,* have been best-sellers since their publication in 1993 and 1988, respectively. In 1975, Prentice-Hall published his leading book in the field of physical distribution management, *Administering the Company Warehouse and Inventory Function.* His articles on various quality and business management subjects have appeared in numerous publications and professional journals.

Dr. Spechler has served as a Senior Examiner for the Malcolm Baldrige National Quality Award and is currently a Judge for the State of Florida's Sterling Quality Award and for the U.S. Department of Energy's Quality Award.

He originated the concept of modeling excellence in business and is a certified Trainer in Neuro Linguistic Programming (NLP).

The Role of the President's Committee on Employment of People with Disabilities and the Americans with Disabilities Act

1

An Interview with Richard Douglas,
Executive Director, The President's Committee

The President's Committee was established in 1947 to provide government agencies and businesses with information and guidance on returning World War II veterans with disabilities. It was first called the President's Committee on the Employment of the Handicapped. An early initiative of the committee was the creation of "Hire the Handicapped Week," which was discontinued when it was recognized that the term "handicapped" was a symbol of American poor thinking, exclusion, and paternalistic attitudes toward individuals with disabilities; it was one of the problematic symbols of the past. The word handicapped was first used in Britain after the Crimean War. Medicine had advanced to a point where large numbers of soldiers returned home with injuries that would have proved fatal in earlier wars. To aid the severely disabled men, Parliament made it legal for war veterans to beg on the streets; they could keep a "cap handy" to accept donations from passersby. Because the word handicapped thus implies making beggars out of people with disabilities, the term is not acceptable. The preferred term is "people with disabilities."

The President's Committee underwent a revolution in its approach in the late 1980s with development of a format of independence; it began to draft the

1

Americans with Disabilities Act (ADA) with the publication of a document entitled "Toward Independence" in 1986. It was drafted by members of the National Council of the President's Committee, including, among others, such notables as Justin Dart, the best-known disability rights leader in America; Joe Dusenberry, a well-known rehabilitation specialist in America; and Len Frieden, noted independent living advocate, who was the executive director of the National Council on Disability at that time. The document served as a blueprint for empowerment and civil rights for persons with disabilities. "Toward Independence" created particular excitement within the disability community because it was published during a conservative administration, and it included a letter of support signed by President Reagan. Justin Dart and others began to recognize that this was a civil rights issue and needed to be addressed from a civil rights standpoint, with a view toward ending discrimination in the workplace, in transportation, and in communications. Senators Harkin, Dole, Kennedy, and others lent their support to a draft of the ADA in 1988. This created a maelstrom of support which was originally initiated by House majority whip Tony Coelho, whose lifelong experience with epilepsy made him an excellent choice to begin the process of drafting its subsequent refinements within Congress. Bipartisan support helped pass the act in 1990. President Bush said that if Congress passed the act, he would sign it, and by saying so overcame conservative opposition. The president was assisted by Dick Thornburg, attorney general at the time, whose son had a traumatic brain injury; Evan Kemp, who is disabled by muscular dystrophy and was then chair of the Equal Employment Opportunity Commission; and Justin Dart, who was appointed chairman of the President's Committee on Employment of People with Disabilities. On July 26, 1990, at the largest ceremony ever held on the White House lawn, with over 3000 in attendance, President Bush signed the bill which brought the ADA into existence.

How did you come to be involved with the committee?

I have had multiple sclerosis for over 20 years and am the first executive director of the President's Committee to have a disability. In fact, for the first 40 years of the committee's existence, the disability community's leadership was largely excluded from the committee due to paternalistic views at the time.

For me, when over 20 years ago I became physically disabled, I felt that something was very wrong with public policy. Why couldn't I get on the bus? Why couldn't I find a place to park? Why were the bathrooms so difficult? Why couldn't I get into the mall? Why when I looked through the personnel manuals of the companies that I worked for were none of my issues covered, while those of women and minorities were. Eventually, it became clear to me that those government agencies that were supposed to help the disabled were in fact victimized by negative social attitudes.

I began as a volunteer who had a disability with a business background and eventually became my state's vocational rehabilitation director. After six years there, I moved to the President's Committee as executive director in 1991.

What is the President's Committee doing today?

Today, the President's Committee is composed of 35 staff members and several hundred volunteers. With the passage of the ADA, the President's Committee became much more involved with the issues faced by individuals with disabilities. The President's Committee also administers the Job Accommodation Network (JAN), which provides information on accommodation technologies, equipment, and systems for people with physical or mental disabilities on the job. In the month that I joined the President's Committee, March 1991, JAN received 800 calls. A symbol of the interest and change in American business toward individuals with disabilities can be seen in the fact that the number of calls received by the JAN in March 1994, just three years later, was 6000!

The mission of the President's Committee is basically to focus on the empowerment through employment of persons with disabilities and to help the business community in understanding, applying, and communicating the needs of individuals with disabilities. The purpose of the President's Committee is to address the fears, myths, misinformation, and prejudices associated with the disabled community and to provide a forum for business, labor, and others to deal with the significant employment issues.

What are some of these issues?

One example of implementing the committee's mission can be seen in a 1993 teleconference project report of the President's Committee on Employment of People with Disabilities. This report, titled "Operation People First: Toward a National Disability Policy," is based on over 60 teleconference meetings with more than 1000 disability community leaders in all states and territories. It points to the need for a cohesive national policy on disability. The nation lacks coordinated and comprehensive policy and laws which are consistent with and supportive of the ADA and which can bring people with disabilities into the political, economic, and social mainstream of our culture. The ADA provides the legal framework for achieving equality and empowerment for America's 49 million citizens with physical and mental disabilities. Coordinated policy and programs consistent with the purposes of the ADA would establish the foundation on which individuals with disabilities can build in reordering our society from one which fosters exclusion, dependence, and paternalism to one which promotes inclusion, independence, and empowerment. Here are some of the report's conclusions and recommendations.

Disability Action Plan—The report states that, as a nation, we lack a coordinated and comprehensive policy toward disability that is in accord with the ADA. The ADA has been a major first step toward creating a structure of empowerment for people with disabilities to maximize their potential. But it is not by itself enough. America needs a comprehensive disability policy. Laws, regulations, programs, and services on both the federal and state level need to be revisited to ensure that they are philosophically and programmatically in tune with the spirit and letter of the ADA. Everything should be put on the table: state workers' compensation laws, healthcare reform, Social Security Administration disability programs, housing services, transportation services, welfare programs, tax code provisions related to disability, vocational rehabilitation, developmental disability laws and programs, etc. They should all be reworked as needed to develop a coordinated, philosophically consistent national disability policy that empowers people with disabilities and puts them in control of their own destiny. The fragmented array of services now available need to be coordinated and made more easily accessible to people with disabilities. Government jurisdiction over disability needs to be rationalized and ordered to ensure clear communication of national priorities and goals.

The primary recommendation of this report is that the federal government undertake the development of a coordinated, comprehensive national disability policy that is driven by and consistent with the ADA. This policy should be developed over the next several years, complete with legislative language, regulatory and programmatic change, and budget recommendations. It should then be presented to the President and the Congress.

The report commented on ADA implementation and its effect. Though significant advances have been made in many areas due to the ADA, participants in nearly every state complained of a slow response by state and local government officials in implementing and enforcing the law and by the business community—particularly small business—in complying with its provisions.

Numerous states were specifically named by participants as taking a "wait-and-see" attitude toward ADA enforcement and implementation.

Participants in the teleconference meetings developed a list of recommendations for the federal government to increase the effectiveness and efficiency of the ADA:

1. Improve and increase efforts to educate employers and state and local government officials about the ADA.

2. Provide strong leadership from the White House on ADA enforcement.

3. Develop, refine, and better communicate methods of "reasonable accommodation," in particular, the accommodation needs of people with mental

health conditions, developmental disabilities, learning disabilities, brain injuries, chronic fatigue syndrome, and multiple chemical sensitivity.

4. Develop and institute alternative methods of dispute resolution and mediation to speed the enforcement and implementation of the ADA.

5. Provide larger staffs for Department of Justice and the Equal Employment Opportunity Commission for ADA enforcement and claims investigation.

Furthermore, recommendations to government were made. Government should lead by forming partnerships with business, state and local governments, the schools, and the disability community to create integrated programs that meet the needs of everyone.

Government could also facilitate employment by establishing a national database or archive of job opportunities and training programs for people with disabilities.

The current administration should immediately take steps to change Medicaid waiver procedures to allow states to pursue innovative strategies for more community-based services for people with disabilities and to mandate the closing of inappropriate, dehumanizing institutions for people with developmental and psychiatric disabilities. Special initiatives need to be designed to improve the whole spectrum of services available in rural areas. In particular, more transportation services should be established for people with disabilities.

Likewise, initiatives targeted at other underserved populations, including elderly persons and minorities with disabilities, need to be developed.

The disability leaders made recommendations to business. Business should take proactive steps to comply with the ADA and to recruit, hire, train, and retain people with disabilities.

Employers should seek out more information on the ADA and become better informed about different kinds of "reasonable accommodations," particularly for people with cognitive and psychiatric disabilities. The JAN, sponsored by the President's Committee on Employment of People with Disabilities, is a valuable resource which can play an important role in this educational process.

Recommendations to media were made as well. The media should seek to cover people with disabilities in a responsible, dignified manner and eschew coverage which condescends, pities, or demeans people with disabilities.

The media should focus coverage of people with disabilities on positive accomplishments, successful integration into the mainstream, and the civil rights struggle of the ADA. People with disabilities must be covered as people first, not as representative "disability types."

Film and television media should seek to include people with disabilities as real, central characters in programming. People with disabilities need to be seen as normal, capable, three-dimensional individuals with human needs and human problems, including involvement in romantic and sexual relationships.

The advertising community should include people with disabilities in advertising imagery and media. The 49 million Americans with disabilities represent an enormous potential market to which the advertising and business communities should appeal directly.

Like every other sector of the employment community, the media should provide opportunities for qualified people with disabilities to work as reporters, anchors, editors, and correspondents.

Finally, recommendations were also made to the disability community. People with disabilities should empower themselves by becoming fully educated about their rights and responsibilities under the ADA and actively seek to defend those rights and advocate on behalf of themselves in all public forums, including the media and governmental arenas.

People with disabilities should consider greatly expanding an existing national organization, or creating a new one, to advocate their civil and social rights. Although various disability constituencies have excellent advocacy representatives in Washington, there is no organization with the staff and the responsibility to represent the disability community as a whole.

All disability constituencies and organizations should work together, building effective coalitions and presenting a united front in order to be maximally effective in political struggles at all levels of government, particularly the state and local levels.

What else is business doing on ADA implementation?

It is important to note that the companies that have developed a diverse work force do so more for economic reasons than for social reasons. These companies tell us that they develop diverse work forces which include people with disabilities not for reasons of compassion but because it makes economic sense.

In recent years, there has been a significant positive shift in attitude about persons with disabilities. Surveys show that 90% of Americans believe that hiring persons with disabilities is a good thing. The media is beginning to treat us as normal people rather than objects of pity or courageous heroes. In further support of this positive trend is the increasing confidence on the part of the disability community that they can be successful.

Of course, there have been and continue to be barriers to the successful advocacy and empowerment of people with disabilities. These barriers include:

1. The possibility of discouragement and apathy in the disability community. The disability community cannot slacken its efforts with the passage

of the ADA; it needs to be an advocate and use every opportunity to demonstrate and point out where change is needed.

2. More focus needs to be given by the media to their treatment of persons with disabilities. For every story that is balanced and shows persons with disabilities living normal lives and working at ordinary jobs, there are many more that are not focused that way. There are no courses in journalism at the college level that provide instruction on how to interview the disabled or how to present a balanced view of their lives. A liberal, TV station in Minneapolis recently ran a story of a man in a wheelchair having his pocket picked. The station was all for inclusion of people with disabilities and thought that this would make an appropriate story. A disability leader in the community called the station and asked, "Why did you cover that? Would you have covered the story if the man hadn't been in a wheelchair?" The news broadcaster replied that he saw the point that it could have happened to anybody.

3. There is concern over attacks on the ADA and suggestions that it should be repealed. In recent months, there has been a lot of controversy over the ADA being an unfunded federal mandate. The United States Conference of Mayors said that it was, and that the costs of implementing the ADA in municipalities and making a municipal building accessible, meaning the Title II requirements, was wrong in passing the costs on to the states and cities. The answer to that is that the costs of implementing civil rights laws have always—since the writing of the Declaration of Independence—been passed on to the states, cities, counties, and municipalities. Some mayors still take the position that exercising civil rights for their citizens is too expensive. This is a tremendous worry, and the disability community must be alert to and challenge that position whenever it is presented.

4. We are concerned about any possible momentum away from including persons with disabilities and that negative attitudes will become hardened through a backlash effort.

5. Businesses need to be convinced that including persons with disabilities is an economic advantage. Based on many years of operating experience and after analyzing tens of thousands of actual accommodation cases, the President's Committee's JAN has discovered that the costs of accommodating a person on the job are negligible.

   - 88% cost less than $1000

   - 69% cost less than $500

- 50% cost less than $50

- 31% of accommodations cost nothing

Where costs are involved, substantial public funds are available to assist businesses. Interestingly, many accommodations are readily adopted by the non-disabled population. For example, when given a choice between steps and a ramp, 80% of people without disabilities choose to use the ramp.

6. Legislative issues such as universal healthcare, better education for disabled children, and social security legislation encourage people to work their way off benefits rather than making it virtually impossible for them to do so.

A key point that everyone needs to know is that the disability issue is a very personal issue. We all know persons with disabilities, and most people have disabled individuals in their families. The economic, social, and personal costs of not including persons with disabilities in the mainstream of business and personal affairs is enormous. We all need to be vocal advocates for people with disabilities.

The Americans with Disabilities Act—Here is some guidance to business persons who want to know the key elements of the ADA.

1. The ADA was enacted to prohibit discrimination against people with disabilities. It is intended to help eliminate attitudinal barriers (prejudice, myth, stereotype) toward people with disabilities in employment and inclusion in mainstream America.

2. The ADA was created to eliminate architectural, transportation, and communication barriers.

The federal government is covered by the Vocational Rehabilitation Act of 1973, Section 501. The ADA is a timely reminder of what the feds should have been doing for almost 20 years.

If you put the ADA and the Vocational Rehabilitation Act to work using common sense and a "treat others as you want to be treated" attitude, you would be moving closer to meeting the requirements of the laws while creating a more competent and diverse workplace. What's more, you might also find that you have become closer to your customers and developed new and growing services that enrich your·effectiveness and productivity.

Some Demographics—There are an estimated 49 million Americans with disabilities. About one-third work, but many millions more are capable and willing. The cost of neglecting people with disabilities as a viable work force has been enormous—an estimated $200 billion annually in public and private payments, according to White House statistics. What's more, another $100 billion is lost each year in unrealized wages and taxes—a very unfortunate bottom line, most executives agree. Not to mention the waste of human potential.

These economic factors along with the civil rights issues of discrimination toward people with disabilities were the prime driving factors in the passage of the ADA.

If your information and services are not reaching Americans with disabilities, you are not doing your job. Researchers who study the size of the market of persons with disabilities claim that one out of eight Americans currently has a physical or mental disability (close to 20% of the population). Because of improvements in trauma care, better medical interventions and rehabilitation, prenatal and neonatal care, and improved geriatric medicine for our growing population of elders (soon to be us), it is estimated that by the year 2000, one out of five Americans or 20% of our population will have a disability. This is a huge customer base to consider.

What must I know about hiring?

Most executives are familiar with the Civil Rights Act of 1964 and its anti-discrimination provisions for women and minorities. The ADA provides similar protection for people with disabilities.

You need to know the definition of disability under the ADA. Disability is defined as a physical or mental impairment that substantially limits one or more major life activities, such as walking, talking, seeing, hearing, learning, breathing, or working, or having a record of such an impairment or being regarded as having one. Most people say they can much more easily understand this definition which focuses on the functional limitation rather than the disability label which can be vague or confusing.

There are many resources at the state level, including the public vocational rehabilitation program, and unions provide not-for-profit rehabilitation organizations. They are in your phone book.

Next, remember that *a person with a disability must be qualified and able to perform the essential functions of the job.* Those "essential functions" are the tasks that are fundamental and intrinsic to the job. Many employers are looking at job descriptions to be sure they describe what is done and how it is done. Understanding essential functions is particularly important to prepare for applicant interviews.

It will help you to know about reasonable accommodation. Reasonable accommodation on the job, when needed, assists the person with a disability to perform job duties. I use a wheelchair, so reasonable accommodation is first being able to access the building, the office, and the files, and that may mean ensuring that a desk is the right height. Raising a desk to accommodate my wheelchair may mean using wooden blocks to prop it up and moving furniture so I can get around the office. The applicant or employee is responsible for requesting an accommodation. This may mean restructuring the job, modifying work schedules, or providing aids or services. Employers who have experience with reasonable accommodation have found that the cost of a job or work environment accommodation is not high, with the average being $500. Close to 90% of accommodations cost less than $1000.

What about the hiring process?

A few do's and don'ts might be helpful here:

- *Do* focus on the job requirements and the person's abilities.
- *Don't* focus on the disability.
- *Do* ask candidates if they can perform the essential job functions.
- *Don't* ask whether the candidate has a disability or the severity of it.
- *Do* allow potential workers to describe how they can perform a job.
- *Don't* assume that doing the job is impossible.
- *Do* allow the candidate to request reasonable accommodation. It is the responsibility of the job candidate to inform the employer of any accommodation needs.
- *Do* expect the same job performance of an employee with a disability as anyone else.

Simply put, the ADA and the Vocational Rehabilitation Act are really about just two things. They are about *opening your mind* and *opening your facilities and services*. And finally, what they are about once again is attitude. An executive who understands this will look for the ability and not the disability.

A Ten-Step Process for Implementing the Americans with Disabilities Act Criteria

2

The model outlined below has been developed from the successful strategies applied by the companies profiled in this book. Several of the chapters include detailed outlines and content of training programs that can be used in developing a training program that is appropriate for your own organizational needs. The case studies can also serve as excellent sources for benchmarking key issues as you move to implement new or enhance existing efforts to comply with or go beyond the requirements of the Americans with Disabilities Act (ADA).

The Ten Steps

1. Consider the Existing Organizational Framework

Research into the best practices of and positive results achieved by leading companies in the field of disability management indicates that these companies thoughtfully evaluated three organizational factors as they implemented their processes. The evaluations resulted in well-balanced approaches that set the stage for success.

The first factor considered is the *culture* of the organization, which is represented by the sum of beliefs and resulting behaviors that take place throughout the organization. All of the companies discussed in this book have a strong belief in the value-added contribution that persons with disabilities can make toward achieving the mission of the organization. This belief is projected throughout the organization—at all levels and in all functions. The result of this strong belief is enhanced profitability and organizational morale.

Several companies whose cultures are heavily team oriented have taken a bottom-up approach toward building programs to introduce persons with disabilities. In these cases, middle managers take initiatives for pilot programs, training efforts, and working with community agencies. Resulting success stories are informally communicated throughout the organization and implementation efforts are expanded. Other companies whose cultures are highly structured take a more formal approach. In these cases, senior management plays a major role in the start-up phase and on an ongoing basis. Through senior management's visibility, the organization recognizes that employing persons with disabilities is an important objective. Implementation is swift and efforts are well documented. Continuing efforts are often given additional support by staff members trained in disability management and accommodation techniques.

Several companies whose management would have liked their disability processes to have been included in this book, but are not, were found to be lacking in the cultural attributes necessary for success. Their people did not believe that employing people with disabilities meant anything other than strict, minimum compliance with the law. Passive resistance and avoidance of the issue was apparent.

The second factor considered is the company's **technological structure**. This factor encompasses physical infrastructure and includes items such as computer software and hardware configurations, ergonomic considerations, and the level of automation. New technologies for the disabled have opened up opportunities for blind and physically disabled persons to participate in the most highly sophisticated computer-intensive operations in both manufacturing and service organizations. The levels of productivity and quality performance of employees with disabilities are often higher than their non-disabled peer group. The case studies in this book demonstrate this time after time.

Finally, the company's **management system** needs to be taken into account. The management system defines the effectiveness of those processes by which an organization manages its human and physical assets. Effectiveness is defined by the following algorithm:

$$\text{Effectiveness} = \frac{\text{Productivity} \times \text{Quality}}{\text{Investment}}$$

The case studies in this book demonstrate the many ways in which management and all employees are achieving greater operating effectiveness (which translates into greater profitability) through retaining and hiring persons with disabilities. Most accommodations require a modest investment that has a fast payback.

The early return-to-work programs discussed in several of the chapters, for example, cost little or nothing to implement but have been documented as savings millions of dollars. Another example can be seen in the retention of a scientist with a severe back impairment through ergonomic redesign of his office (which included a water bed). His creative designs were a major factor in his company's (USBI) winning a NASA contract.

2. Management Policies and Values

Virtually all of the companies included in this book have developed formal management policies and value statements that cover the ADA and persons with disabilities. Many also include in their policy statements how their values bear on the subject in terms of human relations. The policy statements clearly portray what the companies wish to achieve; the value statements cover the ways in which people should work together as they strive to get there.

3. Assessment

Most successful implementations have been preceded by an assessment of the status of disability management programs and employing persons with disabilities. In some cases, the assessment is conducted by trained internal staff and in others by outside consultants; some companies utilize the services of rehabilitation agencies. Where consultants are used, they are often disabled persons themselves. Models of assessments covering physical access and reasonable accommodations are presented in several of the chapters.

4. Implementation Design Team

Implementation design teams or task forces are frequently used to ensure complete and coordinated efforts toward assuring full compliance with both the letter and the spirit of the ADA. These teams are composed of representatives from human resources, safety, finance, data services, legal, corporate communications, operations, and other key departments.

5. Implementation Planning

Implementation planning involves the preparation of formal project plans that show tasks, persons, or departments responsible and respective completion dates. Periodic progress meetings are held, with written status reports explaining reasons for any delays in the schedule and revised completion dates if necessary. Examples of implementation planning formats are provided in the chapters.

6. Training

Virtually all of the successful companies have introduced some level of training for management and other employees. Training runs the gamut from familiarization with the ADA to sensitivity and awareness training. In some cases, well-designed videotape presentations are used along with workshops or seminars. Many companies utilize training programs provided by rehabilitation organizations.

Several of the companies profiled in this book generously contributed the details of their training programs.

7. Benefit from Professional Resources and Liaisons

Union–management liaisons have been particularly effective in the design and implementation of early return-to-work programs. The Industry-Labor Council's National Center for Disability Services, the National Leadership Coalition on AIDS, state and private rehabilitation agencies, and others can provide valuable assistance in developing successful training programs. Other resources such as the Marriott Foundation's "Bridges...From School to Work" program and Miami-Dade Community College's MEED Program for microcomputer education and training offer participation in internship and recruitment. Additional resources are listed in Appendices I and III.

8. Use of Technologies and Systems

Included in this book are numerous examples that demonstrate how individuals with a broad range of disabilities can be accommodated through the use of new technologies and integrated computer systems. These technologies have come into use within the last few years and have opened up a vast new world of opportunity for employers to hire exceptionally well-qualified people who were previously difficult to position in companies. For example, totally blind telephone customer service representatives working in high-tech computer database environments are able to perform as effectively as their non-disabled peers. They are able to perform in this capacity because of speech synthesis and supporting technology along with their "speed listening" capability. Speed listening enables the blind customer service representative to simultaneously *hear* information appearing on computer screens while listening and responding to customer inquiries. Customers are unaware of the fact that they are speaking to a blind person. See Chapters 7 and 13 for additional details. Other chapters also include examples of accommodations that make use of similar systems and technologies.

9. Develop a Communications Plan

Supporting all of the above actions is a communications plan that informs all persons in the company about the steps being taken toward implementing or enhancing disability management efforts. A variety of media are used for this purpose, including annual reports, videotapes, company newsletters, distribution of articles on disability subjects, brochures and bulletins from outside agencies, group discussions in departments where persons with disabilities will be introduced for the first time, and publication of implementation planning progress reports.

When starting from scratch in developing a plan for disability management and employing persons with disabilities, a time line covering the introduction of various aspects of the plan is created. The time line may span an initial period of two or more year, with ongoing efforts beyond that time. One of the first items to be communicated is a top management policy statement (several are shown in the chapters). Other items that are typically publicized include ADA requirements and conformance schedules, statistical profiles of persons with disabilities, proper etiquette in speaking to employees and customers with disabilities, education on AIDS in the workplace, case histories and success stories of persons with disabilities within and outside the company, outside resources available to persons with disabilities, internal resources available, listings of educational programs, and descriptions of accommodations made, among many other items.

Some companies have created newsletters dedicated to the subject of disabilities. Honeywell's is called "CHED Cable" (Council of Honeywell Employees with Disabilities).

10. Follow-Through

One of the least heralded factors in successful efforts is following through on employee perceptions of program success. One measure of success is the rate at which individuals disclose their disabilities. Many of the companies participating in this work can provide the number of persons with disabilities as a percentage of the total work force, and they also break that statistic down by type of disability. High disclosure rates indicate a corporate culture embedded with mutual trust.

Some employees who were interviewed said that they wished that management would ask them what they needed and commented further on how company effectiveness could be improved if they were asked for their ideas on access and other accommodations. These employees indicated that they are reluctant to volunteer information but would gladly give it if asked.

At least one company employs a disabilities ombudsman to encourage disclosure and a free exchange of information. Several organizations have disability specialists on their human resource staffs who follow-up on how well accommodations made are working out and what people's needs and perceptions are.

CASE STUDIES: COMPANIES

AT&T **3**

Elizabeth P. Dixon, Manager,
Corporate Equal Opportunity/Affirmative Action

Before you can understand the process of making "reasonable accommodations" at AT&T, you need to understand a bit about the background of the company and its philosophy. As of September 1993, AT&T was made up of approximately 260,000 employees. This is a dramatic decrease in population since the 1984 break up of the Bell System. The corporation is organized along business Unit lines with administrative functions decentralized, receiving direction from a small centralized corporate policy group. Such employee services as benefits and health affairs are also provided by a corporate-wide organization. Portions of the AT&T employee population are also represented by two labor unions, the Communications Workers of America and the International Brotherhood of Electrical Workers. It is therefore easy to see that there are many places to which an individual employee can turn for assistance, depending on the nature of his or her concern.

AT&T, as a federal contractor, has been subject to the requirements of Section 503 of the Rehabilitation Act of 1973, as amended, since its inception. Therefore, the advent of the Americans with Disabilities Act of 1990 (ADA) had little effect on AT&T's policy of providing reasonable accommodations for applicants and employees with disabilities. The company places ultimate responsibility and accountability for making reasonable accommodations within the normal duties of each manager and supervisor. However, recognizing that most managers do not have the knowledge or expertise to research complex accommodations for their employees with disabilities, AT&T makes available a group of trained and company-certified Job Accommodation Specialists to assist with this process.

Job Accommodation Specialists

This is a good place to describe AT&T's network of Job Accommodation Specialists (JAS). As mentioned, these individuals are available to assist managers and supervisors when they need or are asked to make reasonable accommodations for applicants and employees with disabilities. They hold positions in many of the AT&T Business Units and in the more centralized National Personnel Services Organization, which delivers many human resource services to Business Units on a contract basis. Being a JAS is often only part of any individual's duties, but some will say it is the most interesting and sometimes the most rewarding part.

The JAS program was started at AT&T in 1982 and thus pre-dates the ADA. It is, however, of great assistance to AT&T in complying with the act. Over the years, the training and certification program has evolved into its present three-and-a-half-day format of lecture, discussion, classroom exercise, and hands-on practice. Speakers from within AT&T and from outside discuss a variety of topics, including disability legislation, the consumer's role in making reasonable accommodations, AT&T corporate policies and practices, using medical resources, internal and external resources and technology, developing a job analysis technique, accommodation alternatives, and upper management support for making reasonable accommodations. Former seminar participants also meet with the students to discuss their experiences and any unique accommodation situations they have encountered.

The most important, and some say the most useful, part of the training occurs on the final day. In the morning, students are divided into teams, and each team is given an accommodation situation to work through. This in itself is not unique. What makes it special is that each team works with a volunteer AT&T manager with an actual AT&T job description. Each team also works with a volunteer AT&T employee who has a disability. The assignment is to determine what accommodation alternatives may be appropriate for that individual in that job. Students have an entire morning to begin working through the process. They are encouraged to use resources they have learned about, to make a site visit, to tour the building with the employee with the disability, and to talk to peers and co-workers. Some management volunteers have really gotten into the spirit of the exercise by calling mock staff meetings to discuss the situation and by insisting that the accommodation team discuss accommodation alternatives with their upper management. Other management and disabled volunteers have met beforehand to develop their own scenario for the morning discussions. The afternoon is spent in team readouts of the morning's findings and discussion of what was done well and some alternate approaches. In some ways, the volunteers get as much out of the training as the students. Managers get a chance to interact with employees with disabilities and learn from them. Disabled volunteers broaden their AT&T contacts and sometimes discover new accommodation alternatives which they can take back to their regular jobs and discuss with their management.

To date, about 150 individuals have gone through the program since 1982. Currently, 125 individuals are on the JAS list, and approximately 75 perform the JAS function as part of their assigned responsibilities. Through electronic mail and other contacts, AT&T's JAS share information among themselves on unusual accommodation situations, local sources of technical assistance, and other areas of interest. They also may form ad hoc teams to work on specific issues of concern to their various Business Units or the corporation as a whole.

General Philosophy

AT&T does not hire people with disabilities because it is a nice thing to do, nor does the company have specific jobs for people with disabilities. AT&T hires and retains qualified people with the skills and expertise to move the corporation ahead; if these individuals happen to have disabilities, AT&T makes the appropriate reasonable accommodations if possible. It is in fact possible that some individuals with disabilities may possess skills and knowledge not as likely to be found in the non-disabled population. For example, when AT&T began staffing its various telecommunications relay centers throughout the country, the company was interested in people who had an intimate knowledge of deaf culture to fill community outreach positions in these centers. While such knowledge may be found in the hearing community, it is much easier to find qualified people to fill such positions who are themselves a part of the deaf community. When one of the Business Units needed to evaluate how compatible its computer technology was with assistive devices for blind computer users, it hired an individual with excellent computer skills who also happened to be blind and had a good working knowledge of the available assistive technology.

In keeping with AT&T's stated policy of hiring qualified people to fill available jobs, it is possible to find people with disabilities in a variety of positions within the company. The vice president–data processing services for AT&T Universal Card Services happens to be blind, but he holds the position because he was the best qualified person to do the work. People who are blind serve in other areas such as customer service and billing, telecommunications relay services, training sales personnel, computer programming, electrical engineering, and equal opportunity/affirmative action/diversity work. Aside from working in the Telecommunications Relay Centers, people who are deaf or hard of hearing work as secretaries to AT&T executives, clerks in international finance operations, computer technicians, and human resource specialists. People with various forms of mobility impairments fill positions as specialists in financial management, telemarketing, and equipment sales and troubleshooting for large companies and the federal government.

Although it would seem, from this brief recitation of the types of jobs AT&T employees with disabilities hold, that the company only accommodates physical disabilities, that is far from true. However, mental or emotional disabilities are much more difficult to describe, although accommodating them may take the same amount of effort and cost less. For example, an autistic individual does data entry work at a corporate training facility, and an individual with Down's syndrome performs various tasks in the main mailroom at the New Jersey headquarters building. The accommodations for this individual will be discussed in greater detail shortly.

Examples of Specific Accommodations

Now that you understand the corporate structure and general philosophy of making reasonable accommodation at AT&T, a discussion of some specific situations will be easier to understand.

Chief Financial Officer's Organization

An individual who is quadriplegic was interviewed and hired for a job in the chief financial officer's organization. During the hiring process, certain accommodations were made: a table was raised high enough for him to get his wheelchair under so he could take the standard management employment tests, and he was granted additional time to complete the tests to accommodate his limited ability to write quickly. After he was hired, the group with whom he would be working expressed some concerns about various aspects of his employment. Over a period of approximately a year, these issues were worked out with the assistance of various groups and organizations, including the local JAS, health affairs, benefits, and the corporate law division.

One of the easiest things to do was to provide an additional set of hand splints. The individual had designed his own, but wanted an extra set so he would not have to carry them back and forth between home and the office. The splints make it possible for him to use the computer more efficiently. The most important thing, however, was establishing a level of understanding within the work group. Before the newly hired individual actually reported for work, he visited the work site and met his co-workers. Since many of them had never worked with anyone who had a visible disability, they had many questions and concerns. The local JAS arranged a meeting at which the group could discuss concerns and ask questions. What was scheduled as a one-hour introductory meeting turned into a four-hour question and answer session, but the result was that everyone felt more comfortable. The opportunity to communicate made co-workers more comfortable and more willing to provide additional assistance, such as pulling reports off the printer or retrieving needed medication from a shirt pocket.

During the next two years, additional accommodations were made, mostly by the employee himself. These included the purchase of a new powered wheel-chair and a new van with a lift. Additional meetings were held to discuss accommodations needed when the medical facility in the employee's work location was closed for budget reasons. The employee had been relying on personnel from that office to assist with personal care needs, but an alternative was found through discussions with the employee.

One important matter which is often overlooked was discussed very early in the accommodation process—the need for an evacuation plan in case of emergency. Both internal and community safety personnel were notified and an evacuation plan was established and, most important, practiced so all would know what to expect. Fortunately, there has been no need to put this plan into effect, but it is still practiced whenever there is an emergency drill at that facility.

Human Resources

The accommodation situation was somewhat different for a vision-impaired employee who works in the AT&T Corporate Human Resources organization. Over the years, she has used various assistive devices to magnify both printed material and characters on the computer screen. Recently, computer equipment within her organization was upgraded for the rest of the work force. However, due to the limitations of her assistive devices, which were only compatible with the old 6300 type computer, it was not possible to upgrade her equipment unless additional assistive technology was also purchased. Because the employee had over the years developed relationships with accessible technology vendors, locating appropriate hardware and software was simple. Management agreed that the new equipment would enhance the employee's productivity, and a means of funding the purchase was determined.

When the new equipment (a board for the computer and some additional software) arrived, company computer technicians were called upon to ensure compatibility of all systems. The new equipment has allowed the employee to increase her use of the computer, although compatibility problems still exist which make it impossible for her to access a specific reports system. This issue is still being worked on and is expected to be resolved by the time additional network software is installed.

Building Services

So far, accommodations for physical disabilities have been discussed, although some of these accommodations have more to do with attitude than technology or access. Accommodating a mental or emotional disability may take a great deal less technology, but it often involves more thoughtful consideration and ingenuity. An individual with Down's syndrome is a productive member of the employee team working in the main mailroom at the AT&T New Jersey Headquarters building. This team is responsible for receiving, sorting, and delivering mail for over 3000 people, and the mailroom is always a hive of activity.

In this instance, AT&T and the local JAS received extensive help and support from the New Jersey ARC, which provided a job coach and some sensitivity training for the team. Since most team members are at the same salary level and have the same overall job responsibilities, it was fairly easy to restructure the job tasks to provide the individual with Down's syndrome with a full and meaningful job while ensuring that no tasks were beyond his capabilities. Because employees working in this mailroom are represented by the Communications Workers of America, it was necessary to ensure union cooperation when restructuring his job. Management has always been pleased with the employee's performance, and he is taking advantage of his co-workers' willingness to teach him additional skills, such as basic computer operation, when there is time.

Performance Standards

It is important to emphasize that no matter what accommodations are made for a particular individual, lowering expected performance standards is not one of them. All AT&T employees are expected to meet performance standards set by their management during periodic discussions. Accommodation issues are always treated separately from performance issues unless the failure to accommodate, or the inadequacy of a particular accommodation in a given circumstance, caused the performance problem. In that case, accommodation options are addressed, with the assistance of a JAS, if appropriate.

Communication and Follow-Up

Whenever you make a reasonable accommodation, good communication is a key factor in its success. Management must communicate expectations to the employee or applicant requesting the accommodation. The individual with the disability must communicate his or her needs, what will and will not work for him or her, and realistic expectations. JAS, disability case managers, and other personnel must share pertinent information which will allow everyone to make the most informed decision possible.

After an accommodation has been made, some follow-up is usually important. If an accommodation is made to assist an individual to attend and fully participate in a company-sponsored training seminar, the fact that the training has been completed is usually sufficient. However, in the case of the human resources employee with computer compatibility problems, follow-up at regular intervals is keeping everyone advised of when the new network software will be available to allow her full access to all reports systems. JAS keep in touch with the employee in the finance organization to make sure that the accommodations are still adequate. For example, when he purchased his new powered wheelchair, it was discovered that the position of the joystick on the chair made it difficult for him to get close enough to his desk to reach the computer keyboard. The JAS arranged for a building services worker to slightly modify the desk to allow for easier access.

Such follow-up is usually simple, like a phone call every few months to see how things are going or a word in passing in the hallway. It can, however, make all the difference in the comfort level of both the individual with the disability and his or her manager. The employee, who may for any number of reasons be shy about approaching his or her manager if things are not working exactly right, knows there is someone available to assist. Managers understand that they are not alone when it comes to accommodation situations; there is a place to go for answers they cannot find on their own. It is important to note that while a JAS may facilitate communication, he or she never takes on the manager's responsibilities in terms of career development and performance feedback and appraisal.

The process of making reasonable accommodations for employees and applicants with disabilities can take many forms; some require a good deal of research and involve many people/organizations, while others need only a brief discussion between manager and employee. AT&T recognizes its responsibility to make accommodations when appropriate and acknowledges that it makes good business sense to do so.

BankAmerica Corporation

4

BankAmerica Corporation and its consolidated subsidiaries provide diverse financial products and services to individuals, businesses, government agencies, and financial institutions throughout the world. BankAmerica Corporation is the second-largest bank holding company in the United States based on total assets as of December 31, 1994. With banking affiliates in ten western states, BankAmerica has the largest presence of any banking institution in the West.

As the bank has grown and diversified, it has recognized that its responsibility for good corporate citizenship should also grow. BankAmerica has, therefore, undertaken a broad-based effort, encompassing community reinvestment, philanthropy, environmental responsibility, affirmative action, accommodations for people with disabilities, and responses to unexpected emergency needs in the communities it serves, such as those stemming from the recent floods in northern California and earthquakes in Los Angeles and Kobe, Japan.

BankAmerica has also taken the lead in meeting its environmental responsibilities. In 1991, a corporate-wide task force recommended environmental principles which management has integrated into the company's day-to-day business activities with positive results. Credit policy guidelines have been developed to encourage loans to environmentally beneficial businesses and to help promote environmentally responsible behavior. In addition, the bank now requires that environmental issues be addressed as part of all contacts relating to properties it occupies. The bank has also completed two historic debt-for-nature swaps that will help support rain forest conservation in Latin America, initiated a series of rain forest checks to raise the visibility of conservation issues with domestic customers, and helped fund efforts to conserve endangered ecosystems.

When Congress passed the Americans with Disabilities Act (ADA) in 1991, BankAmerica wanted to be a leader in accommodating the special needs of its employees and customers with disabilities. Using its environmental activities as a model, BankAmerica again established a corporate-wide task force to identify what could be done. Like its environmental predecessor, the ADA task force recommended and management agreed that staff be allocated to the effort on a full-time basis, supported by other departments throughout the company. They worked to enhance access to facilities, products, services, and employment by people with disabilities, and their efforts have been cited as models by other institutions in the United States.

BankAmerica views these and other corporate responsibility efforts both as good business practice and as important to the maintenance of its franchise and to the social and economic health of its communities. Its efforts are also part of its heritage, stemming from the views of the bank's founder, A.P. Giannini. Nearly a century ago, he believed, and demonstrated, that banking had tremendous potential for those who had the vision and ability to promote the economic development of communities and serve people who had not had access to banking services before.

BankAmerica's ADA Accomplishments to Date

A new office was established to lead the bank's ADA efforts and coordinate its activities with many other departments throughout the organization. An important initiative taken by Ms. Terri Hanagan, vice president of ADA Programs, was to form an alliance with the Marriott Foundation's "Bridges...From School to Work" program (this program is covered in detail in Chapter 32). This innovative program provides job training and learning internships to high school students with disabilities.

Some of BankAmerica's accomplishments to date in dealing with issues related to the ADA are as follows.

A Manager's Guide to Managing Human Resources—Revisions to the guide have been recommended to reflect compliance requirements with ADA and are under review by the Legal Department.

Application for Employment (EXEC-1)—The EXEC-1 has been revised to eliminate any illegal pre-employment inquiries.

Essential Functions Project—U.S. Compensation in conjunction with the Legal Department and Equal Opportunity and Diversity Programs has implemented an extensive action plan to outline the essential functions of every position in the company. Positions have been prioritized according to their level of potential liability: (i) those with high physical demands (e.g., couriers), (ii) those having high turnover (e.g., cash handlers), and (iii) those jobs with large populations (e.g., tellers). The project was completed at the end of 1993.

Pre-employment Tests—The five validated in-house tests that the company currently uses to prescreen non-exempt applicants have been evaluated on the basis of appropriate accommodations. The five tests are the Teller Test, Cash Handler Test, Proof Operator Test, Secretary/Clerical Test, and Teleservicing Test.

Public Accommodations (Title III) Video—The first title of the ADA to become effective was to be the one impacting customer accessibility to goods and services. Because the deadline for Title III was imminent, ADA Programs turned to Human Resources for help in quickly producing a video that not only addressed the letter of the law but also reflected the sensitivities of BankAmerica's culture. Equal Opportunity and Diversity Programs in partnership with HR Communications and Creative Services produced a training video to assist in complying with the awareness and accessibility aspects of Title III, which became effective January 26, 1992. The video and a meeting leader's guide were distributed to all U.S.-based units in January 1992. Although the video was specifically designed to be viewed by employees who directly serve customers, managers were encouraged to share it with all other employees as well to help increase general sensitivity and awareness.

The video has been shown at various external seminars and forums and is recognized as one of the most effective and professionally produced videos on the subject of public accommodations. In fact, it was the first video known to address this issue. BankAmerica has sold 40 videos to large and small employers (including a number of financial institutions), the Department of Justice, physicians, and others. While not a large profit-maker in dollars and cents, the positive public opinion engendered through BankAmerica's proactive approach is incalculable.

ADA Training for Human Resources: Phase I—From August to December 1991, three articles on ADA appeared in the *Human Resources Bulletin*. In addition, in December 1991 and January 1992, two articles for employees appeared in *On Your Behalf*. For BankAmerica's human resource community in particular, these five articles have provided resource information on:

- Overview of the ADA
- What managers need to know: interviewing and hiring
- Customers with disabilities
- Interviewing techniques
- Interviewing etiquette
- Myths and stereotypes
- Statement of BankAmerica's ADA principles

- Positive language
- Working with people with disabilities

A compilation of these articles in brochure form has been disseminated extensively at external seminars and meetings. In fact, the Department of Labor purchased several hundred brochures.

ADA Training for Human Resources: Phase II—A two- to three-hour seminar for appropriate human resource professionals was launched in August 1992 to emphasize the nuts and bolts of the law, what to do, and guidance on how to do it right. In addition, the seminar provides Human Resources with modular training components that allow the training of line managers specifically on interviewing and etiquette (attitudinal barriers). These two components include resources (video and materials).

Disabilities Accommodation Fund—A central accommodation fund to support accommodations in excess of $300 has been administered by Equal Opportunity and Diversity Programs since 1985. Since the enactment of the ADA, the level of requests to access the corporate fund has risen steadily; however, appropriate counseling has resulted in many of these requests being supported with no- to low-cost solutions.

Assessing the Impact of the ADA on Bank Operations

Based on a charter from the bank's chief executive officer to conduct an assessment of how the ADA would impact reasonable accommodations for employees and customers, a 22-member task force was formed with representatives from a wide range of bank operations. A key to the success of this task force was a letter drafted by the chief executive officer to all its members stating his belief in and support of their mission. In addition, he also attended the task force's first meeting. Finally, in a videotape for all employees, he introduced the bank's ADA efforts and his desire to meet the *spirit* of the act. The task force's recommendations are as follows.

Recommended Actions

---

1. Endorse the proposed BankAmerica Corporation ADA Position Statement (see below).

2. Designate Consumer Banking Group (CBG) as having initial authority and responsibility to implement, coordinate and administer a comprehen-

sive company-wide ADA program through year-end 1991. Subsequently, Corporate Community Development (CCD) will assume responsibility for the program.

3. Establish a toll-free customer information and service number (1-800-2-ENABLE) to complement our Corporate Outreach Program and develop an awareness brochure.

4. Charge Corporate Real Estate and Versatel Businesses, in conjunction with CBG, with responsibility for developing and executing a prioritized plan to make all facilities and ATM locations accessible to people with disabilities. Where practical, facilities and ATM locations should be made accessible to customers with disabilities prior to January 26, 1992.

5. Charge Human Resources, in conjunction with CBG, with developing and implementing an awareness and training program for all customer service personnel, prior to January 26, 1992.

6. Charge Human Resources with developing and implementing an awareness and training program for appropriate management to address ADA employment provisions which become effective July 26, 1992.

Corporate Position on
the Americans with Disabilities Act

BankAmerica Corporation is committed to serving the needs of all customers and employees, and fully supports the Americans with Disabilities Act.

BankAmerica believes the goals and objectives of the ADA will enhance the quality of our society. We also believe that the American economy is made stronger by businesses that reach out to include all segments of the population. We believe the ADA ultimately will help invigorate the economy by bringing more individuals with disabilities into the employment and consumer mainstream.

Accordingly, wherever practical, BankAmerica pledges to:

1. Provide access to existing facilities and services.

2. Treat applicants, employees and customers with disabilities with dignity, and offer them the same opportunities we extend to the non-disabled.

3. Seek out and listen to the concerns of people with disabilities. Incorporate those concerns in employment policies, design and renovation of facilities, and in the delivery of products and services.

4. Make appropriate investments of time and resources to serve the needs of people with disabilities.

We realize that even the best efforts of the business community will not remove every barrier faced by all people with disabilities, but we believe that meaningful efforts to do so will offer many more opportunities to participate fully in the economic and social mainstream.

Planning for Implementing Task Force Recommendations

The Managing Committee adopted the task force's recommendations in their entirety. A project management approach was then taken toward assuring the successful implementation of the recommendations. This approach exhibited three main features:

1. Assignment of responsibility to specific individuals for each element of the implementation effort

2. Clearly defined action steps with due dates where appropriate

3. Specific deliverables

The following is an example of the task force's control sheet for managing the implementation of its recommendations.

Americans with Disabilities Task Force Control Sheet

Action Steps	Deliverables
1. Obtain and analyze information as to the programs of other large financial institutions, large corporate employers, and/or public accommodation oriented companies. (Scope to include both gathered employment and facilities.)	Summarize other programs. Draw conclusions on information gathered.
1a. If you can assist in providing input as to the contents of questions to include in the survey of other programs or if there is information that would be particularly valuable to assist you with your assignment, please forward material to Terri Hanagan by 6/14.	

Action Steps	*Deliverables*
2. Establish dialogue with organizations representing various types of disabled persons, discuss ways banking products, services, and facilities may be modified to be more responsive. (Scope to include both employee and customer perspectives.)	Summarize the characteristics of people with disabilities by type of disability and identify perceived needs.
3. Review customer and employee concerns related to access, facilities, services, or allegations of discriminatory treatment toward people with disabilities. Seek input from focus groups of employees with disabilities.	Summarize the concerns of customers and employees with disabilities.
4. Review employment policies and practices related to people with disabilities and recommend changes to employment policies.	Identify areas where policy clarification is needed.
5. Develop an approach for a coordinated review of facilities to evaluate the degree of barrier free access. Identify modifications needed to facilities to improve customer and employee access.	Submit a methodology and preliminary estimates of costs and timing for all domestic locations.
6. Identify the types of needs we can address by modifying products and services.	Recommend changes to current products and services and appropriate auxiliary aids.
7. Document that those needs we are unable to meet represent either an undue burden or a fundamental alteration of our products or services.	To be addressed based upon information developed from action steps 1–6 above and input from Social Policy Committee.

Communicating and Training for Effective ADA Policy Implementation

Following top management's expression of support and personal commitment to implement an innovative and far-reaching program to address the needs of persons with disabilities, a series of ongoing communication efforts was introduced. These communication efforts were designed to familiarize all of the bank's management employees with the ADA and information that they would need to implement new initiatives. Communications were also designed to convey the values and beliefs which were to drive the relationship between the bank's entire staff and persons with disabilities.

Video Presentation

A special videotape presentation was developed to assist employees in understanding the needs of customers with disabilities. The video introduces the ADA; describes issues regarding customer access to bank facilities; shows the impact of the ADA on employment, transportation, telecommunications, and sports; addresses typical employee concerns in relating to customers with disabilities; demonstrates how employees can exercise proper etiquette in communicating with customers with disabilities; and presents management's values and policy on the subject.

The video is accompanied by an ADA orientation meeting for employees. A meeting leader's guide was also created. BankAmerica makes the video available to other interested organizations for a small fee.

BankAmerica's Training Program for Human Resources

In order to ensure the effectiveness of Human Resources personnel in dealing with the many subjects relating to the ADA and persons with disabilities, the department created a special training program. An outline of the program's content is shown below and serves as a model for other human resources organizations.

BankAmerica's ADA Training Program for Human Resources

The program (presented in a three-hour seminar):
1. Provides the participants with the basic information necessary to guide their respective line managers on ADA.
2. Is designed as a train-the-trainer program to communicate the nuts and bolts of the law, what to do, and guidance on how to do it right. Participants receive copies of the instructor's outline and overheads.
   - In addition, two take-away modular components are provided to assist Human Resources in training line managers specifically on interviewing and etiquette. These components include videos and facilitation materials.

Target audience:
- Human resource managers
- Human resource representatives
- Staffing representatives
- Personnel services specialists
- Employee relations consultants

Expected outcomes:
1. Understand and communicate ADA regulations and the impact on BofA line managers
2. Communicate and define ADA terminology and its application to line managers
3. Identify risks of non-compliance
4. Inform managers on compliance requirements related to:
   - Interviewing
   - Essential functions
   - Accommodations
5. Assist managers with accommodation requests, processes, and available resources

The Training Program Outline

I. Why ADA?
- Attitudes about the ADA
- Myths and misconceptions

II. Overview of the law
- Introduce case studies
- ADA: the law
- Terminology
- Employer defenses
- Employment inquiry
- Medical confidentiality
- Drug and alcohol
- Debrief of case studies

III. Workplace implications
- Video on interviewing
- Reasonable accommodations: how to at BofA
- Disabilities Accommodation Fund
- Essential Function Project

- Drugs and alcohol in the workplace and the ADA
- Workers' compensation and the ADA

IV. Performance management issues
- Attendance
- Performance appraisals
- Layoffs
- Staff development
- Peer employee interactions

V. Summary
- Etiquette video and workbook
- Fact packets (numerous handouts and resource information)
- "Human Resource Professionals Quick Reference Guide to ADA's Impact on the Employment Life Cycle"
- Contacts within BofA can answer ADA-related questions

Training Program for Interviewing Job Applicants with Disabilities

A special training program for interviewing job applicants with disabilities, titled "Gateway to Opportunity," was prepared to assist managers in their interviewing efforts. An outline of the content of the training program is shown below. A specially prepared video is used as part of the training program.

Interviewing Job Applicants with Disabilities

I.   Preparing to Train
- Why a Training Session on Interviewing Job Applicants with Disabilities?
- Program Objectives
- Program Elements
- Teaching Plans

II. Getting Started
- Warm-Up Exercise

III. Showing the Visual Presentation
- Visual Presentation Synopsis
- Summary of Guidelines and Teaching Points

- Review Breaks
- Preparing Participants
- Showing the Videotape

IV. Talking It Over
- Why Is Interviewing So Important?
- What Do You Need for the Interview?
- What Are the Etiquette-Related Prerequisites?
- Appropriate Terminology
- Effective Communication Strategies
- Providing Information
- Arrangement of Physical Space

V. Practicing Key Skills
- Practicing Skills: Why?
- Practicing Skills: How?
- Preparing for Practice Exercises
- Implementing Practice Exercises
- Following Up Practice Exercises

VI. Wrapping Up
- Personal Benefits
- Closing Comments

VII. Participants' Resource Handout Introduction
- Participants' Resource Handout

Acknowledgment
Part of this material is based on the publication *Disability Etiquette in the Workplace,* by Patricia A. Morrissey, Ph.D., prepared for the Employment Policy Foundation.

Copyright ©1992 Advantage Media Inc.

Training Program for Disability Etiquette in the Workplace

A major concern voiced by many managers and employees is how they should communicate with, and what terms and phrases they should use in speaking with, persons with disabilities. BankAmerica has prepared a special training program and video presentation for this purpose. Used with the training program is a "Language Guide on Disability," developed by the California Governor's Committee for Employment of Disabled Persons. Both the outline of the training program and the language guide are provided here.

Disability Etiquette in the Workplace

I. **Preparing to Train**
   - Why a Training Session on Disability Etiquette in the Workplace?
   - Program Objectives
   - Program Elements
   - Teaching Plans

II. **Getting Started**
   - Warm-Up Exercise

III. **Showing the Visual Presentation**
   - Visual Presentation Synopsis
   - Summary of Guidelines and Teaching Points
   - Review Breaks
   - Preparing Participants
   - Showing the Videotape

IV. **Talking It Over**
   - When and Where Is Disability Etiquette Most Important?
   - Appropriate Terminology
   - Effective Communication Strategies
   - Providing Information
   - Arrangement of Physical Space

V. **Practicing Key Skills**
   - Practicing Skills: Why?
   - Practicing Skills: How?
   - Preparing for Practice Exercises
   - Implementing Practice Exercises
   - Following Up Practice Exercises

VI. **Wrapping Up**
   - Personal Benefits
   - Closing Comments

VII. **Participants' Resource Handout Introduction**
   - Participants' Resource Handout

Acknowledgment
Part of this material is based on the publication *Disability Etiquette in the Workplace,* by Patricia A. Morrissey, Ph.D., prepared for the Employment Policy Foundation.

Language Guide on Disability:
A Primer on How to Say What You Mean to Say

**Developed by The California Governor's Committee
for Employment of Disabled Persons
(MIC 41, P.O. Box 826880, Sacramento, CA 94280-0001)**

Introduction

Language is powerful! It reflects, reinforces, and shapes our perceptions of people. Words which reflect positive attitudes and awareness help develop positive communications.

Words about disability have been strongly affected by legal, medical, and political terms. Consequently, our daily language is filled with technical terms which often do not convey our intended social message and which are further complicated by personal styles and preference.

The suggestions in this brochure are provided as a guide to improve language usage. Most suggestions are just common sense; but others are a matter of becoming aware of appropriate, **current** terminology. Using the right words can make a dramatic difference in both our private and public communications!

Examples of Good and Bad Usage

Language should accurately portray an individual or situation. It should emphasize the person rather than the disability.

> *Don't say...*
>
> "Mr. Lee is a *crippled teacher* and *confined to a wheelchair*. All of his students are *normal*."

> *But instead say...*
>
> "Mr. Lee is a *teacher with a disability*. He is a *wheelchair-user*. All of his students are *nondisabled*."

> *Don't say...*
>
> "A large bank in Southern California modified its building for its *handicapped employees and customers*. Subsequently, the bank initiated an on-the-job managerial training program which included *afflicted college seniors*. Participants included those *stricken with various conditions*."

But instead say...

"A large bank in Southern California modified its building for its *employees and customers with disabilities*. Subsequently, the bank initiated an on-the-job managerial training program which included *college seniors with disabilities*. Participants included *individuals who had either cerebral palsy, mental/emotional disability, or hearing impairment*."

Preferred Terms and Expressions

These words and expressions are currently preferred and reflect a positive attitude. Some language is "trendy" and meanings may vary depending on context or locale.

blind	mobility impaired
deaf	nondisabled
developmentally disabled	paralyzed, paralysis
differently able	persons with cerebral palsy
disabled	persons with disabilities
hearing impaired	persons with paraplegia
mentally/emotionally disabled	seizure
mentally restored	visually impaired
mentally retarded	wheelchair-user

Again, the ideal is to incorporate these words into our language in a way that expresses the dignity of the person.

Outdated/Inaccurate Terms and Expressions

We are often not aware of the biases or negative attitudes expressed in our language. Eliminating the bad words is as important as using the good words.

These words and expressions have strong negative, derogatory connotations. Avoid using them and discourage their use by others:

afflicted	deaf mute
cerebral-palsied	defective
confined to a wheelchair	deformed
crazy, insane	gimp
cripple, crip	handicapped
deaf and dumb	invalid

lame	spastic, spaz
maimed	stricken
paralytic, arthritic, epileptic	victim
poor unfortunate	wheelchair-bound
retard	withered

What Can We Do About Language?

- We can educate
- We can inform
- We can politely correct inaccurate use of language
- We can seek positive use of communication media
- We can encourage a societal attitude where only positive accurate words are acceptable in the context of any conversation!

An ADA Progress Report to All Employees

BankAmerica places great value on keeping its employees informed on a broad range of business issues. A special memorandum was issued to all employees on January 10, 1994, describing significant areas of progress in the bank's ADA implementation program.

Special Accommodations and New Technologies for BankAmerica Employees

The ADA requires that companies provide reasonable accommodations to persons with disabilities. However, in many companies, management plays a passive role in providing accommodations to its employees. These companies meet the letter of the law but not the spirit of it. They are missing an opportunity to enhance employee morale, increase total productivity and quality, and improve customer satisfaction (which results in greater profitability).

BankAmerica has taken an aggressive, positive approach toward providing accommodations for its employees with disabilities. As a result of this consistent, positive attitude toward persons with disabilities, employees have a greater trust relationship with management, and many more individuals disclose their disabilities. They know that disclosing disabilities will not affect their promotability or retention with the company. Employees whose accommodation needs are met are more productive. Interestingly, non-disabled employees also find that adapting specific accommodations enhances their job performance. Significantly, the cost of accommodations for employees averages only $1000.

A number of disability categories and the respective accommodations that the bank has provided for its employees are listed below.

Visual Disabilities

- Software to generate computer, braille, and voice output.

- Enlarging software and supporting equipment for people with minimum vision. Information on computer screens can be magnified to a maximum of 40X, in different colors and contrasts, plus various background colors can be introduced. One visually impaired person uses this system to design company forms. The company also provides portable units for employees to use while traveling.

- Flexible work schedules are used to enable visually impaired persons to arrive home before dark. Occasionally, an employee may sleep in the office overnight if he or she cannot, in their judgment, arrive home before dark. Employee lounges are available for this purpose.

- Customizing lighting and window shades for individuals with sensitivity to certain light levels and conditions.

- Use of photocopier magnification in providing printed matter to persons with visual disabilities.

- For totally blind persons, tape recordings, braille, or readers are used.

- In order to ease the concerns of employees in departments where a totally blind employee is joining the group, a preliminary introduction is made, with an open discussion among the parties. In a typical case, a new blind employee and his dog were introduced to the group. Employees were advised on how the dog was to be treated and given the opportunity to develop a rapport with the new employee. Concerns evaporated and the employees voluntarily established a special area for the dog to rest in. The dog impressed everyone with its ability to assist the blind employee by picking up dropped material, guiding the individual to various parts of the office complex, and even punching the proper elevator button when arriving at work.

Hearing Disabilities

- Accommodations include the following: special headsets, voice amplifiers, hearing-aid-compatible headsets, assistive listening devices for conference rooms, TDDs for persons who are totally deaf, headsets that block out white noise in the office, equipment that enables a telephone user to hear only the voice at the other end of the line, elimination of background noise, and use of laptop computers at conference meetings where recorders enter comments to be viewed by individuals with hearing disabilities.

• Use of American Sign Language interpreters at conferences and meetings.

Mobility Impairment

• Accessibility for both horizontal and vertical file cabinets.

• Use of a joystick to enter computer data.

• Use of service dogs trained to pick up dropped items, open doors, and perform other tasks.

• Encourage non-disabled employees to try out equipment that mobility-impaired individuals use on the job. This helps to build team spirit and greater awareness of the needs of disabled persons.

Multiple Sclerosis

• Special armrests, keyboard trays at appropriate heights, grippers for paper, and special chairs.

AIDS, Cancer, and Heart Conditions

• Modified work schedules.

• Fax equipment, computers, and dedicated telephone lines are provided to enable persons with these disabilities to telecommute.

Ergonomic Factors

• Special chairs are designed for various physical disabilities. Designs are developed by the Stanford University Rehabilitation Center.

Developmental Disabilities

• Job coaching in partnership with community agencies such as the Association for Retarded Citizens.

• Use of enclaves (i.e., dedicated areas in which the special needs of these individuals for training, development, work, and supervision can be provided) where community agencies provide supervision.

- Organizing work into smaller elements to enable individuals to follow task requirements more easily.
- Reengineering work to simplify effort.

Learning Disabilities

- Use of task timer stopwatches.
- Use of color coding (versus alpha-numeric coding) for filing activities.
- Use of multiple-color pens.

Quality and Productivity Performance

BankAmerica's experience supports the findings of research into the job performance of persons with disabilities. Given reasonable accommodation coupled with top management, peer, and supervisory support, the performance of persons with disabilities in terms of quality and productivity is, on average, equal to that of non-disabled employees.

Expanded Application of ADA Implementation Results

The ADA extends its coverage to U.S. citizens who are employed abroad. The Social Policy Committee, composed of the bank's top management, has directed that the same facilities and reasonable accommodations applied in the United States be implemented at its operations globally.

The Boeing Company and the International Association of Machinists and Aerospace Workers Union

5

The Boeing Company is well known for having built more airplanes than any other company. But airplanes are only part of the company's story. Boeing is also involved in space vehicles, helicopters, electronics, computing services, and telecommunications.

The company believes that one key to its success in so many technologies lies in the diversity of its employees. Its management maintains that each of the company's achievements comes as a result of the dedication, effort, and combination of skills represented by the Boeing work force. The following Boeing policy statement gives special attention to the disabled segment of its work force:

> It is the policy of the Boeing Company to take affirmative action to employ, advance in employment and otherwise treat qualified individuals with a disability without discrimination based upon their physical or mental disability in all employment practices such as advertising, recruiting, hiring, promotion, demotion, transfer, layoff, termination, rates of pay or other forms of compensation, and selection for training including apprenticeship.

Boeing has a long history of hiring and promoting qualified persons who have disabilities. Its experience has shown that it is not disability but rather productivity and results that count. The company believes that encouraging people with diverse skills, talents, and backgrounds keeps it strong.

Organizing to Assist Persons with Disabilities

Recognizing the advantages of hiring individuals with disabilities, Boeing established the office of disability services. Disability services, the corporate office of equal employment opportunity, and the operating organizations have a responsibility for maintaining an effective affirmative action program for individuals with disabilities. The disability services office works with equal employment opportunity administrators and line managers for the purpose of assisting in evaluation and facilitating possible placement.

When an applicant has the education, training, and work experience to qualify for the skills the Boeing Company is seeking, the disability services office frequently coordinates on a case-by-case basis the evaluation for reasonable accommodation. The goal of reasonable accommodation is to enable an individual with a disability to become a fully productive employee.

In 1989, Boeing and the International Association of Machinists and Aerospace Workers Union (IAM) decided to create a landmark project whereby a joint effort would be conducted to assist disabled workers in returning to work as soon as possible. Site committees were established to implement the early return-to-work concept. Prior to the establishment of this creative initiative, an injured employee had to be completely recovered without limitations before returning to work. Under the new agreement, each case would be evaluated individually, with appropriate accommodations to enable an employee to return to work early. The results of this joint effort have been extraordinary. In a two-year period, one Boeing division reduced disabled employee time lost by half and reduced workers' compensation expenses by approximately half. The positive impact on the morale of the employees involved is beyond calculation.

Reasonable Accommodations

In implementing the IAM/Boeing agreement, it was sometimes necessary to break long-held attitudes and stereotypes regarding disabled employees. Prior supervisory performance evaluations and budget constraints sometimes worked against supervisor acceptance of employees who were not fully productive. In order for the return-to-work program to be successful, it was important that supervisor pressure for productivity be relieved. This issue has been addressed, and in some cases, such as a disabled person working at a new job, management provides a grace period to facilitate the employee reaching full productivity.

The various strategies and reasonable accommodations used at Boeing and the respective roles of the unions, IAM CARES (Center for Administering Rehabilitation and Education Services) representative, and company personnel are depicted in the following case studies.

Case Study I

A 55-year-old male aerospace machinist who worked on a large engine lathe originally injured his back at work in February 1992. His diagnosis was sprain/strain. He was off work for about 90 days and returned to work on the same machine. In September 1993, he again hurt his back and was off work. He first underwent a physical therapy program and then a work hardening program for several months. His doctor released him to work in January 1994 with no restrictions, and he was placed back on the same lathe.

To operate this machine, the worker was required to bend forward at the waist and twist slightly to the side while changing cutters, some of which weighed up to 32 pounds. The employee had been back to work only about two weeks when he was assigned to machine some castings that require eight different tool setups and thus multiple requirements to lean over the machine to change heavy cutters. He again severely strained his back, sought medical treatment, and was taken off work by his doctor.

At this point, the company made an IAM CARES vocational rehabilitation counselor (VRC) available to assist the employee and coordinate services and his eventual return to work. The VRC did a detailed job analysis of the employee's duties on all the various types and sizes of engine lathes that he ran from time to time in the shop. The job analysis delineated the varying physical demands of running the different machines. This was presented to the employee's attending physician who recommended that the employee only run the smaller lathes when he returned, which would allow him to stand closer to the point of operation on the machine and avoid forward bending and twisting. However, the attending physician stated that the release date was as yet undetermined and recommended that the employee be seen by a physical medicine specialist. This specialist prescribed a different program of physical and occupational therapy.

After the employee completed this program of work conditioning, including education in body mechanics, posture, pacing, and activity tolerances, the IAM CARES VRC met with him, his wife, and the physical medicine specialist. Terms of the upcoming release to work were discussed and the doctor recommended a gradual return, starting with four hours per day and, if well tolerated, an increase of one hour per day per week up to eight hours; he also recommended working only on the smaller lathes which required less bending and lifting. Moreover, he recommended alternating sitting, standing, and walking; use of an ergonomic stool and industrial-type lumbosacral support; no bending, crawling, or climbing; and no lifting/carrying over 24 pounds.

The VRC arranged for the company to provide an ergonomic stool and for management to keep the employee off the large lathe. She also counseled with the employee's wife, who was concerned that the job would make her husband's condition worse and eventually require him to be in a wheelchair. The medical diagnosis was explained to her in terms which she could understand, and eventually she felt more confident about her husband returning to work.

The first week of June, the employee returned to work for four hours per day and was reevaluated weekly by the company's medical department physicians before increasing his number of hours. He sat on the ergonomic stool as much as possible while the machine was running and continued to wear the lumbar support which reminded him to use better body mechanics if he started to bend over at the waist. He was up to a full eight-hour day by early July and in follow-up visits by the VRC seemed to be tolerating the job well.

Unfortunately, the employee experienced back pain again on August 3 and attributed it to the fact that even on the smallest lathe, running the smallest parts, he had to bend forward due to his 6'1" frame. The VRC met with the employee and his specialist again, and the doctor recommended raising the lathe four to six inches off the floor to accommodate the man's taller than average height. The VRC contacted the shop management about raising the lathe; a company ergonomist was consulted who recommended raising the equipment eight inches. The shop received an estimate from facilities that the accommodation would cost $2600; there was some reluctance about incurring this expense.

The VRC explained to management that the company was spending over $2400 per month to keep the employee home and non-productive. With this logic in mind, the accommodation expense was approved. When the work was not accomplished after several weeks, the VRC began making phone calls to learn what was holding up the process; she suspected that the paperwork had fallen through the cracks. Sure enough, the plans had been mislaid on a design engineer's desk and had not been approved. The work was soon completed, and the doctor released the employee to return to work.

Upon the employee's return, he was very pleased with the change, as were his co-workers who also used the machine from time to time. At the new height, he and the rest of the machinists could stand up straight when using the machine, and all felt less fatigued at the end of their shift. As of this writing, the employee is still at work on this machine and is tolerating the job very well. The chronic sprain/strain cycle fostered by working on ergonomically unsound machinery seems to have been broken.

Case Study II

A 49-year-old female employee had worked as a microelectronics packaging operator since 1981. On November 12, 1987, a locker fell on her at work, causing a neck injury. She was out of work from December 7 until December 14. She was out again on March 8, 1988, had neck surgery January 23, 1989, and returned to her regular job in May 1989. The static neck flexion aggravated her condition. Extensive accommodations were made, but she was still unable to perform the essential functions of the job, and alternative placement was investigated. Her medical recommendations prohibited working with a microscope, repetitive or sustained neck flexion or extension, visual and precise hand movement, and lifting over ten pounds.

In November 1990, the employee was approved to work as a blueprint file clerk and accepted this position on November 5. Because she was also unable to perform the essential tasks of this job due to increased neck pain, she was then placed as a unit buyout contract compliance clerk for two months. She was out of work again on September 20, 1991 due to back pain resulting from a non-industrial accident which occurred in June 1991.

On April 12, 1994, the employee was once again cleared to return to work with the following medical recommendations: occasional lifting, pulling and pushing not to exceed 5 pounds, sitting not to exceed 30 minutes at a time or 3 hours per shift, may alternately sit/stand as tolerated, no overhead work, occasional bending, limited kneeling, and no work with neck in flexed position. This time, there was an IAM CARES VRC available to assist in placing the employee. She completed a written job analysis and assisted in obtaining a videotape of the job. Both were submitted to and approved by the employee's attending physician with the following recommended accommodations: ergonomic chair, foot rest and stool, slanted work tables, adjusted document holders, wrist rest, and electric stapler. The physician also recommended working initially only Monday, Wednesday, and Friday and job coaching by an occupational therapist as long as needed for at least two hours per day during the first month of employment.

During mediation to allow her to return to the contract compliance clerk job, management stated that she lacked the required typing skills to do the job. Although she had previously worked in that position for two months and therefore had rights to the job, management had been planning to send her for training in typing just as she went on leave the last time. When she was tested for her ability to type, she typed 29 words per minute with 1 error. The requirement for the job was 40 words per minute. The IAM CARES VRC made arrangements for a computer programmed with Typing Tutor to be placed in her home, along with a table and ergonomic chair, so she could work on her typing skills at home on the days she was not at work.

The VRC drafted the return-to-work plan detailing the responsibilities of all parties involved and obtained the signatures of the supervisor, employee, outside VRC, attending physician, occupational therapist, and herself. The VRC then coordinated the ordering and placement of all the ergonomic equipment and monitored the employee's progress closely with the assistance of the occupational therapist, who provided job coaching to ensure proper body mechanics and correct use of the ergonomic equipment.

The employee returned to work part time on October 14, 1994 and full time on December 5, 1994 at her own request. Her attendance and job performance have been good. The VRC obtained the support of the attending physician, management, and the employee and her spouse and coordinated placement of all the equipment and other support services necessary for this complex return-to-work plan. Without her efforts, it is unlikely that all of the necessary elements needed to return the employee to work would have been accomplished.

Case Study III

Ms. X has a back and knee injury. She also has a weight problem, which aggravates her condition. Mobility is the issue in returning to work.

Ms. X first injured her back in 1992; she was able to return to work after several months of physical therapy and water therapy. Her job was sedentary for the most part, but she needed to be able to go to daily staff meetings. The VRC was able to help her obtain a walker through the agency that administers the Labor and Industry claims for the company. She returned to her job and was able to use the walker to get to her staff meetings. A handicapped parking pass was obtained for her so she could park near the building where she worked.

A few months later, Ms. X injured her knee while walking to the rest room. She was off work several more months and received treatment for her knee. Surgery was not necessary and physical therapy and water exercises were recommended. It was clear that Ms. X could do her job if the mobility problem could be resolved; the walker would only work for very short distances. A wheelchair or a scooter along with a walker were considered as possible options. The safety department, the supervisor in her shop, the claims manager, the nurse consultant, and her physician were all consulted.

The vocational rehabilitation counselor and Ms. X were able to convince all parties involved that a scooter, a lift for her van, and a walker would best meet her needs. The counselor explored resources in the community for purchasing a scooter which could accommodate Ms. X's weight and van lift. After many telephone calls, the counselor found a company that could provide the appropriate scooter and van lift at a reasonable price. The next step was to find a way to pay for these aids. The counselor worked with the claims manager and Ms. X to work out a plan. The claims manager agreed to pay for half of the expense, and Ms. X agreed to pay the other half from her settlement when her claim was closed.

As a result, Ms. X was able to return to work and is doing very well since her mobility problem has been resolved. An added benefit is that Ms. X's quality of life has greatly improved; she now has the freedom to live a more normal life in her home and in the community. She is able to do her shopping and go places without the help of others. Her self-esteem has soared as a result of her new independence.

Case Study IV

Until recently, it has been very difficult to design rehabilitation solutions for workers with limited use of their hands. There are four reasons for this: (1) Many people have difficulty understanding and empathizing with limited hand use. Rehabilitation solutions include giving the injured person "easier" work appropriate for limited lifting (i.e., filing, stapling, etc.). (2) Technological solutions, when available and effective, are expensive. (3) There has been reluctance to admit that some overuse syndrome hand injuries are permanent. (4) This then requires that we look at how we are accomplishing some work tasks, particularly in office situations.

As of this writing, Boeing has developed a very gratifying rehabilitation solution utilizing some start-of-the-art accommodations. Ms. X has been a computer programmer and systems analyst for a number of years. She is a bright and creative individual, whose hard work and long hours were rewarded by rapid promotion within the company. However, by the late 1980s, she had symptoms of overuse syndrome. Carpel tunnel release surgery did not resolve the problem. By 1991, she was in hand braces and had a 100% keyboard usage restriction.

Because she was a valued employee, the company accommodated her with a voice recognition computer system and gave her a job as an estimator. (This was "easier" work which could be accomplished with then start-of-the-art technology, but which no longer made use of some of her best skills as a programmer.) The price for this accommodation was $5000.

However, by late 1994, her system was outdated. It did not work in the Windows environment (which she watched being added to all the computers around her). Also, due to company downsizing, her job description now required clerical duties, including filing and stapling (using a mechanical stapler). Ms. X adapted by using the keyboard to fill in where her voice-activated system was deficient and tried to staple by pressing down the lever with her forearm. A further complication was that her workstation was an ergonomic nightmare; it lacked even the ordinary appropriate alignments of worker–monitor–chair–lighting. And management was unhappy because she was not getting the work done.

Ms. X was depressed and angry. She had lost her career. After accomplishing much creative and useful work for her company, she was now reduced to doing work that did not make the best use of her abilities and which she could not physically do. She could see that she would soon be out of a job altogether.

The first task for IAM CARES was to support Ms. X emotionally. Surprisingly, after a very brief period of venting her frustration, she quickly became an energetic and major part of her own rehab team. Through her expertise in software, she was able to advise the company that new solutions were available. Coordinating with hardware people who knew of other recent technological innovations, it was determined that her workstation could be updated for about $400.

The first problem was to convince management that stapling and filing were not appropriate work for her (certainly not with a mechanical stapler!). She was not getting the work done because she did not have the proper tools. Accommodation was necessary. An ergonomist was brought in to make the obvious standard lighting and equipment adjustments. (Ms. X now routinely adjusts the workstations of other people around her.)

Because the new updated software and hardware are start-of-the-art (and may need further "adjustments"), it did not take long to come up with the concept that Ms. X (being the only person in the company with three year's experience with voice-activated office equipment) could quite possibly be better utilized helping to coordinate the installation of other such systems within the company. At present, representatives from corporate insurance, workers' compensation administration, computing technology, and medical services are talking about whether this solution might be integrated into the system.

The plan would be to accommodate workers, either temporarily because of present injuries, or because they are already symptomatic and injuries could be prevented, or permanently because returning to keyboard usage is not recommended. Ms. X could certainly help evaluate which software would be most appropriate in each situation, could help train the users, and could program additional functions whenever needed. Her new software will allow her to return to programming. This is a win–win situation for everyone. Injured workers can be accommodated. Potential injuries can be prevented. Workers' compensation costs are reduced. And Ms. X is back on track, where her creative skills and proven abilities are once again an asset to herself and to her company.

Case Study V

Ms. X has worked for the Boeing commercial airplane group for the past 18 years. For the much of the last ten years, she has worked as a developer prover electrical, which involves extensive work with computers and making handwritten notes. Over the past two years, she began to experience swelling, numbness, and pain in her right hand and arm. These symptoms became progressively worse apparently due to overuse. This caused her to be on industrial leave twice. The exact etiology of her problem is still being determined. Her doctors have considered several diagnoses, from carpal tunnel syndrome to reflex sympathetic dystrophy. Cortisone injections, a course of non-steroidal anti-inflammatory medication, and physical therapy helped reduce her symptoms to the point where she was ready to try returning to work, with significant restrictions on use of her right hand, particularly relating to work on a computer keyboard or mouse. She continued to have problems with her right upper extremity and received further restrictions from a Boeing Company clinic doctor.

A return-to-work team consisting of a nurse case manager and a vocational rehabilitation counselor was assigned, and her workstation was evaluated to determine if any ergonomic modifications would allow her to do her job without increasing her symptoms. She uses a computer-aided drafting system that has several additional keyboards, dial controls, and a complex mouse controller. She had transferred some tasks from her right to her left hand, but there was some concern that she would start to experience repetitive motion symptoms in her left hand. Some changes, such as forearm supports, were considered; however, it became apparent that in light of the complexities of her workstation/computer, further evaluation of her work area by a hand-function specialist was needed.

Working with the claims adjuster for the insurance company that handles Boeing workers' compensation claims, an occupational therapist with extensive experience in evaluating work sites and recommending ergonomic modifications was brought in. Initial recommendations were to lower her monitor and relocate her copy holder to directly below her monitor. This would allow her to hold her head and neck in a more comfortable and natural position. Also recommended were a keyboard holder with a low-profile wrist rest and a foot rest. Due to all the different keyboards and controllers on her computer system, forearm support devices that clamp on to the desk were not practical. Instead, the occupational therapist recommended an ergonomic chair with height and back rest adjustment, seat pan tilt, and movable arm rests that swing in toward her body and help support her forearms.

Except for the chair, which had to be specially ordered, the other workstation modifications, such as the wrist rest and foot rest, were already available within the company's normal material requisition system.

The employee has indicated that these modifications have helped her perform her work without the fatigue and discomfort she experienced in the past. She plans to slowly increase the use of her right hand and arm. She is now more aware of changing positions and tries to modify how she accomplishes tasks so that repetitive movements are reduced.

Case VI

Mrs. X was first diagnosed with bone spurs in 1992. She went on a leave of absence to have surgery for this condition in late 1992. The following month, she had surgery for a bunion on the same foot. She continued to experience swelling and discoloration in her foot after the cast was removed and was given a foot brace. Four months after the first surgery, she started attending physical therapy and began using a cane for walking. Six months after the initial surgery, Mrs. X was diagnosed with reflex sympathetic dystrophy.

In total, Mrs. X was off work for 21 months. During this time, she received nerve blocks and an electronic stimulator was implanted. She was confined to a wheelchair for approximately 12 months. In an inpatient pain program, Mrs. X improved to the point where she could walk unassisted by even a cane.

The vocational counselor, nurse case manager, and Mrs. X worked with management to arrange a graduated return-to-work program where she would perform paperwork duties for a few hours a day and then perform light-duty inspection work for the rest of the day. Mrs. X started out working two full days a week for four weeks. She worked three days a week for two weeks and then graduated to four days a week. She has been working four days a week for three months.

Mrs. X's doctor is not yet ready to release her for full-time work. Mrs. X continues to work and is independent. She has good and bad days, but she is very happy to have the chance to be a productive worker and be with her family of friends at work again.

Supported Employment

To further illustrate Boeing's commitment to a diversified work force, a pilot program was established in the late 1980s to evaluate whether supported employment for people with developmental disabilities was practical in a large, complex industrial firm. The results of the program were positive. According to Boeing, supported employment makes good business sense.

Supported employment at Boeing is no longer a pilot program. Supported employees hold jobs in the commercial airline group wire shop, the support services print shop bindery, and in other areas in the Puget Sound region.

The disability services and supported employment office administrators co-ordinate reasonable accommodation arrangements and education programs and identify tasks suitable for developmentally disabled persons.

Community outreach is another aspect of disability services and supported employment. These offices interact with local agencies concerning how potential qualified applicants with disabilities can best apply at Boeing. They also act as a contact with government and social service agencies to stay abreast of developments made elsewhere and to pass on information gained from Boeing's experience.

The following example illustrates the viability of the supported employment program.

Case Study

This case study demonstrates the success achieved in placing a supported employee in Boeing's print shop. The print shop manager commented that the print shop's bindery had a high employee turnover rate in the past. He would start new employees there, but they would always move on as soon as something else opened up. The constant repetition of the job did not offer enough of a challenge to hold their interest. As a result, the department was in a permanent training mode.

The manager recognized that this was a situation where supported employment might have a good chance of succeeding. A Trillium Employment Services (a non-profit agency noted for its expertise in supported employment) job coach spent a week learning about the operation in preparation for training the shop's first supported employee.

Neither the manager nor others in the department really knew what to expect. When the employee came on board, she started out with only one task. She now handles 14 tasks—almost everything the bindery does.

After a couple of months, the print shop took on a second supported employee. The two have been working in the bindery for over two years. Their job coach was phased out over time, and they interact with their co-workers just like everyone else. The department manager says that he depends on these individuals. If one of them is absent, there is no one else to do the work.

The manager estimates that without his supported employees, his shop would have had to train at least ten new workers in the bindery. "This has been a very positive experience for all of us," he said. "It's brought our crew closer together, and our supported employees have certainly grown while they've been here."

Citicorp Diners Club

6

Pat Giordano and Connie McKenna

Citicorp Diners Club was founded in 1950 and is the international charge card that meets the needs of individuals, business travelers, and the companies for which they travel. Accepted at more than 2.5 million merchant locations in 175 countries, Diners Club serves more than 6.4 million cardmembers worldwide and has relationships with over half of the Fortune 500 companies. The company's 1993 worldwide sales volume was $21 billion.

Beginning with a Corporate Philosophy

"The Right Thing to Do"

As the company's operations center, the Denver office of Citicorp Diners Club performs customer service, credit processing, collections, franchise and establishment services, systems development, and technology services. Other departments in Denver, including human resources and training, quality assurance, finance, and building services, support those functions that ultimately serve the Citicorp Diners Club customer.

In 1991, with a new president and CEO at the helm, Diners Club's Denver facility undertook an initiative to aggressively hire and promote people with disabilities as part of its efforts to champion diversity within its work force and hone its competitive edge.

Robert H. Rosseau came into the company with a strong "people focus," along with a desire to keep the company vital in a fast-paced and changing marketplace. It was under this direction that Diners Club pinpointed a largely untapped source of potential applicants: people with disabilities.

Diners Club knew that the Americans with Disabilities Act (ADA) was to be implemented in a couple of years. But for the management staff, this was not about the ADA. It was the right thing to do for the company.

From Vision to Reality: What Is Do-Able?

In the beginning, Diners Club's human resource managers looked for a relatively simple introductory position—one that would lend itself to any special accommodations in training, equipment, and software—in which to place newly recruited employees with disabilities. The human resources department did not try to tackle every job all at once. At first, a success was needed to demonstrate that people with disabilities could do the job.

To pursue the new initiative, employees with disabilities were brought into the authorizations department as part-time, temporary workers under the employment of a local temporary placement service. Since this 24-hour department was staffed mostly by temporary employees due to fluctuating volumes and a multitude of shifts, it was the likely place to begin.

Authorizations representatives answer calls from merchants seeking verification and approval for charges made on Diners Club accounts. The task involves the use of a multiline telephone, a personal computer, and a software program with four separate screens. Incoming calls usually can be processed within 30 seconds.

Once a starting point for the initiative was established, it was crucial for those leading the effort to gain the support of managers throughout the company.

Lining Up Management Support

In July 1992, the same month the ADA went into effect, human resource managers held a required training session for all Diners Club managers in both the Denver and Chicago offices.

The meeting addressed the ADA and why hiring and promoting people with disabilities is a good business practice. Managers learned about the letter and spirit of the act and its impact on their business. The meeting heightened the managers' awareness. In addition, it reinforced that they should focus on people's abilities. Anyone who needs an accommodation to make the job workable should contact the human resources department so a determination can be made—with the employee's input—as to what the best accommodation would be.

The human resources department also sent out a company-wide memo to inform all employees about the passage of the ADA and its significance to the company.

At the time, the authorizations department had several managers, all of whom were enthusiastic about the hiring initiative. Early on, managers from the authorizations and human resources departments conducted an on-site visit to Projects with Industry, a local non-profit agency, to observe its job training for people with disabilities. The managers who attended stated, "This is something we wanted to make happen once we saw that we could do it, and that there was someone with knowledge and experience who would give us some help."

To ensure a smooth transition into the department, Projects with Industry teamed up with the Colorado Division of Vocational Rehabilitation to hold sensitivity training for non-disabled employees in the authorizations department.

Adapting the Physical Work Environment

Prior to this initiative, Diners Club already had a number of employees with disabilities in its Denver office and had made structural adaptations on an ad hoc basis to accommodate them. Before embarking on a major effort to hire and promote people with disabilities, therefore, it was necessary to prepare the building inside and out to accommodate a wider range of disabilities.

The Diners Club's facilities manager contacted the company's architectural contractor, which made recommendations based on the Building Owners & Managers Association International (BOMA) ADA Compliance Guidebook.* In addition, Diners Club consulted with a local non-profit organization, the Rocky Mountain Federation of Handicapped Athletes, which had an accommodations expert on staff. (The RMFHA is a division of the Pegasus Foundation, Inc., a Denver-based organization that works for the educational and charitable benefit of people with physical disabilities.)

By early 1992, Diners Club was looking to renovate the building's exterior access routes, rest rooms, and cafeteria. The company then sought approval for its plans from the building landlord, which agreed to share some of the costs and responsibilities involved in the renovation.

The most expensive single improvement entailed reconfiguring existing handi-capped rest rooms to create five accessible unisex rest rooms, one on each floor. Each new rest room required an automatic door opener at the entrance, removal of the interior vestibule door, removal of interior stalls and excess toilets, relocated grab bars, new urinals, a locking mechanism, and signage that lights up when the room is occupied. In addition to a $2,000 architectural review, the project cost Diners Club $31,500.

When it came to the cafeteria, Diners Club opted to train the cafeteria service staff to respond to the needs of employees with disabilities. Under the ADA, many of the existing facilities are considered "grandfathered." Diners Club did not have to make these changes, but elected to do so to make the facility an accessible place to work for individuals with disabilities.

Diners Club made other accommodations that were not required by law, including emergency evacuation chairs for each floor, trained employees who

---

* For a copy of BOMA's ADA Compliance Guidebook, contact: BOMA International, 1201 New York Avenue N.W., Suite 300, Washington, D.C. 20005 (phone: 202-408-2662; fax: 202-371-0181).

act as "fire wardens" to help employees with disabilities into the evacuation chairs, additional parking spaces for employees with any temporary disabilities, five Teletype machines for the deaf and amplified telephone equipment for the hearing impaired, and an in-house ergonomics program designed to lower the incidence of repetitive-motion ailments through individual workstation analysis, employee education, and adaptive furniture and equipment as needed. In addition, the company offers a door-to-door shuttle service, contracted through a local firm, which runs during all scheduled work hours.

Outside the building, Diners Club's landlord provided additional handicap parking spaces, signage, and a public sidewalk from the bus stop; trimmed back or removed any foliage that impedes upon the accessibility of walkways; and adjusted the closers on the outside doors to allow enough time for disabled employees to pass through.

In the future, the company plans further improvements, such as replacing existing doorknobs with lever-type openers, installing visual emergency alarms for deaf and hearing-impaired employees (currently, co-workers are assigned to alert these employees in an emergency), remodeling basement locker rooms for accessibility, and locating automatic door openers at the main entrances and exits. It is an ongoing process. The company has focused on the needs of employees who are already on board, but will make additional accommodations as needed.

Getting to Work

Finding Qualified Applicants

With preparations completed, Diners Club was ready to plug into the disabled community in order to find qualified applicants to fill job openings in the authorizations department.

The company's human resource manager began contacting recruitment sources and referral services that specialize in rehabilitation, training, and placement of individuals with disabilities. These included state and federally funded public agencies as well as private organizations. Most of these contacts were made in person by attending job fairs for the disabled; visiting rehabilitation centers, hospitals, and educational facilities; participating on employer advisory committees of rehabilitation organizations; attending national and local conferences on rehabilitation and employment of individuals with disabilities; and inviting job trainers and recruiters to tour Diners Club's Denver office.

From these encounters, the human resource manager culled a list of referral sources, which is continually updated and used today, to ensure ongoing referral of qualified individuals with disabilities for any job openings that arise.

Enlisting Outside Assistance

Diners Club requested expert assistance from these outside sources in the following areas: employee skill-level assessment, job assessment (to determine if the disabled employee can perform the essential functions of the position), adaptive computer equipment and software programming, job coaching, sensitivity training for non-disabled employees, and interpreting business meetings and performance appraisals for the deaf.

When disabled employees came into the authorizations department, Diners Club provided the personal computers and mainframe emulation board, Projects with Industry supplied the JAWS (Job Access With Speech) software application equipment, and the Colorado Division of Vocational Rehabilitation provided the programming.

Today, this system works pretty much the same way: Diners Club provides the computer hardware, the state provides the adaptive software, and both entities negotiate together on the costs of the programming.

A Big Leap

Diners Club's first blind and visually impaired employees were hired into the authorizations department and soon became eligible for other positions within the company. They had an opportunity to move into open positions in the customer service department. This was a more demanding job that entailed the use of up to 66 different computer screens (versus 4 in authorizations) and 600 macro codes to maneuver those screens to process incoming customer service calls. Since they met the qualifications and it was determined in their interviews that they had the skills for the job, the human resources, customer service, and training departments set out to make that position accessible to them as well.

The most extensive accommodation required to open up this next level of opportunity was computer programming and training in the customer service software. This was the company's big leap. If an applicant had the skills to do the job and needed an accommodation, then one would be made. Employees can go as high as their skills will take them and the equipment should not hold them back. Some managers in the Denver office were concerned about the aggressiveness of the plan, but the company forged ahead.

Job counselors from the Colorado Division of Rehabilitation and Colorado Center for the Blind, who had previously worked with these employees on interviewing and employment skills, were on hand to help. They assisted Diners Club's trainers in the accommodation of classes and materials, conducted further sensitivity training for non-disabled co-workers, aided in the process of "job carving" (in which non-disabled workers take over any part of the job a disabled worker cannot do while the disabled employee in turn assumes part of the co-worker's responsibilities), and found a programmer to adapt the software used in customer service.

In-House Training

In May 1993, while the computer fields needed for customer service were being programmed into JAWS, training began. Classes combined sighted employees with blind and visually impaired employees. Initially, the trainer provided a reader for the material that was not yet available in braille, as well as a job coach, but soon found that neither was necessary.

"I had never taught visually impaired people before, so I didn't know how much help they would need," says Genelle Petsch, a Diners Club trainer. "We had set up a lot of helpers for that first class, but by the second class, we were teaching them in much the same way we would train sighted employees."

Trainers, she explains, customarily impart information through three of the senses—visual, auditory, and kinesthetic. "At first, I was concerned about the visual side of training. But I quickly found I didn't have to worry. As long as I concentrated on the auditory information and the kinesthetic aspect, they were fine. Their ability to hone in and work in other ways makes up for the lack of visual ability."

The presence of the disabled students did not bog down the training. On the contrary, Petsch says, "It may have gone faster, because the blind and visually impaired students had already started brailling the material and knew a great deal of information before they got to class. The sighted students were having to keep up with them."

At first, students learned in the classroom through a combination of lecture and hands-on exercises. Then they began to answer customer service calls for a specific product. After a few months, students were brought back into the classroom for additional training.

Early on, the newly trained customer service representatives had the help of an on-floor trainer. Once they settled into their jobs, however, they—like all other employees—had access to an assistant supervisor, whose job it is to answer questions from the customer service representatives, and to an information center they could reach at any time by phone.

All the employees trained for customer service work memorize their most frequently used screens (about 30) and then refer to job manuals when other screens are needed. Although the manuals are available in braille, the JAWS computer system has been programmed to read the on-line reference manuals as well. In addition, all paperwork that employees use for assisting customers is available to the blind and visually impaired representatives on WordPerfect. They can read and fill out such paperwork on their computers.

On the Job

Paul, Nancy, and Jill: Case Studies

The customer service department receives approximately 130,000 calls a month. Positions in the customer service department are very demanding due to the amount of information needed to provide the best service to Diners Club customers. For blind and visually impaired employees, the job is made even more demanding due to the adaptive computer equipment.

While listening to the customer on the right side of his headset, Paul is hearing a voice synthesizer on the left, which relays back the keys he has typed on the keyboard. The voice synthesizer guides him around the screen he is using to process the customer's call, telling him every piece of information a sighted employee would see on the computer screen. The voice speaks quickly, almost subliminally, while the customer talks.

"It's the hardest part of the job," says Paul, who has worked for Diners Club since he completed his training with Projects with Industry more than three years ago and has been a customer service representative for the past year. "I've trained myself to hear different information out of each ear."

Learning the job was a long process, he says, deftly handling the calls that come in one right after the other. He starts with a security screen (every caller undergoes a security check), checks the account balance on another screen, and then gives the customer a charge-by-charge rundown of the account on still another. Later he makes some notes to himself on his braille writer.

Just down the aisle is Nancy, visually impaired and recently trained to process new-application calls. She uses an LP-DOS large-print screen with a voice synthesizer "as a back-up," she notes, "because it would be easy to miss something." As she pans around the card application on the screen, she sees only a part of it at a time. The application appears in blue print; the customer information she types in appears in white. On the walls of her cubicle arc notes printed in extra-large type.

Nancy is a self-taught computer programmer who confesses to enjoying computers. Before Diners Club, where she started as a console operator in authorizations for six months before she moved to customer service, she had worked at a number of jobs, including a nursing home aide, food service worker, and volunteer school aide.

As a new employee, Nancy feels she is starting a career at Diners Club. "I've got another 15 to 20 years of work in me," she says, "and I'd like to do it here."

Jill and her seeing-eye dog have been in customer service for a year. She says that after tiring of low-skill, low-paying jobs, she pursued vocational training at Projects with Industry and then was employed at Diners Club.

Since completing her customer service training, she has appreciated the "constant support system" available to all employees, which includes work-flow supervisors, "leads" (experienced co-workers assigned to help others), the in-house information center, and sighted co-workers who volunteer to exercise her dog for her.

Gauging Success

The performance standard set for disabled employees at Diners Club is the same for all employees: The company will give people the tools they need to do the job, but they must have the skills to do it 100%. "At Diners Club we hire people because we believe they will best serve our customers. We give smart, quality people the opportunity and the resources to serve customers. When that happens, our business prospers," says Robert Rosseau, president and CEO.

Keeping the Initiative Going

Day to Day and Beyond

Diners Club's initiative to hire and promote people with disabilities continues to grow and evolve as each success, and even failure, forges a foundation for the next step.

The company has girded its initiative with employment policies that allow for more flexibility, including moving workers to other positions to accommodate a disability; adjusting work schedules through job sharing, temporary at-home work, and intermittent family medical leave to accommodate a disability; and increasing breaks to allow for medication.

Employees with disabilities are an integral part of the Diners Club corporate fabric and as such are included in its future plans. The company is looking to establish a learning center for people with disabilities at the Denver office. In conjunction with the Colorado Division of Vocational Rehabilitation and the Colorado Center for the Blind, the learning center would provide job training for blind and visually impaired individuals to work in a customer service environment at Citicorp Diners Club and other companies, thereby creating a pool of qualified workers for these positions.

In addition, the company plans to set up internships with the Community College of Denver's Computer Training for People with Disabilities Program. The Denver office also is exploring the feasibility of a formal work-at-home program for people who are unable to work outside of their homes due to their disabilities. In addition, human resource managers continually are on the lookout for new technologies to make the work environment more adaptable to people with disabilities.

A Few Final Words

In order for such an initiative to succeed at Diners Club, it first and foremost required the backing of the most senior people within the corporation, having a human resources manager who has become a "resident expert" on mobility issues, and it takes commitment from the managers of the operational areas.

It also has taken commitment, financial as well as philosophical. On the financial side, funding for an accommodation is provided by the corporation. However, outside resources are also available to provide financial assistance.

On the philosophical side, at Diners Club the attitude is, "We don't have great disabled employees, we have great employees who happen to be disabled." This distinction is the basis of an employment philosophy that has helped Diners Club do a better job in serving customers.

Digital Equipment Corporation

7

Digital Equipment Corporation is the world's leader in open client/server solutions, from personal computing to integrated worldwide information systems. Digital's Alpha AXP platforms, storage, networking, software, and services, together with industry-focused solutions from business partners, help organizations compete and win in today's global marketplace.

Digital's Assistive Technology

Digital Equipment Corporation has demonstrated a long-standing commitment to disabled persons which extends to a number of stakeholders, including employees, customers, community organizations, and others. The passage of legislation such as the Americans with Disabilities Act (ADA) makes Digital's contributions in the field of assistive technology more important than ever.

Digital's Assistive Technology Group, located in Marlboro, Massachusetts, was formed in 1989. The group is responsible for directing the company's engineering and manufacturing resources toward advancing computer-based technology for use by persons with disabilities. The organization employs a multi-faceted strategy and set of programs in order to accomplish this objective. The broad spectrum of activity includes:

- Advancement of the DECtalk speech synthesis technology

- Management of an independent software vendor program

- Establishment of the assistive technology value-added reseller program

- Support for integration of DECtalk technology into third-party products designed for use by people with disabilities

- Operation of Digital's Assistive Technology Access Center (ATAC) demonstration facility

- Development and support of the assistive technology electronic bulletin board system

Digital's commitment to the physically challenged also includes a Vision Impaired Information Services Program Office and Deaf/Hard of Hearing Services.

Each of these elements supports an overall objective of promoting the development of, awareness of, access to, and use of superior quality technology by disabled persons and of maximizing workplace productivity.

DECtalk Speech Synthesis Technology Contributions

Technology and product development efforts are concentrated on the DECtalk speech synthesis technology for two primary reasons. First, the technology offers superior quality speech synthesis, with a high level of natural-sounding and intelligible speech output. Furthermore, the technology offers an expansive range of benefits to individuals with a wide variety of disability types. It is a fundamental element of products and applications that offer computing access and productivity enhancements for:

- People who are blind or have low vision
- People who are non-vocal or non-verbal
- People with learning disabilities
- People with motor skill challenges

Digital's DECtalk PC Speech Synthesizer is one product designed specifically for use by people with disabilities. When used with one of a range of screen access software applications, it offers personal computer (PC) access to individuals who are blind or vision impaired. Material displayed on the terminal screen, as well as keyed material, may be "read" to the user via the speech synthesizer.

DECtalk Express Speech Synthesizer

Digital's high-quality DECtalk™ text-to-speech synthesis technology is now available in an external and portable product. The DECtalk Express Speech Synthesizer can be used with a variety of screen access software applications designed for use by individuals who are non-vocal/non-verbal, are blind or have low vision, or who have learning disabilities. When used in an application of this type, it allows users to hear both keyed input as well as other material displayed on the screen by converting ASCII text to natural-sounding speech output. The serial port allows for use with a PC (IBM or compatible), laptop, notebook, palmtop, workstation, or Apple or Macintosh computer.

Major features of the DECtalk Express Speech Synthesizer include:

- **Portable**   Small, lightweight, and battery-powered for enhanced mobility, with carrying case and other accessories that facilitate transportation

- **Compatible**   Supported by a range of software applications designed for use by people with disabilities; serial communication port interface allows connection to a wide range of desktop and portable PCs as well as PDAs, Apple and Macintosh computers, and workstations

- **Personal**   Headphones included for private listening

- **Accessible**   Braille labeling, audiotape, and braille user information, along with jack differentiation, allow for easy orientation and access for users who are blind or have low vision

- **User control**   Combined on/off and volume controls allow the user to select volume of choice

Supporting software applications can take advantage of the major features of the DECtalk speech synthesis technology, including:

- **Nine predefined voices**   Four male, four female, and one child voice offer a wide selection

- **Speaking rates of 75 to 650 words per minute**   Allows for use from slow spelling to fast scanning

- **Comprehensive pronunciation rules and controls for pauses, pitch, and stress**   Provides for enhanced naturalness and accuracy of spoken text, including proper names and words that are spelled alike but spoken differently

- **Speech options**   Users can elect to have text spoken by letter, word, or phrase and to have some, none, or all punctuation pronounced

- **Unlimited vocabulary**   Comprehensive pronunciation rules allow for pronunciation of any text

- **Word-by-word indexing**   Allows for a direct match between screen viewing and spoken text

Independent Software Vendor Program

The independent software vendor program supports applications developers outside of Digital in developing screen access and other applications to be used with products such as the DECtalk PC Speech Synthesizer. Within this program, resources such as a Developer's Toolkit have been developed, with a goal of supporting the availability and use of a range of choices and applications tailored to the end users' needs.

Value-Added Reseller and Direct Sales Channels

An assistive technology value-added reseller program has also been established to further support the wide range of user needs and interests. For example, the DECtalk PC Speech Synthesizer is available from more than 60 resellers worldwide. The "added value" provided by these resellers can include any of the following:

- System integration
- Technical support
- Consultation
- Documentation
- Training

The value-added reseller program supplements Digital's direct sales channels, which include direct ordering capabilities through the DECdirect and Desktop Direct organizations.

Contributions to Third-Party Assistive Technology Portfolios

Digital's assistive technology is made even more readily available to individuals with disabilities through DECtalk speech synthesis technology licensing arrangements with third-party companies.

This licensing program facilitates the widespread availability and use of Digital's DECtalk speech synthesis technology in a manner that complements the DECtalk-based products that are developed internally. For example, it is licensed for integration in third-party voice output communication aids, commonly known as VOCAs. These devices are extremely useful tools for communicating with DECtalk speech and a variety of forms of input, on behalf of individuals who are non-verbal or have other forms of disabilities which affect the ability to communicate via speech.

Assistive Technology Access Center

The Assistive Technology Access Center provides a supplementary program for facilitating widespread awareness and understanding of Digital's assistive technologies. Employees, customers, community organizations, and others may visit the center, located in Marlboro, Massachusetts, for first-hand demonstrations of the ways in which various assistive technologies and products offer computing access, improved productivity, and tools for employment and personal use.

Electronic Bulletin Board System

Digital's DECtalk PC electronic bulletin board system is available as a method for customers, resellers, and applications developers to gain access to product information. Information about a product can be acquired quickly and easily by users who dial directly into the system via modem from a PC.

Vision Impaired Information Services Program Office

Digital's Vision Impaired Information Services Program Office, located in Nashua, New Hampshire, was developed to meet the documentation needs of visually/print-impaired customers. Services available through Digital's Vision Impaired Information Services Program Office include:

- Vision Impaired On-Line Documentation
- Technology consultation for the visually/print impaired
- Assistive technology consultation, including interpretation of state and federal legislation and adaptive hardware and software integration
- Adaptive technology analysis

Digital customers may purchase translated and formatted documentation by contacting their local sales account representative in the Vision Impaired Information Services Program Office. Documentation may be shipped on the following media:

- Magnetic tape
- Tape cartridge
- Diskette

Formatted documentation for computer braille is available in three forms:

- Printable hard copy/soft copy (ASCII text files)
  o May be printed via bulk braille printer

- o May be read using a braille terminal
- o May be read using various screen magnification utilities

- Voice-generated (DECtalk)
- CD-ROM

Deaf/Hard of Hearing Services

Through its Deaf/Hard of Hearing Services, Digital provides a wide variety of tools and support programs to enhance accessibility for hearing-impaired employees, customers, vendors, suppliers, and other individuals working for or with the company.

Resources includes:

- Awareness training
- Consultation
- Sales support
- Workplace accommodations
- Coordination of American Sign Language classes
- Interpreting services for the employment process

Documentation Service for the Visually Impaired

Strengthening its commitment to physically challenged customers, Digital Equipment Corporation has introduced Vision Impaired On-Line Documentation, a service specially designed to provide blind and visually impaired customers access to electronic information about Digital products.

Vision Impaired On-Line Documentation, in ISO 9660 ASCII format distributed on CD-ROM, offers Digital's customers the flexibility to access product information in the most convenient manner for their specific needs. Documentation can be downloaded and read in a number of ways:

- With screen reader applications combined with a synthetic voice board like DECtalk PC
- In hard copy using a braille printer
- Using a refreshable braille display
- Using various screen magnification utilities

In its first release, in December 1993, Vision Impaired On-Line Documentation included information on the following products:

- ALL-IN-1
- DEC C
- DEC Pascal
- DECset
- OpenVMS
- ULTRIX
- VAX COBOL
- VAX Document
- DEC BASIC
- DEC FORTRAN
- DEC VTX
- DECtalk PC
- RISC C
- VAX C
- VAX DATATRIEVE
- WPS-PLUS

Increasingly, Digital sees that information technology is becoming part of the visually impaired employee's day-to-day work routine. Digital's Vision Impaired On-Line Documentation provides users an easy way to receive information they need about its products. Digital also offers users the flexibility to access the information in the format they prefer, using synthetic voice, braille displays, braille translation software, or screen magnification utilities.

The service is a cost-effective solution for companies that wish to comply with the ADA, which places greater responsibility on employers to invest in assistive technologies.

"Access to timely product information is a key to success in the computer field," says Dr. Daniel Hilton-Chalfen, coordinator of the UCLA Disabilities and Computing Program. "But to many users with visual disabilities, ready access to print documentation has been an impossibility. Digital's Vision Impaired On-Line Documentation sets an example we hope will become standard in the industry by making all Digital documentation readily available in an accessible, electronic format."

Vision Impaired On-Line Documentation, now available in the United States, can be ordered by calling DECdirect (1-800-344-4825) or a local Digital sales representative.

DECtalk PC Application Support

DECtalk speech synthesis is one of the most significant advances in technologies that have enabled a vast number of disabled persons to achieve their human and employment potential. The social welfare of this technological development is beyond measure. In the author's opinion, this is the stuff that the Nobel Prize was designed to recognize. Digital Equipment's management philosophy and support, combined with its creative scientific and engineering expertise, has produced an assistive technology that will positively impact individuals, companies, and governments worldwide.

The wide range of applications of DECtalk may be partially appreciated by the large number of products and companies engaged in developing those supporting products, as shown in Exhibit I. To fully appreciate the impact that DECtalk has made, it would be necessary to see totally and partially blind persons, the deaf and hearing-impaired persons, and others working in engineering, scientific, customer service, healthcare, and so many other fulfilling and important jobs in companies spread across the United States and abroad.

Reducing Costs and Future Directions

Ronald Gemma, a product manager at Digital, explains that,

> Some of the challenges that face the assistive technology market in the future include reduced product costs and size, enhanced technology in the areas of speech recognition and speech synthesis, and access to the computer-based graphical user interface (GUI) for the vision- and motion-limited person.
>
> Improvements are being made constantly. For instance a high-end voice dictation speech recognition system sold for $9000+ several years ago. Today, they can be purchased for under $1K. Similarly, high-quality text-to-speech synthesis cost $4700 several years ago and now can be purchased for less than $1200. OCR (optical character recognition) reading machines were in the $5000 range in the same time period and are now available for under $2000 as add-ons to existing PCs. The cost price curve can be seen in the comparison of a PC system equipped for a blind person. In 1989, a braille-based PC with a braille display and braille printer could cost from $16–20,000+. It also required that the individual be very well versed in braille. In 1991, a PC with a DOS-based screen access program and a stand-alone text-to-speech synthesizer would cost in the $8–12K range. In 1993, a MS Windows-based PC with a GUI-capable screen access program and an integral text-to-speech synthesizer option card cost in the $3.5–5K range. With the text-to-speech technology, the user need only to learn to touch type instead of mastering the usually more difficult to learn braille.
>
> These cost trends are accompanied by technology improvements. Speech recognition dictation rates are faster, OCR is more accurate and less sensitive to types of fonts and page skewing in the reader, speech synthesis is getting more natural, and screen access programs allow a blind person to navigate in a graphical-based environment like MS Windows using a mouse pointing device.

EXHIBIT I

DECtalk PC Application Support
January 22, 1995

Product	Version	Application	Company	Address	Telephone
An Open Book Unbound	V2.0	OCR reader	Arkenstone, Inc.	1390 Borregas Ave. Sunnyvale, CA 94089	408-752-2200 745-6739 FAX 800-444-4443
ASAP (Auto. Screen Access Program)	V1.0	Screen access	Microtalk	917 Clearcreek Drive Texarkana, TX 75503	903-832-3471 832-3517 FAX 832-3722 BBS
Business Vision DT4 Win Vision	V3.08	Screen access/ DOS Screen access/ Windows	Artic Technologies	55 Park Street Troy, MI 48083-2753	810-588-7370
CINTEX		Communication aid/environmental control	NanoPac, Inc.	4833 S. Sheridan Rd. Ste. 402 Tulsa, OK 74145-5718	918-665-0329 665-0361 FAX
EASE (Easy access workstation)		Library information system	Gaylord Brothers	7272 Morgan Road Liverpool, NY 13090	800-272-3414 315-457-5070
Eyegaze		Computer control	LC Technologies, Inc.	9455 Silver King Ct. Fairfax, VA 22031	703-385-7133

EXHIBIT I (continued)

DECtalk PC Application Support
January 22, 1995

Product	Version	Application	Company	Address	Telephone
Flipper	V4.2	Screen access	Omnichron	1438 Oxford Street Berkeley, CA 94709	510-540-6455
HandiCHAT HandiKEY	V2.23 V3.0	Communication aid	Microsystems Software	600 Worcester Road Framingham, MA 01701	508-879-9000 626-8515 FAX 875-8009 BBS 800-828-2600
JAWS (Job Access With Speech) DOS/Windows WordScholar	V2.31 V1.0	Screen access Learning	Henter-Joyce, Inc.	2100 62nd Ave., North St. Petersburg, FL 33702	800-336-5658 813-528-8900 8901 FAX 8903 BBS
outSPOKEN for Macintosh (DECtalk Express) and Windows		Screen access MS Windows	Berkeley Systems, Inc.	2095 Rose Street Berkeley, CA 94709	510-540-5535 540-5115 FAX
ProTalk		Screen Access MS Windows	BioLink Computer R&D Ltd.	4770 Glenwood Ave. N. Vancouver, BC V7R 4G8 Canada	604-984-4099 985-8493 FAX

Product	Version	Type	Company	Address	Phone
QWERTY WORD PROCESSOR		Talking word processor	HFK Software	68 Welles Road Lincoln, MA 01773	617-259-0059
SARAW (Speech Assisted Reading and Writing)		Literacy	Regenisis	1046 Deep Cove Road N. Vancouver, BC Canada	604-929-6663
ScreenPower OsCar	V1.0A V3.0	Screen access OCR reader	TeleSensory	455 N. Bernadino Ave. P.O. Box 7455 Mountain View, CA 94039-7455	415-960-0920 800-227-8418
Screen Reader/DOS Screen Reader/2 (DECtalk Express)	V1.2	Screen access	IBM Special Needs Systems	1000 NW 51st Street Boca Raton, FL 33432	800-426-4832 407-982-6508
Sound Proof		Learning	Humanware, Inc.	6245 King Road Loomis, CA 95650	800-722-3393
Talking Screen EZ Keys	V3.42 V5.09	Communication aid	words +, inc.	40015 Sierra Highway Building B-145 Palmdale, CA 93550	800-869-8521 805-266-8500 266-8969 FAX 266-8896 BBS
Tinytalk	V1.41	Screen access	OMS Development	610B Forest Ave. Wilmette, IL 60091	708-251-5787 251-5793 FAX
Vocal-Eyes	V2.2	Screen access/ learning	GW Micro	310 Racquet Drive Fort Wayne, IN 46825	219-483-3625

EXHIBIT I (continued)

DECtalk PC Application Support
January 22, 1995

Product	Version	Application	Company	Address	Telephone
Vocate Slimware/ Window Bridge	V1.0 V1.3	Learning Screen access DOS/Windows	Syntha-Voice Computers, Inc.	800 Queenston Road Ste. 304 Stoney Creek, Ontario L8G 1A7 Canada	905-662-0565 800-263-4540 263-0568 FAX 263-0569 BBS
VOS (Voice Operating System)	Dialogic Toolkit	Telephone response	Parity Software	870 Market, Ste. 800 San Francisco, CA 94102	415-989-0330 989-0441 FAX 989-0436 BBS
Write Away	V1.2	Communication aid	Institute on Applied Technology	Children's Hospital Fegan Plaza 300 Longwood Avenue Boston, MA 02115	617-735-6998 735-6882 FAX

Eaton Corporation, Hydraulics Division

8

Kurt Langel, Human Resources Manager

In June 1988, Eaton Corporation acquired the Cessna Plant in Hutchinson, Kansas from General Dynamics. Eaton's interest in the facility surfaced because of the compatibility of products with existing products that were offered through Eaton Corporation's Hydraulics Division.

The Hutchinson Plant has been in existence since the early 1940s, when the facility manufactured wooden gliders under the Cessna name. Hydraulic cylinders, gear pumps, and motors were introduced in the 1950s, and valves as well as piston pumps evolved in the 1960s. The Hutchinson Plant continues to manufacture these products today under the Eaton name primarily for major agricultural original equipment manufacturers. Hutchinson employs 700 people under 702,000 square feet of floor space. The bargaining unit is represented by the International Association of Machinists. At the time of this writing, the average employee is 45 years of age with 18 years of service.

Hiring the Disabled

Under Cessna, the Hutchinson Plant had been extremely proactive in hiring and accommodating individuals with disabilities. Cessna's attitude about employing the disabled was a perfect match with the human resource philosophies of Eaton Corporation. The manufacturing boom of the 1970s along with Cessna's relationship with a local rehabilitation center provided the catalyst for meeting production needs and accommodating the disabled. The following is a summary of employees at the Hutchinson Plant who are disabled and performing production operations:

Disability	Job	Years of Service
Hearing	Pump tester	21
Sight	Assembler	29
Loss of arm	Materials handler	21
Loss of arm	Tool maker	34
Hearing	Lathe operator	38
Cerebral palsy	Machine operator	22
Hearing	Bar chuck machine	36
Knee fused	Tool grinder	20
Hearing	Valve tester	29
Sight	Assembler	32
Sight	Machine operator	19
Loss of leg	Machine operator	9

Philosophy Shift

Ironically, while the Hutchinson Plant had been progressive in employing and accommodating the disabled who were hired into the facility, the plant did not seem to be as proactive with employees who may have been injured on the job or developed non-work-related disabilities and had medical restrictions. High workers' compensation costs as well as the introduction of the Americans with Disabilities Act (ADA) pushed the Hutchinson Plant to embrace worker accommodation within its active work force.

In 1992, workers' compensation costs at Hutchinson were $1892 per employee. Also, due to its labor contract and past practice, the plant had no avenues to pursue in returning restricted employees to work. Its position had been that if an employee could not perform 100% on the job, he could not return to work. In 1992, policies, procedures, and accommodations to the facility were reviewed in preparation for the ADA.

In mid-1992, the company and the union began a series of meetings to discuss the ADA and any provisions of the labor contract that might interfere with this new law. The union leadership was dedicated to any changes or improvements that were needed to conform to the ADA. Through this series of meetings, the company and the union agreed to a return-to-work program for people on limited duty.

The company focused on the number of employees off work receiving temporary total disability and what the cost was to the company. At the same time, it was pointed out that some of these inactive employees, who were of full-time status but restricted in what they could do, were union members but were not paying dues because they were not allowed to return to work. While the company was not in a position to create jobs to return people to work, it was pointed out that oftentimes employees can return to their regular jobs or light duty positions with simple accommodations. As a result of the company/union agreement, Hutchinson has a separate department that accounts for employees' time while on light duty assignments. While in this department, employees do not learn specialized skills that may earn them favor over senior employees. This was a crucial issue in the agreement in that specialized skills are used in the labor agreement to determine a successful bidder. Any labor costs associated with light duty work do not get directly charged to the department supervisor. The light duty department is managed by the human resources department and charged as such. This ensures that there is a record of activity if the information is needed in the future. Between employees entering and leaving the program, it continually employs about 1% of the work force. Hutchinson workers' compensation expenses have been reduced $571 per employee (the annualized estimate for 1994) from the 1992 cost of $1892 per employee. This reduction amounts to a total annual savings of $924,700. People who use the light duty program find it a favorable method of rehabilitation for returning to their previous jobs.

Ergonomics

As a result of the company/union agreement on a return-to-work program, the supervisors and engineers found themselves looking at how jobs were being done instead of what was being done. To assist in the learning process of evaluating methodologies to accommodate work, as well as increase the awareness of the cause of cumulative trauma injuries, Hutchinson conducted ergonomics training for all supervisory and engineering personnel. The safety coordinators, who are hourly personnel in the bargaining unit, also took part in the training.

The trainer instructed the group on the causes of cumulative trauma such as poor hand/wrist posture and equipment designed to fit tooling, plant space, and internal componentry without any consideration of the human body. A discussion of carpal tunnel syndrome focused on how the carpal tunnel nerve becomes inflamed due to poor work methods and/or overuse and how the carpal tunnel nerve is surgically repaired.

The trainer also focused on early detection and prevention, which would be a change from the past. Typically the company shied away from wanting to hear and deal with sore arms and hands, and employees were sensitive to that position. As a result, soreness went unreported until it was too late and surgery, as well as additional expense, was the only answer. The trainer emphasized ergonomic and reaction plans that freely permit employees to report the early stages of soreness so that necessary adjustments to the work area can be made. This direction would also eventually result in a reduction of workers' compensation costs and recordable injuries because the focus would be on prevention rather than reaction.

The trainer spent time in the plant videotaping operations that could clearly result in cumulative trauma. In one scene, an operator was forced to bend over to lift parts out of a tub. It was estimated the parts weighed 10 to 15 pounds and the employee would bend over 150 times per day. The group decided that a waist-high half tub may be in order to eliminate bending, as well as a conveyor assist to move the parts to the machine. The supervisors and engineers left the meeting with a different perspective on the causes of cumulative trauma and what can be done to prevent such an injury. Even more important, the company is receptive to employees' comments about soreness and encourages early reporting and corrective action.

While the number of cumulative trauma cases at Hutchinson has not yet declined, the plant continues to be proactive in implementing ergonomic measures as cumulative trauma symptomology is identified. The latest innovation is an ergonomic alert that is completed upon the initial notice of cumulative trauma and forces follow up by the department safety team. There has, however, been an improvement in safety statistics. The lost workday rate has declined from 3.1 in 1992 to 2.5 in 1994. The recordable injury rate was 16.1 in 1993 and is currently at 15.3. Because of the return-to-work program, the most significant reduction has been seen in days away from work, which was 160 in 1991, dropped to 121.3 in 1992, and is currently 57.7.

Examples of Accommodation

Hutchinson employs a blind parts assembler who has 32 years of service. This employee has received accommodations throughout the years in a variety of ways:

- His ride to work is provided by a generous co-worker(s) who also escorts him to and from his workstation and any rest room needs. For this employee, by far the greatest accommodation is the people who work at Hutchinson and their attitude about the disabled.

- His supervisor and co-workers ensure that the parts that he works with are similar and that there are no changes to his work area without informing him first.

- His primary function is to ensure that machined parts have a smooth finish and are properly "deburred." Simple hand-held tools are used to remove burrs. Quality is also assured by his feeling the parts for smoothness.

Another employee with nine years of service had his left leg amputated just below the knee due to a health condition. Just one week after surgery, the employee returned to work, primarily filling out paperwork so he could be seated and allow his leg to recover from surgery. This assignment lasted approximately 30 days, at which time the employee returned to his regular duties in machining while standing on crutches. Eventually, he had a prosthesis made, and crutches were not necessary. After a short duration, this employee was assigned to quality assurance, which required him to travel the facility. The company purchased a stand-up electric cart so he could complete his assignment as required. Another transfer was made back to machine operations, where the entire work area was arranged to accommodate the employee. New roll tables were built, racks were readjusted, and the immediate work area was opened up to provide the employee a safe, productive work environment.

Several years ago, Hutchinson employed an individual in a wheelchair. He worked in the toolroom and eventually retired from that position. The toolroom had an operation where broach buttons were polished. The supervisor determined that the employee could do the work if a lower work bench was built to accommodate the height of his wheelchair. The supervisor moved the employee and any machinery that had to do with the operation into a separate room where the employee could control all service, ordering, and processing of these buttons. In order to do this, all storage racks were reworked to a lower level, and a special "hook" was manufactured so the employee could reach parts at the bottom of the rack. As a result of manufacturing improvements, the need for the broach buttons eventually was eliminated. The company then determined that the employee could sharpen drill bits if the workbench was redesigned and brought down to the level of his wheelchair. All control handles on equipment were redesigned to allow the employee access to whatever he needed to do the job.

The Hutchinson Plant of Eaton Corporation made very few changes with the implementation of the ADA. The attitude of the people, along with a positive relationship with organized labor, put the company far ahead of employers that continue to struggle with the requirements of the ADA. While two of its greatest success stories are the reduction in workers' compensation costs and its return-to work program, its most significant achievement is the realization that active employees with restrictions can be contributing members of the organization.

Federal Express

9

Betty Laevey, Career Planning Administrator

Twenty-one years ago, FedEx was first to reach the market with time-sensitive express package delivery services. The company still sets the standards in the shipping industry for reliability, innovative technology, logistics management, and customer satisfaction. FedEx continues to enhance its network, its equipment, and its services to stay ahead of its competitors. The company consistently works to compress time, putting its customers in touch with their end users faster and helping them to be competitive nationally and internationally. Every 24 hours, two million packages pass through FedEx hubs, meeting time-certain commitments that keep the world economy ticking. For over 100,000 Federal Express employees around the world, "it's all in a day's work."

Federal Express's Responses to Employees with Disabilities Before and After Passage of the Americans with Disabilities Act

Prior to passage of the Americans with Disabilities Act (ADA), Federal Express employed persons with disabilities in professional and administrative areas as well as operational areas.

Central Support Services and Air Ground Terminals & Transportation

In the Central Support Services and Air Ground Terminals & Transportation Divisions, large sorting facilities and ramps are processing points. These areas are where packages are received, sorted, redistributed, off-loaded, and reloaded onto aircraft and readied for distribution to the Ground Operations Division pickup and delivery teams. The primary positions at these sorting facilities are categorized as checker/sorters and handlers. These areas house complicated sorting belt systems, heavy equipment, tugs, cargo container dollies, and fork-lifts, among other equipment.

At its National Sorting Facilities, specifically in Memphis, Oakland, and Indianapolis, FedEx has hired a number of employees with hearing impairments. These employees were first hired in January 1989. In order to create a safe and comfortable environment, management has provided TDD machines and voice relay systems. In addition, American Sign Language classes are held for any and all employees, including managers. A Hearing Impaired Coordinator was hired in November 1991 in order to provide for better communication between employees with hearing impairment and those without. It is interesting to note that Federal Express took these steps before the introduction of the ADA.

At the Oakland facility, TDDs have been installed in the administration area. In addition, a telephone that will automatically call security in case of an emergency has been installed in the elevator. Under consideration is the installation of strobe lights in rest rooms, break rooms, halls, and outside the building in the ramp area of the airport grounds.

Customer Service

Federal Express has also employed persons with hearing impairments in its Customer Invoicing Data Center as well as Customer Research and the professional areas. In the Customer Service Division, an individual with multiple sclerosis along with a hearing impairment was given a quieter work area and phones equipped with lights to indicate they were ringing.

There are a number of visually impaired customer service representatives (CSRs) at FedEx's five regional call centers. They are responsible for taking shipping orders by telephone and committing them to a computer database to be relayed to the ground operations network for pickup and delivery. Following an examination of the needs of the visually impaired against available technology by the Network Systems and Design Group of Customer Service and Planning, the first visually impaired customer service agent was hired in October 1987.

With minor exceptions, the work performed by visually impaired employees is identical to that performed by their sighted counterparts. The employees are enabled to perform their jobs through a system of screen-reading software which interprets information on a computer screen and sends it to a speech synthesizer which in turn speaks to the CSR. Instead of the dedicated terminals used by sighted CSRs, the system requires the use of a personal computer equipped with hardware and software which allows it to interface with the Federal Express mainframe. The CSR uses a specially modified headset which receives input from the customer in one ear and from the synthetic speech device in the other.

Federal Express is currently working on a project that will attempt to resolve the issue of limited access to printed resources by visually impaired employees.

Training/informational products will be referred to a format that will allow the data to be transferred to disks that can be read by the synthetic speech device. Alternatively, the data can be sent to a braille embosser which will translate the material for those who read braille. As a result, visually impaired employees will have access to publications simultaneously with their sighted peers.

Ground Operations

Service agents for FedEx's Ground Operations Division have responsibility for interfacing with customers at stations and business service centers. They accept over-the-counter shipments dropped off by customers. As part of their duties, they are expected to have the ability to lift packages weighing 75 pounds by themselves and maneuver packages weighing up to 150 pounds with assistance. In an effort to enhance the opportunities for employees who are restricted from performing such lifting tasks, FedEx has granted station management the prerogative of waiving the lifting requirements where the operation permits.

Federal Express's philosophy is "People, Service, Profit," and it has demonstrated its commitment to its people over the years in a myriad of ways. A large proportion of its employees are in positions that require driving (e.g., couriers) and heavy lifting. When couriers can no longer meet the certification mandates of the Department of Transportation, they must be removed from such positions. Where possible, FedEx has placed some of these employees in foot courier positions and other courier positions that do not require their meeting the stringent qualifications of the Department of Transportation.

Other Areas

Throughout the corporation, the Properties and Facilities department is responsible for ensuring that appropriate modifications have been made to facilities to comply with the ADA. In the area of ramps, such modifications must also be in compliance with building codes for ramps. For example, in the case of an employee whose mobility depends on his using crutches, which prohibited his maneuvering a ramp that was too steep, the ramp was modified to meet his needs.

Examples of other accommodations currently being provided include:

- Doors are widened to accommodate wheelchairs

- Correctly contoured ergonomic chairs are provided for those who suffer from back problems

- High-tech keyboards are provided for persons who have developed carpal tunnel syndrome

- Shift adjustments may be made where a person's physical condition precludes working at a particular time of day

- "Standing" positions are created for those who cannot sit for extended periods

- Special break schedules are created for those who have digestive, dietary, or exercise problems

Federal Express Corporation Human Capital Management Program

The quickest way to improve earnings is to decrease expenses. Federal Express spent over $100 million during calendar year 1991 on time lost due to employee illness and/or injury. While this is a staggering figure, it does not even begin to account for the indirect costs associated with lost productivity—lower morale, service failures, and, most important, lost energy and thinking power in the work force.

The Corporate Human Capital Management Task Force was charged with developing a solution to this issue. The solution resulted in several changes to policies and procedures and, more importantly, established a team approach to help the manager as well as the employee who is on leave. Effective March 1992, Federal Express implemented the Corporate Human Capital Management Program, which affected existing policies and procedures related to medical leave of absence, attendance, and safety policies, among others.

The Human Capital Management Program was developed not only to contain costs and better manage cases of employee absence due to illness and injury, but also to maintain contact with employees whose extended absence could cause them to feel disaffiliated from the company. Continuing contact ultimately eases the employee's reentry into the work force.

Knowledge of the Human Capital Management Program is mandatory for management as well as Personnel, Safety, and other relevant support groups. Therefore, extensive efforts have been made to prepare all managers corporate-wide for their roles as a result of any procedural changes. Training is conducted by personnel representatives and safety/health specialists. Instructional manuals are updated and recurrency training is conducted to keep management apprised of policies and procedures.

The following is an overview of the basic function of the Divisional Human Capital Management Program Committee. Actual committee procedures and operations are at the discretion of the local teams and are designed to meet specific divisional needs.

The Divisional/District Committees

Standing committee members:

- Designated divisional/district chairperson
- Personnel matrix representative
- Safety/health specialist

Advisors to the committee include corporate staff groups such as Workers' Compensation, Legal, and Employee Benefits as needed.

Divisional Committee Functions

- Establish a process for convening in a timely manner to review cases

- Establish a system to ensure that management maintains appropriate communications and timely information to employees on medical leave of absence

- Review status of specific cases and provide:
  - o Placement of employee returning from leave
  - o Review of employee returning from leave with restrictions/limitations
  - o Employee with letter confirming application preference status or laterals and
  - o Downbids within division
  - o Other placements within the division not requiring corporate committee review

Corporate Human Capital Management Committee Responsibilities

- Resolution of problems that cannot be resolved at local levels (i.e., conflicting medical opinions, recurring injury/illness)

- Placement of employees released for return to work with no restrictions when no positions are available within the division

- Review of employees released for return to work with restrictions and limitations when no modified positions are available within the division

- Proposed position or work area modifications requiring expenses over $2000

- Maintain records to track trends, placements, types of cases by category, etc.

Temporary Return to Work

- Permits a full-time employee on disability leave to return to work in a limited capacity for a maximum period of 90 days

Florida Power & Light Company

10

Florida Power & Light Company (FPL) was established in 1925 and is one of the largest investor-owned utilities in the nation. Its headquarters is in Juno Beach, Florida, and its service territory covers 27,650 miles in all or part of 35 Florida counties, using 58,000 miles of electric lines. The company prides itself in its ability to manage costs to the extent that a typical customer bill was nearly 10% lower in December 1993 than in 1985. It also takes pride in its long-standing and progressive efforts toward effectively addressing diversity issues and its sensitivity in meeting the needs of its 12,000 employees.

Initial Efforts

In an effort to project management's progressive attitude toward implementing a comprehensive equal employment opportunity program, FPL's president issued the following letter to all employees:

> Fellow employees:
>
> FPL has a long-standing commitment to equal opportunity. This helps ensure that individuals are given equal opportunity in employment, advancement and benefits without regard to race, color, religion, sex, age, national origin, disability or because an individual is a disabled veteran or a veteran of the Vietnam Era.
>
> We are proud of our record in this endeavor and are committed to even greater achievements in the future.
>
> FPL's Affirmative Action Program sets forth specific objectives as well as procedures which will translate our equal opportunity policies into deeds.

I am personally committed to the implementation of our Affirmative Action Program. Its success requires a similar commitment from each employee. Your personal dedication to and involvement in Equal Employment Opportunity is required to make this commitment effective.

Stephen Frank
President

With the passage of the Americans with Disabilities Act (ADA) in 1992, the company launched a two-pronged effort to communicate its intent to meet both the specific requirements and the spirit of the act. One effort was directed toward communicating the impact of the act on the company and its employees. This was accomplished through an article entitled "Americans with Disabilities Act: What You Should Know," published in an internal newsletter in July 1992.

In this article, the company announced the passage of the act and its enforcement provision. The company also announced the establishment of a team consisting of 40 employees to consider important ADA issues. The article further outlined the types of disabilities protected by the act, factors related to reasonable accommodations, and the belief that most accommodations would not be too costly.

The second thrust of the company's two-pronged effort was to prepare an ADA training program for all supervisors. The purpose of the training program was to provide supervisors with the education and insight required for their objective and sensitive handling of any issue associated with persons with disabilities. The training program was designed to enable supervisors to realize the following objectives:

- List five employment practices covered by the ADA

- Describe who the ADA protects

- Identify how disability is defined

- Distinguish between essential and non-essential job functions

- Select three examples of reasonable accommodations

- List three selection standards and procedures covered by the ADA

- Identify two types of questions that are not allowed during a pre-employment interview

The company also prepared a special videotape on the ADA and developed a training program for its human resource staff.

Reasonable Accommodations and Special Programs for Persons with Disabilities at FPL

Reclamation and Salvage Department Project

FPL maintains a large, centralized reclamation and salvage facility as a separate profit center and as part of its cost reduction efforts. The latter facility receives a wide variety of worn, damaged, and obsolete materials and parts from power plant, transmission, and other units throughout its widespread operating territory. It then separates and consolidates these materials in order to optimize their salvage value. The facility also has refurbishing shops for the repair of items such as street lights, cut-out switches, and transformers that can be returned to service. Altogether, it contributes significantly to the profitability of the company.

In order to further its relationship with local rehabilitation organizations in support of their objective of providing job training to persons with disabilities, FPL decided to hire a group of people with a wide range of disabilities to supplement its full-time work force at the reclamation and salvage facility. This concept of a supplementary work force also supported management's cost containment objectives, since this group would handle only surge workload requirements where full-time employees would not be economically justified.

In establishing this special group of disabled employees, the company considered two options. The first, which was not adopted, was to contract the work out to an off-site rehabilitation organization. The second option, which was adopted, resulted in the work being performed at FPL's facility, with hiring, supervision, and wage payments made through a rehabilitation organization. FPL and the rehabilitation organization worked together to create the right fit between job functions and individuals. An initial group of 15 disabled workers and 2 supervisors was established, with the workers integrated within various departments. This arrangement proved to be too cumbersome for the supervisors, who had to travel to different departments. The solution was to establish an enclave, or special unit, where all of the disabled employees worked. While the disabled employees are located together to perform their work, all break periods are taken in common areas with all employees at the facility. Special workbenches and other accommodations have been made to facilitate the ability of the disabled employees to accomplish their tasks.

The range of disabilities found in this group includes hearing impaired, emotional difficulties, cognitive limitations, crutch dependent, and quadriplegic. The average productivity of the group is 73% (with a low of 55% and a high of 93%) as measured against the productivity of the regular work force. The quality of the disabled group's work is equal to that of the full-time work force. Importantly, the wages paid to the disabled employees on production jobs are based on their individual productivity levels. Non-production jobs such as janitorial services are paid at the regular company rate. Job functions performed by persons with disabilities include sorting paper, baling cardboard, disassembly of street lights and other devices, assembly of boxes, packaging of salvageable parts, and parts assembly. Management reports that this special work group has demonstrated a very positive attitude, has an excellent attendance record, is well-accepted by other employees, and expresses a deep appreciation for the chance to demonstrate their capabilities. This program is evidence of management's stated belief that every person has value and that it is their job to find opportunities for individuals to be productive.

FPL is one of a handful of corporations selected to receive the Employment Achievement Award from the Florida Development Disabilities Council. The award recognizes FPL's practice of employing people with disabilities at the central reclamation and salvage center with the goal of enabling disabled persons to get experience in the workplace and graduate after one year to full-time employment elsewhere. The company's skills building program began in 1992.

Individual with Severe Allergy

One employee developed a severe allergic reaction to the chlorine used in processing engineering drawings and blueprints. To correct the situation, the company replaced existing processing equipment with a dry Xerox process and contracted out chlorine-based work. Unfortunately, the individual was still sensitive to the vapors which emanated from the paper received from the contractors. A final solution to dealing with these vapors was the installation of a high-efficiency particulate-arresting air purification system. In this example, the company demonstrated sensitivity not only to the allergic employee, but also to the possible effects of chlorine vapors on other employees in the area.

Engineer with Limited Vision

In order to enable an engineer who developed a problem with his peripheral vision to continue to work, the company purchased a computer magnification software program and associated hardware.

Computer Specialist with Muscular Dystrophy

In order to facilitate the continued employment of a computer specialist with muscular dystrophy, the company permitted him to work at home and provided him with the necessary computer and communications equipment. A special phone line was also installed at his home. While the company was willing to have him work entirely at home, the individual expressed a desire to work at the office 50% of the time. Because of the employee's extremely high level of productivity and quality performance, a first-floor office was provided even though his department was located on the fourth floor. His fellow employees have been particularly attentive to his needs by arranging for special access to a manually operated elevator in case of emergency, assisting him out of conference room chairs, and working around his physical limitations.

Motorcycle Accident Victim

A computer specialist who repairs and installs personal computers returned to work after being paralyzed from the waist down in a motorcycle accident. Fellow employees comment that he moves around the building in his wheelchair faster than they are able to. The only accommodation that was required to enable him to perform his job was to raise the height of his desk.

Accommodations at the Company's Fitness Center

The company's fitness center is designed to allow access by all employees. Special equipment and accommodations have been incorporated for persons with disabilities. For example, a polio victim who has difficulty walking utilizes specially designed upper body exercise equipment, individuals with cardiac problems receive special attention and regimens, and individuals with multiple sclerosis utilize special pieces of equipment that are designed for easy access and limited controls, such as limited leg extension, so that they will not exceed their capabilities.

The fitness center's philosophy is to bring persons with disabilities into the mainstream; there is no separation of employees using the facility. The center's staff works with each individual in developing a wellness program that is appropriate to his or her capabilities. Interestingly, the company calculates that it saves $3 for every dollar spent on the fitness center's operation.

Other Accommodations for Disabled Employees

- Special training for a meter reader with dyslexia
- A sign language interpreter is provided at meetings for a hearing-impaired employee
- Amplified phones in the customer service department for use by hearing-impaired employees
- Numerous physical access accommodations

Special Job Descriptions for Return-to-Work Analysis

The company has prepared job analysis descriptions covering all work functions to enable company doctors to properly evaluate an injured employee's ability to return to a specific job. These job descriptions were prepared using the aid of the U.S. Department of Labor's "Dictionary of Occupational Titles" and the Capability Corporation's publication entitled "Characteristics of Occupations."

Where the job description indicates that the individual's disability function is marginal (versus central) to the person's task, his or her return to work is not an issue. A workmen's compensation issues committee, composed of persons from all of the company's business units, has been formed to resolve any unresolved issues between individuals and the company. In those cases where an individual can no longer perform his or her original job function, the company assists in finding a new position. An examples of FPL's job analysis format is shown below.

Job Analysis

The position of **lineman,** at the xxxxxx location (D.O.T. #821.361-026), is a skilled one requiring a four-year apprenticeship and ongoing continuing education in-service courses. A commercial driver's license, "Hilti gun" license, forklift license, and first aid and CPR certification are required.

The lineman works on a two-man crew under the direct supervision of a job foreman, working a regular 40-hour week in 5 days per week or, in some areas, a 40-hour week in 4 days. In major emergency situations, such as hurricanes, the usual routine is 16 hours on and 8 hours off. For other emergencies of lesser catastrophe, whoever has the least overtime posted is called.

The position of lineman is almost entirely outside, exposing the worker to fumes, dust, mist, and environmental changes involving heat, wind, and wet and humid weather. Some night duty is required in emergencies, presenting the added risk of reduced visibility on all types of terrain. The job requires climbing and working at unprotected heights. The worker is also around moving machinery and drives automotive equipment.

Essential Job Functions

The job of lineman is described as being about 50% working aloft on overhead lines and the rest of the time on the ground working on underground cables. The linemen are responsible for constructing new facilities and repairing existing structures.

When installing underground cables, trenches or holes may have to be dug to a depth of approximately 3 to 6 feet to install the cable and conduit. This requires hand digging on various types of terrain including mud, sand, sodded, etc. After the conduit is installed, the trench or hole that was dug is filled in and the sodded area repaired if necessary. Occasionally, a backhoe and trencher are used, depending on the crew mix and where the job is. This involves climbing up and down from the backhoe seat and operating the hand and foot controls. Finally, the cable is pulled through the buried conduit.

Other jobs include switching the cables by going through the transformer using a six- to eight-foot insulated stick "shotgun" on which "elbows" are placed. These are used to pull off energized elbow terminations and put on de-energized bushings. These cone-shaped receptacles are plugged into energized elbows.

When working above ground or aloft, the worker is required to climb up into a lift bucket. The bucket is approximately 24 × 28 inches and about 5 feet deep. It is not possible to squat into a bucket. The worker uses shotgun sticks to undo and move items on the pole he is working with. The work is about 80% in front of the lineman and about 20% above his head. Insulators, which weigh 25 to 30 pounds each, are hung by drilling holes in the pole and hanging one to three per pole. Wire is picked up under tension and transferred from one pole to a new pole. Some buckets have winches to lift the wire, which may be anywhere from 25 to 30 pounds of pull up to 100 pounds of pull. This depends on the wire size, ranging from No. 2 diameter, which is about the size of a pencil, or No. 568 diameter, which is about $1 \frac{1}{4}$ inches in diameter. Some wire is aluminum and some copper, depending on the environmental conditions and if it will be exposed to salt spray. When working in an easement that is inaccessible to the buckets, the lineman must climb the pole. This involves putting "hooks" or climbers on and a belt which holds 30 to 60 pounds of gear and tools. The belt is also a safety belt when up on the pole. Climbing with hooks involves keeping the knees, or at least one knee, locked to keep the hooks in the pole. When up on the pole, the worker will set insulators or drill and may have to reach out to three to four feet to access what is being repaired. Insulated covers are made of rubber and are three inches by four feet. These are hauled up on a hand line with a pulley with someone on the ground assisting. The poles may be anywhere from 35 to 50 feet tall or 65 to 100 feet tall.

Physical Demands

The position of lineman is classified as heavy duty, requiring 6.0 mets of typical energy. It involves occasionally lifting up to 100 pounds and frequently lifting 50 pounds or less.

Activity	*Percent of Time Doing Activity*
Sitting	Occasionally (0 to 33%)
Reaching above shoulder level	Frequently (34 to 66%)
Working with body bent at waist	Frequently
Crawling	Occasionally
Climbing stairs and ladders	Occasionally
Working with arms extended at shoulder level	Frequently
Working with arms above shoulders	Occasionally
Fine hand manipulation	Frequently
Gross hand manipulation	Frequently
Simple grasping	Frequently
Power grip	Frequently
Hand twisting	Occasionally
Pushing	Occasionally
Pulling	Frequently

Discussion

The position of lineman is physically taxing, requiring the worker to be in good physical condition. Modifications of this position are not possible given the particular demands. The worker must be physically fit enough to climb poles supporting his own weight and 30 to 60 pounds of equipment with his knees and back.

General Electric Corporation

11

GE traces its beginnings to Thomas A. Edison, who established the Edison Electric Light Company in 1878. In 1892, a merger of the Edison General Electric Light Company and the Thomson-Houston Electric Company created the General Electric Company. In 1986, GE merged with RCA.

GE is a diversified technology, manufacturing, and services company with a commitment to achieving worldwide leadership in each of its major businesses: aircraft engines, broadcasting (NBC), electrical distribution equipment, electric motors and industrial systems, capital services, power systems, information services, lighting, locomotives, major appliances, medical systems, and plastics. The company employs over 222,000 people worldwide, including approximately 163,000 in the United States. John F. Welch, Jr. is chairman and chief executive officer of GE.

All GE businesses operate on a worldwide basis. In 1994, GE Lighting established two joint ventures in rapidly expanding markets—GE Jiabao Lighting Company, Ltd. in China and PT GE Angkasa Lighting in Indonesia. In 1993, GE Lighting launched Hitachi GE Lighting, Ltd., in Japan and GE Apar Lighting, Ltd. in India. In 1991, GE Lighting purchased THORN EMI's lamp-making operations in the U.K. and in 1990 acquired majority interest in the Hungarian lamp-maker Tungsram.

A consortium led by GE Power Systems acquired a majority interest in Nuovo Pignone, an Italian electrical equipment maker, in 1994. This move strengthened GE's power generation market position in Europe, North Africa, the Middle East, Asia, and Russia.

In 1993, NBC purchased the Super Channel, Europe's pan-European general programming television service which is delivered to 65 million homes.

GE Capital's Aviation Services business became the world's preeminent aircraft lessor and financial solutions provider in 1993, serving more than 100 airlines in more than 50 countries. Also in 1993, GE Capital's Trailer Leasing acquired an extensive European network by purchasing TIP Europe, with 65 branches in 10 countries.

GE Appliances has strong position in two of the world's fastest growing nations through its successful joint ventures—Godrej-GE in India and MABE in Mexico.

GE Plastics acquired Borg-Warner's chemicals businesses in 1988. GE Plastics has 11 manufacturing sites in Europe and Asia, in addition to joint venture facilities in a number of other countries, including a 50/50 joint venture with the India Petrochemicals Corporation.

The acquisition of CGR of France in 1987 and the formation of the joint venture GE Yokogawa Medical Systems of Japan in 1982 made GE Medical Systems a leading global supplier. Key additional joint ventures in China, Russia, India, and Japan have strengthened its position.

CFM International, a joint company between GE Aircraft Engines and SNECMA of France, has been in operation since 1974. Today, it is one of the largest manufacturers of commercial jet engines in the world.

Social Responsibility

GE earned Harvard University's George S. Dively Award for Corporate Public Initiative in 1990 for the involvement of GE volunteers in education programs nationwide. GE was one of only two companies awarded the President's Volunteer Action Award for community service in 1994.

The National Science Foundation presented its first National Corporate Achievement Award to the GE Foundation in 1992, recognizing the foundation's outstanding support of minority students, faculty, and professionals in science, engineering, and mathematics.

In 1993, GE, the GE Foundations, and GE employees contributed almost $68 million to support education, the arts, the environment, and human services organizations worldwide. The financial support is in addition to the hundreds of thousands of hours GE employees annually volunteer to community projects.

As a government contractor, GE fell under the 1973 Rehabilitation Act. A significant number of the provisions of the Americans with Disabilities Act (ADA) had, therefore, already been addressed by the company.

General Electric's Commitment to Diversity and Employing Persons with Disabilities

Corporate Responsibility

In an effort to communicate GE's concern about assuring ethical behavior and integrity among all its employees, John F. Welch, Jr., chairman of the board and chief executive officer, issued a Statement of Integrity in 1993 which applied to compliance with the ADA as well as other issues. The Statement of Integrity is a model for other organizations and is shown below.

Statement of Integrity

For more than a century, GE people have created an asset of incalculable value—the company's worldwide reputation for integrity and high standards of business conduct. That reputation, built by so many people over so many years, rides on each business transaction we make.

Integrity is the rock upon which we build our business success—our quality products and services, our forthright relations with customers and suppliers and, ultimately, our winning competitive record. GE's quest for competitive excellence begins and ends with our commitment to ethical conduct.

For each person in the GE community, I ask you to make a personal commitment to follow our Code of Conduct:

- Obey the applicable laws and regulations governing our business conduct worldwide.

- Be honest, fair, and trustworthy in all of your GE activities and relationships.

- Avoid all conflicts of interest between work and personal affairs.

- Foster an atmosphere in which equal opportunity extends to every member of the diverse GE community.

- Strive to create a safe workplace and to protect the environment.

- Through leadership at all levels, sustain a culture where ethical conduct is recognized, valued, and exemplified by all employees.

Guiding us in upholding our ethical commitment is a set of GE policies on key integrity issues. All GE employees must comply not only with the letter of these policies but also their spirit.

If you have a concern about what is proper conduct for you or anyone else, promptly raise that concern to your manager or through one of the other channels the company makes available to you. Nothing—not customer service, competitiveness, direct orders from a superior or "making the numbers"—is more important than integrity.

GE leaders have the additional responsibility to make compliance a vital part of our business activities. Adherence to GE policy and applicable law is the foundation of our competitiveness. Concerns about appropriate conduct must be promptly addressed with care and respect.

We are all privileged to work for one of the best companies in the world. We must, every day in every way, preserve and strengthen for those who will follow us what has been GE's foundation for success for more than 100 years—the GE commitment to total, unyielding integrity.

Signed
John F. Welch, Jr.
Chairman of the Board
& Chief Executive Officer

The above Statement of Integrity is the leading statement in a guide to GE policies entitled "Integrity: The Spirit and the Letter of Our Commitment." Each employee is asked to acknowledge receipt of the guide by signing a special card. The guide includes policies covering equal employment opportunity; ethical business practices; health, safety, and environmental protection; and several other key areas. Of particular importance to the subject of accommodating persons with disabilities is the company's policy on equal employment opportunity:

> GE is committed to equal employment opportunity, a basic goal of a free society. By continuing to extend equal opportunity and provide fair treatment to all employees on the basis of merit, we will improve GE's success while enhancing the progress of individuals and the communities where our businesses are located.

Requirements:

- Use merit, qualifications and other job-related criteria as the sole basis for all employment-related decisions affecting employees.

- Recruit, hire, train, compensate, promote and provide other conditions of employment without regard to a person's race, color, religion, national origin, sex, age, disability, veteran status or other characteristic protected by law.

- Take affirmative action to provide equal employment opportunity complying with the spirit and letter of all laws, regulations and government contract requirements. Affirmative action should include programs and efforts to ensure that there are diverse applicant and candidate pools of people who are qualified and who have the opportunity to compete for open positions. Selection of successful candidates will then be based on qualifications and merit.

- Demonstrate leadership in programs to increase employment opportunity for all citizens in communities where GE has facilities.

- Provide a work environment free of harassment of any kind based on diverse human characteristics and cultural backgrounds. Sexual harassment, a form of harassment, is prohibited under this policy.

The guide to GE policies goes further and describes the responsibilities of its "leaders" to implement and manage according to its precepts. For example, it states that managers must assure that effective equal employment opportunity and affirmative action plans, programs, and practices are *developed* and *implemented* and are *measured* at least annually.

Additionally, the guide provides examples of equal employment opportunity violations. One example states the following: "Allowing race, color, religion, national origin, sex, age, disability, veteran status or other characteristics protected by law to be a factor in screening employees for hiring, promotion, compensation, or other employment related decisions."

Corporate human resources provides guidance, education, training, bulletins, and procedures for implementing the policy, including requirements for reporting, monitoring, and review.

Altogether, the Statement of Integrity and the supporting structure to make it work reflect creditably on the company's commitment to doing the right thing for all its employees, explicitly including persons with disabilities. The Statement of Integrity is an example of corporate responsibility that embodies the spirit of the best of what America is all about.

Organizational Strategies for Complying with the ADA

GE's formal emphasis on addressing issues concerning persons with disabilities began with the Federal Rehabilitation Act of 1973. Because of the overlapping provisions of the latter act with those of the ADA, the company had a relatively narrow gap to fill in achieving full compliance with the ADA. One of the significant changes in approach required with the introduction of the ADA concerned employment physicals. Prior to passage of the ADA, medical examinations for new hires were administered on a pre-employment basis. Following the passage of the ADA, physical examinations were given on a post-employment basis. A major distinction between prior practice and the procedure followed under the ADA is that a physical examination cannot be given to an individual until the company has made a job offer to him or her. Additionally, under the ADA, medical exams must be specifically structured to address the specific job functions and responsibilities. For the first time it became necessary to inform the company's doctors and clinics as to the job description associated with each prospective employee's job.

GE created two levels of task forces to provide guidance and direction in implementing the requirements of the ADA. One task force was established at the corporate office level and consisted of representatives from human resources, personnel services, legal, communications, facilities, medical staff, and corporate systems and input from persons with disabilities. Additional task forces were created throughout the company. These task forces were structured similarly to the corporate model, with modifications depending on the service or manufacturing nature of each division. An important criterion in structuring the task forces was that they be cross-functional.

The General Electric Capital task force developed an ADA implementation checklist as a guide for its divisional operations. The checklist is representative of those used by other divisions and covers such factors as job applications and interviews, job functions, employment testing and reasonable accommodation process, medical examinations, and facilities. Also included are pre-employment and interview guidelines and a technical resources list.

Communication Plan

In January 1993, GE issued "Integrity: The Spirit and the Letter of Our Commitment." This publication formed a critical base for other communications related to diversity and persons with disabilities in the workplace. The company's Workforce Diversity Program is a synergistic part of its approach toward developing and supporting a belief in empowering employees to act and make decisions. As part of its diversity communications program, GE purchased and tailored to its own needs a videotape entitled "The ADA Maze—What You Can Do." This video has been viewed by employees and managers throughout the company and is directed toward advising them on how to conduct employment and other interviews and providing advice on compliance issues.

To further enhance its communications efforts on the ADA, the company introduced a series of articles in its newsletter, "GE News." Several key articles are reproduced here.

ADA Act Seeks to Improve Equal Opportunity, Access*
(Week of May 4–8, 1992)

Equal opportunity and access for disabled people in all aspects of life. That's the objective of the Americans with Disabilities Act (ADA), passed by Congress in 1990 and which takes effect in stages this year. An attorney and manager with Corporate Staff Human Resources explains in this interview how ADA affects corporate component locations.

Aren't we already doing many of the things that the ADA requires?

Yes. And over the years we've done an excellent job of complying with existing federal and state laws related to the disabled and handicapped. As a federal contractor, under the Rehabilitation Act of 1973, GE was prohibited from discriminating against otherwise qualified individuals. In contrast, the ADA's coverage extends to almost all private employers.

To prepare for Title I (the Employment section) of the ADA which takes effect in July, a task force from various corporate component locations has been reviewing the impact of the law on every aspect of our operations to ensure that corporate components are in full compliance, and that qualified disabled persons will be given equal opportunities at GE.

What are the key drivers behind this new law?

Some 43 million Americans are estimated to have physical or mental disabilities—and that number is growing as the general population ages. Disabled people have historically been the subject of discrimination. It's often based on stereotypes about their ability to participate in and contribute to society. Approximately $150 billion is spent in the United States each year on benefits and support programs for disabled people who would work if given the chance. The Americans with Disabilities Act focuses on assuring equal opportunity and full participation for these individuals.

Is discrimination against disabled persons really a pervasive problem in the U.S.?

Congress has found that discrimination indeed persists in such critical areas as employment, housing, public accommodations, education, transportation, tele-

---

* Questions and answers excerpted from "20 Questions and Answers on the Americans with Disabilities Act (ADA Questions and Answers)." ©Employment Policy Foundation. Reprinted with permission.

communications (thus the need for "closed captioned" TV), recreation, institutionalization, health services, voting, and access to public services. The ADA focuses on all of these areas.

How does the ADA affect corporate component locations?

The main emphasis for the corporate components is on GE's responsibilities as an employer. The ADA prohibits discrimination against "qualified individuals with disabilities" in hiring, advancement, termination, compensation, job training, and other terms and conditions of employment.

Who is a "disabled individual"?

In general, a disabled individual is defined as a person who has a physical or mental impairment that substantially limits a major life activity, such as caring for oneself, performing manual tasks, walking, seeing and/or working. This definition also includes one who is perceived as having a disability or who has a record of such impairment. A "qualified" disabled person under the ADA is one who can perform the essential functions of his or her job, with or without "reasonable accommodation."

What does "reasonable accommodation" mean?

It means buildings are accessible for a disabled person...or providing special work hour arrangements. It could also involve adjusting responsibilities for an employee who isn't able to perform some marginal tasks of the job. For example, if an employee is not able to lift overhead, and that person's job requires that he or she occasionally place a box on a top shelf, that particular task might be assigned to someone else. Reasonable accommodation might also entail holding meetings in locations where disabled persons can attend, such as a ground-level conference room for someone who can't climb stairs. Or it could involve modifying equipment and furniture, such as installing amplifiers on telephones or Braille devices on computer terminals, or providing a special stool to improve access to a machine. GE's corporate components are committed to ensuring accommodations are provided at their locations—and that is what the ADA requires.

Beyond the task force, what else needs to be done to ensure compliance with the ADA?

Every employee has to take ownership for ADA compliance and make sure that GE continues to offer equal opportunity for all. To make that happen, our task force is developing a training package to guide managers in handling circumstances that might exist in their areas. We'll also be communicating more information to all employees. Because ADA is new, every one of us will be learning.

Need assistance?

If you have a disability and need any accommodation for performing your job, contact your Human Resources manager or the GE Medical Center at your site.

Get to Know the ADA*
(Week of July 13-17, 1992)

The Americans with Disabilities Act (ADA) is designed to make it easier for disabled persons to hold jobs, travel on public transportation and use public telecommunications services.

Employers covered by the ADA must make "reasonable accommodations" in their workplaces and employment practices to make job opportunities available to persons with disabilities.

A task force from various corporate component locations has been reviewing the impact of the law on every aspect of operations to ensure that qualified disabled persons will be given equal opportunities at GE.

All managers and employees will be asked to attend special instructional presentations on ADA requirements during the next several months. Look for registration materials from the task force shortly.

Veterans or handicapped may self-identify for consideration under GE's Affirmative Action plans

As a government contractor, GE is subject to Section 503 of the Rehabilitation Act of 1973, which ensures affirmative action in the employment and advancement of individuals who are handicapped. Additionally, government regulations implementing the Vietnam Era Veteran's Readjustment Act of 1974, as amended, require the Company to report on the veteran status of employees.

Confidential information

Both these regulations ask that GE invite employees to voluntarily self-identify either their veteran or handicapped status, if they have not already done so. This may be done at anytime and will remain confidential. For more information or

---

* Questions and answers excerpted from "20 Questions and Answers on the Americans with Disabilities Act (ADA Questions and Answers)" ©Employment Policy Foundation. Reprinted with permission.

to register, employees may contact their component or GE business Human Resources manager.

Details of veteran status

Two types of veteran status are covered under the reporting regulations: The first is *Vietnam Era Veteran*—a veteran, any part of whose active military service was during the period August 5, 1964 through May 7, 1975, who (a) served on active duty for a period of more than 180 days and was discharged or released therefrom with other than a dishonorable discharge, or (b) was discharged or released from active duty because of a service-connected disability.

Employees are invited to voluntarily self-identify their status

The second veteran status is *Special Disabled Veteran*—a veteran who is entitled to compensation (or who, but for the receipt of military retired pay, would be entitled to compensation) under laws administered by the Veterans Administration (a) for a disability rated at 30% or more, or (b) rated at 10% or 20% in the case of a veteran who has been determined under Section 1506 of Title 38, U.S.C. to have a serious employment handicap, *or* a person who was discharged or released from active duty because of a service-connected disability.

GE also records veteran status other than that listed in the definitions above. This would include any persons who served on active duty and who were discharged with other than a dishonorable discharge.

Handicapped status defined

The regulations implementing Section 503 of the Rehabilitation Act of 1973 define "an individual who is handicapped" as "any person who (1) has a physical or mental impairment which substantially limits one or more of such person's major life activities *(such as employment)*; (2) has a record of such impairment; or (3) is regarded as having such impairment."

Question on eligibility?

Employees unsure of whether they fall into any of the categories described here may contact their component or GE business Human Resources manager. Self-identifying for the Company's Affirmative Action plans is both voluntary and completely confidential.

What everyone needs to know about the ADA

To increase understanding of the new Americans with Disabilities Act, the GE News presents this series of questions and answers on how the law affects the workplace. All managers and employees will be asked to attend special instructional presentations on ADA requirements during the next several months. Look for registration materials shortly from the corporate ADA task force.

What is the ADA?

The Americans with Disabilities Act (ADA) is a federal civil rights law that prohibits discrimination against individuals with physical and mental disabilities. The ADA's provisions require equal opportunity in employment, in government services including public transportation, and in the services provided by private businesses, such as stores and restaurants that are open to the public. The ADA also establishes "Accessibility Guidelines" that apply to new construction as well as any alterations made at existing business facilities.

Is the ADA the same as civil rights laws that prohibit discrimination on the basis of race or sex?

The laws on race and sex discrimination require us to ignore those factors in employment decisions. Under the ADA, there will be times when—rather than simply ignoring the disability—the employer must respond to the disability by providing a reasonable accommodation that makes it possible for the individual to take advantage of the equal employment opportunity.

Who is protected under the ADA?

The employment provisions of the ADA apply to applicants as well as existing employees with disabilities. The law will also cover any employee who in the future develops a disability as a result of an illness or injury, on the job or off. The law is comprehensive in that it applies to all aspects of the employment relationship. It covers not only hiring, but also promotions, terminations, compensation and benefits.

What disabilities are covered under this law?

When we think of people with disabilities, we often think of persons whose mobility is limited or who have serious limitations in hearing or seeing. The ADA clearly protects such people from discrimination. But, the ADA's definition of disability goes beyond these conditions. The ADA covers all physical and mental impairments that substantially limit an individual in typical life activities. Thus, the law protects many people with conditions that may not be apparent to others, such as diabetes, epilepsy, heart disease and HIV infection.

The ADA also protects an individual who does not have an impairment now but who has record of such an impairment. So it would be illegal for an employer to refuse to hire a qualified candidate for a job because the individual previously had cancer or tuberculosis.

The law also protects a person who is "regarded" by the employer as having a disability. For example, an employer who refused to hire someone because he or she was rumored to have a disability would be breaking the law even if the person did not in fact have that disability. Generally, temporary impairments, such as a cold or flu, or a broken arm or sprained ankle, are not covered by the ADA.

Author's note—This article was accompanied by a list of ADA team members, and their phone numbers, who were available to answer any specific questions related to the ADA as it applies to corporate component locations. Individuals representing facilities, legal, medical, and human resource functions were included in the list.

Awareness Highlighted at ADA Seminars
(Week of September 21-25, 1992)

All managers at corporate component locations are being asked to attend special instructional presentations on the requirements of the new Americans with Disabilities Act (ADA). Participants at recent seminars have found them especially helpful in better understanding the issues involved when a disabled person is in the workplace.

Managers' Guidelines for Compliance with the Americans with Disabilities Act

A specific ADA educational program was developed for managers. The program covers such topics as company obligations, methods of proper communication with persons with disabilities, compliance with ADA guidelines, and enforcement provisions of the ADA. The program was presented in slide form as part of an educational seminar.

The ADA Six Steps of Reasonable Accommodation (Exhibit I) is used by managers, in conjunction with their human resource manager and the individual with a disability, to select effective accommodations on a case-by-case basis.

EXHIBIT I

ADA Six Steps of Reasonable Accommodation

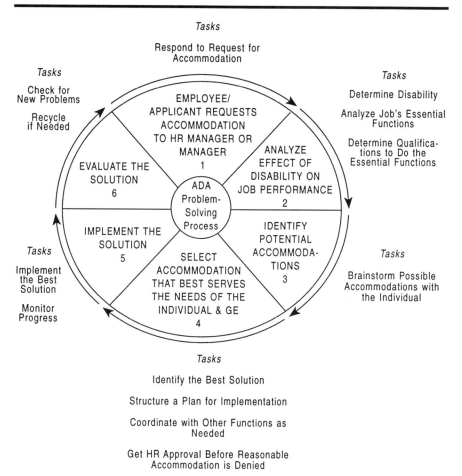

Tasks

Respond to Request for Accommodation

Tasks

Check for New Problems

Recycle if Needed

Tasks

Determine Disability

Analyze Job's Essential Functions

Determine Qualifications to Do the Essential Functions

Tasks

Implement the Best Solution

Monitor Progress

Tasks

Brainstorm Possible Accommodations with the Individual

Tasks

Identify the Best Solution

Structure a Plan for Implementation

Coordinate with Other Functions as Needed

Get HR Approval Before Reasonable Accommodation is Denied

The Cultural Assessment Survey and Dealing with Attitudinal Barriers

GE has developed and uses a cultural assessment survey to further ensure an effective diversity program in its divisions. The survey is specifically designed to measure how various demographic groups within GE, including persons with disabilities, feel about the climate of the company. Compared to other surveys, it includes some unusual and thought-provoking items, as well as a comprehensive list of demographic items.

To assure confidentiality, the completed survey is placed in a preaddressed envelope and mailed to an independent survey firm. No one working for GE sees the individual responses. To further assure anonymity, the consultant's reports to GE are based on a minimum of 25 people of the same sex, race, etc.

Employee focus groups are also used to identify problems and concerns in a confidential atmosphere.

Accommodations to Persons with Disabilities at GE

Accommodations made and affirmative actions taken at GE to enhance the effectiveness of employees include:

- A motorized cart was provided for a female employee who had difficulty walking.

- Special upper body fitness equipment was purchased for an employee paralyzed from the waist down. This equipment was added to the fitness center's inventory.

- Flexible work schedules are provided to facilitate disabled employees' early return to work.

- A list of assistive devices was developed from which employees can select items they feel are needed to facilitate their job performance.

- Employees are provided with access to the Job Analysis Network for information on assistive devices and techniques.

- Ongoing communication to managers demonstrates that persons with disabilities are an asset to their own performance and to the company.

- A major effort is made to communicate the belief that persons with disabilities can work anywhere in the company.

Honeywell 12

Honeywell employs 52,000 people in 95 countries. Its vision for the future is to achieve profitable growth by delighting its customers and thus gain undisputed global leadership in control systems. By fulfilling the world's need for a cleaner environment, greater productivity, energy efficiency, enhanced comfort, and increased safety and national security, the company intends to achieve its vision and realize the greatness it is capable of as a business, as an investment, and as a place to work.

The broad scope of Honeywell's product offerings may be seen in the following applications:

- Industrial automation systems to monitor fuel consumption and emissions at electric utilities

- Building automation systems to monitor and control heating, ventilation and air conditioning, and fire and security systems

- A satellite communications system, providing "office in the sky" capabilities to airline passengers

- Railroad wheel sensors that help safeguard train passengers and motorists by helping to ensure that barriers are lowered at crossings as trains approach

- Development of the first flight management system and receiver that interprets signals from geographic positioning system satellites, allowing aircraft to make curved approaches to airport runways, which increases precision and saves time, fuel, and money

- Automatic test equipment to ensure the working condition of the U.S. Air Force's F-15 electronic warfare systems

- Creation of a digital mapping system for the F-15E which generates a full-color, moving map in the cockpit that provides precise navigation and route selection

Honeywell's formal efforts to address the needs of diversity groups were begun in 1974, with added emphasis for persons with disabilities initiated in 1981. The company has developed an exceptionally well-designed and planned physical facilities requirements program which it has implemented at all of its approximately 300 facilities. The program not only meets the needs of persons with disabilities, but also addresses safety enhancement issues that are important for the well-being of all employees. Honeywell's corporate leadership has demonstrated an unusual sensitivity toward persons with disabilities and encourages their identifying their own needs and solutions. Management provides the moral and financial support to implement reasonable accommodations and to ensure equal access to job and promotion opportunities.

Reducing Barriers for Employing, Retaining, and Promoting Persons with Disabilities

Each Honeywell business unit is responsible for implementing its own plan and individualized program for assuring opportunities for persons with disabilities. A typical divisional approach designed to achieve this objective may be seen in the following letter to all employees issued, along with a training manual, by Mr. John Bailey, vice president and general manager of Honeywell's Protection Services organization in Minneapolis:

> Honeywell has been attentive to the concept of workforce diversity for some time. Workforce diversity is evident in the skills each of use on the job, the experiences and training we bring to the workplace, and in personal appearance. By supporting the concept of workforce diversity, we take advantage of the full complement of human resource skills that is available in our population. Unfortunately, our attitudes about co-workers we perceive as "different" also serve to block careers and limit the company's full use of its workforce.
>
> The affirmative action strategies Honeywell has used to date have demonstrated that people of different racial and cultural backgrounds do work together productively to the ultimate benefit of the corporation. When employees and managers are provided with objective information and concrete experiences, Honeywell has found that commonly held reservations about population segments are really not valid.
>
> One group that remains underutilized in the American workforce is the disabled population. Honeywell has initiated the Windmills training program to create positive attitudes toward people with disabilities and to increase the employment, retention, and promotion

of this population. This manual was developed in conjunction with the Windmills training program, and provides objective information on the disabled population in general, addresses specific employment issues associated with this group, and lists local resources you can consult about recruiting and employing disabled people.

I urge you to read this manual and share it with your staff so that Protection Services can begin to increase our positive efforts to utilize the productivity potential of this able group.

Disabilities Awareness Training Program

An outline of the training program referred to in Mr. Bailey's letter is presented below. The ultimate goal of Honeywell's training program is to increase the employment of people with disabilities. Sixty Honeywell trainers located at divisions around the world tailored a generic training program to their individual environments. Each trainer utilized articles and other communication aids to supplement the basic program.

The training program covers five major subjects:

- A legal summary of the Americans with Disabilities Act (ADA)
- Recruitment and interviewing
- Supervising the disabled employee
- Human resource support
- Resources

Honeywell Protection Services and the Disabled Employee

Introduction
Examining Our Beliefs
   Section 1 ADA Legal Summary
      Americans with Disabilities Act (A Summary)
   Section 2 Recruitment/Interviewing
      Meeting and Evaluating the Candidate
      Interviewing People with Disabilities—Tips
      Recruiting, Hiring and Employing—A list of local resource organizations
         by state
   Section 3 Supervising the Disabled Employee
      Supervisory Considerations
      Supervising Employees with Disabilities (an article by Kirk Birginal)

Reasonable Accommodations at Honeywell

Honeywell has demonstrated an extraordinary sensitivity, creativity, and willingness to support reasonable accommodations for persons with disabilities. Several accommodations implemented at one of the company's 400 facilities are presented below. Many other accommodations have been made at this and the other facilities located throughout the world.

Individual with Epilepsy and Tuberculosis Sclerosis

In order to appreciate this individual's excellent on-the-job performance, some background information on the history of his disability is needed. His condition resulted from an injury at birth caused by the use of forceps and mismanagement of the birth by the doctor, causing injury to the brain and the left temporal lobe. Doctors estimated that he would not live beyond the age of seven, and that if he did, he would have to live in a home for epileptics. Major brain surgery was performed when he was six years old, resulting in the removal of the center of his skull. His parents were loving and sympathetic but not particularly supportive or directive in guiding him toward education and knowledge that would enable him to best utilize his talents. From a very early age, he assumed responsibility for his future. He first convinced his parents that he should attend a public school and requested a chaperon to assist him. Entering school at the third grade level, he proved his ability to do the work. This was no small achievement since at that time people thought of epileptics as very different. Some even thought that they were possessed by demons and incapable of normal behavior. Later, he graduated high school after passing a requirement that he swim 50 yards.

When he was 18 years old, he went to the Stanford University medical library where he accomplished 500 hours of research to gain an understanding of all aspects of seizures. This facilitated discussions with doctors and others with whom he came into contact. When he was automatically given a 4F status by his Selective Service board, he requested a medical exam, and his status was changed to 3A (i.e., permitting him to serve in case of a national emergency).

He felt that it was as important for him to serve his country as it was for non-disabled persons. The Selective Service board looked at his abilities instead of his disability. The ADA was to foster this moral position some years later.

His first job was with Bank of America, and he then worked at night in a restaurant. This individual, who is now 55 years old, found what has become lifelong employment with Honeywell. He has worked for Honeywell for over 27 years. For the last ten years, he has worked as a metal punch press operator on a 150-ton punch press. During this ten-year period, he has produced less than ten defective parts. His productivity, quality, and attendance are among the highest in the department. The only accommodation required for this individual was the opportunity to demonstrate his ability to do the job. Honeywell is the kind of company that gives opportunities to its people, and this attitude existed long before the ADA was passed.

When asked what he would suggest to persons with disabilities who wanted to find a job, he answered with the following advice:

- Be prepared for the interview.
- Know what jobs are available.
- Know what job you want.
- Know the requirements of the job.
- Accomplish any education or skills needed to enhance your marketability.

Totally Blind Person

This person works as a customer service telephone representative and handles requests for information for all systems produced in the United States. In carrying out his responsibilities, he uses voice and on-line services such as voice mail, LAN, WAN, and servers. He accesses the company's mainframe computer and a smaller open system. In accessing various databases, he uses speech synthesis technology produced by Digital Equipment Corporation and Artic Technologies. With these technologies, he is able to listen and respond to a customer's inquiry while virtually at the same time hearing the information on his personal computer from scanned hard copy. He uses two headsets and a hands-free microphone. His customers are unaware that he is blind. He is able to control the speed at which he listens to information and listens so fast that a normally sighted person cannot understand the transmission. With a combination of hardware, software databases, and "speed listening" capability, this blind individual performs as effectively as any other person in his department.

As companies migrate to a paperless environment, more job opportunities are becoming available to blind persons. The individual described here estimates that it requires only one month to learn how to use the speech synthesizer and related equipment. The newest system installed for him required two weeks to program. Honeywell looks at his needs as productivity tools as opposed to extra equipment needed because he is disabled.

Honeywell has also managed to create a positive atmosphere toward persons with disabilities. There is an extraordinary team spirit and attitude in connection with persons with disabilities. When the blind customer service representative requested a four foot by four foot area for his guide dog, the company provided the dog with his own desk, a rug, and the same space allocated to a customer service representative. The blind representative's co-workers even had a desk nameplate made with the title D.O.G., for dedicated optical dog, and they treat him like a member of the team. This very special relationship appears to be the norm at Honeywell.

Quadriplegic

An employee who worked as a group leader in a spray painting unit became a quadriplegic as a result of an automobile accident. He had worked at Honeywell for ten years prior to his accident. Following eight months in a rehabilitation center, he returned to work as a production planner. He now works 20 hours per week both at home and at Honeywell's facility in Minneapolis. The company has provided him with a laptop computer with a handicapped user's keyboard for home use, a trackball for his computer, extra power cords for use at home and the office, a home computer, and a printer.

He is now studying for a two-year college degree, taking nine credits per semester. His co-workers assist him with his studies, and the company makes any necessary software available to him.

Crutch-Dependent Individual

This polio victim is presently employed as a spot welder and assembler on freezer controls, thermostats, and other electronic components. He has worked at several other jobs at Honeywell while using two crutches. The only accommodations required to assist this individual are doors that open automatically and a scooter to transport him from the facility entrance to his work area.

Disabilities Assessment and Recommendations

Honeywell's management took a significant step toward enhancing its awareness of the status of its practices vis-à-vis persons with disabilities by creating the Honeywell Handicapped Employees Council (now named the Council for Honeywell Employees with Disabilities). The council's first task was to conduct an assessment of practices at Honeywell and to offer recommendations. The recommendations serve as a model for companies oriented toward empowering their employees to analyze, recommend, and implement solutions to business issues. The recommendations emphasize six major areas of opportunity: awareness, self-identification, hiring, development, accommodations and accessibility, and self-help. In many cases, the recommendations were simply an expansion of existing Honeywell policy and practice.

The Handicapped Employee in the Diverse Workforce Report and Recommendation

---

- **Strategic Issues**
  - Awareness
  - Identification
  - Hiring
  - Development
  - Accommodations and accessibility
  - Self-help

- **Recommendations**
  1. Collaborate with the Diverse Workforce effort.
  2. Develop and present awareness, education, and training programs.
  3. Develop and implement a goal and tracking system.
  4. Develop a recruiting program.
  5. Develop a placement system.
  6. Develop efficacy, mentor, and self-help training for handicapped employees.
  7. Develop a system for planning and implementing accommodations.
  8. Develop a link to available community services.
  9. Assist other corporations in developing handicapped employee programs.
  10. Share recommendations with the federal government.

- **Goals**
  1. Maximize handicapped employee contribution and development.
  2. Create a barrier-free environment.
  3. Attain workforce and occupational parity.

- **Needs**
  1. A three-year implementation period.
  2. Staff to develop and manage program and objectives over the implementation period.

Issue I Awareness

- **Recommendations Concerning Awareness**
  1. Develop a Company-wide awareness campaign on disability.
     a. Focus on abilities and contributions of handicapped employees.
     b. Develop disability awareness activities for all employees.
     c. Use established communication channels to reach all employees.

  2. Provide a knowledgeable resource for any person needing information on disability.
     a. Provide pertinent, factual information on particular disabilities to hiring managers.
     b. Develop a brochure on disability issues for managers hiring a handicapped person.
     c. Provide methods for employees, both disabled and non-disabled, to obtain information about services that are available in the company.

  3. Develop training on Handicapped Employee Issues.
     a. Include information on handicapped issues in all currently used seminars on minorities.
     b. Develop and include training on supervising handicapped employees in supervisory and middle management development courses to reduce tokenism in hiring and to focus on abilities instead of disabilities.
     c. Include handicapped employee issues in Diverse Workforce Training modules.
     d. Develop and present awareness courses for all employees.
     e. Include pertinent information on disability issues in all new employee literature.

  4. Ensure the Honeywell Handicapped Employees Council is included as a resource on handicapped issues.
     a. Provide input for awareness campaign.
     b. Provide input to development and design of training and awareness courses.
     c. Provide input to company policy concerning handicapped persons.
     d. Clarify and rewrite Honeywell definition of a handicapped person.

  5. Develop a mechanism to make top management's commitment to the handicapped employee more visible to line management.

• *Benefits to Employee:*	• *Benefits to Honeywell:*
Awareness of barriers to achievement is essential to reduction of these barriers. Barriers must be defined and	Helping people understand the full potential of the handicapped employee—to concentrate on abilities

• *Benefits to Employee:*	• *Benefits to Honeywell:*
then recognized by both handicapped and non-handicapped employees. People must understand the effects of their behavior and be offered alternatives before they can change.	and the quality of potential contributions—will significantly increase the productivity of both the handicapped person and those with whom the handicapped person interacts.

Issue II Identification

• **Recommendations Concerning Identification**
  1. Investigate on a one-to-one basis, or in "sensing sessions," the causes for the reluctance to self-identify.
  2. Create an incentive for handicapped people to self-identify.
  3. Develop an identification, goal, and tracking system that can feed into the Honeywell minority goal system.
  4. Develop a method to categorize and track handicapped employees to ensure Honeywell employees a diversity of handicapped people.

• *Benefits to Employee:*	• *Benefits to Honeywell:*
Willingness to self-identify is a sign of both trust in the corporation and healthy self-esteem. Identifying more handicapped employees will both help integrate the individual handicapped employee and empower his or her collective effort for greater achievement in the corporation.	An employee who feels secure and can share information about a disability will be a loyal employee. It is particularly important that people can come forward with disability-related problems that affect productivity so they can be solved. The skills learned in helping people share and solve personal problems which affect productivity can benefit all employees.

Issue III Hiring

• **Recommendations Concerning Hiring**
  1. Develop mechanisms to increase the number of disabled Honeywell employees.
     a. Identify and reward managers who do a good job of hiring handicapped people.
     b. Develop training for all Human Resource staffs to increase awareness of disabilities and available resources.
     c. Recruit qualified handicapped people for professional and management positions.

d. Design and implement recruiting programs with organizations that provide job placement for people with disabilities.

e. Develop and implement recruiting programs with colleges and universities that have large handicapped student populations.

f. Design a review system for job descriptions to identify and change qualifications and responsibilities that automatically eliminate disabled applicants.

g. Design a job structuring system to modify jobs to best utilize handicapped people's abilities.

2. Design and implement programs to ensure Honeywell will have a qualified pool of disabled workers to draw from in the future.

a. Develop a centralized comprehensive link with rehabilitation and social service agencies to provide information to enable them to counsel disabled clients into careers that coincide with Honeywell business requirements.

b. Develop a program with high schools to encourage students with disabilities to pursue technical careers.

c. Set up scholarship/internship programs with select educational institutions to provide resources for disabled students to obtain post-secondary education and experience in appropriate technical fields.

3. To facilitate hiring more handicapped people begin by targeting staffing, Human Resource reps, and EEO Specialist positions in all divisions to be filled by qualified handicapped persons or by persons with strong backgrounds in disability-related issues.

4. Identify one position in each division to be held responsible for handicapped employee support, tracking, and development.

• *Benefits to Employee:*	• *Benefits to Honeywell:*
Honeywell can serve as a national leader and model in the effort to significantly reduce the number of unemployed disabled Americans. There are many bright, talented and skilled handicapped individuals looking for jobs who would be thrilled to work for Honeywell.	The company could tap into a talented, skilled pool of people who have learned to persevere and succeed despite unusual difficulties they face. If these people are properly integrated into the company, the potential for loyalty and achievement is enormous. The effort to create a truly diverse workforce will be enhanced as Honeywell learns to integrate handicapped employees into the fabric of the company.

Issue IV Development

- **Recommendations Concerning Development**
    1. Promote greater movement of handicapped employees.
        a. Design and implement a formal counseling approach for developing disabled employees.
        b. Develop efficacy courses for disabled employees.
        c. Develop incentives for line management to hire, develop, and promote disabled applicants.
        d. Create an award similar to the Lund Award specifically for developing handicapped employees.
        e. Identify management positions that can be filled by handicapped employees.
        f. Design a system to ensure Honeywell will have qualified disabled employees to promote into managerial ranks.
        g. Use tracking system to monitor progress towards workforce occupational parity.
    2. Provide a support system for managers and employees.
        a. Develop a consistent, problem-solving mechanism to be used by employees who have difficulties on the job due to a disability.
        b. Develop a support system for supervisors of disabled employees.
        c. Develop mechanisms to provide all Human Resource Departments with a background in rehabilitation and disability issues.
    3. Work with EEO Specialists to develop a centralized monitoring and support function in each division.
    4. Develop a method to make Honeywell training courses, communications, and meetings accessible to all Honeywell employees.
    5. Design a system for:
        a. job tryouts.
        b. duty sharing.
        c. job restructuring.

• *Benefits to Employee:*	• *Benefits to Honeywell:*
Developing increased abilities, and the self-esteem that follows, can start a new upward spiral in the lives of people accustomed to a downward spiral or relegation to mundane jobs or positions. It obviously gives the	Learning practical ways to develop people who face extraordinary barriers will enhance the company's abilities to develop all employees. In addition, well-developed employees tend to be more motivated and carry

• *Benefits to Employee:*	• *Benefits to Honeywell:*
Honeyweller key insight, hope, and greater belief in the system. The employee simply feels—and is—more valuable.	through the development process of co-workers. People who face greater than normal difficulties and have been given the opportunity to develop will become key links in the developmental process for all employees.

- **Recommendations Concerning Accommodations and Accessibility**
  1. Staff will serve as a centralized accommodation specialist on a national level for not less than two years.

  2. Investigate whether or not the function of providing accommodations can be developed efficiently in the divisions. If that is not possible, create a permanent corporate position that directly serves the divisions' needs.

  3. Develop a corporate or group-level budget that pays for accommodations so the cost does not come out of the hiring manager's department budget.

  4. Allow the accommodation to travel with the employee when a job changes within Honeywell.

  5. Investigate the possibilities of programs to create a flexible work environment for those whose disability causes easy fatigue.

  6. Provide facts about the costs of accommodations to all managers.

  7. Develop a consistent Honeywell policy for accessibility for all buildings.

  8. Develop a method to allow handicapped employees to consult on new construction and renovation of present buildings to ensure accessibility.

• *Benefits to Employee:*	• *Benefits to Honeywell:*
Accommodation helps the handicapped employee feel more a part of the team and gives them the tools they need to be productive. The handicapped employee will feel a personal concern from the manager, which will easily translate into better rapport.	Providing needed accommodations has a direct effect on productivity. Without them, people cannot function effectively. Most accommodations are inexpensive, and merely supplying them helps managers and co-workers become more familiar with a particular handicap. In addition, many accommodations developed for specific handicapped employees will benefit other handicapped employees. It is a simple way to increase on-the-job efficiency.

- **Recommendations Concerning Self-Help**
  1. Facilitate formation of effective handicapped employees councils in each division or organization.
  2. Develop a working relationship between divisional committees or councils and the Honeywell Handicapped Employees Council.
  3. Assist Honeywell Handicapped Employees Council to establish an active presence at company activities.
     a. Special Olympics.
     b. Plaza night.
  4. Self-help activities for handicapped employees.
     a. Create networks for support.
     b. Use consultant to help establish internal support groups.
     c. Identify appropriate persons in the medical community specializing in disability issues to be used for referral when necessary.
     d. Use successful handicapped Honeywellers as role models.
  5. Help EAP personnel learn about disability issues.
  6. Create training/awareness for handicapped employees concerning assertiveness and rights and responsibilities as employees.
  7. Develop a publicity campaign that makes Honeywell employees aware of the Council, its functions, and activities.
     a. Poster campaign.
     b. Newsletter.
     c. Articles in company publications.

• *Benefits to Employee:*	• *Benefits to Honeywell:*
Doing something positive for oneself both individually and on a collective basis greatly increases learning skills, co-worker interaction skills, and self-esteem. This leads to greater achievement, orientation, productivity, and loyalty to one's job and oneself.	Self-help groups make maximum use of both their members and existing resources. The company will realize greater use of its existing developmental programs and less reliance on managers' budgets. These groups contribute to the strengthening of the individual and reduce or eliminate the need for formal organizations, such as a Diverse Workforce effort. Honeywell can look forward to increased employee confidence and willingness to participate.

Descriptions of Disabilities

Descriptions of various disabilities used at Honeywell are provided below. Remember, however, that this is only a partial list. Many other impairments are not listed. Also, the fact that a person has a certain impairment does not necessarily mean that he or she cannot handle all or any of the work requirements. Seek expert consultation when you encounter any specific impairment to assure proper placement of the job candidate. Proper placement means using the "whole person" concept—evaluating the person on the basis of his or her total capacity, which includes his or her experiences, training, skills, and qualifications.

Descriptions of Disabilities

Amputation	The surgical removal of a limb or a portion of a limb. The functional level can often be restored by the substitution of a proper prosthesis.
Arthritis	A disease which affects the joints and is often characterized by joint pain, swelling, weakness, stiffness, and fatigue.
Cancer	Malignant growth of cells affecting part(s) of the body. Cancer is currently thought of not as one disease but rather a group of diseases having basic similarities in terms of development and effect upon the body. There are over a hundred identifiable types, with each having its own life history.
Cardiovascular impairment	Impairment affecting the heart and blood vessels.
Cerebral palsy	Disturbance of motor control or loss of sensation in the body, usually occurring at birth, due to damage or injury of the motor control centers of the brain. The symptoms range from mild to severe, causing muscle coordination problems.
Diabetes	A persistent and inordinate increase of sugar in the blood. Mild diabetes may be controlled by diet alone. A more severe condition requires medication and carefully regulated diet.

Epilepsy	Neurological disorder that occurs when the brain cells discharge too much electrical energy. Most cases of epilepsy are controlled by drugs. There are three principal kinds: (1) "Petit Mal" describes a clouding of consciousness that lasts from 1 to 30 seconds, after which the person is usually alert or resumes activity; (2) "Grand Mal" is characterized by a loss of consciousness for one or several moments and muscle contractions; (3) "Psychomotor" describes an attack where the person acts automatically as though sleepwalking.
Hearing impairment	Persons with profound hearing loss of a neurosensory type are usually referred to as deaf if they are unable to hear or understand speech, even with a hearing aid. Individuals with a conductive hearing loss may benefit by surgery or the use of a hearing aid and are considered to be hearing-impaired. Speech impairment may be associated with a hearing loss.
Paralysis	Complete or partial loss of function, especially involving motion or sensation in a part of the body.
Paraplegia	Paralysis of the legs and lower part of the body.
Polio (poliomyelitis)	A disease of the spinal cord which may cause permanent paralysis of the muscles or part or all of a limb, several limbs, the back, or the breathing muscle called the diaphragm.
Quadriplegia	Paralysis of all four extremities.
Tuberculosis	An infectious disease that affects the lungs.
Visual impairment	An individual may be considered blind if he has complete loss of sight or legally blind if the corrected vision is less than 20/200 (Snellen) in the better eye. In other words, a person is said to be blind if he can see no more at a distance of 20 feet than a person with normal sight can see at a distance of 200 feet.
Mental retardation	Subnormal intellectual functioning manifested during the developmental period. It may affect motor

skills, language development, ability to learn, or self-management and may range from mild to severe.

Mentally restored   Person who has had a severe emotional condition for which special psychological and/or psychiatric care was secured and which resulted in an improved ability to function in task performance and/or interpersonal relationships.

International Business Machines Corporation (IBM)

13

IBM'S international objective is to become and be recognized as the high-technology company most concerned about the needs of people with disabilities and to use its technology and products to enhance their employability and quality of life. Toward achieving this objective, IBM has established a Special Needs Systems unit whose stated mission is to enhance the quality of life and employability of persons with disabilities through the use of IBM technology.

In 1974, through local community service organizations, IBM set up programmer training centers for persons with severe physical disabilities. Equipment, curriculum, instruction, and job placement are supported by IBM and other companies. Today, more than 40 such centers exist across the country, with over 3000 graduates and an 80% placement rate in positions with an average salary of over $20,000. This program has expanded to include training in other computer-related skills, such as word processing, data entry, desktop publishing, and computer-aided design.

As early as 1979, IBM strengthened its commitment to assuming an active role in developing products for persons with disabilities by funding research and through joint development projects. Products developed for the blind resulted in part from a desire to help fellow IBM blind employees. At IBM, approximately 50 blind and vision-impaired persons are employed as lawyers, programmers, hot-line customer support representatives, business planners, engineers, and administrators. These individuals use the products described in this chapter to enhance the quality of their work and their productivity. Few companies have done as much as IBM to both develop products for and employ persons with disabilities.

In late 1986, IBM created the Special Needs Systems organization as part of its Entry Systems Division in Boca Raton. This group develops, markets, and oversees the manufacturing of products under the Independence Series trademark. They are a very dedicated group of people.

The IBM Independence Series is a group of products designed to help individuals with disabilities achieve greater personal and professional independence through the use of technology. There are currently ten products in the series, five of which are designed specifically to increase accessibility to voice and computer communications.

The Independence Series of Products and Case Study Application

For Vision-Impaired Individuals

Screen Reader/DOS

IBM comments that the people who appreciate this technology the most never see it. Screen Reader enables people who are blind or visually impaired to hear the words on a display screen, allowing them to use a computer as a sighted person would. Several of the companies discussed in this book have successfully applied Screen Reader to accommodate persons with vision impairments. It is apparent that this technology has enabled a large body of people to achieve their work and professional potential and to contribute significantly to their companies' missions. Interviews clearly show that individuals using Screen Reader (and other products in the Independence Series) have productivity and quality levels that are equal to and in many cases superior to those of non-disabled persons performing the same work.

Some of the major features of Screen Reader include:

- Autospeak monitors the screen and alerts the user when changes, such as status or error messages, occur.

- Dedicated 18-function keypad controls Screen Reader functions to enhance productivity by reserving the keyboard for application functions.

- Powerful reading functions allow the user to read complete screens, paragraphs, sentences, words, or letters. Importantly, the user reads only the information needed.

- User-defined dictionaries can be created for acronyms, abbreviations, and other specially pronounced words.

- Host/LAN support enables connectivity.

- Windowing provides easy access to many display formats featured in today's popular applications.

Screen Reader/2

Screen Reader/2 is a tool capable of converting screen information to speech to make IBM's Graphical User Interface available to persons who are blind or visually impaired. It is designed to work with IBM's OS/2 operating system.

Screen Reader/2 and Screen Reader/DOS have many of the same features. The following important features, however, are unique to Screen Reader/2:

- Provides voice output of all OS/2 screen information, including messages
- Runs with OS/2 2.1 in all sessions, including Windows applications.
- Recognizes and verbalizes objects (icons) to keep the user informed of screen activity and cursor movement at all times
- Emulates mouse functions such as point and click

In the following case study, the needs assessment for blind associates at Sears, Roebuck and Company and the resulting use of Screen Reader/2 are discussed. For additional strategies and accommodations made at Sears for persons with disabilities, see Chapter 21.

A Case Study:
Breaking the Graphical User Interface (GUI)
Accessibility Barrier*

Technologies of the Past

Prior to 1992, headquarters associates of Sears, Roebuck and Company used a mixed set of technology platforms. Some used personal computers, some used mainframe terminals and many had no terminal at all. The types of technology solutions provided were based on the requirements of the individual's position. The twelve home office associates with disabilities were also provided with a variety of technology solutions based on their unique circumstance and available technology at the time.

Part of this group is comprised of blind associates. The blind associates working in the Information Systems areas performing programming functions used either personal computers with voice synthesis or talking 3270 mainframe

---

* The contribution of Marc Stiehr at Sears and Frank DiPalermo from Ability Consulting in preparing the above case study is acknowledged. The article appeared in the March 1994 issue of "The Screen Reader Newsletter," published by IBM.

terminals. The blind associates in business roles requiring them to read large numbers of documents used Kurzweil readers and scanners. The visually impaired associates used larger screens on their terminals as well as a closed circuit TV system in one situation to enlarge the text on printed documents.

In 1991, Sears made the decision to standardize the home office associates on a common technology platform. Each associate was provided a workstation attached to a local area network (LAN). The company selected OS/2 2.0 as the operating system, utilizing its workplace shell to provide a common look and feel. A standard set of GUI (Graphical User Interface) software was selected to insure consistency both within and between business units. This would provide a new multi-talking way for people to work. However, that presented Sears with the challenge to find the tools that would enable its blind associates and associates with physical disabilities to integrate with the standard GUI platform.

While their current tools were the best solutions that the company could find up to that time, they were limiting from a functionality standpoint. In many cases the tools still did not allow the disabled associates to perform the same functions as their fellow associates. In cases where they could perform the same functions, the software did not allow them to work as quickly or easily as others in the work group.

While the platform was being developed in 1992, an equipment plan was formalized for the disabled associates. The new platform was to be rolled out in conjunction with the move of the entire home office staff to a new physical location. At that time, however, Sears was faced with several problems. The required technology was not yet available in the marketplace and the operating system and LAN were not stabilized. The company said that both of those situations would be resolved by the time the move to a new site in a northwest suburban area of Chicago was completed in late 1992. It was determined that these associates should continue to use their existing technologies until then. In November of 1992, the move was completed and the platform was stabilized. Sears then began the process to integrate its associates using special technology solutions with the common platform.

One of the greatest challenges was to find a way to migrate the blind associates out of the DOS world and into a graphical environment with the rest of their work group. Another challenge was to identify better ways to adapt visually impaired associates to this environment. In addition, updated technology tools needed to be put into place for the associates with physical disabilities to enable them to function more effectively.

In January 1993 Sears contracted with Frank DiPalermo, of Ability Consulting Services, to conduct an evaluation of its needs and to find appropriate technology solutions. Following is the process that was followed from evaluation through installation and training of the associates. Mr. DiPalermo worked with Sears representative Marc Stiehr in conducting the evaluation.

Evaluation

The first task of any good evaluation is to discuss the jobs done by each user with his management. At Sears each of the managers was contacted and their input on job requirements obtained. Sears then tried to determine what, if any, limitations would be associated with their environment. The following questions were asked:

- *What physical space will be assigned to the applicant?* It was necessary to know if there was sufficient space for whatever specialized equipment we might recommend.

- *Are there financial goals expected?* It was important to understand what financial restrictions were posed.

- *What is the current level of technology used in this job?* An understanding of computer technology used in the job is essential. Even though Sears has a standard workstation that all associates use, each department uses it in different ways.

- *Are there technology upgrades in the near future?* We had to plan for the upgrade to OS/2 2.1 in the near future.

The next step was an on-site appraisal of each workplace. Each of the associates with disabilities was interviewed to discuss the following:

- *What are the routine duties of the job?* First activities were prioritized so that the most important activities were known.

- *How is information acquired?* Information is the most important part of any job. It is important to make sure that all necessary information is covered in the evaluation.

- *How is the current technology used by non-disabled associates?* Usually employees only use a portion of the technology in computer systems.

There is usually one person in each area who is the acknowledged expert. He or she is the one everyone else turns to when they have questions about how things work in the department. The Sears team and their consultant endeavored to find out who that was for each area so that when installing the new systems, someone was available to answer the question, "How does your group do this operation?"

Research

During this phase it was important to start with what sort of access technology is available for the systems that Sears uses. There are many access products out there, but not many of them would work in the complex Sears environment. In one case it was necessary to suggest a DOS-based system because there was no way to accommodate this particular employee with OS/2. It was possible, however, to suggest ways to improve his productivity tremendously.

Report

This is the most important phase of job evaluation. The management of the company will respond most favorably if the report covers every aspect of accommodation as well as the costs involved. The following describes how the report was structured.

- Each associate had a separate section
  Level and type of disability
  Job requirements
  Current equipment
  Recommended workstation

- General information
  Deviations from Sears standard needed

- Assistive technology
  Blindness
  Screen Reader/2
  Speech synthesizers
  Refreshable braille
  Braille embossers
  Special profile work

- Vision impairments
  Screen enlargers
  Closed circuit TV

- Mobility impairments
  VoiceType
  On-screen keyboards

The report attempted to give Sears management a clear picture of the entire process, the costs and leave nothing to chance. The authors tried to answer every question before it was asked and tried to ensure that each employee with a disability would be competitive with his peers and able to meet his career objectives.

Installation and Training

Before installing systems for the associates who were blind, we had to start with creating special profiles for Screen Reader/2 to work smoothly with Sears in-house applications. That was accomplished by meeting with the blind associates and having them help to prioritize what pieces of the applications were most important and how they wanted Screen Reader/2 to deal with them. In the case of the Email system, Sears chose to add levels of voicing so that inexperienced users could hear more detail than expert users.

We worked with each associate separately because there was a wide difference in computer experience. First the system was installed and then one-on-one training performed based on individual needs. Initial training was kept small enough so as not to overload the user. Programmers got a thorough grounding in all aspects of OS/2 and the Communications Manager while the associate who had never used a computer was only taught the basics and Email.

All blind associates were provided systems with voice and braille output as each was a proficient braille reader.

One associate, who is a quadriplegic, was provided two means of access: voice recognition and on-screen keyboards. He quickly decided that he was more productive with the voice recognition and so most of his customization and training centered around that concept.

After all associates were up and running, Sears requested a training class to assist the programmers in learning to customize their own system functions later.

Current Status

Great progress has been made. Sears successfully implemented the OS/2 platform for eleven of the twelve associates addressed by the study. The remaining associate received a new voice recognition system using IBM's Voice Type II software. His job involved communicating via electronic mail with the field organization. The system significantly improved his productivity by giving him the ability to issue complete words to the system when composing a document, rather than composing character by character using its phonetic representation (e.g., alpha, bravo, etc.). Sears is continuing to look for better alternatives to the mouse or trackball for associates with physical disabilities.

As discussions with the blind associates regarding their migration to the new platform began, they were very apprehensive. They felt that it was going to be impossible for blind individuals to work in this graphical environment. There was a fear that the new environment was going to jeopardize their careers by adversely affecting their productivity. What they have found, however, is that they are able to work much better. The complement of voice and braille, along with the profiling that was done with their key products, offered them a way to work at a performance level with their peers. For the first time, they are able to use the same programs and systems used by their work groups and perform their functions in much the same manner. The training that the programmers received in writing and modifying profiles has provided them the independence and flexibility to adapt their systems as they wish, thereby increasing their effectiveness.

Management is very pleased with the solutions provided for a number of reasons. With the standardization, the company can now plan and budget more effectively to hire and provide technology for people with special requirements. They now have much more flexibility to offer work assignments to that associate just as with any other associate without a disability.

Screen Magnifier/2

Screen Magnifier/2 enlarges applications running under IBM's powerful OS/2 2.1 operating system. Users can magnify OS/2, DOS, and Windows applications running under OS/2 2.1. The magnification level ranges from 2 to 32 times the normal size, and users can make the words and images on the screen the exact size they need.

Screen Magnifier/2 has other special features, including:

- A "reading mode" that pans the cursor along the lines of magnified text. The reading speed can be controlled with the touch of a finger.

- Screen colors that can be reversed for greater contrast.

- Focus tracking, to ensure that the mouse pointer always moves to the area of interest—so if an error message pops up on another part of the screen, the user will see it immediately.

- A locator that lets the user see just where the magnified window is on the system.

Dennis O'Brien, product manager for Special Needs Systems, said, "Screen Magnifier/2 is a simple tool that can improve the readability and usability of systems for everyone. But, for the visually impaired, it is the key that provides access to the world of OS/2."

For Mobility-Impaired Individuals

VoiceType Dictation for OS/2 and Windows

VoiceType is a flexible speech recognition program that provides freedom from having to use the keyboard. This freedom is achieved by using voice commands to utilize the computer. VoiceType lets the user control the system and many popular software applications through voice commands. Among its many unique advantages are the following:

- Adaptive learning capability responds to each user's speech patterns.

- Multiple user speech files are supported on a single system.

- Large flexible vocabulary of over 22,000 words that allows for user-specified words and commands, and a large backup dictionary that aids in word production and spelling accuracy.

- Built-in voice commands for controlling popular applications.

- Voice macros that allow up to 1000 keystrokes to be entered with a single utterance.

- Voice-accessible on-line documentation.

AccessDOS

AccessDOS provides extended keyboard, mouse, and sound access for IBM DOS users. Because of the specialized control it offers, AccessDOS is particularly useful for persons with disabilities. Among its key features are the following:

- The StickyKeys feature allows the user to separately press each key for multiple key operations. For example, the user can press Ctrl, then Alt, then Del to reboot his or her system, instead of the usual method of holding down the Ctrl and Alt keys while pressing Del.

- MouseKeys is a feature that makes it possible to use the keys on the numeric keypad to move the cursor around the screen, simulating the use of a mouse.

- RepeatKeys allows the user to set how fast keys repeat when held down. This feature may also be turned off to suspend the repeat function.

- ToggleKeys causes a beep to sound, indicating when the Caps Lock, Num Lock, or Scroll Lock keys are activated.

- ShowSounds causes the screen to blink or display a small musical note in the upper left-hand corner of the display when the computer makes a sound.

KeyGuard

KeyGuard is a molded keyboard overlay with holes that expose and isolate each keytop. It attaches securely so the keyboard can be positioned at any desired angle. By pressing keys through the corresponding holes on the KeyGuard, mobility-impaired users can achieve greater control when using a typing stick or fingers. The KeyGuard also provides a handrest, an important feature for users with palsy or other motor coordination conditions.

SpeechViewer

This system is designed to increase the efficiency of speech therapy and speech modification.

SpeechViewer II

SpeechViewer II integrates motivating exercises, powerful speech analysis, and automated record keeping. Using IBM multimedia technology, it provides both visual and auditory feedback synchronized with the graphic display of speech patterns. Fifteen modules are grouped according to the clinical objectives of awareness, skill building, and patterning.

For Attention/Memory-Impaired Individuals

THINKable/2

This system is used in direct therapy and allows a teacher or a clinician to create a structured environment in which students and clients can practice thinking skills in four critical focus areas: visual attention, visual discrimination, visual memory, and visual sequential memory.

John Alden Financial Corporation

14

John Alden Financial Corporation is an insurance holding company that, through its subsidiaries, is principally engaged in providing group life and health insurance and managed care services. John Alden is one of the largest providers of group insurance in this market. The company also markets annuities, life insurance to individuals, credit life and health insurance, extended service contracts, and other health-related risk management services and products.

John Alden Financial Corporation employs 1700 persons at its headquarters in Miami, Florida, and employs an additional 2000 persons in locations throughout the United States. The company's operations are organized into ten regions with a human resources manager located in each region.

The company's diversity program has been successful and sustained over a long period of time and continues to be expanded due in large part to the following belief voiced by Glendon E. Johnson, chairman of the board and chief executive officer: "We have a fundamental belief in the importance of giving back to the community. Individuals cannot succeed where families fail, nor can business succeed where the society around it fails."

Strategies Toward Success and Implementation

John Alden's diversity efforts preceded the introduction of the Americans with Disabilities Act (ADA). The passage of the act did create an enhanced initiative and focus on persons with disabilities. One of the first steps taken to assure compliance with the act was the hiring of an ADA specialist. Much of this individual's time was initially devoted to assuring that physical access requirements were met. The company voluntarily spent $250,000 on physical renovations in 1992. Simultaneous with the physical renovations, the company increased its networking with community agencies and rehabilitation organizations toward expanding the hiring of persons with disabilities. John Alden regularly submits an open position log to these agencies and has been successful in receiving many qualified candidates for its internship program and for full employment opportunities.

An ADA training program for managers (see Exhibit I) was prepared to provide guidance in interviewing, communicating with, and supervising persons with disabilities. This excellent training program uses a videotape and workshop exercises. Topics covered include a legal overview of the ADA, facts about the disabled population, public reaction to individuals with disabilities, a section on preparing job descriptions to meet ADA requirements, interviewing candidates under the ADA, and helpful pointers on interacting and communicating with persons with disabilities. A new program has also been prepared and introduced for all employees and has resulted in increased team spirit.

A special sign language course was offered to all employees in the headquarters location. Forty persons took the course, which was accomplished on their personal time, twice a week over a period of six weeks.

The company's initial efforts in hiring the disabled focused on physically disabled persons. Having successfully worked through the many issues connected with that group, a new initiative toward hiring the developmentally disabled has been introduced.

Special Recruitment of Disabled Applicants

As a company committed to improving the quality of life in its community and utilizing the diverse skills available, John Alden actively recruits people with disabilities. The company works closely with local agencies to identify applicants, to provide internships, and to set up permanent or temporary employment assignments. Alden's Advantage, a program which was established to place talented disabled applicants in temporary to permanent positions, has been very successful and is being duplicated at other companies. Employees have an opportunity to learn about John Alden while gaining invaluable experience. Disabled applicants receive first consideration for new positions.

In 1993, recruitment efforts resulted in placing seven candidates with disabilities at the company's headquarters office alone. On a weekly basis, John Alden notifies 13 local agencies of open positions within the company. The company also assists agencies with various special events, from fund-raising to career fairs.

John Alden has a special recruitment relationship with the following agencies:

- Deaf Services Bureau
- Abilities of Florida

- Division of Blind Services
- Program-Ability
- Jewish Vocational Service, Inc.
- D-Sail
- Division of Vocational Rehabilitation
- Easter Seals Society
- MEED (Microcomputer Education for Employment of the Disabled) Program
- Goodwill Industries of Florida
- Lighthouse for the Blind
- Miami Dade Community College–Employment Services for the Disabled
- Business Coalition for Americans with Disabilities

Training

Not only does John Alden have management development training programs for all its employees and managers, but its classes have been made available to agency clients as well. On a space-available basis, agency clients can attend various training classes on-site with John Alden personnel. This, the company feels, provides training opportunities and exposure to John Alden.

In addition to offering managers a special training program titled "Guide to Managing the ADA," employees received a training program called "ADA: Integration of People with Disabilities in our Workplace." Both programs were offered to employees nationwide.

Special Awareness Program

National Disability Employment Awareness Month—Every year, John Alden celebrates National Disability Employment Awareness Month, which is kicked off with a proclamation from the company president. In 1993, this month-long celebration included sign language classes; video presentations; a panel presentation and discussion by six community experts; an open house with agency exhibits, equipment demonstrations, and computer displays; an article in the company newsletter; and display and distribution of posters and other information throughout the company to increase awareness and to educate.

Examples of Reasonable Accommodations

John Alden has developed a well thought-out and implemented incremental strategy in employing disabled persons. Its initial efforts were concerned with the physically disabled; having been successful in that area, the hiring program is being expanded to other groups. The following examples are representative of accommodations for disabled persons:

- A totally deaf person was initially brought into the company as a temporary employee working in a computer data entry, proofreading, and file updating position. After four months of demonstrating levels of productivity and quality performance equal to those of his peer group, he was offered full-time employment. The only equipment accommodation required for this person was a TDD unit with a message recorder. Occasionally, an interpreter is used to translate at staff meetings. Communications with his peers were enhanced through their voluntarily taking advantage of a course in sign language offered by the company. Some shifting of job responsibilities including elimination of telephone communications with non-TDD users was also accomplished.

- A totally deaf legal secretary was introduced into the company through the Alden's Advantage program and is now a full-time employee. This female employee went through the MEED program located at Miami-Dade Community College in Miami, Florida. Her initial assignment was to provide secretarial service to two paralegals. Her responsibilities were subsequently increased to support four paralegal staff members. She reports to an office manager and uses a date/time stamping system to prioritize her work. In addition to the latter accommodation, her manager makes special accommodations with respect to her hours of work as the need arises. She is reported to be exceptionally quick and accurate in her work, which is performed in a fast-paced and stressful environment.

  In order to accomplish her work in such a superior manner, this individual developed lip-reading skills in both Spanish and English and rarely utilizes an available interpreter. At the beginning of her employment at John Alden, she had to overcome some peer insensitivity toward her disability. Some individuals unknowingly used inappropriate methods in attracting her attention whereas she had requested that they get her attention by touching her on the shoulder or arm. With a little education, coaching, and her manager's support, peer behavior changed. The relationship with her peers is team oriented, businesslike, and professional.

- The company employs a quadriplegic as an analyst in a computer help-desk function. He schedules personal computer maintenance and performs programming that his managers say cannot be performed by anyone else in the department. He works five hours each day and is scheduled to work the busiest time of day. His department is a high stress area.

This individual graduated at the top of his class at MEED, served as an intern, worked in a temporary position, and finally moved into a full-time position. He uses a voice-activated computer and a breath-activated phone. His computer software required special programming for voice recognition. Sensitivity training was provided to his manager before the employee began working at John Alden. The peer group was very cooperative when they saw his ability to handle difficult assignments and his initiative to tackle new projects.

- A developmentally disabled woman was hired through Goodwill Industries to work as a general office clerk in the human resources department. She works from 11 a.m. to 4:30 p.m. because public transportation necessitates three hours of travel both to and from work. Her duties include filing, sorting, opening, and distributing mail, photocopying, and running errands. She is reported to be very accurate in filing confidential personnel files and has retrieved previously misfiled documents that others could not locate. She has an excellent attendance record, good interpersonal relations, and is a participative member of the human resources team. Accommodations for this employee included giving her simple instructions for one task at a time after her supervisor first plans her work for the day. A job coach accompanied her to work initially, but it was soon found that this service was not needed.

- The company's claims department had to hire and quickly train nine claims representatives. A six-week intensive training program was to be held. One of the trainees was totally deaf, and the claims department manager believed that it would not be possible for a deaf person to learn the job at the same pace as the other trainees. Further complicating the situation was the need for a sign translator. A translator was found and the deaf person successfully completed the training along with the other individuals.

A list of special recruits and their respective positions at John Alden follows. This list and the examples above demonstrate the company's proactive and professional approach in employing persons with disabilities.

Developmentally disadvantaged	File clerk and mail
Deaf	Office services and mail services clerk
	Data entry

	Legal secretary
	Claims processing
Visually impaired (legally blind)	Sales representative
Physically impaired	Programmer
	PC support and programming
	Computer operator trainee
	Computer (technical) operations support

EXHIBIT I

Workplace Diversity Series
Guide to Managing the ADA
(Americans with Disabilities Act)
1992
John Alden Financial Corporation
Human Resources

Agenda

8:00 a.m.	Begin workshop
12:30 p.m.	Adjourn

Purpose

As a result of attending today's workshop we will:

Explore our attitudes about individuals with disabilities.

Dispel common myths associated with people with disabilities and the ADA.

Become educated on Title I—Employment.

Learn how to prepare job descriptions that comply with the ADA.

Learn what to do and what not to do when interviewing a disabled applicant.

Provide guidelines and procedures for handling accommodation requests and employment actions.

Create awareness and appreciation for individuals with different abilities.

Warm-Up Questions

Class will organize into their assigned groups to discuss and answer the following questions. Be prepared to share your answers with the class.

1. Have you heard about the Americans with Disabilities Act (ADA)? Write down what you know about this law.

   _____
   _____
   _____
   _____

2. If you were told that a person with a disability would be joining your work group next week, how would you prepare?

   _____
   _____
   _____
   _____

3. What barriers exist in the workplace that might hinder a new employee with a disability?

   _____
   _____
   _____

4. What exposure have you had to a person with a disability?

   _____
   _____

   What was your relationship to that person?

   _____
   _____

   How would you describe that person?

   _____
   _____

5. Can you name any famous or notorious people who have or had a disability?

   _____
   _____
   _____

Begin Viewing Video

View first part of video. Write any questions that come to mind while viewing the video here.

_____
_____
_____

Discussion: Questions/Comments. Briefly discuss your responses to the video. How did the video made you feel? Which people or facts make a special impression on you? Is there anything you would like to add?

_____
_____
_____

Legal Overview

The ADA, signed by President Bush on July 26, 1990, is based on the Rehabilitation Act of 1973. The Rehabilitation Act requires federal contractors and subcontractors with contracts of $2,500 or more not to discriminate against the disabled in all employment matters.

ADA requires employers with 15 or more employees (see compliance effective dates below) not to discriminate against the disabled in all employment practices. The Americans with Disabilities Act comprises five titles. While this workshop focuses on Title I—Employment, a brief outline of the other titles is provided:

Title I—Employment	Prohibits discrimination in employment against a qualified individual with a disability in all terms and conditions of employment.
Title II—Public Services	Prohibits discrimination by a public entity (state or local government services) in providing public services to individuals with disabilities. This title also requires that certain forms of public transportation be made accessible to individuals with disabilities.
Title III—Public Accommodations and Services Operated by Private Entities	Prohibits private entities from discriminating on the basis of a disability in providing public accommodations and services. The title also requires new commercial facilities and public accommodations to be designed and constructed so they are readily accessible to and usable by individual with disabilities unless it is structurally impractical to do so.
Title IV—Telecommunications	Requires that common carriers of interstate wire or radio communications provide technological accommodations for individuals with hearing and speech impairments.
Title V—Miscellaneous	Contains various additional provisions of the ADA. Among these is a prohibition from retaliation against or coercion of individuals who seek to enforce another's or their own rights under the ADA. Title V also amends sections of the Rehabilitation Act of 1973 to exclude current alcohol and drug abusers from its coverage.

Compliance Effective Dates

The effective dates for the five titles differ. Compliance with Title I—Employment phases in over a two-year period:

1. The compliance effective date is July 26, 1992 for employers who have 25 or more employees, for each working day in each of 20 or more calendar weeks in the current or preceding calendar year.

2. The compliance effective date is July 26, 1994 for employers who have 15 or more employees, for each working day in each of 20 or more calendar weeks in the current or preceding calendar year.

3. Title III—Public Accommodation was effective January 1, 1992.

Note: Employers with fewer than 15 employees are not subject to the ADA's Title I legislation.

Title I Terms and Definitions

The purpose of Title I is to require equal employment opportunities for qualified individuals with disabilities. It is unlawful to discriminate on the basis of a disability against a qualified individual in regard to any terms and conditions of employment including, but not limited to:

1. Recruitment, advertising, and job application procedures.

2. Hiring, promotion, demotion, transfer, termination, layoff, and rehiring.

3. Compensation and changes in compensation.

4. Job assignments, job classification, organizational structures, position descriptions, lines of progression and seniority.

5. Sick leave or any leaves of absence.

6. Fringe benefits available by virtue of employment.

7. Selection and financial support for training, apprenticeships, conferences and other related training activities.

8. Employer-sponsored activities, including social and recreational programs.

9. Any other term, condition, or privilege of employment.

From a human resources perspective, this means you must consider the possibility of discrimination against a disabled employee or applicant for every activity performed by human resources or management. To help you understand the law, this section provides some of the primary definitions included in Title I.

A "qualified individual" with a disability
must meet all of these criteria:

1. The individual must have a "disability" as defined by the ADA. An individual is considered disabled if he/she:
   a. has a physical or mental impairment that substantially limits one or more major life activities (such as caring for oneself, performing manual tasks, walking, seeing, hearing, speaking, breathing, learning, and working), or
   b. has a record of such an impairment, or
   c. is regarded as having such an impairment, even if the individual does not actually have such an impairment.
   d. In addition, persons who have a relationship with an individual (parent, child, spouse) with a disability are also protected from discrimination based on this relationship.

2. To be "qualified" the individual must satisfy the job-related requirements of the position held or desired, which include, but are not limited to:
   a. job skills
   b. experience
   c. education

3. To be "qualified" the individual must be able to perform the "essential functions" ("fundamental job duties" of the position).

4. The essential functions may be performed by the disabled individual either with or without a "reasonable accommodation."

5. An employer is required to provide "reasonable accommodation" unless it creates "undue hardship" to the organization. An "undue hardship" is a significant difficulty or expense incurred by an employer.

Failure to abide by the requirements of the ADA may result in applicants or employees filing discrimination charges with the EEOC (Equal Employment Opportunity Commission), the enforcement agency for the ADA.

It is the employer's responsibility to comply with the ADA. Failure to do so can result in a variety of remedies including hiring the disabled employee, reinstatement with or without back pay, establishment of retroactive seniority, promotion, back pay, injunction, and/or at the court's discretion payment of the claimant's attorney's fees and expenses. With the passage of the Civil Rights Act of 1991, employers may also be liable for punitive and compensatory damages in the case of intentional employment discrimination. Under the ADA, the maximum combined compensatory and punitive damage award for John Alden is $300,000. Under Florida law the damage award may actually be higher.

Facts About the Disabled Population
- 43 million disabled individuals, 68% of which are unemployed.
- 58% of disabled men and 80% of disabled women are unemployed.
- Each year ½ million Americans will become disabled.
- Lou Harris Poll said disabled are the most undereducated, underemployed, and underpaid minority.

Employers Reactions to Workers with Disabilities
Over 900 managers were interviewed by the Harris Poll and they had this to say about people with disabilities who worked for them:

19 out of 20 managers give employees with disabilities a "good" or "excellent" rating on their job performance. They say employees with disabilities work as hard or harder than their employees who do not have disabilities.

39% of line managers rate employees with disabilities as better on attendance and punctuality than non-disabled employees, and 40% rate them about the same.

Public Reaction to Individuals with Disabilities
92% say they feel admiration often or occasionally in such situations.

74% say they feel pity often or occasionally.

58% feel awkward or embarrassed often or occasionally. College graduates are quite a bit more likely, by 17 percentage points, to feel this way than those who have not graduated from high school.

47% say they are afraid often or occasionally, because what's happened to the disabled person might happen to them.

54% asked if they ever feel embarrassed or awkward because they don't know whether disabled people want help crossing the road or performing some other task, 54% of the public say they do.

Attitudes Toward People with Disabilities in the Workforce
65% say they would not have any problems working alongside people with disabilities.

68% of the working public feels their co-workers would support policies that would increase the number of disabled people in their workplace.

72%   think people with disabilities can only find jobs with difficulty, only 4% say they can find jobs easily, and 18% think they can't find jobs at all.

66%   of the public feels the disabled are discriminated against in regard to equal access to employment.

78%   feel overall discrimination against people with disabilities exists.

Job Description Under the ADA

ADA does not require an employer to develop or maintain job descriptions; however if they do exist they will be used as evidence in the event of an investigation. Following are important elements to be contained in written job descriptions:

A. **Essential Functions:** Review current job descriptions before having Human Resources advertise or interview for a position and determine the actual or "essential functions." Elements to consider include:
   1. The employer's judgment.
   2. Does the position exist to perform the function?
   3. The amount of time spent requiring a person to perform the function.
   4. Number of employees available to perform the function.
   5. Specialized nature of the function, and expertise required.
   6. Nature of work operation and organizational structure.

B. **Qualifications:**
   1. Be specific—number of years, depth of knowledge, level of training.
   2. Do not include general characteristics such as strength, intelligence, ability to work with others, or ability to learn quickly, unless they can be linked to specific job functions and are identified as necessary to performing those functions.

C. **Job Specifications:**
   1. Minimum required performance or production levels, e.g., 60 wpm (should be required by all incumbents).
   2. Hours of work: note any requirements other than regular working hours, i.e., overtime required, weekends.
   3. Physical requirements: any unusual or non-routine tasks or functions that require physical ability not obvious or inherent in the description of the function and considered essential to the performance of the job (ability to lift heavy equipment or supplies, run errands outside of property or between buildings).
   4. Mental requirements: example—attention to detail, ability to handle stress, analytical aptitude.

5. Required method of communication: is there a required way in which information must be communicated (verbal presentations to group).
6. Work environment: fast-paced, highly stressful, hot/cold, outdoors, exposure to possible irritants.

Note: It is important not to think in terms of what a disabled person can do when preparing job descriptions, but to provide an accurate description of the position.

Exercise I: Defining your own job

Break into 3–4 groups. Each group will have a common disability assigned to them. Now select one of the jobs held by a member of your group. Think of how your disability would affect the job you have chosen. Answer the following questions and be prepared to share your answers with the class.

A. **What are the essential functions and specifications of your job?**
Complete handout. 10 minutes. _____

_____

B. **What elements of your job, if any, would be affected by your disability?**
Describe how they would be affected. 5 minutes._____

_____

Interviewing Applicants with Disabilities

1. Focus on the ability of the "individual."

2. If a disability is visible or the applicant volunteers information, you may **not** ask about:
   a. The nature of the disability. "Why are you in a wheelchair?"
   b. The severity of the disability. "How serious are your injuries?"
   c. The condition causing the disability. "How did you become disabled?"
   d. Any prognosis or expectations. "Is your disability permanent?"
   e. Whether special treatment or leave will be necessary. "Will you require any special assistance or time off?"

   Note: The best policy is to simply ignore the person's disability and ask questions only related to the ability to do the job.

3. You should describe or demonstrate the essential functions of the position and then ask whether the applicant can perform the function with or without reasonable accommodation.

4. You cannot disqualify a candidate based on an inability to perform the "marginal functions" of a job. Marginal functions are defined as those miscellaneous duties that could be eliminated without changing the nature or purpose of the job. These duties should not be included on a formal job description or be a part of the qualifying criteria. However, the job description is not meant to set limitations on what duties an employee is required to perform and a supervisor may direct an employee to perform any job-related duties he or she feels is required.

Examples: A file clerk position description may state that the person holding the job answers the telephone, but if in fact the basic functions of the job are to file and retrieve documents, and the phones are usually handled by other employees, a person whose hearing impairment prevents use of a telephone and who is qualified to do the basic file clerk functions should not be considered unqualified for this position.

5. You may not ask a disabled applicant to demonstrate how they will perform a function unless it is required of everyone who interviews for the job, unless the applicant has a known disability that would appear to interfere with or prevent performance of a job. If the applicant requires an accommodation to perform the demonstration, then one must be provided or the applicant should be permitted to explain how they would perform the function.

Example: You may not ask an applicant in a wheelchair to take a simulated telephone sale test unless it is required by all applicants.

You may ask an individual who has applied for a position as a mail sorter to demonstrate or describe how they would process the mail with one hand since the applicant's disability of having only one hand would appear to interfere with his ability to perform the job.

6. You cannot refer to a person's disability when asking questions regarding attendance. You may inform the applicant of the work hours, leave policies, or any special attendance needs of the job (i.e., two nights late a month) and ask them if they can meet the requirements of the job.

7. If possible, the interview should end with a tour of the work area.

8. Accommodations for interview: Human Resources will provide you with the following accommodations if necessary:
   a. accessible location
   b. sign interpreter
   c. reader for the blind

Interacting and Communicating

Following are some basic guidelines to help you feel more comfortable when interacting with an individual with a disability for the first time. Remember, these are guidelines; because all people are individuals, you may want to adapt your behavior to the specific individual or situation.

Interviewer(s) need to know whether or not the job site is accessible and should be prepared to answer accessibility-related questions.

Use a normal tone of voice when extending a verbal welcome. Do not raise your voice unless requested.

When introduced to a person with a disability, it is appropriate to offer to shake hands. People with limited hand use or who wear an artificial limb can usually shake hands.

a. Shaking hands with the left hand is an acceptable greeting.

b. For those who cannot shake hands, if you wish, you may touch the person on the shoulder or arm to welcome and acknowledge their presence.

Treat adults in a manner befitting adults:

a. Call a person by his or her first name only when extending that familiarity to all others present.

b. Don't patronize people using wheelchairs by patting them on the head or shoulder.

When addressing a person who uses a wheelchair, never lean on the person's wheelchair. The chair is a part of the body space that belongs to the person who uses it.

When talking with a person who has a disability, look at and speak directly to that person, rather than through a companion who may be along.

Observe the individual for clues as to whether or not they require assistance. Don't assume that they need your help and proceed to do something for someone without them having requested it. Respect the independence and ability of the individual just as you would any other person.

If it appears assistance is appropriate, offer assistance in a dignified manner with sensitivity and respect. Be prepared to have the offer declined. Do not proceed to assist if your offer to assist is declined. If the offer is accepted, listen to, or ask for, instructions.

Offer to hold or carry packages in a welcome manner. *Example:* "May I help you with your packages?"

Relax. Don't be embarrassed if you happen to use accepted, common expressions, such as "See you later" or "Walk this way, please," that seem to relate to the person's disability.

Expect the same measure of punctuality and performance from people with disabilities that is required by every potential or actual employee.

People with disabilities expect equal treatment, not special treatment.

Exercise II: Role Playing

Break into your groups once again and read the text that relates to your group's previously assigned disability.

A person from the group will need to be selected to play the following roles:

- disabled applicant
- applicant companion, if applicable
- interviewer
- co-worker

Prepare for the class a role play illustrating the following situations:

- Interviewer greets applicant and companion (if applicable).
- Interviewer walks with applicant and companion to office.
- Once in office, ask the applicant three interview questions that relate to filling the position your group selected for the previous exercise.
- Thank the applicant and walk with him/her to front door.

Explain to the class the relevance of your actions in the role play.

Interviewing Persons Using Mobility Aids:

1. Enable people who use crutches, cane(s), or wheelchairs to keep them within reach.

2. Be aware that some wheelchair users may choose to transfer themselves out of their wheelchairs, into an office chair, for the duration of the interview.

3. When speaking to a person in a wheelchair or on crutches for more than a few minutes, sit in a chair. Place yourself at that person's eye level to facilitate conversation.

Interviewing Persons with Vision Impairments:

1. When greeting a person with a severe loss of vision, always identify yourself and others who may be with you. Say, for example, "On my right is Penelope Potts." When conversing in a group, give a vocal cue by announcing the name of the person to whom you are speaking. Speak in a normal tone of voice, indicate in advance when you will be moving from one place to another, and let it be known when the conversation is at an end.

2. If the person does not extend their hand (to shake hands), verbally extend a welcome. *Example:* "Welcome to the City of Chicago, Department of Personnel."

When preparing to move to another location, advise the person and ask how you may assist them. Some individuals may prefer to be led on the right side; others may prefer the left side.

Allow a person with a visual impairment to take your arm (at or about the elbow). Never grab a blind person's arm. This will enable you to guide rather than propel or lead the person.

When you arrive at your destination, it is helpful to describe the area so that the person can have a relative view of the room. "We are entering my office. My desk is facing us in the center of the room. There are two chairs in front of the desk where you may be seated." "I will place your hand on the back of the chair."

3. When offering seating, place the person's hand on the back or arm of the seat. A verbal cue is helpful as well.

4. When an individual is accompanied by a guide dog, do not attempt to engage the dog. The dog is in a work command and should not be distracted from his duties.

Interviewing Persons with Speech Impairments:

1. Listen attentively when you're talking to a person who has a speech impairment. Keep your manner encouraging rather than correcting. Exercise patience rather than attempting to speak for a person with speech difficulty. When necessary, use short questions that require short answers or a nod or shake of the head.

2. When interviewing a person with a speech impediment, stifle any urge to complete a sentence for the interviewee.

3. Never pretend to understand if you are having difficulty doing so. Repeat what you understand, or incorporate the interviewee's statement into each of the following questions. The person's reaction will clue you in and guide you to understanding.

4. Do not raise your voice. Most speech-impaired persons can hear and understand.

Interviewing Persons Who Are Deaf or Hearing Impaired:

1. To get the attention of a person with a hearing impairment, tap the person on the shoulder or wave your hand.

2. Look directly at the person and speak clearly, naturally, and slowly to establish if the person can read your lips. Not all persons with hearing impairments can lip-read. Those who do will rely on facial expressions and other body language to help in understanding.

3. If the interviewee lip-reads, look directly at him. Speak clearly at a normal pace. Do not exaggerate your lip movements. Speak expressively because the person will rely on your facial expressions, gestures, and body movements to understand you. Maintain eye contact. (Note: it is estimated that only four out of ten spoken words are visible on the lips.)

4. Show consideration by placing yourself facing the light source and keeping your hands, cigarettes, and food away from your mouth when speaking. Keep mustaches well-trimmed.

5. Do not shout at a hearing-impaired person. Shouting distorts sounds accepted through hearing aids and inhibits lip reading. Do not shout at a person who is blind or visually impaired—he can hear you!

6. In the United States, most deaf people use American Sign Language (ASL). ASL is not a universal language. ASL is language with its own syntax and grammatical structure. When scheduling an interpreter for a non-English-speaking person, be certain to retain an interpreter who speaks and interprets in the language of that person.

7. If an interpreter is present, speak to the person who has scheduled the appointment, not the interpreter. Always maintain eye contact with the applicant, not the interpreter.

8. If an interpreter is present, it is commonplace for the interpreter to be seated beside the interviewer, across from the interviewee.

9. Interpreters facilitate communication. They should not be consulted or regarded as a reference for the interviewee.

VIEW VIDEO

Reasonable Accommodation: New Access to the Workplace

An employer must provide a reasonable accommodation to the known physical or mental limitations of a qualified applicant or employee with a disability unless it can show that the accommodation would impose an undue hardship on the business.

A. Generally, it is the responsibility of the employee to request an accommodation, although you may ask if an accommodation is required to perform the functions of a job.

   The time to determine specific accommodations needed to perform the job is after an individual is determined qualified as a potential candidate. The purpose of the interview is to determine qualifications and the need for accommodations.

B. An accommodation may be necessary in an employment practice, work environment, or in a modification or adjustment in the job.

Examples of Reasonable Accommodations:

- Making facilities accessible to and usable by individuals with disabilities.
- Restructuring a job by reallocating or redistributing marginal job functions.
- Altering how or when an essential job function is performed.
- Part-time or modified work schedules.
- Obtaining or modifying equipment or devices.
- Modifying training materials or policies.
- Providing qualified readers or interpreters.
- Reassignment to a vacant position.
- Permitting use of accrued paid leave or unpaid leave for necessary treatment.

C. When determining a reasonable accommodation, consult with the individual in identifying potential accommodations, effectiveness, and comparative costs. If the benefits and costs are relatively equal, it is best to let the employee decide which accommodation they would prefer.

D. The responsibility to provide a reasonable accommodation is an ongoing obligation. You may request documentation of the necessity of an accommodation.

E. "Undue Hardship"—an accommodation would require significant difficulty or expense, would be disruptive to other employees, or would fundamentally alter the nature or operation of the business. Three factors should be used when determining whether an accommodation would cause an undue hardship:

- The size of the office, i.e., the number of employees.
- The financial resources of a company.
- The nature of the work environment.

F. John Alden has established an "Accommodation Fund" that will cover the cost of purchases or adaptations required to accommodate the placement or retention of a disabled employee or applicant. An Accommodation Request Form should be forwarded to Human Resources for approval.

> *Note:* 50% of individuals with disabilities do not require an accommodation and for the 88% of those who do, the accommodation costs less than $1000.00.

Exercise III

As a group, refer to your completed job description and think of any accommodations or adjustments that would allow you to continue performing the essential functions of your job effectively.

_____

_____

_____

Incentives for Hiring a Disabled Employee

Program	Incentive	Restrictions
Targeted Jobs Tax Credit (TJTC)	Tax credit of 40% of first $6,000 earned per employee provided the employment lasts at least 90 days or 120 hours.	May not claim TJTC and OJT for same wages. Certification must be requested on or before first day of work.
Tax Credit on Architectural & Transportation Barriers	Tax deduction on up to $15,000 spent to make a workplace more accessible for employees and customers.	Improvements must meet Treasury Department standards.
Association for Retarded Citizens of the USA	Reimbursement of 50% of entry wage for first 160 hours of on-the-job training; 25% of entry wage for second 160 hours.	Worker must be mentally retarded with IQ below 70, at least 16 years old, underemployed or unemployed over 7 days. Position must be at least 20 hours a week, pay minimum wage, and the employer intent must be to hire that individual on a part-time basis. All males between 18–30 must be registered with Selective Service.
Vocational Rehabilitation On-the-Job Training Program (OTJ)	Shared payment of the disabled employee's wages for a limited time on a negotiated schedule.	Worker must be a VR client. Position must be permanent, full-time, and pay minimum wage.

Selected Disabilities and Common Ways to Accommodate Them

Following is additional reference material you may read alone or refer to as needed. This information can help you think about providing reasonable accommodations to workers with different kinds of job-related limitations. It is not comprehensive; people with similar disabilities may require completely different accommodations, or none at all. But those suggestions may give you an idea of the possibilities.

Sensory Impairments

Hearing Impairments

- Can range from mild to total deafness, with loudness and/or clarity difficulties.
- Some people with severe hearing impairments can read lips (called "speech reading"); most rely on some form of sign language.

Common assistive aids: Hearing aids; TDD (telecommunication devices for the deaf), which makes it possible to use available telephones (both parties must have the devices); alerting devices or alarm systems that signal by light or vibration; interpreters for special meetings.

Speech Disorders

- Can include difficulty in articulating sounds, general use of voice, and fluency.

Common assistive aids: Speech therapy (with possible adjustment in work schedule, if needed); the use of written messages rather than spoken ones; patience on the part of co-workers.

Visual Impairments

- Can range from total to partial loss of sight.
- A person who is legally blind may have some limited sight.

Common assistive aids: Rearrangement of space for worker's guide dog; typewriters, calculators, and computer terminals that "talk"; braille typewriters and computer; printers; scanners that read printed materials and convert them into raised print; hand-held magnifiers.

Developmental Disabilities

Learning Disabilities

- Can include dyslexia (developmental reading disability), dyscalculia (developmental math disability), or aphasia (language disability).
- Can vary widely in degree of severity.

Common assistive aids: Modifying instructions or procedures to compensate for the job-related limitation; consistent and appropriate feedback to avoid misunderstanding.

Mental Disabilities

- Can include mental retardation, Down's syndrome, mental illness, autism, and neurological disabilities.
- May affect the ability to absorb information and to learn; however, people with developmental disabilities often learn and perform well on a level that corresponds to their intellectual ability.

Common assistive aids: Restructuring procedures or tasks; demonstrating tasks rather than explaining them in abstract terms; repeating and reinforcing instructions; extra supervisory assistance as needed.

Hidden Disabilities

AIDS (Acquired Immune Deficiency Syndrome)

- A progressive failure of the immune system; usually fatal.
- Transmitted only when the virus passes directly from the body of a person with AIDS to one without it via bodily fluids or blood.
- People who test positive for HIV may develop AIDS, but do not automatically have AIDS.

Common assistive aids: Vary widely by stage of condition; in early stages, flexible schedules and employee/supervisor training about the facts of AIDS.

Cancer

- Describes more than 100 diseases, none of which is contagious.
- Not necessarily fatal—almost half of all people with cancer live for five or more years after being diagnosed.

Common assistive aids: Vary widely by type of cancer; for those undergoing treatment, flexible schedules or scheduled rest periods.

Cardiovascular Diseases

- Include heart attacks and strokes.
- Employers are advised to require clearance from a physician before the individual returns to work.

Common assistive aids: Modification of job tasks to offset any physical disability; schedule accommodations to permit the worker to manage medication, diet, or fatigue.

Diabetes

- Chronic disorder that can be managed with proper treatment and regular eating schedule.
- Not all diabetics require insulin injections; "maturity-onset" diabetes is treated mainly through diet and body weight control.

Common assistive aids: Schedule accommodations to permit the worker to manage medication, diet, or fatigue.

Epilepsy

- Also known as a "seizure disorder," characterized by a sudden overload of electrical energy passing between brain cells.
- Seizures may range from barely noticeable facial twitching to "grand mal" seizures with brief loss of consciousness.
- Often mild and controllable—some 65% of all people with epilepsy have no seizures while the rest have infrequent, minimal seizures if properly medicated.

Common assistive aids: Education of co-workers about seizures and what to do if one occurs; supervisor or co-worker training to recognize pre-seizure signs (called "auras") so that workers can be helped away from the work area; rearrangement of furniture and equipment to minimize injury in case of a fall.

Head Trauma

- "Invisible" yet common—about 3 million Americans have head injuries each year, but most injuries are minor.
- Major head trauma can manifest itself in headaches, dizziness, uncharacteristic behaviors, and personality changes.
- Lasting effects may include difficulties in seeing and thinking, limited ability to plan or organize activities, inability to control emotions.

Common assistive aids: Varies widely by worker's capacities; modification of tasks or schedule; extra supervisory assistance for a set period while individual readjusts to work.

Musculo-Skeletal Disorders

Arthritis

- Includes more than 100 diseases that involve inflammation of the joints, such as gout, lupus, and scleroderma (thickening of skin).
- The #1 physically disabling condition in the U.S.

- Chronic condition with no known cure; affects all ages.
- Can be controlled with medication, rest, and exercise.

Common assistive aids: Varies widely; break times for rest or exercise; use of joint-protecting devices such as splints.

Cerebral Palsy

- Loss or deficiency of muscle control due to permanent, non-progressive brain damage believed to occur before or at time of birth.
- Characterized by some or all of these conditions: difficulty in walking, balancing, and sometimes speaking, hearing, or using the hands.
- Only a small percentage of people with cerebral palsy have mental retardation (not 100 percent as was once believed).

Common assistive aids: Varies widely; possible rescheduling of work hours; accessible work site and facilities if mobility a problem; use of devices such as lap boards and automatic phone dialers.

Multiple Sclerosis

- Disease of the nervous system.
- Symptoms can come and go; may be mild or severe; may include partial or complete paralysis of arms or legs, numbness, slurred speech, loss of coordination.
- Usually strikes adults from ages 20 to 40.

Common assistive aids: Varies widely; possible rescheduling of work hours; accessible work site and facilities mobility a problem.

Paraplegia and Quadriplegia

- Paraplegia is paralysis of both legs, usually caused by traumatic injury or disease to the spinal cord.
- Quadriplegia is paralysis of legs and arms, usually caused by injury or disease to the spinal cord in the neck.

Common assistive aids: Varies widely; adaptation of physical environment to remove barriers that impede mobility by wheelchair.

Alcoholism and Substance Abuse

Important Note: An employer may discharge or deny employment to current illegal drug users, on the basis of such drug use, without fear of being held liable for disability discrimination.

Persons addicted to drugs but no longer using drugs illegally and receiving treatment for drug addiction or who have been rehabilitated successfully are protected by the ADA from discrimination on the basis of PAST drug addiction.

While current illegal drug users have no protection under the ADA if an employer acts on the basis of such use, a person who currently uses alcohol is NOT AUTOMATICALLY denied protection simply because of the alcohol use. An alcoholic is a person with a disability under the ADA and may be entitled to consideration of accommodation, if she/he is qualified to perform the essential functions of the job.

Alcoholism

- Alcoholism is a chronic, progressive, and potentially fatal disease (not a character flaw or lack of will power as it was once regarded).

Common assistive aids: Often not necessary; possible rescheduling of work hours for treatment or counseling; access to Employee Assistance Programs.

Substance Abuse

- Most mental health professionals also regard substance abuse as an addictive disease.

Management of Individuals with Disabilities

A. *Awareness/Education*—Changing attitudes is the first step in ensuring that the ADA and its promise to integrate disabled individuals into the mainstream are realized.

   1. *Preconceived ideas as to abilities*—Given the multitude of disabilities that exist and the varying degrees of abilities, it is important to treat each person as an individual when determining what their capabilities are.

   2. *Offering assistance*—Never assume a need exists. People with disabilities often do things differently and it may take them longer or appear difficult for them to accomplish something, but it is important to acknowledge and respect their independence. If you wish to offer assistance, ask in a positive way and do not insist if your offer is not accepted.

   3. *Special treatment*—Do not allow a person's disability to change or alter your expectations. Be consistent in your treatment of your disabled and non-disabled employees.

   4. *Co-workers*—While it is beneficial to dispel myths and address concerns, try not to focus on what makes the employee different, but on what qualities and experience he or she will be contributing to the team.

A person's disability and any work-related functional limitations caused by that disability should be held in the strictest confidence and only be discussed or shared with persons having a legitimate need for that information.

B. *Benefits*

1. *Employee activities*—Be sensitive when planning employer-sponsored activities so that they do not exclude disabled workers or relatives of employees who may be disabled.

C. *Performance Evaluations*—You may wish to discuss the performance appraisals with a Human Resource representative prior to conducting the appraisal to increase comfort with the appraisal process.

If job performance problems occur, try to identify if the problem is related to the disability and make adjustments or accommodation as needed. You may want to involve a medical or rehabilitative specialist as necessary. Your Human Resources representative can involve these resources and help you find a solution if one exists.

If the performance problem is one not related to the disability, it is important that you treat the employee in a manner consistent with your management style and address deficiencies accordingly.

D. *Termination*—Prior to any termination, Human Resources must be contacted and consulted. Human Resources must approve any termination decision. If it is determined that poor performance is not related to a disability and an accommodation is not needed, try to establish that there are no psychological, interpersonal, or communication barriers that may be causing the problem. Is the employee not adjusting to his environment or is he or she unhappy because of perceived or actual discrimination? Is there a conflict with a particular supervisor that is causing the problem? The situation should be carefully analyzed prior to deciding to terminate as in any other termination decision. If termination is appropriate, the employee should be handled according to established procedure.

ADA Documentation

1. *Personnel file:* Any employment records including requests for reasonable accommodation, performance appraisals, disciplinary action, selection for training.

2. *Any information* that is not directly related to the job and is of a more sensitive nature should be sent to Human Resources (i.e., discrimination or harassment complaints). Also any information you receive, efforts, actions or involvement with regard to the ADA should be copied to Human Resources for the general ADA Compliance File at headquarters.

3. *Any information* or documentation that is of a medical nature must be kept separate and confidential and may only be kept by Human Resources. All medical information will be kept confidential with strict limitations on its use unless information is used for purposes of safety, necessary accommodation for work duties, insurance requirements, or by governmental officials investigating compliance.

Employer Models

Many preferred employers have already integrated the disabled into their workplace to the benefit of the company and the individual. Those employers who receive federal grants or contracts have been required under the Federal Rehabilitation Act of 1973 to actively affirm the abilities of the disabled in their companies. Other companies, responding to the ADA, have taken similar, voluntary proactive steps to encourage qualified disabled employees to apply and grow with their companies.

We would like you to view some real life examples of successful employment profiles from one of our own business partners, EDS. EDS has produced this video for their own manager training and we would like to share some of their employee profiles with you.

VIEW VIDEO
10 minutes

Above and Beyond

In order to accomplish our mission to bring about the successful implementation of the ADA, we have developed the following strategies that are currently being implemented or are planned for future implementations.

- *Audit all owned and leased facilities* and make necessary alterations for barrier-free workplace.

- *Establish telecommunications link* between John Alden (particularly Human Resources) and the hearing or speech disabled.

- *Develop Reasonable Accommodation Fund* (sample form passed out).

- *Participate in community-based committees* and organizations that support the training and employment of individuals with disabilities.

- *Communicate all job openings to recruiting sources* who serve the disabled community.

- *Develop original initiatives* to facilitate placement and awareness of individuals with disabilities. Examples include: Career Counseling Program, Intern Programs.

- *Educate JALIC* on issues relating to individuals with disabilities and disability management.

Until this point, laws throughout history have mainly served to call attention to the differences of the disabled rather than looking beyond them. This landmark civil rights legislation promises to challenge our learned attitudes, confront our fears and discomfort and lack of understanding, and allow opportunities for all individuals regardless of differences within our organization. John Alden has always supported an equal and diverse workplace and has benefited from this policy with our growth and success. It is with knowledge of the law and understanding of the advantages to our organization that we accept the challenge of becoming a leader in the affirmation of the talents and contributions of individuals with different abilities and encourage their inclusion in the John Alden corporate family.

John Hancock Mutual Life Insurance Company

15

Robert Taber

John Hancock Mutual Life Insurance Company is a major diversified corporation that includes the Life Company and 22 subsidiaries involved in a broad range of financial services including mutual funds, securities brokerage, real estate, and venture capital. Assets in 1994 totaled $83 billion. Hancock has 15,000 employees, 4,300 at the home office and the remainder scattered among sales/services offices in all 50 states, Europe, and Asia.

The company was chartered in Massachusetts on April 21, 1862. John Hancock was chosen as the namesake for his efforts in working toward the independence of the United States. The company began a major diversification trend in 1968, introducing mutual funds and realty services and launching its International Group Program. In the 1980s, John Hancock stepped up its diversification by entering virtually every major financial services industry. It diversified into Asia and opened an operation in Taiwan in 1992.

The Life Company is divided into seven sectors: executive, retail, corporate, investment and pension, financial, business insurance, and law. Each sector is further divided into cost centers. Within the corporate sector is the human resources department. This is where the workforce diversity unit is located. This unit is responsible for the company's affirmative action plan, responding to discrimination charges, and conducting training on such topics as disability awareness, the Americans with Disabilities Act (ADA), and the Family and Medical Leave Act. The unit also monitors ADA compliance.

In preparing for the ADA, the workforce diversity unit reviewed the law and developed an implementation plan for the organization which included:

- Educating all levels of employees by conducting ADA workshops throughout the company.

- Developing a disability policy that became part of the human resources policy guide.

- Identifying resources to assist with accessibility and accommodation issues. Resources included the Job Accommodation Network, the Massachusetts Rehabilitation Commission, the Massachusetts Commission for the Deaf and Hard of Hearing, Carrol Center for the Blind, and New England Rehabilitation Hospital.

Since the initial implementation, John Hancock has developed a comprehensive ADA program that includes:

- Conducting workshops on such topics as disability awareness, ADA, and ergonomics.

- Removing architectural and communication barriers—John Hancock has developed a compliance strategy and began implementing it by placing TDDs (telecommunication devices for the deaf) throughout the company, constructing handicap-accessible bathrooms throughout the home office complex and the John Hancock Tower Observatory, renovating office and meeting rooms to provide full accessibility, constructing a ramp at the garage in the home office complex to provide access from the street to the elevator lobby, installing power-assisted doors and audible/visual fire alarms, and providing interpreters at company events and meetings.

- Providing reasonable accommodations for employees returning to work and active employees—For example, accommodations for visually and hearing-impaired employees have been in place for years. These include:
  o Voice synthesis systems for personal computers, such as VertPro from TeleSensory
  o Magnification systems, such as Vantage or Voyager from TeleSensory
  o Key-modifier software, such as Outspoken for Windows
  o TDDs, such as those offered by AT&T
  o Interpreters from the Massachusetts Commission for the Deaf and Hard of Hearing

- Involvement with local private, state, and federal rehabilitation organizations to facilitate outreach and recruitment of individuals with disabilities—Many disabled employees are successfully employed at John Hancock. Individuals who are visually impaired are employed as customer service representatives, computer programmers, and word processors. Individuals who are hearing impaired are employed as a bookkeeper, cook, controller, and administrative assistant. Individuals with physical disabilities are employed as a lawyer, security officer, and administrator.

John Hancock's return-to-work program has been in existence for over ten years. The program serves as a means to return disabled employees to work. A disability claim analyst manages each case and involves the rehabilitation coordinator once a return-to-work date is known. If accommodations are necessary, the workforce diversity consultant is contacted. The consultant performs a job analysis and submits it to the treating physician. Any reasonable accommodations recommended by the treating physician are put in place. When an employee returns to work on reduced hours, disability payments offset the part-time wages until the employee can earn more than what full disability pay would be. The workforce diversity consultant maintains contact with the employee and supervisor to facilitate a smooth transition back to work.

Ergonomics is part of John Hancock's integrated approach to disability management. The company's ergonomics program is proactive and address a variety of employee disabilities. The program identifies, evaluates, and reduces problems due to poor workstation design. The benefits of the program include improved employee health, fewer injuries, and improved production. John Hancock has seen less time lost to injuries and fewer medical and disability claims as a result of this program. Components of the ergonomic program include:

- *Ergonomic worksite evaluation*—An evaluation of the worksite to identify ergonomic risk factors and develop practical solutions, such as adapting equipment, modifying work schedules, or changing work methods.

- *Medical management program*—John Hancock's health services unit is available for employees to report problems with worksite design, such as lighting, equipment setup, or chair design. The unit also medically monitors employees who request ergonomic accommodations. If necessary, the employee can be referred to an appropriate treatment provider, such as a neurologist, physiatrist, or orthopedist.

- *Education and training*—Training programs on ergonomics are offered to management and employees by the workforce diversity staff and training staff.

Examples of Reasonable Accommodation

The following case studies demonstrate the process of enabling employees to return to work and providing active employees with reasonable accommodations at John Hancock.

Case Study I

This case illustrates the coordination between the disability claim analyst, rehabilitation coordinator, workforce diversity consultant, employee, and treatment provider.

Ed was a senior accountant in the controller's department. He recently celebrated 25 years of service with John Hancock. One cold and snowy January morning, while Ed was shoveling a path to his car to get to work, he experienced some numbness in his right arm. When he went in the house to say good-bye to his wife, he experienced tightness in his chest. His wife called an ambulance, and Ed was admitted to the hospital and diagnosed as suffering a heart attack. After numerous tests, the cardiologist performed an angioplasty, and Ed remained in the hospital for three weeks.

At the beginning of Ed's hospital stay, the disability claim analyst sent out disability claim forms for Ed and his physician to complete. The disability claim analyst continued to stay in contact with Ed and his physician throughout Ed's hospital stay. Upon discharge, Ed was admitted to a cardiac rehabilitation program. During his four weeks there, the disability claim analyst wrote to the cardiologist to determine when Ed could return to work. The physician recommended Ed begin working part time before returning to full-time work. The disability claim analyst then involved the rehabilitation coordinator. The rehabilitation coordinator spoke to Ed, his physician, and Ed's manager to plan a work schedule. All parties agreed on the following schedule:

1. Monday, Wednesday, and Friday from 9:00 to 12:30 for two weeks

2. Five days a week from 9:00 to 12:30 for two weeks

3. Monday, Wednesday, and Friday from 9:00 to 12:30 and Tuesday and Thursday from 9:00 to 2:30 for one week

4. Five days a week from 9:00 to 2:30 for one week

5. Five days a week from 9:00 to 4:00 for one week

6. Five days a week from 9:00 to 5:00 for one week

Ed's physician and the rehabilitation coordinator felt that changes needed to be made Ed's worksite. The rehabilitation coordinator contacted the workforce diversity consultant, who conducted a worksite evaluation and submitted it with Ed's job description to his physician. The workforce diversity consultant and Ed's physician agreed that it was important to reduce fatigue for Ed, and the following accommodations were put in place: an ergonomic chair, footrest, adjustable keyboard tray, and a break every two hours. Because Ed's return-to-work program was coordinated before the end of the rehabilitation program, he had a smooth transition back to work. Both the rehabilitation coordinator and the workforce diversity consultant maintained contact with Ed for a period of time after he started back to work. Ed was eventually able to return to full-time work and is doing well.

Case Study II

This case study involves a 37-year-old employee named Alison. When Alison was 18, she was involved in a diving accident and sustained a head injury which resulted in a seizure disorder.

Alison began working at John Hancock as a cook in 1986. Due to numerous seizures and accidents on the job, some involving self-inflicted injuries with knives, she was unable to perform the essential job functions of a cook. It was therefore necessary to determine if she could be reassigned to another type of work. She had no recent medical information to assist the workforce diversity consultant in determining her functional abilities and limitations. The consultant referred Alison to a physiatrist (physical and rehabilitation medicine physician). The physiatrist recommended she be seen by a neuropsychologist, to determine her cognitive strengths and weaknesses, followed by a vocational rehabilitation counselor. The neuropsychologist found that Alison had strong verbal/language skills but had problems with concentration and coordination. With the assistance of the vocational rehabilitation counselor, possible jobs that best fit Alison's strengths were identified. She appeared to be a candidate for a position as a mail processor. Her responsibilities would be delivering and sorting mail. The vocational rehabilitation counselor served as Alison's job coach. The following accommodations were identified: instructions were posted on the wall near the mailboxes, Alison was to verbalize the location of mail stops so that over time she would encode the locations into her memory, and she worked with an experienced mail processor until she was able to work independently. The consultant evaluated Alison's progress on a regular basis. She has been performing the job independently for over a year and has achieved established productivity and accuracy standards.

Case Study III

Disability management programs are more effective when a cooperative relationship is established with the employee's treatment provider. A partnership among the employer, the employee, and the treatment provider must focus on the goal of keeping the employee connected to the workplace. This case demonstrates the importance of such a partnership

Roger had been on short-term disability because of a muscle disorder that produced neck twitching and resulted in his holding his head in abnormal positions. His physician was able to minimize the effects of the problem with medication. Roger's supervisor maintained contact with him while he was on disability leave and knew when he was able to return to work. The supervisor contacted the company's workforce diversity consultant a few weeks before Roger was released to return to work. The consultant told Roger that he would be in contact with his doctor to discuss any job limitations and accommodations. Roger was eager to return to work and agreed to sign a release so that the consultant could speak to his physician. A job analysis which included the essential/non-essential job functions and physical requirements of the job was submitted to the physician. The physician responded that Roger must keep his head in such a position that it did not tip forward. With this information in hand, an ergonomic worksite evaluation was completed on Roger's workstation. The following accommodations were then put in place: an adjustable keyboard tray, an adjustable monitor arm, an ergonomic chair, and a copy holder attached to the monitor. Upon returning to work, Roger was shown how to use this equipment. He now works full time and is able to perform all his job duties.

John Hancock is a company that is socially responsible. It continues to work with organizations to facilitate employment of individuals with disabilities. John Hancock recognizes that its ADA program helps prevent disabilities and rehabilitates employees so they can return to a productive work life.

Marriott International, Inc.

16

Marriott International became a public company in October 1993, when Marriott Corporation split into two separate companies. Marriott International manages lodging and service businesses. It has operations in 50 states and 24 countries, with approximately 170,000 employees. It has annual sales of about $8 billion.

Marriott International owns the trademarks, trade names, and reservation and franchise systems that were formerly owned by Marriott Corporation. The new company has two operating groups. Their divisions are leaders in their respective businesses and enjoy strong customer preference.

The Lodging Group is composed of Marriott's four hotel management divisions: Marriott Hotels, Resorts and Suites, which manages or franchises 254 full-service hotels (plus 6 managed hotels under construction); Courtyard, the company's moderate-priced lodging division (229 hotels); Residence Inn, the leader in the extended stay segment (186 inns); and Fairfield Inn, Marriott's economy lodging division (161 inns). In total, the group manages or franchises 830 hotels with approximately 177,600 rooms. Also included are Marriott Ownership Resorts, which operates 28 time-share properties with over 59,000 interval owners, and Marriott Golf, which manages 17 golf facilities.

The Service Group has three principal divisions. Marriott Management Services provides food and facilities management for business, education, and healthcare clients, with over 3000 accounts; Marriott Senior Living Services manages 19 retirement communities (plus 8 under construction) which offer independent and assisted living for older Americans. Marriott Distribution Services provides food and related products to the company's operations and external clients through seven distribution centers.

Marriott International's Program for People with Disabilities

Marriott has a long-standing commitment to employing people with disabilities. Its business units actively seek people with disabilities who will benefit from their association with the company and who can help it achieve its business goals. As a result of the company's aggressive program, people with disabilities work in a broad range of job categories.

Marriott's program for training, hiring, and supporting persons with disabilities is based on the philosophy that properly matching an individual with a job, followed by appropriate training and support, can benefit both the company and the associate. The components of the program include employment training, a job referral network, corporate giving, management training, school/business partnerships, liaisons with organizations for persons with disabilities, and the Marriott Foundation.

Some of the positions held by associates with disabilities include:

- Senior vice president
- Vice president
- Director
- Cook
- Secretary
- Security officer
- Engineer
- Manager
- Telephone (PBX) operator

Marriott's Programs and Contributions to Support People with Disabilities

Marriott has always been committed to the recruitment and hiring of people with disabilities. This ongoing commitment is a beneficial business practice as well as "the right thing to do." Nearly 6% of Marriott's work force is comprised of people with disabilities. This strong commitment is reflected in Marriott's policy statement on equal opportunity for Americans with disabilities (see Exhibit I).

Since 1968, Marriott has received more than 100 awards from various federal, state, and local organizations for training and employing persons with disabilities. At the time the Americans with Disabilities Act (ADA) became effective, the company had operations in all 50 states comprised of nearly 4000 business units and approximately 175,000 domestic associates and 20,000 managers.

Unlike many companies of its size, Marriott is affected by both Title I and Title III of the ADA. In order to formulate effective strategies to ensure compliance with the requirements of the law, the company organized independent

EXHIBIT I

Marriott International, Inc.
Equal Opportunity for Americans with Disabilities
Policy Statement

Marriott International, Inc. has always been committed to the employment of people with disabilities. It is the Company's policy to provide Equal Employment Opportunity for persons with disabilities in full compliance with the AMERICANS WITH DISABILITIES ACT OF 1990 and the regulations of the Equal Employment Opportunity Commission in connection with, but not limited to, hiring, training, accommodating and promoting individuals with disabilities. Further, Marriott will promote their participating in social or recreational functions and the use of associate facilities.

The Company's Equal Employment Opportunity Program affirms the Company's longstanding and continuing commitment to fair employment of persons with disabilities. It is the responsibility of all managers and officers to ensure that the Program is implemented in all Company operations. It is the responsibility of the Corporate Vice President of Equal Employment Opportunity/Affirmative Action to monitor compliance with this Program and to assist managers and officers in meeting their Equal Employment Opportunity obligations.

J.W. Marriott, Jr.
Chairman, President and
Chief Executive Officer

---

task forces for Title I and Title III to develop an implementation plan for each (see Exhibit II).

Marriott's primary concerns were:

- Training 20,000 managers as well as numerous supervisors and associates in direct customer-contact positions
- Reviewing and revising approximately 600 job descriptions
- Revising human resource policies and procedures
- Identifying and removing barriers
- Meeting transportation requirements under Title III

EXHIBIT II

Americans with Disabilities Act
Implementation Plan 1991–1992

Major Activity Recommendations Title I	Responsibility	Completion Date								
		Oct	Nov	Dec	Jan	Feb	Mar	Apr	May	Jun
Obtain, develop and validate new pre-placement evaluation.*	SBU designator				31					
Discard all applications dated prior to 2/91.	SBUs		29							
Review and revise job descriptions to include essential functions and non-essential functions.	SBU designator						20			
Review and advise regarding new job descriptions.	Corp. EEO Corp. Legal								1	ongoing
Training modules completed.	Gary Dave		18							
Finalize LOA policy language.	Dave Bob		18							
Disseminate application memo to field.	Dave		18							

Action	Responsibility	Timeline
Disseminate ADA policy statement and ADA posting requirements to all SBUs.	Dave	16
Ensure all ADA posting requirements are met.	Vice Presidents of HR	1
Provide ADA updates to all SBUs.	Dave, Edward	ongoing ↑ ↑ ↑
Provide ADA training for HR managers, interviewers and hiring managers.	Vice Presidents of HR	15
Assist SBU's ADA training initiatives.	Dave, Edward Sloan, Janet Tully	ongoing ↑ ↑ ↑ ↑ ↑
Provide reasonable (case-by-case) accommodation advice.	Corp. EEO, Corp. Legal, SBU designator	ongoing

Title III

Action	Responsibility	Timeline
Develop strategy to address Title III issues.	SBU designator	15
Ensure vehicle accessibility requirements are communicated and addressed.	SBU designator	18

*To be discussed and reviewed with Corporate Legal and Corporate EEO.

Marriott's innovative Community Employment & Training Programs Department, whose main purpose is to assist in the training and placement of persons with barriers to employment including disabilities, provides linkups to referral agencies for company units and the field. Marriott has numerous projects around the country, many of which are customized to meet the needs of specific units and/or persons with disabilities.

One of its larger projects is at the Atlanta Marriott Marquis Hotel, a 1600-room property in downtown Atlanta. This is a Community Based Work Adjustment Program in partnership with Goodwill Industries of Atlanta. The project is in its third year and 80 people have completed the program. More than 67 individuals have gone on to full-time employment with Marriott. In addition, the Division of Vocational Rehabilitation and the United Way are also working with Marriott on this project.

The program in Atlanta is "disability neutral," which means that it is open to people with any type of disability. Almost every position in the hotel qualifies. It is called a full-circle program because not only do persons with disabilities receive training, but Goodwill representatives learn what business expects from employees.

Because of the positive exposure to persons with disabilities and the accompanying sensitivity and awareness training, managers have learned to look beyond the disability to the abilities of the applicant. As a result of this successful effort, a staff position is dedicated to transitioning people with disabilities into the workplace.

Other successes are numerous. More than 60 individuals with disabilities are employed at the New York Marquis Hotel. Special computers with an audio system to accommodate visually impaired reservationists have been installed at the Marriott Reservations Center in Omaha.

Marriott also invested heavily in auxiliary aids for its lodging customers with hearing impairments. Each full-service hotel was issued one auxiliary kit per hundred rooms. Other lodging products including Courtyard/Fairfield Inn and Residence Inn received one kit per unit. The kits included:

- Closed-caption decoder for Spectradyne-operated TV
- Door knock alert with strobe light
- Clock and pillow vibrator
- Telephone alert with strobe light
- Telephone-amplifying device
- Two TDDs (telecommunication devices for the deaf)

Marriott is the only major hospitality company that is a member of the President's Committee on Employment of People with Disabilities. In 1990,

Marriott received the Exemplary Voluntary Efforts Award given by the U.S. Department of Labor, Office of Federal Contract Compliance Programs. The award was given in recognition of an outreach, recruitment, and training program for high school students with disabilities. In 1992, Marriott received the Labor Investing for Tomorrow Award from the U.S. Department of Labor.

Marriott has instituted two programs aimed at helping young people with disabilities adapt to the working world. In 1989, the Marriott Foundation for People with Disabilities was established by the Marriott family to foster the employment of youth with disabilities. The "Bridges...From School to Work" program develops internships with local employers for students with disabilities in their last year of high school. Since 1989, more than 1600 students have participated. The Bridges program has placed 1291 of these students with some 550 employers. The program operates in San Francisco, Washington, D.C., Chicago, and Montgomery County, Maryland, where Marriott is headquartered (see Chapter 32 for further details).

Marriott also initiated the School/Business Partnership Program with Walter Johnson High School in Bethesda, Maryland. In this program, 33 Marriott associates were matched with either mentally retarded students from the Bridges program or students with learning disabilities from the Learning Center at Walter Johnson. The objective of the program is to help students make a successful transition to the world beyond the classroom.

Employing People with Disabilities

At Marriott, work force diversity is valued and respected. The company's commitment to the development of human potential and the principle of equal opportunity dates back more than 66 years.

Marriott places strong emphasis on abilities rather than disabilities. The company's experience has shown that people with disabilities can be productive members of the work force. This experience corroborates other findings which indicate that job accommodation costs are generally minimal and often cost nothing at all, that people with disabilities are no more difficult to supervise than employees without disabilities, that they have safety records that equal their non-disabled peers, and that they perform their jobs as well as other employees in similar positions.

The passage of the ADA provided Marriott the opportunity to carefully examine company facilities and employment practices to ensure that they not only comply with the law but fulfill the expectations and needs of people with disabilities. Through the company's Equal Employment Opportunity Department, an ADA task force developed a comprehensive training program entitled "Breaking Down Barriers," which is relevant to associates at all levels. While the ADA ensures that people with disabilities will not be overlooked, this program helps Marriott provide an environment that meets both the letter and the spirit of the act.

Several principles guide Marriott's efforts to effectively employ people with disabilities: open communication of expectations and standards is key to an effective program; awareness and education in both management and staff are critical to hiring and retaining employees with disabilities; and most significant, matching individual skills, abilities, and interests with job requirements is central to a long and mutually beneficial employment relationship.

Marriott believes that it simply makes good business sense to hire the best performers, regardless of whether they happen to be disabled. The company plans to continue to provide equal opportunity for all employees and to be a leader in employing people with disabilities. As each person gains, so does Marriott. The efforts and commitment of every individual contribute to the company's success.

Reasonable Accommodations

Marriott is a leader among leaders in implementing a robust program of reasonable accommodations and in its proactive attitude in attracting persons with disabilities.

Marriott has hired persons with disabilities to fill jobs in virtually every major department. Representative examples of positions and accommodations related to persons with disabilities include:

- Work sharing is used in the housekeeping area to reduce the number of rooms for which individuals with certain disabilities are responsible.

- An infrared listening system was purchased by the human resources department for a hearing-impaired affirmative action technician to facilitate that individual's participation in meetings. A TDD unit was also installed for that person.

- A blind person operates a grill in a Marriott restaurant without any accommodations.

- An air-conditioning, general repair, and maintenance position is staffed by a person with one arm. This individual needs no special accommodation to accomplish his work.

- A blind secretary to the general manager of a major hotel uses screen-reading technology to accomplish her work.

- Persons with cerebral palsy work in housekeeping, a sports bar, gift shop, and other areas. These individuals require no special accommodations.

- A multiple amputee who is wheelchair bound works in an upholstery repair function and requires no special accommodations.

These examples demonstrate that, on average, accommodations for persons with disabilities involve very low cost. Where costs are incurred, the payback period is short.

Marriott has a useful tracking device to record request and implementation of accommodations (see Exhibit III).

Training for Managers

While Marriott has been recognized as a leader in the employment and accommodation of individuals with disabilities, the enactment of the ADA was seen as having far-reaching effects on the company. As part of its overall strategy in continuing as a leader in this field, Marriott decided to prepare its managers for implementing the employment and public access provisions of the ADA through a special training program. This initial training program and a subsequently developed advanced training program represent a state-of-the-art product.

The ADA training program is called "Breaking Down Barriers—Working Together." It contains a leader's guide for line managers, numerous quizzes, role-playing activities, handouts, and slides and is presented in five units or modules.

Unit 1: Raising Awareness about Disabilities—This unit is intended for all managers and supervisors, especially those responsible for hiring. It is a prerequisite for Units 2, 3, and 4. Participants identify their personal beliefs or assumptions about people with disabilities and the potential negative impact of these beliefs or assumptions on employment decisions and customer service.

Unit 2: ADA's Employment Provisions for Line Managers—This unit is intended for front-line managers and supervisors who are directly involved in hiring and supervising others. Participants learn the essentials of the employment provisions of the ADA, specifically with regard to avoiding discrimination against people with disabilities and reasonably accommodating employees and applicants with disabilities.

Unit 3: ADA's Employment Provisions for Human Resource Managers—This unit is intended for human resource managers or others who are called upon to establish policies or advise line managers in implementing the

EXHIBIT III

Reasonable Accommodations Documentation Procedure

1. Division _____ Unit _____

2. Name of person requesting the accommodation: _____

3. Date requested: _____ Applicant _____
   Associate _____

4. What limitations were to be accommodated? _____

5. What was the accommodation requested?

   _____

   _____

   _____

6. Approximate cost of accommodation: _____

7. Was the accommodation approved?   Yes ____   No ____
   a) If "Yes," please describe the accommodation made and its cost.

   _____

   _____

   b) If "No," please explain why it was refused, keeping in mind the undue
      hardship criteria. _____

   _____

   Who made the decision?   Name: _____
                            Position: _____

8. Were alternative accommodations discussed with the individual?
   a) If "Yes," please list alternatives. _____

   _____

   b) If "No," why not? _____

   _____

9. Which internal and/or external resources were used in considering the
   accommodation? _____

   _____

10. Name of manager completing this form: _____
                            Date: _____

employment provisions of the ADA. Participants examine the detailed employment provisions of the ADA, including guidelines for reasonable accommodations, inquiries into employee disabilities, the use of medical examinations, and the management of drug abusers and alcoholics in the workplace.

Unit 4: ADA and Public Accommodation—This unit is intended for line managers and those who are responsible for facilities design, maintenance, and alterations. Participants learn the essentials of the public accommodation provisions of the ADA, specifically with regard to the removal of barriers to the full and equal enjoyment of goods and services by customers, employees, and job applicants with disabilities.

Unit 5: Customer and Employee Relations—This unit is intended for all employees, especially those in high customer contact positions. Participants learn ways of interacting with customers and fellow employees who have disabilities in order to promote sensitivity and acceptance.

About the Modules—Each module has a leader guide and is designed to be conducted by line managers (with the exception of Unit 3) in a two-hour time frame. Unit 3 is conducted by human resource professionals who have EEO-related expertise. Unit 1 is used as a prerequisite for Units 2, 3, and 4. Unit 5 has some awareness-raising activities built into it.

Motorola, SPS

17

Gail A. Majors, Workplace Diversity Manager
Peter D. Niemuth, Benefits Manager
Frankie Palmer, Manufacturing Manager

Motorola is one of the world's leading providers of wireless communications, semiconductors, and advanced electronic systems and services. Major equipment businesses include cellular telephone, two-way radio, paging and data communications, personal communications, automotive, defense and space electronics, and computers.

The fundamental objective of the company is total customer satisfaction. To reach this fundamental objective, the company acts within a framework of key beliefs, goals, and initiatives. Key beliefs include conducting business with uncompromising integrity and constant respect for people. Company goals are to develop "best-in-class" people, marketing, technology, manufacturing, service, and products, including hardware, software, and systems; increase global market share; and provide superior financial results.

Motorola Semiconductor Products, headquartered in Phoenix, Arizona, designs, produces, and distributes a broad line of discrete semiconductors and integrated circuits, including microprocessors, RF devices, microcomputers, memories, and sensors. Major facilities supporting the sector are also located in Austin, Texas; Irvine, California; Durham, North Carolina; Mexico; Asia; and East Kilbride, Scotland. While the domestic population is 24,000, the population in Phoenix is approximately 14,000, located in seven major facilities in the Phoenix metro area.

The following policy/procedure statements apply directly to those employees located in the Phoenix Semiconductor Products Sector (SPS) of Motorola, although policy similarities are found throughout the company. As a federal contractor, the implementation of the Americans with Disabilities Act (ADA) was viewed as an extension of the Rehabilitation Act. The advent of the ADA prompted SPS to unify and document processes throughout the Phoenix area, solidifying and reinforcing the philosophy/practice of providing equal employment to those who are differently able.

The three most notable changes specifically brought about by the ADA were:

- The development and implementation of a four-hour training class
- Site-specific facility accessibility improvements
- Documentation of the accommodation process for those who declare a disability

The ADA class provides training for supervisors and managers on the impact of the ADA, especially in the interviewing and accommodation process. The course was developed and instructed by in-house diversity managers and a consultant who is differently abled. To date, over 2000 employees have been trained.

The site-specific plans were developed by members of a cross-functional task force representing facilities, diversity, human resources, legal, safety, security, occupational health resources, training, compensation, and staffing. The entire team reviewed all sites to recommend improved access to public and non-public areas. They developed an implementation plan and began to make accommodations as required (see Exhibit I). The cross-functional team recommended changes that not only complied with the law but also improved accessibility for all employees. The team continues to meet on an ongoing basis to continually review accommodations and facilities.

The third, and possibly the most complex, portion of implementation was in documenting the accommodation process for existing or potential employees. While accommodations had been made for years, no one process was uniformly utilized or shared among the various facilities. The team charter became anticipating where accommodations would be requested, based on historical and future needs, and then flowcharting the "next" step. Additionally, seven "help" questions (Exhibit II) and a flowchart (Exhibit III) were published to assist in the accommodation process.

Special Accommodations

Motorola, Phoenix SPS has employed a number of hearing-impaired individuals for the past two decades. Many of the employees worked at the 52nd Street facility. In 1991, the Signs of Silence Team was formed and initially chartered to identify and implement solutions to problems in the work environment which were unique to the hearing-impaired population. Team members consisted of both hearing-impaired employees and hearing employees who have hearing-impaired children. The hearing-impaired team members had service dates ranging from 7 to over 20 years.

EXHIBIT I

Facilities Plan of Implementation for ADA Issues

SITE: _____   DATE: _____

NON-CONFORMING ISSUE AND ESTIMATED COST	PRIORITY	START DATE	COMPLETION DATE	RESPONSIBLE NAME

ATTORNEY-CLIENT PRIVILEGE

EXHIBIT II

Employment of People with Disability: Seven-Step Decision Process

There is a seven-step process, which is summarized here, that may help you to evaluate whether an applicant or an employee is a qualified person with a disability.

1. Is the individual disabled? Does the person have a *physical or mental impairment* that substantially limits one or more major life activities such as walking, seeing, etc.? Do they have a *record of such impairment* such as a recovered cancer patient? Or are they *perceived to have an impairment* such as a severe facial disfigurement or are suspected of having the HIV virus? In the latter case, the individual may not be disabled except for the perception of others, which protects them under the ADA.

2. Does the individual meet the basic qualification standards for the job?   Do they have the knowledge, experience, skills, education, college degree, licenses and certifications needed for the job? If they do not, they are not qualified for the job. The ADA does not require employers to lower their standards by hiring someone who is not qualified.

3. Can the individual perform the essential functions of the job without reasonable accommodation?   If yes, they are qualified. If they cannot perform *non-essential functions* of the job, the job may be restructured by trading or assigning *non-essential functions* to another employee.

4. If the individual cannot perform the essential functions of the job without reasonable accommodation, can they perform the essential functions of the job with reasonable accommodation? Transferring an *employee* to another *open position* is a reasonable accommodation. For assistance in identifying reasonable accommodations, you may ask the applicant or employee what they need. They may know better than anyone else or you may contact the Job Accommodation Network (JAN) by calling 1-800-526-7234 for additional ideas. Workforce Diversity will assist you as well. The ADA *does not require* that you assign *essential functions* to another employee, only that you make reasonable accommodation which will enable the individual to perform the essential functions of the job.

5. Would providing the necessary accommodations cause undue hardship on the employer?   Some of the measurements of undue hardship include the employer's size, financial resources, funding available from corporate or rehabilitation agencies, percentage of the budget that would need to be used for accommodation, whether the accommodation would benefit more than one person, would the employer face plant closure or job loss if required to provide the accommodation and whether the accommodation would hinder other employees in the performance of their job.

6. Would placement of the individual into the job with or without accommodation pose a direct threat to the health or safety of themselves or others?   If no, the person is qualified for hire. If yes, the person is not qualified for hire. Disqualifying an individual for employment under this question must have supporting medical and safety information to confirm.

7. Can an accommodation be made that would minimize the direct threat to the health or safety of themselves or others?   If yes, the person is qualified for hire. If no, the individual is not qualified.

EXHIBIT III

Employment of People with Disability Decision Chart

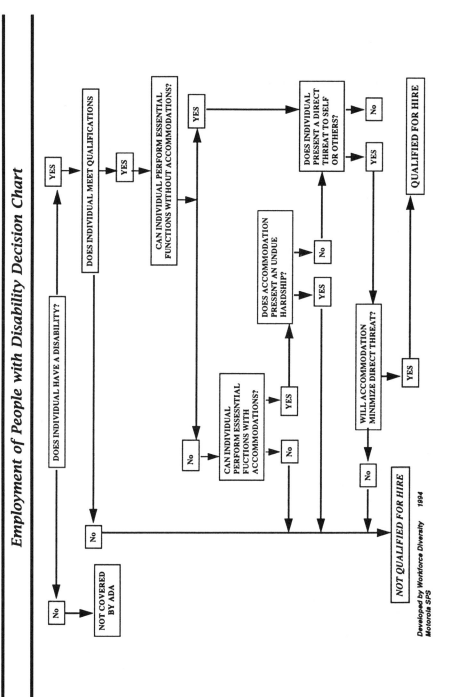

Developed by Workforce Diversity   1994
Motorola SPS

The team researched and documented the four most critical problems within the work environment which created a difficulty:

1. Evacuation procedures
2. Healthcare issues related to medical emergencies
3. Two-way communication with family
4. Ordering and paying for meals in the cafeteria

The evacuation procedure problem, caused by the inability to hear the warning siren, was quickly resolved. All hearing-impaired employees were provided with alphanumeric vibrating pagers. Each pager was programmed to activate simultaneously with the evacuation sirens and read "Evacuate, Evacuate. Please leave the building." Additionally, flashing lights were installed within the facilities to alert the hearing impaired.

Expanding on the use of pagers, one hearing-impaired material handler used his pager to communicate as he performed his job throughout the facility. Codes were established which told him when to go to certain areas within the factory or what supplies to bring. He was also provided with a personal computer so that he could communicate through the e-mail system.

The issue of healthcare related to medical emergencies. Hearing-impaired employees were concerned that in the event of accident or illness, no one would be available to interpret sign language or understand the nature of the problem. Information cards were developed to provide information about the employee, including the name of his or her doctor, an interpreter's name and pager number, and other medical information as necessary. These cards were attached to the Motorola employee badge which must be worn while in the facility. Health services representatives were also taught key words and phrases in American Sign Language.

The need/desire to talk with a member of the employee's family was identified as another problem. Although one TDD was available in the cafeteria, it was frequently in use. Additional TDDs were installed throughout the facility, including in the team's home department. The cafeteria phone was then relocated to a more private area. Part of the strategic plan also included classes for hearing employees to learn how to operate the phones.

Daily communication with the hearing-impaired population was awkward for some hearing employees. Classes in American Sign Language were offered by Motorola to the team's peers and supervisors. An interpreter was contracted to assist with daily communications in meetings or conferences. Ultimately an interpreter was hired to support ongoing functions within the department.

The final problem addressed by the team was ordering and paying for food in the cafeteria. Lip reading and signing were confusing for both the hearing-impaired and the hearing population. The team sought alternatives to simplify the process. To overcome the confusion, paper and pencils were provided at each food section and signs were positioned for easy reading by both the hearing impaired and the food servers. Also, a new digital display feature was added to the registers, which delighted all of the employees.

The team successfully addressed and presented its project during the 1992 Motorola Total Customer Satisfaction (TCS) competition. Two issues were abundantly clear to the audience. First, the project had improved daily communication between the hearing-impaired and the hearing population in the work environment. Second, a much wider audience of Motorolans had been educated on the impact of loss of hearing. The presentation dispelled such myths as all hearing-impaired people can read lips or loss of hearing impairs one's ability to drive a vehicle or communicate on the telephone. Identifying the individual's abilities in the workplace, as opposed to the perceived disability, is a valuable lesson for all who have seen the presentation. The actual TCS team also served a third function, which was to allow team members to feel accepted and supported within the larger departmental team. This sense of pride and acceptance formed future bonds.

The team was so successful in both its TCS showcase and solution implementation that word of its accomplishments has been widely publicized throughout the community. The team members continually represent Motorola to other hearing-impaired individuals and organizations throughout the Metro Phoenix area.

Reach Out Efforts Outside of Motorola

At Phoenix SPS, the passage of the ADA has brought about a renewed commitment to work with the differently abled within the community. In conjunction with its pledge to affirmatively utilize diversity within the community, Motorola, in cooperation with the University of Arizona Department of Special Education and Rehabilitation School, developed a practicum for graduate students to research issues and accepted practices in human resources, especially as such policies and practices affect the hiring of persons with disabilities. The internship was designed to provide students with a working knowledge of employer evaluations and expectations for the subsequent placement of differently abled employees. One student learned how to evaluate the use of a clean room wheelchair which could be utilized in a semiconductor manufacturing area. The project required investigating semiconductor manufacturing processes, the need for clean room equipment/attire, accessibility to and from the manufacturing area, and the feasibility of easily adjusting a workstation to accommodate both a wheelchair and a regular chair. The resulting evaluation was provided to a Motorola team for further evaluation and the University of Arizona as the student's semester project.

Motorola continually seeks ways to work with all members of the community, including the differently abled. As the need for skilled professionals increases, the diverse qualified talent within the community will continually be utilized. Motorola's intent is to provide appropriate opportunities for all employees, matching the skills and abilities to the placement. Partnering in this way provides a healthier community for all.

Philip Morris Companies, Inc. **18**

Philip Morris Companies, Inc. is the world's largest producer and marketer of consumer packaged goods, providing over 150,000 jobs worldwide. The company's origin dates back to 1847 when Mr. Philip Morris, a London tobacconist, produced tobacco in a then new form—cigarettes. In addition to its tobacco products, the company is a major producer of food and brewery products.

Philip Morris U.S.A. is America's number one cigarette manufacturer. Its flagship brand, Marlboro, is the leading brand of cigarettes in the United States and the world. Marlboro Lights is the leading low-tar cigarette. Virginia Slims is the leading cigarette made especially for women. Benson & Hedges 100's is America's leading freestanding 100mm cigarette.

Miller Brewing became part of Philip Morris in 1969 and soon surged into second place among the world's brewers with distribution in approximately 80 countries and territories. Together, Miller Lite, Lite Ice, Miller Genuine Draft, Miller Genuine Draft Light, Icehouse, and Red Dog account for almost a quarter of the U.S. premium beer segment. Other popular brands include Molson, Foster's Leinenkugel's Meister Bräu, and Milwaukee's Best. Miller also markets Löwenbräu, the super premium brand that originated in Germany.

Kraft Foods, Inc. produces such well-known brands as Jell-O, Velveeta, Kraft Miracle Whip, Post, Oscar Mayer, Philadelphia Brand, Kool-Aid, Entenmann's, Tombstone, Lender's, Cool Whip, Stove Top, and Shake 'N Bake. At least ten cents out of every dollar spent on brand-name foods in the United States is spent on Kraft Foods products.

Compliance with the Americans with Disabilities Act

Philip Morris's operational diversity offers the opportunity to see how a company with both staff and broad-based manufacturing operations approaches implementing the spirit of the Americans with Disabilities Act (ADA). The company's employing persons with disabilities actually predates the ADA. The passage of the ADA did bring a new focus to the subjects of accessibility, accommodations, and other aspects of the law.

The company's subsidiaries retained consultants, several among them persons with mobility limitations, to evaluate facility access and related issues. In addition to the latter assessments, several training and ADA awareness programs were implemented.

The first program presents a series of comprehensive questions and answers regarding the ADA. The questions and answers (which are quite thoughtful and complete) cover such important subjects as the kind of employment decisions affected by the ADA; reasonable accommodations; the possible need to modify policies, practices, and/or procedures; the extent to which structural barriers need to be removed; and the consequences of not complying.

The second program is a slide presentation intended for human resource professionals. It covers the following four major factors connected with the ADA:

- Background and purpose of the ADA
- Reasonable accommodation
- Key issues
- Enforcement

The first part of the presentation describes the content of the five titles of the ADA, describes key provisions of the ADA, and defines what is and what is not considered to be a disability. This part also provides a matrix comparison between the ADA and Section 503 of the Rehabilitation Act.

Part two covers such matters as the job application process, the work environment, and defenses to claims of discrimination.

Part three is presented as a series of areas of concern and their respective issues. Using job standards as an item of concern, for example, the issues are up-to-date job descriptions, identification of essential functions, and job-related criteria. Part three is an excellent checklist covering pre-employment, employment, and post-employment issues.

Finally, part four covers enforcement provisions of the ADA and what types of organizations are covered under the act.

Accommodations for the Differently Abled

Philip Morris U.S.A.

This major subsidiary of the Philip Morris Companies manifests the same considerations for persons with disabilities as has been observed in the other subsidiaries. Representative accommodations include the following:

- An employee who incurred a spinal injury uses a computer in his work as a design engineer. While he was recovering in the hospital, the company installed a computer in his room in order to build his confidence in his ability to perform his work. His supervisor and a representative from the human resources department worked with hospital rehabilitation personnel until his return to work.

   Upon his return to work, a complete review of physical access issues was conducted, along with an evaluation of how his personal needs would be attended to. His productivity and quality have been excellent since his accident in 1990. Early concerns on the part of management regarding many perceived personal care needs turned out to be non-issues. Several employees volunteered to assist him; however, a minimum of personal care was needed. He had a catheter, which obviated the need for attention to bowel or bladder needs. Virtually the only accommodations provided to this individual were a heated ramp for wheelchair access and couriers to bring material to him.

- Employees with degenerative diseases or terminal illnesses are given alternative, flexible work schedules for as long as they are able to work.

- The company makes every effort to provide opportunities to work at home for individuals with long-term illnesses such as cancer patients taking chemotherapy.

- Visually impaired persons working in Computer Information Services have been provided with computer equipment that magnifies both printed and computer-generated information (see Chapter 13 for a detailed description of this type of equipment).

- Hearing-impaired persons working in areas where forklift trucks maneuver are assisted by special lights installed on the trucks.

- A totally deaf person working in production operations is assisted in day-to-day needs by a fellow employee who learned sign language. A professional sign interpreter is made available to assist at formal training sessions.

- Visually impaired persons are assured of being given assignments during the daytime shift.

Miller Brewing

Miller Brewing also shows evidence of a commitment to assisting and employing persons with disabilities. Representative examples of accommodations are as follows:

- A senior executive who works closely with the local school system and Goodwill Industries' rehabilitation organization to employ persons with disabilities as computer programmers also fosters their employment at Miller Brewing. A product of this relationship can be seen in the case of a programmer analyst who is wheelchair bound due to a degenerative muscular disease. The company arranged for a voluntary "buddy system," where fellow employees bring the employee to and from work. His work area has been redesigned to provide wheelchair access, and he uses a standard personal computer and keyboard. The only other accommodation has been the preparation of an emergency evacuation plan.

- Believing that work is therapeutic, the company has developed an effective "Transitional Return to Work" program. This program applies to individuals who have a short-term disability where a doctor does not maintain that they should remain at home. Some of these employees are given jobs commensurate with their physical limitations without a loss in wages. After 30 days, individual cases are reevaluated.

- A female employee who was with the company for three months became paralyzed from the waist down as a result of an automobile accident. She also had limited use of one arm as a result of the accident. She has been reassigned to the training department, where she was given training in supervisory responsibilities and in the use of various pieces of equipment.

- In 1994, the company's recruiting department retained Goodwill Industries to train its entire staff. Employment applications are prepared in braille for vision-impaired individuals.

Kraft Foods, Inc.

Recognition of the special needs and opportunities in employing persons with disabilities at Kraft Foods goes back 20 years. The company has developed a strong, positive reputation in this area. A key to the company's high level of involvement over an extended period of time has been the support of top management for recruitment of persons with disabilities. The culture at Kraft Foods reflects its managers' flexibility in working with persons with disabilities and their appreciation of the abilities they bring to the workplace. This cultural orientation which is accepting of and encouraging to persons with disabilities is manifested in a variety of ways. The company retained a hearing-impaired reporter to provide ADA awareness training for its managers and brought in wheelchair-bound consultants to assess physical access at its headquarters facility.

Examples of accommodations at Kraft's Oscar Mayer headquarters and production facilities include:

- A quadriplegic employee who works as a computer programmer and who uses a mouth stick to perform his work was given a special keyboard (see the Chapter 13 for a full description of this device) and a flexible work schedule. He works three days per week.

- The company employs individuals with a wide range of disabilities in both exempt and non-exempt positions where virtually no special accommodations are required. Sight-impaired, arthritic, and other mobility-impaired persons work in such diverse areas as computer systems, loading dock, graphic arts, accounting, and as a research assistant.

- A hearing-impaired individual with 20 years seniority works as a head telephone operator in scheduling and supervising operators. This position does not require answering phone calls.

- A wheelchair-bound employee with 10 years seniority who has difficulty speaking (he can only say hi or hello) delivers high-priority mail throughout the headquarters building. The company is experimenting with a special portable keyboard and display to facilitate his communicating with other employees.

- Through cooperation with Yahara House, a rehabilitation agency in Madison, Wisconsin, the company employs emotionally troubled persons in part-time positions. New individuals are brought into the company every six weeks, and Yahara House counselors learn their clients' jobs so that they can substitute for them if necessary.

- Height-adjustable workstations that are ergonomically designed are used in production operations for mobility-impaired employees.

- A person with one hand was hired to slice turkey meat. A special device was fabricated to allow him to hold a knife.

- A female employee who originally joined Kraft as a food scientist developed multiple sclerosis. Her work as a food scientist required extensive travel to plant facilities and restricted operations and navigating difficult areas such as catwalks. When she became wheelchair bound after being employed for a year and a half, she could no longer work as a food scientist.

    The company and the individual reviewed other employment possibilities and agreed on packaging design as an appropriate alternative. This change of job function required a year and a half of training. The employee now works in a computer environment as a senior research designer, designing structural packaging for Kraft products. Special accommodations for her include the following:

o   A wheelchair lift was installed to permit access to a second work level.

o   A dedicated parking space was provided.

o   The company arranges special transportation during inclement weather when the employee feels it would be difficult to access the facility unassisted.

o   The company pays for special transportation needs when business travel is required.

Kraft further promotes the ADA in the following ways:

•   All employees are required to take diversity awareness training that includes a special section on persons with disabilities.

•   Recognizing that some of its customers are blind or severely sight impaired, the company has a totally blind employee who prepares its recipe booklets and food preparation directions in braille.

Summary

The positive attitude of management at all Philip Morris facilities has resulted in practical, low-cost accommodations that range from simple workplace redesigns to the use of state-of-the-art technologies. The results have been outstanding in terms of the quality of life of affected employees and their peers and the high levels of productivity and quality generated by disabled employees. Philip Morris serves as an inspirational model for those companies responding to the spirit of the ADA criteria.

The Prudential Asset Management Company

19

Dennis Butler, SPHR

The Prudential Asset Management Company (PAMCO) is a subsidiary of The Prudential Insurance Company of America. PAMCO is a leader in the institutional asset management industry, offering a wide range of pension administration and investment management services to more than 800 companies and other institutions. PAMCO employs more than 1500 people in positions ranging from entry-level clerical to information systems to advanced financial and administrative functions. Most employees work in northern New Jersey or northeastern Pennsylvania.

PAMCO has long been committed to equal opportunity and affirmative action. However, prior to 1989, most individuals with disabilities were employed in very basic clerical functions. Few, if any, disabled individuals were employed in professional-level positions. Faced with the challenges of an increasingly competitive job market, PAMCO management decided to go beyond the minimum requirements of the Americans with Disabilities Act (ADA) by targeting people with disabilities in recruiting efforts for professional positions. This group was viewed as a largely untapped source of quality candidates to meet projected staffing needs.

To start the initiative, PAMCO's human resources executive sent a memo to the management staff informing them that PAMCO's human resources area would be making significant efforts to recruit, promote, and retain qualified individuals with disabilities. Reactions were cautiously positive. It was clear that if these efforts were to be successful, PAMCO associates needed more information about what "working with the disabled" would mean. The human resources area then sought ways to start breaking down some of the attitudinal barriers which had historically made management reluctant to hire such individuals.

Awareness Training

PAMCO's earliest awareness training involved the human resources area contacting the County Office of Disability Services. They explained that while they were interested in recruiting within the disabled community, they were concerned that many associates would be uncomfortable about what to expect. The director of the county office, who uses a wheelchair, agreed to make a lunchtime presentation on disability etiquette in the workplace. The presentation was advertised around the office and attendance was strictly voluntary. The room was filled with associates from various departments and of various ranks. The director discussed some of the common "do's" and "don'ts" in a very personal and often humorous manner. Reactions to the presentation were overwhelmingly positive. As a result of greater awareness and understanding, many myths and concerns of this small group were dispelled.

Realizing that more education was needed, PAMCO retained the services of a consultant who had extensive experience working with corporations to recruit, employ, and promote qualified individuals with disabilities. The consultant served as a general resource and conducted various training sessions for management and staff.

One of the programs was a full-day experiential workshop called "Widerviews," which provided a forum for discussing the nature of various disabilities and the capabilities of the individuals who have them. Participants had the opportunity to hear from and speak to individuals with disabilities. They also had the chance to participate in exercises intended to highlight some of the challenges which these individuals face in the workplace. For example, to illustrate some of the challenges faced by people in wheelchairs, participants were given wheelchairs and asked to do simple tasks around the building, such as making a phone call at a pay phone, retrieving a paper towel in one of the so-called "handicap-accessible" rest rooms, or negotiating the access ramp. The workshop was very enlightening and the response was overwhelmingly positive as understanding increased.

PAMCO also used the services of the consultant to conduct pre-employment training sessions in areas where individuals with disabilities were being hired. These sessions provided additional information about disabilities and taught associates how to interact appropriately with the new hires. One hearing-impaired associate, whose area had received the training before he arrived, commented that he probably would not have left his previous employer if such training had taken place.

PAMCO's human resource professionals have received additional training in ADA compliance, disability awareness, and interviewing techniques so that they can work with line management to increase their understanding of, and comfort level with, the special workplace needs of individuals with disabilities. Supervisory courses offered in-house include information for supervisors about the ADA. (*Note:* While PAMCO paid for the services of a consultant to conduct awareness training, similar services can be provided at little or no cost by organizations such as supported living centers and vocational rehabilitation agencies.)

Involving All Employees

To further assure the success of its efforts relative to the employment of individuals with disabilities, PAMCO established a Disability Awareness Committee as part of its overall managing diversity effort. Membership on the committee is voluntary and includes associates ranging from clerical assistants to financial executives. The mission of this committee is "to create a work environment where individuals are able to perform to the fullest of their ability and to raise consciousness and increase sensitivity of all people when dealing with individuals with special needs." With this mission in mind, the committee has sponsored a variety of activities including posting notices on the e-mail system which highlighted an individual with a disability who made a difference, sponsoring an art exhibit in the employee lunch area which featured works by individuals with disabilities, presenting lunchtime sessions about various disabilities, and identifying resource materials available about disabilities.

The Disability Awareness Committee also set up a suggestion box and urged all associates to point out potential barriers within the workplace. While PAMCO's facilities were generally in compliance with current building code requirements relating to accessibility, the suggestion box uncovered water fountains that were too high for individuals in wheelchairs (easily remedied by installing a cup dispenser next to the fountain), plants located near stairwells which were potentially hazardous for a blind person (the plants were moved), and aisles that were not readily passable in a wheelchair (the clutter was cleared). Not only did these changes make PAMCO more accessible, but the process involved many associates and served to help increase awareness and understanding.

In addition to the activities of the Disability Awareness Committee, a number of PAMCO associates who are deaf or hearing impaired have conducted deaf awareness sessions and offered sign language classes to anyone who was interested. The classes are held during lunchtime and teach both basic fingerspelling and signed English.

Accommodation

Once a person with a disability is offered a position with PAMCO, the individual is asked what accommodations he or she will need to help perform the job duties. Accommodations involving cost are paid for by the Human Resource Division. Accommodations PAMCO has provided run the gamut from the simple to the complex.

Deaf or Hearing Impairment—PAMCO provides telecommunication devices for the deaf (TDDs) and volume control devices to facilitate effective communication via telephone. The company's electronic mail system is used heavily for routine communications by hearing-impaired and hearing associates. Additionally, many of the employment, benefits, and customer service areas of PAMCO and The Prudential have TDDs.

Sign language interpreters are brought in as needed for training, staff meetings, or other group presentations to ensure full participation by all associates. Given the cost and at times scarcity of available sign language interpreters, PAMCO has also used computer-assisted notetaking (CAN) when an interpreter was not available. This involves using a laptop or other personal computer and standard word processing software. When CAN is being used, the notetaker simply types the minutes into the computer as they occur so the deaf associate can read them as they are being typed and participate by typing comments back. Depending on individual typing proficiency, notetakers capture as much of the dialogue as possible, providing a close to verbatim account of what is going on. (They use a lot of abbreviations and are told that spelling doesn't count!)

Videotapes used for training or internal communications are all closed captioned. PAMCO's TVs and VCRs are all equipped with closed-caption decoders to allow playback. (TVs manufactured after July 1992 generally have the decoding technology built in.)

Visual Impairment—PAMCO equipped a visually impaired associate's personal computer with special hardware and software to enlarge the screen image. To help him find a ride to work when his original transportation plans fell through, the human resources area searched the employee database to locate individuals with whom he could carpool, similar to the ride match services many employers are now making available to help comply with the Federal Clean Air Act.

Mobility or Other Physical Impairments—PAMCO provided an electric scooter for one associate whose job required extensive movement around the office. For a recently disabled individual whose position required frequent visits to clients, PAMCO shared the cost of outfitting a van. Existing computer equipment was set up at home for a systems analyst whose disability made a daily commute impossible. Now the associate only travels to the office for occasional meetings. Other accommodations have been as simple as making minor adjustments to workstations or providing footstools.

Recruiting Individuals with Disabilities

Over the past several years, PAMCO has hired several individuals with disabilities in a variety of positions, ranging from financial reviewers to financial analysts to programmers and claims processors.

When recruiting at college campuses, PAMCO lets career services professionals know of its desire to include individuals with disabilities in its regular recruiting activities. Additionally, it recruits at the National Technical Institute for the Deaf and Gallaudet University (the only four-year college for the deaf and hearing impaired). PAMCO has also participated in career fairs and other information forums targeted at the disabled community to make it known that it is looking for highly qualified individuals.

PAMCO has also worked with a number of disabled and college placement service organizations to provide an employer's perspective of what is expected of college hires and what the students with disabilities can do to enhance their chances for success in a corporate environment. These types of outreach activities are particularly important for students with disabilities who are liberal arts or behavioral science majors who may not have a good understanding of the opportunities available to them in a corporate environment. From an employer's perspective, these types of activities help expand the network through which qualified candidates can be found.

Access to qualified candidates with disabilities can also be increased through affiliations with local ADA business groups or through organizations such as the National Center for Disability Services Industry Labor Council.

Management Accountability and Recognition

To foster understanding and support for recruiting, promoting, and retaining a diverse work force which includes individuals with disabilities, PAMCO modified its performance appraisal process so that all members of management are recognized and rewarded for their efforts in this regard. Additionally, PAMCO's overall performance as part of The Prudential enterprise includes an evaluation of how well the diversity of the work force has been managed. This evaluation has a direct impact on management's annual incentive compensation.

Reynolds Metals Company

20

Founded in 1919, Reynolds Metals Company is the second largest aluminum company in the United States and the third largest in the world. The company serves global markets as a supplier and recycler of value-added aluminum and other products. Reynolds Metals operations are vertically integrated into two areas.

Finished products and other sales includes the manufacture and distribution of value-added finished products. This encompasses aluminum beverage cans; Reynolds brand aluminum foil and plastic consumer products, including Reynolds Wrap; aluminum foil and plastic packaging materials for food, pharmaceutical, confectionery, food service, and industrial markets; and aluminum and vinyl building products.

Production and processing includes refining alumina from bauxite and producing carbon products and primary and reclaimed aluminum, principally to supply internal needs. Reynolds manufactures rolled, extruded, drawn, and cast products for fabrication into finished products and for sale to others. Examples include can stock and other sheet, plate, and extruded automotive parts and wheels. This area also includes the sale of gold and other non-aluminum products.

Reynolds employs 29,000 men and women at more than 100 locations worldwide. Through its wholly owned operations and others in which it has varying interests, the company conducts business in 22 countries throughout the world.

Accommodations at Reynolds Metals Company

Reynolds Metals' formal concern in addressing the needs of persons with disabilities dates back to 1964 at which time it established an equal opportunity affairs (EOA) office. The company's EOA corporate director participated on the President's Committee on Employment of Persons with Disabilities and has also assisted the Job Accommodation Network (JAN) in developing its database on accommodations. The JAN provides a free accommodations reference service to any organization.

The EOA office hired an individual to serve exclusively in coordinating the company's conformance to Section 503 of the National Rehabilitation Act of 1973 and to the needs of disabled headquarters employees, applicants, organizations, and plant locations throughout the United States. In 1974, the office conducted an assessment of barriers that might prevent the employment or upward mobility of persons with disabilities in the company. The assessment included a review of all company policies and procedures relating to persons with disabilities and their effective use. A number of accommodations for both sighted and vision-impaired persons resulted from these assessment efforts.

One of the outcomes of the disabilities-related assessment was the realization of a need to determine the physical and mental job qualification requirements of all job classifications in the company. The EOA office conducted a benchmarking effort to determine what specific information was needed for this purpose and came up empty handed. It could find no company that had developed an approach to document its physical and mental job qualification requirements and therefore developed its own.

A representative sample of accommodations made for persons with disabilities at Reynolds Metals includes the following:

- Assurance that all wheelchair users in the headquarters operation could access any part of the building. One change that resulted from this review was the installation of buttons to automatically control the opening of two sets of double doors at the building's main entrance. Previously, a company guard had to be called to open the doors.

- Another front-entrance problem that surfaced at the company's headquarters building was the difficulty that mobility-impaired individuals had in navigating four steep steps. The solution to this problem was to install an electrically operated lift that rises from the street level to the building entrance. Justifiably proud of this accommodation, the company's executives asked the chairman of the Equal Employment Opportunity Commission, who was attending a conference at the headquarters and who was a wheelchair user, to comment on the lift's utility. The chairman replied that the lift had a rated capacity of 45 pounds, while his battery-operated wheelchair weighed 250 pounds and he weighed an additional 250 pounds, totaling 500 pounds, which he thought represented a safety problem. The company increased the lift's capacity to 550 pounds.

- The company is proactive in surveying its employees for recommendations for needed accommodations. It should be noted that research indicates that it is important for a company to seek this kind of information rather than passively waiting for the information to be volunteered. Persons with disabilities are frequently hesitant to make voluntary suggestions for accommodations, even though little or no cost may be involved. When asked for this kind of feedback, however, they often make suggestions that can save the company money in addition to satisfying their needs for accommodations.

- Several sight-impaired computer operators have been given software systems that magnify (up to 40 times original size) information on their computer screens. As a result of this accommodation, the productivity and performance of sight-impaired employees are equal to or better than that of their peer group.

- The company has negotiated terms in its union contract that define its responsibilities in providing assistance with regard to an employee's disability. These responsibilities include the possibility of job redesign. A case in point is a person who had a back injury and could no longer lift the 30- to 40-pound item that was established as being part of the essential requirements of the job. He had no difficulty in pushing or pulling; his limitation was in lifting only. The EOA office asked the engineering department to assist in finding a solution to the problem to facilitate the continued employment of a valuable person. The engineers designed a special lift that enabled the employee to move the material to a conveyor. The cost of this accommodation was a mere $200.

- To accommodate hearing-impaired persons working in production areas, amber flashing lights were attached to equipment that would be hazardous to use until repaired. This safety factor also benefited non-disabled employees; in fact, after installing the amber lights, time lost due to accidents decreased significantly.

- Light-duty work is provided for employees who develop temporary disabilities. The union has facilitated the use of this type of an accommodation by agreeing to exceptions to the usual seniority rules.

- A hearing-impaired librarian has been given an amplified phone with a flashing light.

- A painter who developed a fear of heights was reassigned to work at ground level only.

- A chemist who became a quadriplegic as a result of an automobile accident was reassigned as a laboratory supervisor so that he was not required to handle chemicals.

These examples are representative of a wide range of accommodations made at Reynolds Metals Company—a company that has developed a responsive, proactive, and sensitive attitude in accommodating persons with disabilities.

Sears, Roebuck and Company

21

Mary Jean Houde

Sears, Roebuck and Company, originated in 1886 and incorporated in 1893, today operates approximately 800 multi-line retail stores and 1200 specialty stores in the United States. Stores also are located in Canada and Mexico. Sears employs more than 300,000 people, and its headquarters is located in Illinois.

From a payroll of 80 employees in the mid-1890s, Sears not only increased the number of employees but expanded its interest in personnel matters as well. Expansion was particularly noticeable during the 1940s and as World War II ended. Employment figures for Sears more than doubled between 1939 and 1947, to a total of 178,593. Between 1945 and 1947 alone, there was a net increase of 53,891 employees.

During the post-war years, people with disabilities were noticeably included in personnel considerations nationally. In 1947, Sears and other companies became founding members of the committee now known as the President's Committee on Employment of People with Disabilities. This involvement and commitment on the part of Sears would continue.

After the initial leadership of Richard Warren Sears, company executives prior to 1947 included Julius Rosenwald, who was as well known and respected for his philanthropic endeavors as he was in the business world. Rosenwald was president of Sears from 1908 to 1924 and chairman of the board from 1924 to 1932, during which time he introduced an employee profit-sharing plan and led in the adoption of sickness benefits for employees, vacations with pay, and better working conditions. Like Rosenwald, his successors combined good business with concern for the well-being of Sears employees.

An example of the compatibility of good business and concern for employees is found in Sears' history of employment of people with disabilities. Major programs include the Selective Placement Program, Early Return to Work Program, and an annual ProgramAble Day. These and other programs focus on what people **can** do, instead of what they can't do.

The Selective Placement Program encourages job applicants to apply for any job in the company for which they can qualify. This empowers job applicants by placing the selection process in the hands of the person with the disability and not a recruiter. The program design matches people with disabilities to jobs they are able to perform rather than focusing on what the person may be unable to do. The philosophy is that a qualified person with a disability can succeed. Reasonable accommodations may help assure success.

Sears began tracking accommodations in 1978, and records show accommodations for more than 450 employees. Not all accommodations are reported, however, and most disabled associates require no accommodation. It has been estimated that among the 300,000 employees at Sears, there are 20,000 persons with disabilities, physical or cognitive. Self-identification of employees as disabled is voluntary.

An Early Return to Work Program, developed in 1991, has been implemented in all Sears locations. An extension of the company's safe work practices, this program makes possible the provision of modified or temporary duty in order to shorten the length of absence resulting from work-related injury. The goal of the program is to convert what might become a permanent and total disability to a temporary/partial absence, while assuring a productive work force. For example, an associate who works in a physically demanding position and develops a disability that could be considered permanent might return to work in a non-physical position (e.g., office worker).

In addition to modified or temporary work duty, the program permits an injured employee who expects to be absent more than 20 work days to become a member of a "sponsor team." The team consists of the injured worker, a co-worker, the injured worker's supervisor, the unit manager, and a carrier claims manager. The co-worker's responsibility is to help the injured employee's recovery. This allows the injured employee to continue to feel a sense of "community" within the company during the often isolated recovery stage and keeps the company informed of the injured employee's status.

Sears hosts a ProgramAble Day annually as an addition to traditional hiring and recruitment efforts like visits to college campuses and participation in a wide variety of job fairs. ProgramAble is a unique, public/private computer training program located in the city of Chicago for students who have severe disabilities. The students are able to learn about Sears as a corporation, a community participant, and a prospective employer all in one day. Following breakfast and introductions, ProgramAble students hear a history of Sears as a major force in American retailing and learn the layout of a Sears store and its in-store systems. Each student spends time with a Sears associate in his or her work environment. Afternoon activities include a panel discussion by systems and human resource managers, as well as former ProgramAble students who are Sears employees. The panel discussion is followed by an in-depth question and answer period which gives students a better opportunity to explore possible interests in Sears as an employer.

Among those who joined Sears following a ProgramAble experience is Don Mott, who was promoted in late 1994 to the position of programmer/analyst in Human Resources Management Systems. After losing his sight in a 1981 accident, Mott was seeking a new career (he had been an owner-operator trucker and operations manager for a trucking company). He spent nine months in ProgramAble and was interviewed by Sears and hired. Special computer equipment was provided by Sears (an Alva braille display, Screen Reader/2 software, and Accent voice synthesizer) at a total cost of $16,225. With accommodations, Mott's work record equals that of non-disabled employees. Bill Brannen, department manager of Human Resources Information Technology at Sears, calls Don "extremely creative and innovative" and adds that he has been "a great asset to the company."

Mott also exemplifies the value of the Selective Placement Program, as do many other Sears employees who have been able to identify jobs for which they qualify. This includes three Sears associates who are either visually impaired or blind. Brad Shorser and Mary Ann Stephen have retinitis pigmentosa, a congenital, progressive disintegration of the retina, and Alan Sprecher has been blind since birth.

Mott, Shorser, Stephen, and Sprecher were featured in a recently released case report on Sears by Peter David Blanck, Ph.D., J.D., Senior Fellow at The Annenberg Washington Program in Communications Policy Studies. The report, entitled "Communicating the Americans with Disabilities Act," included costs of accommodations and comments from supervisors. Blanck's study of Sears indicated that compliance with the Americans with Disabilities Act (ADA) does not necessarily mean high costs. The average cost of accommodations related to the act and made between 1978 and 1992 was only $121. Most accommodations at Sears require little or no cost, including flexible scheduling, longer training periods, back-support belts, revised job descriptions, rest periods, enhanced lighting, adjusted workstations, and supported chairs or stools. Some accommodations, like those for Shorser, are more costly.

Shorser is senior manager of import operations at Sears, with responsibility for U.S. customs issues, domestic distribution and billing, ocean carrier logistics, and negotiations with a third-party logistics company managed by Sears. He began employment with Sears as a retail management trainee and has been with Sears for 20 years. Along the way, Shorser, who has some vision, was encouraged by Sears managers to utilize special equipment and technology as his retinitis pigmentosa progressed.

Accommodations for Shorser include a Kurzweil reading machine that scans text and recites it using synthesized human speech and an IBM PC equipped with an Alva braille display, Screen Reader software, and a voice synthesizer.

Total cost of the equipment was $26,225. These accommodations were called "relatively modest" by Bill Ginsburg, director of International Import Operations for Sears. He says that while the benefit of accommodations cannot be measured or quantified, the equipment allows Sears to benefit from Shorser's 20 years of experience and development of expertise. During a Chicago television interview, Shorser mentioned that Sears had given him "the opportunity to be employed in the type of position that is commensurate with my ability." About the ADA, Shorser said that it has "a positive impact on private industry...in providing other disabled individuals with that same opportunity."

Stephen, an administrative assistant in the legal department at Sears, also has some vision and uses both a text enlarger for reading printed material and an oversized, 19-inch, high-contrast computer monitor for reading computer files. These accommodations cost $7500 and allowed her to perform, according to Laura Plank, an attorney in Marketing Practices, "equally with everyone else on the team." Incidentally, Stephen has had four promotions in five years.

Sprecher is a COBOL programmer who creates mainframe sales reporting applications at Sears. He was recruited by Sears through contacts at the Chicago Lighthouse for the Blind, after he earned an associate degree in data processing from the Milwaukee (Wisconsin) Area Technical College. Entry-level programming training was provided at Sears. His accommodations, at a cost of $16,225, consisted of an Alva braille display at $14,500, Screen Reader/2 software at $725, and Accent voice synthesizer at $1000. Commenting on Sprecher's six successful and productive years at Sears, systems consultant and project leader Mike Offerman said, "The accommodation was 'paid for' long ago."

Sears has attempted through the years to provide the best available technology for blind associates, based on need. Those whose responsibilities included the review of a large volume of hard copy mail were provided with Kurzweil readers and scanners. Associates in the programming area used both personal computers and mainframe terminals with voice-activated software to announce the contents of the current screen. They also used a variety of braille printers as output devices. While these tools allowed them to work in the programming environment, the tools had limitations, and those limitations affected their productivity as well as their ability to use the same products as their work group.

Technology Solutions

Marc Stiehr, systems planning consultant for end-user computing at Sears, explained, "The challenge we faced was to find a way to migrate our blind associates out of the DOS world and into the same graphical environment as their work group. In January 1993, Sears contracted with Ability Consulting Services of Austin, Texas to assist in the evaluation of needs and to find appropriate technology solutions. Each associate was interviewed to provide an understanding of job responsibilities and determine what adaptive equipment was being used. Current state-of-the-art technology was researched in an effort to match up equipment that met the needs of each individual associate; a report was then prepared on each associate with specific recommendations. The best solution in the marketplace was IBM's Screen Reader/2 for OS/2, which had just become available."

According to Stiehr, there was initial resistance from blind associates who indicated that it would be impossible for them to work in this graphical environment. They feared that this environment would jeopardize their careers and leave them behind as others moved ahead.

"We quickly determined," said Stiehr, "that Screen Reader by itself would not provide the solution, dispel fears and improve productivity." He went on to explain, "While Screen Reader can read entire screens as well as any portion of a screen, the mainframe systems used by blind associates to access their work would need clearer interpretations. We decided to write programs called Screen Reader profiles, which would clearly announce what screen they were on and what actions were expected of them. Meetings were held with the associates to determine what was important from a voice feedback standpoint. These profiles were completed before we rolled out our solution."

Individual attention provided for each associate included setup and training with the new workstation. The first three weeks of system use indicated that while the solution provided the blind associates with the capabilities of the GUI (graphical user interface) environment that they had known in the DOS environment, they would still be unable to use the systems as effectively as their sighted counterparts.

"The missing piece was braille," said Stiehr, "and they were all strong braillers." Sears acquired 83-cell Alva braille displays (at $14,500 each) for the four blind associates in the headquarters program. For the first time in a production mode, braille displays were integrated with Screen Reader in an OS/2 2.0 environment.

Those unable to use their hands to operate computers were provided with a voice recognition system called VoiceType from Dragon Systems. With this system, an associate can speak in words (instead of individual characters as in previous systems) to interact with the computer. At a cost of $2400, this system allows the user to create "macro" commands whereby specific single words can be designated to represent frequently used word combinations.

Blind associates finally are allowed to be truly competitive with their sighted counterparts using the OS/2 platform. They can perform programming work and initiate, modify, and respond to e-mail documents much more quickly, often in half the time, according to Stiehr. He adds, "The total solution of braille and voice coupled with OS/2 has enabled our blind associates to work in the same environment as their counterparts, has improved their productivity, and has provided a greater degree of self-reliance."

To encourage self-reliance, Sears developed and provided for blind programmers a training class on the basics of writing and modifying Screen Reader as well as other customization procedures.

Work situations faced by disabled persons were well understood by Paul L. Scher, who managed the Sears program for employees with disabilities for 21 years before retiring from the company in 1993 and developing a consulting business of his own. Scher has been totally blind since 1968 as a result of glaucoma.

When Scher joined Sears' Equal Opportunity staff in 1972, he brought with him 15 years of experience in the field of rehabilitation. He worked to increase hiring and upgrading of associates with disabilities and spearheaded the development of the Selective Placement Program at Sears. Interviewed in 1990, Scher said, "We take the position that a person with a disability is potentially capable of doing any job that the company has available." When asked about attendance and performance of disabled employees, Scher said, "We find that disabled associates' attendance and performance records are equal if not better than non-disabled persons."

Sears activities relating to people with disabilities, which predate the ADA by 45 years, have gone beyond employing people with disabilities and providing opportunities for achievement and advancement. Sears is a charter member in Project Access, an organization designed to help businesses comply with the ADA and deal with the issues involved in the employment of people with disabilities. Project Access disseminates information on the experiences of companies that employ large numbers of persons with disabilities in an effort to help lower the learning curve for other companies, share information on actual experiences, and identify useful businesses designed to serve as ADA compliance resources. Other programs include a pilot effort with the Department of Labor to catalog organizations that locate and train employees with disabilities.

Store Modifications

Consistent with a long history of providing individual accommodations, Sears was aggressive in making its stores accessible to associates and customers with disabilities. Associates received training on how to best serve customers with disabilities, and store modifications included widening door entrances, adding power-assisted automatic doors, lowering sinks and vending machines in washrooms, and providing mini-kiosks with volume control for the hearing impaired. Signs urging customers with disabilities to seek assistance from a sales associate (if needed) are displayed prominently. Employees are asked to encourage personal requests from individual customers who might need something altered or adapted.

Modifications resulted from an extensive survey sent to each store regarding existing accommodations for people with disabilities. A specially formed Corporate Council on the ADA reviewed the responses and finalized an 81-page compliance booklet with an action plan for Sears stores. The compliance booklet includes a section on serving customers with disabilities. The primary author of that section was Paul Scher.

During the design process for the Sears headquarters at Hoffman Estates (a complex called Prairie Stone), Sears used Peer Review, a consulting firm, to assess the needs of its home office associates with disabilities. Research provided information used to address design issues ranging from the height of coat racks in the hospitality suite to shower stall and grooming counters in the fitness center.

Sears also received recommendations from Paralyzed Veterans of America/ Paradign Design Group, which worked with the building architects to help Sears make Prairie Stone as barrier free as possible. All areas, including overall site design, office buildings, and parking structures, were designed to optimize accessibility and mobility for individuals working at or making visits to Prairie Stone.

Sharing Experiences

Requests for information concerning ADA compliance experiences have come to Sears from individuals, organizations, and other businesses. In the process of sharing, meetings have been held and tours conducted.

Tours have taken visitors to workstations of employees with disabilities. Using company experience as a guide, Sears associates emphasize that compliance, which can be simple and inexpensive in many cases, is really an investment in the future of a company and society in general. Also, they point out that associates with disabilities have been excellent performers, as well as loyal and dependable.

Sears employees with disabilities frequently have been interviewed. One such employee is Tony Norris. His story begins with years of working his way up through the ranks at Sears until he was traveling around the world buying shoes. He ran the Chicago marathon and played rugby. Then, one day in 1986, he felt a numbness in his right leg. Surgery to remove a tumor from his spine left Norris a quadriplegic. After 20 months in the hospital, he received a call from his former boss at Sears. Sears wanted him back at work.

Norris is a senior systems specialist in Family Footwear for Sears. He receives about 4000 inquiries and requests for assistance each month and is able to perform his job responsibilities with the aid of a voice-activated computer and a breath-controlled telephone. Minor modifications have been made to his cubicle to accommodate his motorized wheelchair.

His attitude, as well as his accomplishments, have been applauded by print and broadcast media. "What I experienced," says Norris, "was the vanguard of things to come. We [people with disabilities] are becoming part of society...and we contribute. People are finally recognizing that and giving us a chance. All we want is a chance to get ahead."

Recognition

Sears has been recognized on numerous occasions through the years for employment of and its work with people with disabilities. Recent awards include the National Easter Seal Society award for corporate leadership, presented in September 1992, and the Infinitec Corporate Leadership Award, presented by the United Cerebral Palsy Association of Greater Chicago in June 1993.

The Easter Seal Society award, called EDI (for Equality, Dignity, and Independence), was the first of its kind to be awarded for corporate leadership. It went to three corporations—Sears, Lane Transit District, and U.S. Bancorp. The EDI designation reflects the National Easter Seal Society's mission of achieving independence for millions of Americans with disabilities. The society is a non-profit, community-based health agency with 160 affiliates. It provides rehabilitation and preventive care services, computer and other technological assistance, and camping, recreation, advocacy, and public education programs that reach more than a million people each year.

Leadership to increase independence for people with disabilities was also the basis for the 1993 Infinitec Awards which went to Senator Robert Dole and Sears. The Infinitec Awards are named after a national center which is being built by the United Cerebral Palsy Association of Chicago to increase access to existing technology products that enable people with disabilities to live life on their own terms. Those products range from easy-to-handle dinner utensils to computers that help people read, write, and talk.

Sears also was commended by Attorney General Janet Reno during a 1993 speech marking the third anniversary of the Americans with Disabilities Act. Reno cited Sears' commitment to making stores accessible to the disabled.

The bottom line for Sears was expressed in 1994 by Edward A. Brennan, Sears chairman and CEO: "When we help people with disabilities, we help Sears and we help our customers."

Texas Instruments   22

Texas Instruments, Incorporated, headquartered in Dallas, Texas, is a high-technology company with sales or manufacturing operations in more than 30 countries. Its products and services include semiconductors, defense electronics systems, software productivity tools, printers, notebook computers and consumer electronics products, custom engineering and manufacturing services, electrical controls, and metallurgical materials.

Texas Instruments (TI) believes that attention and consideration to the needs of its diverse work force make good business sense. The company has determined that it can cost $150,000 to train a professional employee to a point where he or she is fully productive. That bottom-line reason is why TI expanded its employee diversity initiatives in 1994. Its TI Diversity Network includes more than 20 employee committees established for women, Chinese, Blacks, Hispanics, Mexicans, Asian Indians, and the disabled.

Examples of Accommodations for Persons with Disabilities

TI has a long-standing involvement in programs to assist disabled persons find employment. The company participates in community business advisory councils (BACs) as a means of providing guidance and work internships to persons with disabilities. TI's experience with rehabilitation and training organizations demonstrates that it makes good business sense to hire the disabled. The following example of a disabled computer programmer is a case in point.

Case I

Linda Neufeld had stopped at a convenience store to add oil to her car's engine when another driver backed a pickup truck into her and crushed her knees. That accident, and the rehabilitation that followed, ended her involvement in the business she had built with her former husband. Before the accident two years ago, she had helped him in a home repair business. "There's no way I could still climb up a ladder and carry roofing supplies," she said.

217

Instead, she turned to an intensive training program at El Centro College for people who have disabilities. That eight-month program, Computer Programmer Training for the Physically Challenged, led to an internship with TI and a job offer from the company. She started her new job on June 22, the same week she graduated from the course. She now is a member of the Customer Service Systems team.

Linda does not consider herself disabled, and one cannot tell from watching her that she ever sustained a serious injury. However, she qualified for the El Centro program because she could no longer perform her previous job.

Linda met Anita Hawiszczak during the course. Anita is a staffing administrator at the Spring Creek site. She serves on the program's BAC and frequently helps students prepare resumes and hone job-hunting skills. "Our goal is to help physically challenged people into our work force and help them get started on a new career," Anita said. "It's important to attract qualified people to TI. It's a good business practice."

Anita is one of two active TI employees involved in the program's BAC. Three former employees also serve on the council. "This is an excellent way for TI to recruit people who have disabilities," Anita said. "Not only are we making an impact in the community, but this is a very good source of computer programmers who are qualified for our jobs."

Since the program began six years ago, TI has hired six graduates. Four, including Linda, are active TI employees.

Intensive Training

El Centro's program is intensive and requires eight months of full-time training, followed by a two-month internship. The program also provides training in business communications, resume preparation, job seeking, and job maintenance skills.

Students are selected by El Centro through a rigorous testing and interview process. Sixteen people graduated in Linda's class.

The BAC, made up of representatives from businesses in the Dallas area, oversees the program. Because of the heavy involvement of the council, the course gives students the skills required by business.

"This is a very intense, very difficult class," Anita said. "It is one of the top programs such as this in the nation."

New Law

"TI has always encouraged and helped employees who have disabilities," said Tamira Griffin of Corporate Employee Relations. Programs such as the one at

El Centro will help ensure that TI continues to make a positive impact on the disabled community.

"The Americans with Disabilities Act (ADA) reinforces what TI has been doing all along," she said. The ADA protects qualified people with disabilities from discrimination if they can perform the essential functions of their jobs with or without reasonable accommodation. Accommodation is not required if it would impose undue difficulty or hardship on the company.

Two sections of the ADA are particularly applicable to TI, according to Tamira. One section deals with employment requirements. The primary focus in this section is understanding the essential job requirements, a person's ability to meet those requirements, and any need for accommodation. This section covers an employer's hiring process, promotion practices, and other employee-related activities.

Another section sets standards so that buildings are accessible to people with disabilities. It was written to make sure that structural barriers do not exclude people with disabilities.

"Although this law is new, TI has always been committed to employees who have disabilities," Tamira said. "TI is actively involved in this area of our community and makes an effort to find and recruit qualified employees who happen to have disabilities."

Case II

Debbie Smelko doesn't know the words "I can't" even exist in the English language. And she prefers it that way.

Debbie injured her spinal cord in a car accident in 1978 and has been in a wheelchair ever since. Despite a painful rehabilitation, Debbie was determined to let nothing slow her down. Within the year, she was hired by TI in Dallas, Texas. Leaving the security of her home and friends, she moved unassisted to a new city, a new job, and a new life.

Starting out as a software design engineer, Debbie moved on to other positions within TI. Currently, she is administrator of a software engineering department with 650 employees and responsibilities in 6 different locations around north Texas. Over the years, she has helped pioneer changes at TI in parking lots, bathrooms, and ramps, long before the ADA was even a figment of someone's imagination. Later she served as an active member on the ADA team at TI, as well as on the board of directors of the company's activity and fitness center. Currently, Debbie serves on the Mayor's (Dallas) Committee for Employment of People with Disabilities.

In the meantime, Debbie's social life became as active as her career. There was travel to the Bahamas and the Caribbean (complete with snorkeling, scuba diving, and deep sea fishing), camping in Montana, football games at the Astro-dome, and dancing at Gilley's. Then, while working as a volunteer scorekeeper for the TI softball team, she met and married her husband, Tom Smelko.

The couple decided they wanted children and were blessed with a first son, T.J., in 1986. But the birth was premature and, because of complications, T.J. was diagnosed with cerebral palsy as well as hearing difficulties. Once again, courage and optimism became the operating forces in Debbie's life. With no books, magazines, literature, or even other mothers on hand for help or advice, Debbie designed a changing table, modified a crib, and became efficient with an infant car seat. Now she has become not only a one-woman advocate on "chal-lenged" motherhood but is an inspiration to many others. While it has been a very long road full of surgeons and physical therapists, T.J. walks, talks, and interacts beautifully with his second-grade classmates.

Two years after T.J. was born, Peter came along, and then, four years later, the Smelko's had a baby girl, Katie. The children have each grown up riding in mommy's wheelchair and now have become her little helpers in their weekly visit to the supermarket, where the yogurt is sometimes too high for Debbie to reach.

Life in the Smelko household is pretty typical of any two-career family. There are lots of trips to IHOP and McDonald's on weekends, although Debbie prides herself on her Tex-Mex cooking and Italian specialties. The kids swim and practice sports. They have classmates and playmates and play dates, which all make for a hectic schedule. There are family vacations and day trips to the zoo. Debbie is reaping the rewards of motherhood and family. In a profile done by her alma mater, Boston College, she is quoted as wanting to be named the "Best PTA Mom in Texas" and, in fact, considers motherhood to be her most important accomplishment.

Debbie has achieved recognition in her career and her personal life for her intelligence, her tenacity, and her capabilities. She has made a difference not only in the lives of those who know and love her, but also in the lives of many others whom she has been able to help and touch. In her Christmas letter last year, she added: "For the first time in 7 years, there is no medical update. No news is Good News!!"

Debbie Smelko is anything but typical. But you'd never know it by listening to her or watching her. To many, her struggles may have seemed insurmount-able. To Debbie, they were all just another challenge to be met and overcome.

Other Accommodations

The following list of disabilities or restrictions and respective accommodations is representative of accommodations made at TI:

Disability or Restrictions	*Accommodation*
Mobility	Motorized scooter
Diabetic	No overtime hours
Wheelchair	Power door openers at several locations
	Installation of a door to mini-auditorium and seat removal for wheelchair
No manual torquing or clinching	Automatic tools
No walking long distances, cannot walk and carry, no lifting over 30 pounds (from sitting position only), no standing for long periods of time, crutch walking as tolerated, wheelchair/cart for longer distances	Uses motorized carts
Take short walk every 45 minutes, need elbow supports on work chair	Installed elbow support at workstation, employee to take stretch breaks every 45 minutes
No lifting over 15 pounds, no repetitive gripping or pinching with left hand	Employee transferred to package inspector job in security
No bending, stooping, or lifting over 40 pounds	Lifting to be handled by co-workers
No prolonged sitting, stooping, or standing, raised workstation and orthopedic chair with high back needed	Orthopedic chair provided at cost of $700
No lifting greater than 15 pounds, must have 15-minute break every hour, light duty only, no use of manual torque tools, no twisting of left forearm or wrist for intervals greater than 20 minutes	Employee is to utilize a "buddy system" for lifting and long test sequences, employee has access to torque tools and special cart for transporting parts
Peripheral neuropathy	Motorized cart
Back limitations	Job modification (lifting/carrying requirement)
Hearing impaired	Use interpreter to sign at all meetings, telephone with blinker, telephone with loud ring

Texas Instruments Implementation Time Line

The following time line shows the primary implementation elements for introducing the ADA at TI:

Implementation Element	Month 1	Month 2	Month 3	Month 4
Process development	>--------------X			
Forms creation/revision	>--------------X			
H.R. Opportunity Center HROC approve direction	X			
Training & communications plan development	>--------------X			
Dallas site articles		X	X	X
Review team evaluates process		X		
Revisions needed based on feedback?		X----------X		
Creation of communications package	X--------------------------X			
Delivery of materials & training for HR reps and medical			X	
Training for staffing & EEO				X----X
Delivery of bulk materials			X	
T NEWS				X---X

Supervisor's Guide

Texas Instruments has developed a very professional and one of the best supervisor's guides as an aid in implementing and administering the ADA. The guide includes such important items as an overview of the ADA and important definitions of key elements in the act, TI's compliance process described in flowchart form, job analysis forms with instructions in their use, the procedure to request an accommodation, medical information, an explanation of the supervisor's role related to the ADA with case situations, examples of accommodations, a slide presentation for supervisors to use in explaining the ADA, and the supervisor's role in its successful implementation.

Union Pacific Technologies

23

Union Pacific Technologies (UPT) develops sophisticated computer software for the corporation's operating companies and aggressively pursues research in new technologies. The company also has expanded the scope of its commercial activities outside of Union Pacific.

UPT continues to assist the Ferrocarriles Nacionales de Mexico (FNM), the national railway of Mexico, with the installation of computer software similar to that used by Union Pacific Railroad. During 1993, UPT installed a new yard management system at the FNM's 17 largest yards. The system maintains an inventory of freight cars in each yard and generates switching instructions for the assembly of outbound trains.

UPT also helped the FNM upgrade its central computer facility in Mexico City. Over the past two years, the FNM has more than doubled the capacity of its computers, which are now electronically linked with the Association of American Railroads' computer systems. This allows for a detailed exchange of information on trains and shipments moving across the U.S.–Mexico border.

Domestically, UPT continued with the implementation of the advanced train control work order system on the Union Pacific Railroad. Nearly 1700 of Union Pacific's locomotives have been equipped with on-board computers capable of receiving and sending car pickup and placement information, and over 5000 conductors have been trained in their use. By 1995, all of Union Pacific's trains will be equipped with on-board computers.

At Overnite Transportation, a subsidiary of Union Pacific Corporation, UPT is assisting with the installation of a centralized billing system that uses imaging and other leading-edge systems. UPT also modified USPCI's (USPCI was a subsidiary of Union Pacific Corporation that specializes in the disposal of hazardous and non-hazardous waste materials) Facilities Information Management System (FIMS) for use at its new incinerator in Clive, Utah. FIMS tracks shipments from arrival through treatment and disposal.

UPT's commercial sales continue to grow. Shipment Management Service, the industry benchmark for shipment tracking, is the company's fastest growing commercial product. More than 150 companies subscribe to this service.

UPT's Strategy for Employing the Disabled

UPT's program for employing the disabled predates the Americans with Disabilities Act by several years. Several of the most successful disability employment programs focused initially on employing persons with one type of disability. UPT focused on persons with limited or no vision. These individuals go through a year's training and job hardening program called ADEPT (Associates for Disabled Programmer Training), provided by Goodwill Industries. Following this training, UPT's chief executive officer and president personally interviewed the initial group of graduates and selected individuals for a three-month internship in the company's programming department. As a further commitment to this effort, UPT's chief executive officer sits on ADEPT's advisory board.

During the year-long training program, students attend classes at a Goodwill Industries facility utilizing IBM computers. Goodwill pretests students' abilities and provides disability awareness training to company supervisors. When ADEPT program graduates are assigned to their internships, monthly evaluations are prepared by their supervisors and self-evaluations are completed by the interns. The two evaluations are compared in a progress review session between the supervisor and the intern, and both agreements and differences in perceptions are discussed. It should be noted that the same monthly evaluation procedure is followed with non-disabled new hires. Following the three-month internship, the company may offer successful candidates full-time employment as entry-level programmers. Interestingly, the program's first intern demonstrated a faster learning curve than the average sighted entry-level programmer. At the very beginning of the company's programming training, both sighted and disabled persons are trained together. Persons with vision disabilities are teamed with sighted persons in a "buddy system" approach to both training and working.

The following cases are representative of the successful adaptation to computer programming being accomplished at UPT.

Case I

One of the first entry-level computer programmer candidates was a woman who had lost most of her vision due to Masin's disease. Prior to her vision loss, she had worked as a microfiche filing clerk. After completing Goodwill's ADEPT program, she required only normal job counseling. Using an IBM screen reader and a magnifier, she has achieved an "exceptional level of quality and productivity."

Case II

Another successful graduate of the ADEPT program who is partially blind uses an array of assistive technologies purchased by the company in 1991 at a cost of approximately $8000. UPT requested the assistance of Adapt Ability, an agency located in St. Louis, Missouri, to evaluate this individual's requirements and to make equipment recommendations. This highly regarded agency recommended the use of equipment produced by TeleSensory Corporation coupled with appropriate software. First, TeleSensory's Vista II and Lynx adapter cards were needed for his computer. These cards game him complete access to all computer material, including graphics that might be used for flowcharts. Vista II is a computer enlarger that magnifies text and graphics up to 16 times normal size. Vista is a powerful color text and graphics magnification system for IBM PC and PS/2 computers and compatibles. It is the only screen-enlarging system that is completely mouse controlled. The Vista mouse puts magnification, automatic scrolling, and location of text and cursor at an individual's fingertips. Presentation views display an enlarged image overlaid on the entire unmagnified screen. Lynx links computers and closed-circuit television systems. Together with the Vista computer magnification system, Lynx displays an image from a video camera on a VGA or multi-sync monitor. The image can be enlarged, moved, frozen, or saved to disk. Lynx brings split-screen video to high-resolution VGA monitors and works with any video camera. A special digital contrast enhancement feature makes light colors brighter and dark colors darker to improve text readability.

This combination of computer hardware allows the sight-impaired programmer to view a program that he is writing while supporting print documentation is displayed simultaneously on his computer monitor.

Two camera systems were recommended for this individual. The first, called Vantage (also manufactured by TeleSensory), is a desktop camera that includes its own monitor. This second monitor can be used to display additional print information and to provide further access to the volume of print information needed by the programmer. The second camera is an ingenious device called MEVA. It is a portable camera that has its own portable, four-inch monitor and also connects to either the Vantage or Lynx. This portable camera offers increased versatility to the programmer's workstation. The portable capacity of this magnification unit helps him locate files and manuals and function in meetings and training settings, whether in-house or on the road. If he were expected to participate in a meeting, he could use the standard print material used by other participants.

Adapt Ability also worked closely with this programmer to identify a software package that would function with all of the above equipment and would allow him to perform all of his written functions without changing programs. This individual has a need for a maximum of three screens open at the same time to allow retrieval of information from two screens and programming on a third screen. He successfully tested a program called Sprint, published by Borland. The program has the capacity to perform all of the necessary functions at a 1991 cost of about $200. Sprint also supports a mouse, which makes him more efficient as he moves through large listings of codes. The IBM PS/2 computer has a mouse port. In this case, the programmer preferred the Logitech mouse, which plugged directly into the existing mouse port.

Adapt Ability also recommended the purchase of a keyboard/mouse pad drawer since the programmer uses two mice and has additional clutter on his desk due to the low-vision hardware. A monitor holder was also recommended to allow easy access to and adjustment of the position of the monitor. Finally, an ergonomic chair with adjustable lumbar support, adjustable back height, adjustable seat (forward and back), and angular adjustment was recommended.

Case III

A totally blind programmer was initially hired as an intern and subsequently remained with the company as a full-time employee. Her three-month internship was extended to six months due to low initial productivity. This low productivity resulted from her having to adapt to the "screen reader" which provided her with an audio output of information shown on the computer monitor. Using the screen reader device, she had to listen to a translation of the entire screen in order to select individual words. Within six months, she was able to achieve normal programming productivity and quality levels. This individual now works in a team environment comprised of three to twelve programmers assigned to the development and maintenance of major programs.

Case IV

An employee who injured his back was accommodated through the company's work at home program. Due to a back injury, he had to alternate between sitting and standing and could not work continuously. Prior to his injury, he had worked as a project manager for ten years. UPT sent a complete computer and telecommunications system to his home, where he worked successfully for a year before returning to a normal routine at the company. His only ongoing requirement at the office is an adjustable computer monitor for sitting or standing and a special ergonomic chair.

Through a combination of proper training and job hardening strategies, assistive technologies, and a management team that is sensitive to the special needs of persons with disabilities, UPT and its employees have benefited from having disabled persons on the team. UPT is an excellent example of how much can be accomplished in terms of both company profitability and employee well-being with a lot of heart and a relatively small dollar investment.

United Services Automobile Association (USAA)

24

William B. Tracy, Senior Vice President,
Human Resources

In 1922, a small group of Army officers who had difficulty obtaining reasonably priced, reliable automobile insurance coverage because of their mobile lifestyle founded a member-owned reciprocal insurance association in which members insure each other and share in profits and losses. Originally called the United States Army Automobile Association, the name was changed to the United Services Automobile Association in 1924 when officers of the other military services became eligible for membership. Today, known as USAA, the company is an insurance and diversified financial services organization that provides a complete line of insurance and financial products services. With a membership of over 2.6 million, USAA owns and manages assets worth more than $33 billion and is ranked among the top 50 U.S. diversified financial companies in the Fortune Service 500.

USAA has a work force of nearly 16,000 employees. The home office is located on 286 acres in northwest San Antonio, Texas. About 30% of USAA's total work force works outside of San Antonio, most in regional offices located in Tampa, Florida; Norfolk, Virginia; Colorado Springs, Colorado; and Sacramento, California. USAA also has offices in London, England, and Frankfurt, Germany, to serve the needs of members residing in Europe.

At the heart of USAA's corporate culture is the employees' commitment to service—service to USAA's membership, service to each other, and service to the communities in which they work and live. This notion of service derives from the heritage of the personal and professional ethics of the military officer corps, which forms the base of its membership. USAA has an international reputation as a leader in America's service sector.

Employee contact with USAA members, one on one, day after day, is the foundation of this reputation. USAA hires the best people possible, provides the right tools and technical training, and offers an outstanding working environment. In addition, USAA encourages all employees to participate in self-development activities to enhance their own skills and self-image and to make them more productive. This combination of the service ethic and the positive attitude toward employees carries over easily to serving employees who fall under the provisions of the Americans with Disabilities Act (ADA).

Throughout its 72-year history, USAA has employed disabled workers and provided appropriate accommodations for them when needed and where possible. With the advent of the ADA, however, USAA took further steps to ensure the fullest possible measure of compliance and to continue to provide fair and equitable support to employees and job applicants.

Among the first steps taken in this regard was to establish a full-time Job Accommodation Specialist position in the Employment and Placement Office. The purpose of this position is to help coordinate matters related to compliance with the ADA. The incumbent considers the needs of current employees and facilitates the resolution of potential problems for job applicants who may be disabled. In addition, USAA set up an ADA Accommodation Committee with designated representatives from the following functional areas:

- Compensation
- General Counsel
- Education
- Employment and Placement
- Employment Relations
- Facilities
- Health Services
- Job Accommodation Specialist (chairman)
- Manpower
- Safety
- Training

This committee works to meet the requirements of the ADA across the broad spectrum of USAA's activities and addresses ADA-related matters as they arise. The committee initially met on a monthly basis, but later began meeting at the request of any committee member or at the call of the chairman.

The leadership and senior management of USAA support the provisions of the ADA through the statement of equal employment opportunity contained in the USAA Personnel Policies Manual. The statement reads:

USAA recruits and employs the best-qualified personnel available and provides equal opportunities for the advancement of all its employees. This applies not only to employment but also to training, upgrading, and promotion in a manner which will not discriminate against any person because of race, color, religion, age, sex, disability, veteran status, national origin, or as otherwise provided by state and local anti-discrimination laws. USAA maintains a working environment free from any type of discriminatory intimidation.

To ensure that all managers and supervisors within the company fully understand this policy, the human resources department undertook a series of measures that included such activities as housecalls, seminars, and other training.

Housecalls are mini-classes brought to the work area which last approximately one hour. The ADA housecall consists of the following three modules:

1. *Employment Module*—Presented by the Job Accommodation Specialist, the topics covered include Job Specification Form, Job Accommodation Request Form, do's and don'ts of interviewing individuals with disabilities, disabilities awareness survey, and the employment provisions of the ADA.

2. *Legal Module*—Presented by the Labor Counsel attorneys, the topics covered include seven kinds of discrimination prohibited under Title I of the ADA, individual with disability vs. qualified individual with disability, disability coverage and exclusions, reasonable accommodation, and essential functions.

3. *Attitude/Awareness Module*—Presented by the Employee Relations Advisor, topics covered include disability language and etiquette (do's and don'ts), sensitivity issues, and role playing.

Seminars include sensitivity training taught by a local not-for-profit organization that specializes in disability issues and services. Sessions last for approximately four hours and include modules on the hearing impaired, the vision impaired, and the mobility impaired.

Other training includes FLEX training classes offered to managers and supervisors to help them understand the interview/selection process in terms of the ADA. The "New Manager's Survival Course" is offered to new managers and supervisors during their first six months in the position. This course is also available to experienced managers as a refresher. Managers are also provided a "Selection Handbook," which covers ADA information. USAA continues to offer these forms of education and assistance as requested or required on a recurring basis.

When a job vacancy occurs, the initiating supervisor must complete and sign a Job Specification Form (in addition to other pertinent paperwork) and forward it to the Employment and Placement Office. The purpose of the form is to identify the essential job functions as described in the ADA, the Equal Employment Opportunity Commission's (EEOC) Title I Final Regulations, and the EEOC's Technical Assistance Manual. The form captures the physical and mental requirements necessary to perform the job successfully and the required demands and equipment skills necessary to accomplish those essential functions. The form assists in the development of a job description that accurately incorporates the essential functions of the job.

To help ensure complete fairness in the interviewing and hiring process, USAA has provided ADA awareness training to interviewers and others involved in the hiring process. This training provides information about disabilities and emphasizes the importance of individualized assessments. It also informs interviewers of the basic requirements regarding pre-employment inquiries and the types of questions prohibited during the interview procedure. It is also aimed at helping interviewers feel more at ease in talking with people with various disabilities.

USAA also makes sure that employees involved in the selection process treat those with disabilities fairly in any testing required for a specific position. For example, USAA gives pre-employment testing for all clerical and entry-level jobs. Such evaluation may include testing of typing skills or aptitude, or both. USAA provides appropriate accommodation in the testing process to job applicants when requested and warranted.

Occasionally, after hire, a disabled employee may feel that a specific accommodation would enhance his or her job performance/capability. When this occurs, an Accommodation Request form is completed. The Job Accommodation Specialist handles this request with appropriate functional representatives. Based on their input, a corporate decision is made as to whether to approve or disapprove the request.

The decision to approve an accommodation most often results in adjusting the work environment or modifying equipment or procedures. Examples include:

1. Enlarging testing material for an applicant with vision impairment

2. Providing assistance with the completion of an application for an applicant with mobility impairment

3. Providing a laptop computer, modem, and communication software package for a visually impaired programmer analyst required to perform on-call duty at home

4. Removing fluorescent lighting above the workstation of an employee with seizure disorders (who was adversely affected by fluorescent lighting)

5. Providing an electric wheelchair to be used in the workplace by a mobility-impaired employee

6. Providing a replacement vehicle with a six-way adjustable car seat for a back-impaired physical damage field manager

7. Adjusting the work schedule of a diabetic employee to permit a consistent dinner time encouraged as part of the worker's treatment program

8. Procuring a "light touch" keyboard to alleviate repetitive motion demands for an employee with wrist tendinitis

9. Turning down speakers playing music located above a hearing-impaired employee's desk to relieve the ear discomfort caused by high notes

10. Providing a color monitor with white and turquoise characters on a dark background as requested by a visually impaired employee

11. Providing a sign language interpreter to assist in the application process for a hearing-impaired employee

In the area of training and development, USAA has experienced situations in which students attending classes require accommodations. At the time employees sign up to take a specific course, they are asked whether they anticipate a need for accommodation based on any physical condition over the course of the training. They receive a name and phone number to call in the event they have any questions. Questions might include what the course entails, what equipment is used, and how the classroom is configured. This helps individuals to determine if any special help will be required to permit successful attendance and accomplishment of learning objectives. Exploring this well in advance of the beginning of the class allows for planning to meet a student's individual needs. Examples of accommodations provided in training include:

1. Arrangements are made to move computer equipment for visually impaired employees attending Information Systems classes. These PCs have audio boards or magnification devices installed in them. Because most classes are four hours per day, the equipment must be returned to the employee's desk for the remainder of the day, which means moving the equipment twice each training day.

2. Signers are sometimes used for hearing-impaired employees attending training. Although several internal employees are able to sign, USAA has

found that it is more cost effective to bring in signers from outside the company. In some classes, particularly those involving a substantial amount of interaction, several interpreters are sometimes required to keep up with multiple conversations.

3. A module on the ADA is included as part of the training for new instructors. This module heightens awareness to help the instructors prepare for individuals who need special accommodation(s) to complete the class successfully. To sensitize them to the subject, "Nobody Is Burning Wheelchairs," a video produced by Easter Seals, is shown.

As mentioned earlier, continuing education for self-development is an important part of the corporate culture of USAA. To assist those who are disabled in participating, USAA has done the following:

1. Provided signers and notetakers in courses for hearing-impaired and physically disabled employees. (The signers were provided by the Community College District with state-level support, at no charge to USAA.)

2. Offered and funded a class in sign language for two units in which employees wanted to learn to communicate better with fellow employees.

3. Set up an ADA counseling desk at the front of the main education office to facilitate access of employees with disabilities to education advisors.

4. Provided PC software in the Skills Enhancement Lab to assist hearing-impaired employees who require or seek basic skills training.

5. Designed the Skills Enhancement Lab with oversize desks to accommodate students in wheelchairs.

6. As part of its commitment to continuing education, USAA provides facilities for evening and weekend college classes for the benefit of both employees and the general public. Procedures have been set up to better enable students with disabilities to access the building and parking area (although parking for handicapped employees or guests is available at all times). Staff members are available during the scheduled class hours to help students who need assistance with locating and getting to classrooms.

USAA's in-house health services provides valuable assistance to all these services. Clinic personnel support employees with disabilities in the following ways:

1. When medically required, clinic personnel assist with monitoring blood sugar, urine dip sticks, nutrition, and exercise

2. Assist in coordinating work restrictions required by physical limitations with appropriate parties through use of a Confidential Work Status Form

3. Work closely with Texas Rehabilitation to return injured/disabled employees to work

4. Loan wheelchairs (including motorized) to employees in need

Given the opportunity and some accommodations, disabled individuals can make significant contributions to USAA. The day-to-day actions of the Job Accommodation Specialist and the ADA Accommodation Committee are key. Their efforts demonstrate that helping the disabled pays dividends in terms of both the workplace and the bottom line.

United Technologies Corporation, USBI Company

25

Lisa Cunningham

USBI Company, a subsidiary of United Technologies Corporation, is responsible for the design, integration, manufacture, and refurbishment of the non-motor components of the solid rocket boosters for the NASA, Marshall Space Flight Center space shuttle program. USBI has approximately 1200 employees located in Huntsville, Alabama; Kennedy Space Center, Florida; and Slidell, Louisiana.

USBI designed and operates the NASA, Marshall Space Flight Center's 44-acre Shuttle Booster Assembly and Refurbishment Facility at the Kennedy Space Center, Florida. This facility processes shuttle booster components with time-saving, cost-effective methods. The work involves precision robotic application, removal, and reapplication of multi-layered protective coatings and insulation; testing, servicing, and installation of electrical, mechanical, and hydraulic systems; and systems testing. USBI designed, developed, and installed the software and hardware for the shuttle's Automatic Booster Assembly Checkout System. The company has developed a wide variety of specialized ground support equipment and new methods to reduce corrosion. USBI also developed effective support systems to manage the 5000 components used for each flight in assembly, 3000 of which are refurbished after each flight and reused.

Case Study

USBI has worked diligently over the years to accommodate employees with disabilities. Accommodations have been provided before and after the implementation of the Americans with Disabilities Act (ADA). USBI takes the position that accommodation is not just the law, it is the right thing to do. The company does not like to use the term "reasonable accommodation," because it implies doing just what is required to comply with federal regulations. In many cases, USBI's accommodations have gone beyond the required "reasonable."

While the accommodations provided by USBI have been fairly inexpensive, the tangible and intangible benefits have more than outweighed the costs. One of the most important accommodations a company can make does not cost anything. Fostering an environment of support, sensitivity, and understanding within the organization is perhaps the most important action a company can take. USBI has accomplished this through top management support and employee awareness.

When an employer does everything possible to accommodate employees with disabilities, everybody wins. Employee self-esteem and motivation increase, and optimum performance levels benefit the employees and the company. Most, if not all, employees with disabilities are very determined, due to the daily challenges they face. If they are given opportunities and accommodations, there is no limit to what they can achieve. To cite an example, one USBI engineer recently helped the company obtain a multi-million-dollar NASA contract with his ideas and research on improving the parachutes for the solid rocket booster, as part of the space shuttle program. This accomplishment required a great deal of time, dedication, and persistence. The employee has received awards from the company, including the Manned Flight Awareness Launch Honoree Award, which is the highest award presented. He has also been recognized by the Governor's Committee on Employment of People with Disabilities at the local and state levels. The employee responsible for these accomplishments performs most of his work from a water bed, due to a musculoskeletal disorder. He is limited to about 20 minutes of sitting and 60 minutes of standing per day.

Other USBI employees with disabilities have maintained excellent and superior performance, despite daily challenges that are not faced by able-bodied employees. These employees perform a variety of job functions, including management, engineering, and administration. Many have received individual and team awards for significant accomplishments. Several have received the Manned Flight Awareness Launch Honoree Award for successful work on the space shuttle program. Recipients of this award are flown to Kennedy Space Center or Johnson Space Center to view a launch or landing and to participate in various award festivities. One employee received the Silver Snoopy award, which was presented at the employee's workstation by an astronaut. The Silver Snoopy is the astronaut corps' personal award presented to NASA and contractor employees for significant contributions to the space shuttle program. These employees perform their jobs with a great deal of determination, motivation, and personal strength. USBI is proud of the contributions made by these employees and the inspiration they provide to the entire organization.

The responsibility for making accommodations is not just a human resources function at USBI. The human resources department invites employees with disabilities to self-identify on a regular basis, to determine what accommodations may be needed. The department then reviews the responses and contacts the appropriate departments to initiate the accommodations. Follow-up contacts are made on a regular basis to determine whether additional accommodations are needed. The accommodations are made possible through the work of the facilities, safety, and medical departments. Top management also plays a key role, because without strong support from the top down, these accommodations would not be possible. As cited earlier, management at USBI strongly supports accommodations for employees with disabilities and recognizes that all employees are an important part of the team. All employees deserve the opportunity to reach their full potential.

Employee support from the entire organization has been strong. USBI employees have provided assistance by escorting physically challenged co-workers to a safe place during fire drills and emergencies, helping co-workers to and from the rest room, checking on co-workers periodically to see if they need anything, traveling on behalf of co-workers who are unable to, and most importantly, treating their colleagues with respect and dignity. Teamwork and support from the entire organization are essential in providing accommodations for employees with disabilities.

Support for employees with disabilities is often a result of awareness. To help increase awareness, USBI offered sensitivity training for managers and supervisors during 1992. This training focused on accommodations as well as support for employees with disabilities, and the managers learned how to make these employees feel more comfortable. They also received tips on how to interact comfortably with physically challenged applicants during an employment interview. In 1994, all employees received diversity awareness training. This program included a section on persons with disabilities and how physical ability can make people different from one another. The participants were encouraged to focus on a person's *ability* rather than disability.

The same message was expressed during a recent seminar conducted by an employee with a disability. His mission was to help other employees understand the challenges and triumphs that he and his peers face daily. The seminar was part of a company-wide observance of National Disabilities Month during October 1994. The employee was joined by a local disability employment specialist. The speakers urged the audience to keep an open mind and not to prejudge anyone's abilities. The primary focus of the seminar was to convince those who deal with physically challenged individuals to evaluate them based on their abilities and not their disabilities. The speakers also indicated that persons with disabilities have made adjustments to increase their capabilities and productivity. Additional disability awareness training continues.

USBI has made accommodations in several areas, the most prevalent of which are mobility assistance and personal safety. The case of the employee who works from a water bed was cited earlier. He suffers from a musculoskeletal disorder, which was recently diagnosed as advanced Lyme disease, and has limited mobility. His water bed has been installed and relocated several times, and his computer is adjusted to the right height to accommodate him. He has been included in meetings via telecon, and on several occasions, his colleagues have volunteered to travel on his behalf. This employee recently made his first trip in over five years from the Alabama location to the Kennedy Space Center. He traveled on an airline that provided a direct flight, rode with a colleague to work every day, and worked out of a chaise lounge while in Florida. With a few very simple accommodations, this employee's trip was enjoyable and productive.

Upon his return, the employee was awarded the Manned Flight Awareness Launch Honoree Award for his accomplishments on the parachute project cited earlier. As a result of this award, the employee again traveled to Florida, where he attended an awards banquet, viewed a launch, met with astronauts, and toured the Kennedy Space Center. Accommodations for this trip included a direct flight to Florida; a chaise lounge to use throughout the tour, launch viewing, and other activities; and extra space in the tour vehicle so he could lie down.

USBI has assisted employees who suffer from multiple sclerosis by providing a motorized wheelchair and a walker for mobility in the workplace. USBI also provided physical assistance for getting in and out of vehicles. One employee was relocated to the first floor for better access to the rest room, and an emergency buzzer was installed in the rest room. Door tensions were adjusted for this employee. Despite these challenges, this employee maintained excellent performance in a key role which involved regular interface with the customer.

All employees with mobility challenges have been provided with special assistance during fire drills, hurricane drills, tornado warnings, or any other emergencies. These employees have also been relocated to the first floor or near elevators, depending on the severity of their disability. Special parking spaces have been designated at all company buildings to ensure better access. In several cases, employees with mobility challenges have been provided with training at their workstations. This eliminated the need to attend mandatory training classes that were conducted in the training center located in another building.

For hearing-impaired employees, USBI has offered assistance based on the degree of hearing loss. Interpreters have been provided for meetings and training sessions. The company installed a headset into the telephone for one employee to amplify sound and also installed a warning buzzer in his office to alert him to emergencies. This employee has performed very well as a section chief and has been cited several times for his contributions and outstanding performance.

An employee with macular degeneration has difficulty with tunnel vision, but can see with peripheral vision. His job required him to look at small, detailed prints of hardware, which was not possible with his condition. The employee was provided with enlargement equipment, which magnifies data 60 times. The machine is a desktop video-magnifier with a monitor, which projects the material placed under the unit onto the screen. The equipment better enabled the employee to maintain excellent performance in his position as a senior engineer.

All employees with vision and hearing difficulties have been provided with assistance during drills and emergencies.

One employee has a form of dyslexia that limits his capacity to read or retain any written material. This condition has made it difficult for him to obtain the certifications required to perform his job as a technician. However, with the help of his supervisor and teammates, the employee recently received his commercial driver's license and also became certified in welding and aluminum processing. The employee is extremely talented in the mechanical area and can build various types of tools and equipment. His supervisor and co-workers recognize this talent and help him utilize his abilities to the fullest extent. The employee regularly receives verbal instructions and is provided with tutoring when an assignment or certification test requires reading. He keeps a tape recorder handy to tape any instructions or assignments. During required certification training classes, the employee is given oral, rather than written, tests.

Employees with serious or chronic back problems have been provided with ergonomically designed chairs to make sitting more comfortable. Some have also received altered job classifications to eliminate heavy lifting. Footstools and armrests have been provided for employees with low back pain and wrist problems.

Employees with serious or chronic diseases have been provided with altered work schedules and altered job classifications. Many employees have worked part-time schedules after surgeries or hospitalizations.

If a disability becomes so severe that an employee feels he or she cannot continue to work, USBI's corporate-wide benefits program provides financial support until age 65.

Substance abuse is probably the most challenging disability to address, because it is a multi-faceted issue. USBI has a policy that clearly prohibits the use, sale, possession, or manufacture of illegal drugs or alcohol on company premises. However, if an employee has a substance abuse problem, the company will give the employee an opportunity to overcome this problem before taking any disciplinary action. Not only is it the law, but this practice can also benefit the employee and the company. In some cases, employees have corrected the problem and become valuable team players with good performance. In other cases, employees did not overcome the problem after months of treatment and numerous opportunities.

This subject was covered during a recent supervisory course on "Recognizing and Handling Work Problems" at USBI. Managers and supervisors were advised that substance abuse may be covered under the ADA and that reasonable accommodations should be made. This was not a surprise, because USBI has followed the same approach for years, even before the ADA was implemented. The managers and supervisors were advised to give the employee a reasonable, realistic period of time to undergo treatment and try to correct the problem. They were also told that their support is crucial to the employee's success. However, if the employee's work performance is still affected by the substance abuse after a reasonable opportunity period or if the employee is guilty of related misconduct (i.e. possession, sale), then disciplinary action must be taken.

USBI offers support for employees with disabilities in several ways. Employees are invited to self-identify on a regular basis, and follow-up contacts are made as needed. Flextime and makeup time are offered to all employees. These policies have been helpful to employees who require medical treatment on a regular basis.

USBI is represented on the Huntsville Area Governor's Committee on Employment of People with Disabilities in Alabama and on the Disability Action Awareness Working Group in Florida. Each year, the Huntsville Area Governor's Committee accepts nominations for various awards. In 1993, USBI nominated three employees, one of whom was named Employee of the Year. In 1994, USBI received the Large Business/Industry Award.

USBI believes in accommodating employees with disabilities, because these employees are strong assets to the organization. They take a great deal of pride in their work and do not back away from challenges. With their strong "can do" attitudes and contagious enthusiasm, they inspire their fellow employees. Employees with disabilities have suggested ideas that have saved the company money and brought in new business.

USBI strongly supports the hiring and accommodating of employees with disabilities, because it is a win–win situation for everyone involved.

UNUM Life Insurance Company of America

26

UNUM Life Insurance Company of America is the largest subsidiary within the UNUM Corporation. It is an insurance company whose core business is group employee benefit products, and it is the nation's leading provider of group and individual disability insurance. Based in Portland, Maine, UNUM Life Insurance Company of America employs 4700 people.

UNUM Life Insurance Company of America has an extensive commitment to disability management at the employer level. This commitment is articulated in a statement of the company's "Disability Management Philosophy."

The invigorated disability management program is under the leadership of the manager of disability and benefit administration. The individual holding this position is accountable for overall profitability through effective disability risk management at the employer level while maintaining appropriate risk-relieving disability plans that support early return to work for employees with disabilities. The manager is the core position and is the direct resource for effectuating this goal.

The functional purpose of the disability management portion of this position is to work directly with employees, managers, supervisors, human resource personnel, and key decision makers within UNUM America, as well as with other internal areas of the organization involved in disability and prevention, in order to positively impact profitability and performance issues pertaining to employee disability and disability-related costs.

This position also created and chairs the ASAP (Accommodation, Safety, and Prevention) Committee, which meets on an as-needed basis. The purpose of the committee is to proactively address the needs of any person hired who has a disability. Examples include insuring that all ergonomic issues are addressed and changes are made prior to the date the employee starts work and determining if there are any barriers that need to be removed so the person can operate in a safe environment (i.e., sidewalks are clear, elevator doors are slow enough for the person to enter, etc.).

A key to success for UNUM Life Insurance Company of America, a specialty holding company with $12.4 billion in assets, has been its ability to set and meet ambitious goals. In 1992, the company set its most ambitious goal ever: to be the worldwide leader in its chosen markets by 1998, its 150th anniversary. UNUM America's Robert Ostrander, senior vice president of individual disability, says that the company realized that it could only achieve its vision through sustained superior performance. A Customer Value Team (CVT) was established to create a new business architecture that would both provide a competitive advantage and enhance the value of the company's offerings to its customers. In carrying out its ambitious mission, the CVT gathered input from employees, customers, and outside experts and enhanced existing key efforts such as "Operating Excellence," a total quality initiative.

UNUM's Disability Management Program

Research indicates that UNUM Life Insurance Company of America has created the most professionally developed, operationally tested, and financially documented disability management program in the United States. In keeping with its total quality management process, the company has achieved an alignment of its employee needs, management vision and philosophy, customer requirements, and a businesslike concern for financial integrity.

Understanding the Costs and Consequences of Disability in the Workplace

How much does disability really cost? The answer to this question is not simple. However, the better the costs, causes, and changing nature of disability in the workplace are understood, the better costs can be controlled.

UNUM has developed a way to measure the *full* cost of disability. This approach can help employers, both small and large, gauge the cost of disability in their organizations and shape target cost management tactics.

The Full Cost Study

Most managers would agree that the cost of disability is high—but how high is it? The cost is difficult but not impossible to quantify. In 1991, UNUM completed a research project designed, in part, to find out. The UNUM Full Cost Study was conducted by university-based researchers and professional staff from the Washington Business Group on Health.

The "full cost" is the direct cost of disability, plus the hidden cost, plus the costs of disability management. This study did not calculate the cost of disability to the individual, which is usually substantial.

In 12 diverse organizations collectively employing more than 160,000 individuals, the full cost of disability averaged $2285 per employee, with

- $1134 (4% of payroll) in direct costs
- $748 (3% of payroll) in hidden costs
- $403 (1% of payroll) in disability management costs

The full cost of disability averaged 8.0% of payroll—a significant cost of doing business. Half this cost was "direct" and easily quantified and allocated by benefits managers.

Direct Costs

Direct costs of disability include:

- Benefits for medical absence (sick leave)
- Short-term disability (STD) payments or premiums
- Long-term disability (LTD) payments or premiums
- Disability pensions
- Workers' compensation
- The disability component of social security taxes
- Miscellaneous accident insurance
- Employer's administrative costs

In the few cases where data were available, the extra medical costs associated with disability were also considered but were not included in the summary calculation. However, these costs can be a major incremental expense. For example, at one large company, the average annual medical expense for an employee receiving LTD benefits was $13,348—7.4 times higher than a non-LTD employee. At a smaller company, the differential was 16.5 times greater.

Hidden Costs

As the heading implies, some costs are more difficult to pinpoint—but no less real. These expenses are incurred when an employee is absent because of disability. Examples of hidden costs include the added expense of using replacement workers and lower productivity. Productivity typically declines:

- Prior to an employee going out on disability

- When a replacement worker is not available
- With the initial use of temporary workers
- When an employee returns to work after a period of disability and must be retrained

Even in the most sophisticated organizations, data are rarely available to precisely measure these types of costs. An approximation can be developed based on the economic principle that compensation is the best estimate of the value of lost production, which makes the baseline equal to days absent times average compensation (salary plus fringe benefits).

Disability Management

As used in the Full Cost Study, disability management encompasses a variety of activities and programs intended to prevent disabilities from occurring and/or minimize the impact of disabilities on employers and employees. Included in these costs are:

- Wellness programs
- Employee assistance plans
- Medical clinics geared toward minimizing disability
- Employee safety programs
- Activities of claims management
- Return-to-work programs

These and related topics are discussed in the next section.

Getting Down to Cases: McCrone, Inc.

To understand how disability-related costs add up, consider the case of McCrone, Inc., one of the participants in the Full Cost Study. This firm is representative of a substantial portion of UNUM's client base in both industry and size. At the time of the study, McCrone had about 250 employees. Headquartered in Annapolis, Maryland, the firm provides engineering, planning, and surveying services to private and government clientele in the mid-Atlantic region.

The study revealed that in 1989, McCrone's full cost of disability was about $329,000, or approximately 6% of payroll, and significantly less than the 8.6% average cost among study participants.

Direct Costs—McCrone's direct costs were $149,687. Of that amount, about $100,000 resulted from sick leave as workers' compensation costs. McCrone also paid $44,498 in STD and LTD premiums to UNUM. However, actual STD claims paid were $33,167, and total LTD losses incurred (paid claims plus reserves) totaled $43,383.

Hidden Costs—The hidden cost of sick leave, STD, and LTD was computed by adding full wages paid (representing the value of work performed) plus 35% for fringe benefits. Approximately $153,000 was estimated as the hidden cost of employee absences during periods in which disability benefits were paid.

In addition to the wages-plus-benefits measure, however, companies like McCrone must consider such costs as continued financing of the pension plan for disabled employees who accrue service credits while on LTD and the costs of continuing health benefits. For McCrone, these additional costs were minimal in 1989, but could become significant in the future.

Disability Management Costs—At the time of the study, McCrone's only formal disability management program was its absence-control policy. McCrone's direct disability costs include an unusual five-day-per-year, 100% of salary sick leave plan that also allows employees to use accumulated vacation days. Sick leave, however, is paid and accounted for whether or not it is used, a policy designed to minimize absences. As a result, 90% of sick leave is included in direct costs and 10% is included in the cost of disability management. About 25% of these costs resulted from sick time paid but not used. Additional amounts reflect a percentage of the company's supervisory and human resource management costs relating to time spent on disability-related issues throughout the year.

McCrone Then and Now

In 1989, McCrone was a rapidly growing firm. Had the curve continued upward, the company would have tripled its employment in a decade, requiring it to institute a range of more formal procedures and plans to better manage the costs identified in the study. Specific recommendations included the development of a better database, especially for sick leave absences, and a more proactive approach toward disability that would seek to reduce disability events and manage costs more effectively when they did occur.

The Full Cost Study revealed that the hidden costs of disability at McCrone exceeded direct costs, as is the case at most companies.

Direct Costs		Hidden Costs		Disability Management		Total
$149,687	+	$153,402	+	$26,301	=	$329,390

McCrone adjusted to the 1990–92 economic downturn by trimming its work force, as did many firms. Regardless, STD experience has improved greatly as a result of hands-on work by the company's human resource manager and close coordination and communication between UNUM and the company.

LTD claims continue at a higher level than expected, largely as a result of three very serious illnesses that could not have been prevented. The high level of claims and reserve requirements led to an expected increase in premiums. To boost employee awareness of benefits and costs, and to encourage greater employee involvement in cost-control efforts, the company moved to an employee-pay-all LTD benefit to maintain coverage.

UNUM has continued to work with McCrone—and, of course, to pay claims—as the company's financial footing has changed. UNUM's size has allowed it to pool risk across many small employers and to continue to offer coverage when other carriers might have refused renew.

Bringing Cost Savings to the Bottom Line

By generalizing the results of the McCrone case and the eleven other participants, the Full Cost Study identified six key factors within a company's control that should be considered when analyzing, understanding, and controlling the costs of disability. These factors include:

- *Employee Incentives*—Reducing benefit levels may be at odds with the attract-and-retain human resource strategy of most companies. Yet, effects can be moderated by adjusting other human resource strategies and programs and by instituting wellness and prevention efforts. Also, performance measurement systems that reward attendance as well as productivity encourage employees to return to work and thereby reduce costs.

- *Employer Incentives*—The study found that the corporate commitment to control disability costs often was not fully reflected in the organization's operations. Senior managers may want to return an employee to work as soon as possible, while a line supervisor may fear a loss of productivity that will impact his or her compensation. The solution is clear communication of the organization's goals, as well as team-building incentives.

- *Information*—Lack of systematic information about employee disability characterized many participants in the study. Relatively low-cost computer systems make an integrated information approach as feasible as it is desirable. However, the system must be geared toward interaction instead of just periodic reports. Managers must be able to query the database if disability considerations are to become a standard part of the decision-making process. This is an example of applying total quality management to disability management.

- *Coordination*—Disability must be viewed and managed on a coordinated, programmatic basis rather than as a set of separate and distinct events. Candidates for integration into a comprehensive program include occupational and non-occupational disabilities, absence control programs, procedures that help supervisors minimize disruptions caused by employee absences, disability management, insurance purchasing, and self-insurance administration.

- *Disability Management*—The study showed that successful cost-control programs include a significant disability management component—an integrated program that is proactive as well as reactive.

- *Organizational Culture*—In organizations with a bureaucratic or even hostile relationship between employees and management, disability benefits and return-to-work issues were often just another point of contention. On the other hand, the study found much less resistance to disability management initiatives in organizations characterized by employee empowerment, compensation arrangements that tied individual rewards to organizational success, and a sense of teamwork.

Managing Disability and Its Costs: The UNUM Response to Disability Risk

Effectively managing the costs of disability requires an understanding of the progression of disability risk. More importantly, it requires a strong ally who is constantly investing in learning more about the causes, prevention, and alleviation of disability.

This section covers the valuable lessons learned from UNUM's experience in managing disability for clients and their employees and from UNUM's role as an employer. These lessons are at the core of UNUM's industry-leading disability risk management capabilities—skills and services that have become the foundation of its customers' disability management plans.

The UNUM Disability Risk Continuum illustrates the close link between costs and disability. It simply adds an employer cost line to show that costs and employee ability are inversely related. As an employee's health declines, the employer's (and, for that matter, the employee's) costs rise. As an employee's health returns, employer costs drop.

The goal of disability management, and UNUM's goal, is to lower the cost of employee disability. As an employee's ability to work declines, costs increase. As the employee regains the ability to work, as a result of either recovery or learning how to function with a disability through rehabilitation or accommodation, costs drop.

Management Strategies and the Continuum

Disability management in the workplace has changed rapidly over the past 20 years. Insurers such as UNUM and disability benefits administrators have been in the forefront of developing disability management services to mitigate the costs and impact of disability.

Initially, disability management efforts focused primarily on individual disability events after the fact. These efforts were intended to:

- Accurately document the existence of disability
- Restore the working capacity of individuals
- Get individuals back to work through a variety of intervention and job modification approaches

Today's efforts are more broadly based. They take place at the organizational as well as individual level. This shift reflects increased understanding of complex cost relationships including medical, workers' compensation, employee benefits, and lost productivity. As a result, disability management is more frequently a comprehensive, systematic spectrum of organizational strategies. These strategies help control costs at various points on the disability continuum.

Today's most effective disability management programs incorporate:

- *Plan Design*—Definitions of disability, the level and length of benefit payments, and return-to-work incentives are all carefully considered in designing a UNUM benefit plan. Sound plan design takes into account past disability experience and reflects the company's human resource philosophy while meeting the organization's cost objectives.

- *Prevention and Health Promotion*—Programs that reduce risk in the workplace and encourage employee health are far and away the most effective strategy for managing disability costs.

- *Stay-at-Work Programs*—These initiatives encompass a wide range of activities from employee assistance programs to highly individualized efforts designed to accommodate an employee's ability to work. Such accommodations may include changing the way work is done or changing the tools used in the job.

- *Early Detection and Intervention*—Claims management, coordinating with the employee's physician, and even planning for appropriate rehabilitation can begin as soon as a potential disability case is identified. Clear-cut duration control can set the stage—and expectations—for an early return to work.

- *Rehabilitation and Return-to-Work Efforts*—Getting an employee back to work reduces the direct costs of disability benefits and the indirect costs of lost productivity and replacement workers. UNUM offers a full range of return-to-work services, claims settlement alternatives when appropriate, ergonomic consulting, and workplace analyses, all designed to help manage the costs and impacts of disability for employers and employees alike.

- *Individual Support*—If an employee is permanently disabled, support can take many forms, including:
  o Assistance with filing (and in all likelihood appealing) a social security disability claim
  o Regular contact with the claimant to answer questions as well as monitor the case
  o Helping a disabled employee make the transition to a long-term care program

- *Ongoing Organizational Support*—The legal and regulatory environments are constantly changing, and one of UNUM's most important services is the constant monitoring of new legislation and regulations. As a result, UNUM has become an information resource for its clients.

Disability Management in Action: Travel Management Group, Inc.

To understand the positive impact that just a few disability management initiatives can have on an organization, consider the case of a large (6000-employee) regional travel services company.

In 1991, the company spent more than $7 million on employee illness and disability costs. Managers sensed that disability-related costs were excessive, but lacked the skills to accurately analyze or effectively manage the situation. They addressed the problem in two ways:

- They asked UNUM to undertake a study of the company's disability policies and programs and to make tactical and strategic recommendations that could help manage costs.

- They asked UNUM for assistance in managing their self-insured STD program in conjunction with the existing UNUM LTD plan.

The Disability Management Services Study

UNUM maintains a team of disability experts who specialize in disability management services (DMS). The team undertook an in-depth analysis of the organization's disability policies, procedures, and costs. The corporate disability analysis from DMS revealed that:

- Incidence of STD claims was approximately 94 per 1000 employees, which is high for this type of business.

- Almost a third of disability claims, particularly among high-production workers, were stress related (a rate well above the industry norm), and many other claims were for back injuries and accidents.

- A disproportionate number of both psychiatric and back-related claims were alleged to be work related.

- Following a disabling injury or illness, employees often had little contact with managers/supervisors and seldom had any restrictions or limitations when they returned to work.

Based on these findings, the DMS team recommended concrete steps to reduce the cost and incidence of disability. Among these were:

- *Increase manager and employee involvement* by forming a task force to identify disability management opportunities

- *Reduce claims incidence* by encouraging employees to better utilize the existing employee assistance program

- *Encourage early return to work* by developing formal light-duty programs

- *Leverage disability efforts across the company* by coordinating insurance carrier and internal risk management programs

- *Unify the organization* behind disability management goals by developing written policies and procedures and through improved communication and training

Better Management of STD Claims

The company believed it could develop appropriate procedures to administer its self-insured STD program. However, management wanted to maximize its internal operational capabilities with duration-control guidelines and assistance with more complex claims.

The client installed UNUM's PC-based Duration Control System, which gives on-line access to duration guidelines for nearly 2000 causes of STD absence. These guidelines show expected claim duration and facilitate fair and consistent benefit approvals. The system provides a proven method to control claims by verifying absences that are longer than normal.

Measuring the Results

As of this writing, the company's disability management program had not yet been in place for a full fiscal year. Results have already been significant, however, when viewed on a month-by-month or case-by-case basis.

- The DMS study recommended that the client immediately allow employees to return to work even with activity restrictions. The company implemented the recommendation, and four employees are now back at work on a restricted basis. This action improved the plan's experience by reducing LTD benefit payments by thousands of dollars per month.

- In the first three months of its involvement, UNUM's recommendations and procedures produced savings as well. In two cases involving complications of pregnancy, for example, UNUM's duration guidelines saved the company more than $5500.

- Because UNUM helps manage the "flow" of STD claims into LTD claims, LTD experience is expected to improve as a result of early intervention.

- The organization now demonstrates greater concern for and commitment to employees. New human resource policies are expected to result in shorter disabilities and increased productivity.

The UNUM Case: A Million-Dollar Example

The financial benefits of a coordinated disability management program have been amply demonstrated by UNUM itself, which became one of the twelve participating employers in the Full Cost Study. The company's commitment to pioneering the practices it advocates was also instrumental in its decision to contract its own DMS unit for an in-depth analysis of its disability management strategies and needs.

The specific objectives of the corporate disability analysis were to:

- Identify disability management alternatives and programs to improve disability experience

- Provide support to the policyholder for the introduction and implementation of stay-at-work and return-to-work incentives

The DMS review and Full Cost Study complemented one another. Under the plan, the results of the Full Cost Study would provide a baseline against which to measure the cost effectiveness of ongoing investments in disability management, including DMS recommendations.

UNUM's Full Cost of Disability

Although the Full Cost Study was conducted in early 1991, it only considered data from 1989, prior to the implementation of any corporate disability analysis recommendations or significant new disability management initiatives developed through a partnership with the human resource department and DMS. The study measured the costs of disability, which were about $7 million, or 5% of payroll, a surprisingly high amount considering the inherent safety of the workplace and the relative youth of UNUM's 5500-person labor force.

Direct costs totaled about 2.8% of payroll and indirect costs 2.4%. Direct costs included self-insured salary continuance and STD and LTD premiums based on case experience paid by UNUM as an employer to UNUM as an insurer. An additional $600,000 was spent on various forms of disability management. This consisted of primarily the medical department's health risk reduction program, which included training in areas ranging from use of video display terminals to proper lifting to stress management. Including disability management expenditures, the full cost of disability was 5.7% of payroll.

UNUM America's Disability Management Philosophy

In 1990, UNUM America adopted a disability management philosophy which states, in part:

> **UNUM's vision of leadership in our chosen businesses** depends on the capabilities of our people. As a business and as an employer, effective Disability Management makes sense. Our business strength lies in our ability to attract and retain quality people. As an employer, **we value and respect our employees** and are committed to helping them contribute to their fullest potential.
>
> Disability Management includes a strong emphasis on safety and prevention as well as continued efforts to employ and support those employees with restrictions or limitations. We are committed to providing accommodations that will allow an employee to be a productive member of UNUM's work force.

The DMS Analysis

The DMS analysis included on-site interviews with key staff members responsible for management and benefits, as well as a review of nearly 100 LTD claims and 200 STD cases. The study found higher than expected incidence and duration of disabilities, particularly related to normal pregnancy and complications of pregnancy. DMS recommendations included:

- More aggressive risk management intervention on selected claims
- Better overall monitoring and analysis of absences
- Targeted stay-at-work and return-to-work programs
- Plan design changes based on experience, including changes in the salary continuation feature of the STD plan, and greater utilization of partial disability benefits
- Dedication of resources to disability management
- Employee and management education

Positive Response

Armed with the findings from DMS and the Full Cost Study, UNUM's disability management team met with UNUM's corporate management and proposed a specific plan of action, which included:

- Review and revision of current programs (for example, the full-salary continuation program was changed to encourage early return to work, and absence reports were modified to make information more accessible and useful to managers)

- Improved prevention efforts, including closer coordination with the medical department to manage required ergonomic changes and a more active role for the existing safety committee in identifying problems and educating managers

- Implementation of a formal return-to-work program for employees with disabilities

- Training for managers and supervisors

- Regular monitoring of savings using the full cost model

Bottom-Line Impact

UNUM's savings have been, in a word, impressive, even though the full disability management program has only focused on UNUM's largest affiliate to date. In its first 18 months, the program demonstrated net savings of more than $1.5 million, including a 20% reduction in LTD premium paid by UNUM as an employer to UNUM as an insurer.

The Disability Awareness Workshop

As part of UNUM's own disability management strategy, the company developed an in-house training program that can serve as a model for any organization. The Disability Awareness Workshop was intended to increase both awareness of and sensitivity to employing people with disabilities in order to foster more effective interaction between employees with and without disabilities and thereby promote a better working relationship. More importantly, the workshop encouraged managers and supervisors to think in terms of an individual's *abilities* rather than disabilities.

Quarterly sessions examine a range of topics, including:

• Myths, misconceptions, and realities of disability

• UNUM's commitment to employing people with disabilities

• New technologies available to people with disabilities

• Understanding specific disabilities

• Placing workers with disabilities in the right jobs

Increased awareness of these issues among managers and supervisors was a significant factor in UNUM's substantial decrease in disability costs.

UNUM: An Authority on Accommodations and Interventions on Behalf of Employees with Disabilities

UNUM's extensive experience in accommodating persons with disabilities in the workplace can be seen in the following case histories.* The company has prepared an excellent booklet covering its recommended approach toward companies accommodating persons with disabilities. The booklet is titled "ADA Guidebook: Navigating the Americans with Disabilities Act of 1990." Copies can be obtained from local UNUM offices or by writing to UNUM Corporation, 2211 Congress Street, Portland, ME 04122.

Easing an Attorney's Return to Work

Accommodating a disability does not always mean dealing with a physical limitation. Occasionally, an employee is prevented from performing job duties

---

* Cases are true, although claimant and company names have been changed to preserve confidentiality.

because of an emotional problem such as depression, which is what happened to Joan Dawson, an assistant trial attorney with a growing law firm. One of 30 lawyers at the company, Joan was 36 and making her way up the corporate ladder. Job pressure comes with being a trial attorney, and Joan's work situation was compounded by personal problems.

Joan began having difficulty concentrating on her cases and meeting important deadlines. To make matters worse, she and the partner to whom she reported had a troublesome working relationship that was creating additional stress.

About three years after she joined the firm, Joan filed a disability claim with a diagnosis of depression. During the next 10 $\frac{1}{2}$ months, she was unable to work and continued to see a psychologist. At the end of that time, Joan felt she was ready to return to work. Her psychologist, however, advised against returning full time. A UNUM rehabilitation counselor met with Joan and her psychologist and negotiated a part-time return to work that was acceptable to both.

When Joan contacted the firm, she found a great deal of support for her proposal to return to work part time and a stated willingness to accommodate her needs. Her employer reduced her case load so she could work fewer hours, and together they developed a graduated return schedule. The firm also changed her reporting relationship to eliminate the conflict with her former manager.

Although Joan experienced some setbacks during her return to work, she did not have to go on total disability again. After six months, she was able to increase her time at work, and two month later she resumed working full time in her capacity as a trial attorney.

Joan reports that her employer and co-workers have been cooperative and supportive during her transition back to a full case load and that the firm's accommodations were essential to her recovery and the return-to-work process.

A Back Problem Brings New Career Possibilities

A disability that prevents an employee from performing required job duties does not have to mean a dead end. When an employee wants to return to work and is flexible about occupational opportunities, employer support can often lead to placement in a different position.

Consider the case of Alice Brown, a 34-year-old supervisor in the kitchen of a regional hospital with approximately 1500 employees. Alice's job requires her to be on her feet for the better part of the work day and occasionally lift heavy food trays and move large stove pots.

More than a year ago, Alice slipped and fell down her front steps during an ice storm. The accident left her confined to bed for two months due to a ruptured disc in her spine. When doctors suggested surgery to help reduce her continuing pain, Alice agreed. The operation was successful in relieving her discomfort, but

Alice's doctor permanently restricted her from prolonged standing or lifting. As a result, Alice can no longer perform the essential duties of her job as kitchen supervisor.

Alice's recuperation has been a long one; she is still at home after more than 14 months. While she realizes that she will not be able to return to her previous position, she definitely wants to continue working in some capacity. Because her employer values her past contributions and is required to comply with the ADA, the hospital is retaining Alice as an employee.

Well before her disability benefits were scheduled to end, the hospital's human resource manager suggested that Alice complete a skills assessment. After evaluating the results, the human resource manager encouraged Alice to enroll in a general clerical course at the local community college, which she did. Alice also elected to take an additional course in medical terminology. Costs for course fees and books were $300, which UNUM provided. Her training in administration and general clerical duties will enable Alice to explore a variety of positions within the hospital. In fact, her employer is now looking for an available position that takes into account Alice's new skills and abilities, as well as her limitations.

The hospital has gone one step further. It is in the process of enrolling Alice in a technical training course where she will learn to read results from an electrocardiogram. She expects to complete this course over the summer. This kind of job requires little standing or lifting and would allow Alice to remain seated while performing many of her duties.

Thanks to the accommodations the hospital has made, Alice is looking forward to returning to work in the near future. While there are currently no clerical or support staff openings that match her current abilities, she is optimistic that by working closely with the human resources department and with UNUM, she will soon find a permanent position that is right for her.

Helping a Teacher Continue to Teach

When an employee has invested 20 years in a career, it is not easy to give it up because of a disability. That's how Richard Wood feels about his position at the large private school where he teaches history and English. Richard, 46, has a degenerative disease that is hereditary and results in the slow, steady decline of muscle function. Currently, he is partially disabled, with the loss of all fine motor dexterity and most manual dexterity.

As a teacher, Richard is required to create tests, develop lesson plans and study guides, and visually present materials to his students. Due to his deteriorating condition, he can no longer perform these tasks. Despite this challenge, he wants to stay on the job and remain as productive as he can for as long as possible. His school system, with a staff of 185, is supportive of Richard's efforts to remain at work. To date, he has not lost any work time and has not filed a disability claim.

In the fall, Richard began to use adaptive equipment at home which allowed him to work despite his limitations. The equipment enabled him to prepare his classroom presentations outside of school, which he did willingly, not realizing that the school would be willing to accommodate him in the classroom. The school system contacted a UNUM rehabilitation counselor, who helped the school purchase a voice-activated computer, a printer, software, and a projector for classroom use that will enable Richard to perform all his duties and stay on the job.

The cost of the accommodation, approximately $5000, is being shared by the school and UNUM. UNUM sees the accommodation as an investment in the future, and the school sees the purchase as a long-term solution to Richard's limitations. As long as he has his voice, he will be able to use the equipment and continue to teach.

This accommodation by his employer means that Richard will be able to remain a productive and contributing member of the school's staff for the foreseeable future, despite his increasing limitations. It will allow him to continue in his chosen career for as long as he is able.

Staying on the Job with Multiple Sclerosis

A team approach to rehabilitation can often help keep a valued employee on the job despite increasing limitations. That is what happened at State Data Company, a computer programming and consulting firm with fewer than 450 employees. Efforts by an accommodation assistance team, the company, and UNUM (the insurer) are making it possible for John Stevens to stay at work.

John, 44, was originally hired as a computer engineer. He was later diagnosed with multiple sclerosis and experienced loss of vision, as well as general weakening and fatigue, as a result of his condition.

A little more than a year ago, it became clear that John could no longer perform the essential duties of his job—the reading, writing, and analysis that require excellent eyesight and intense concentration. John filed a disability claim, but indicated he wanted to remain at work, even though fewer hours and different responsibilities would mean a significant reduction in his salary. A team that included John's supervisor, a human resources representative, and a state rehabilitation counselor evaluated his position and assessed John's skills. With John's agreement, they determined that he could best use his abilities as a research and development specialist. John was transferred to the research job, where he had fewer management responsibilities, worked fewer hours, and could continue making a contribution to the company.

Because John was unable to work in his own occupation but continued to work at another job, he was eligible for UNUM's work incentive benefit, which made it financially feasible for him to move to the new position with its reduced hours and income. This financial accommodation enables him to receive 100% of his predisability earnings for up to 12 months by providing the difference between his disability benefit and the actual earnings from his new job. After 12 months, a partial benefit will be paid if his current earnings are less than his predisability income. In addition, the company has provided other assistance for John by purchasing a computer, special software, and a visual scanner to help him perform his job duties. The total cost of the equipment is expected to be approximately $7200 and will be shared by UNUM and the company.

John's health has continued to deteriorate, further affecting his abilities. He has made it clear, however, that he wants to keep working for as long as he is able. His supervisor continues to follow the action steps of the accommodation process by regularly monitoring John's performance and limitations to see what alternatives are possible and discussing them with him. John now works as an information researcher, where his responsibilities and hours are even less demanding. His supervisor also allows him to take advantage of flexible hours so he can keep doctors' appointments and attend to his medical needs.

Wausau Insurance Companies

27

Wausau Insurance is an integral part of Nationwide Insurance Enterprise, which is composed of the following organizations: Nationwide Insurance, Nationwide Financial Services, Farmland Insurance, West Coast Life Insurance, NEA Valuebuilder Investor Services, Colonial Insurance, Public Employees Benefit Services Corporation, Scottsdale Insurance, Nationwide Communications, Financial Horizons Distributors Agency, Neckura Insurance, Gates McDonald, and National Casualty.

Wausau's vision is to be recognized by its customers as the very best name in the commercial insurance and risk management services business. Wausau's mission is to help businesses and institutions protect their financial, physical, and human resources with property, casualty, and employee benefits products and services of exceptional value and to grow profitability as part of these endeavors.

In its efforts to provide "exceptional value," Wausau has embraced the total quality management precept of listening to its customers and is responding to their needs in the following ways:

- Being a financially strong partner capable of helping customers manage the challenges of risk management

- Helping to manage costs, particularly healthcare costs (Wausau's employee return-to-work program is particularly noteworthy and is described in detail in the next section)

- Handling the complex problems of international insurance coverages

- Being flexible in finding solutions to problems

- Providing clear communications to assist customers in keeping on top of risk management challenges

Wausau's return-to-work (RTW) program is a model of cost containment and reduction. It places heavy emphasis on employee well-being through a

261

combination of personal supervisory attention to people's needs, medical evaluation, ergonomic factors, and reasonable accommodations. The company has created a successful RTW program for itself and, having fully tested the program internally, makes it available to its customers. Those of its customers that adopt the program may experience significantly reduced insurance premiums.

Wausau's Return-to-Work Program

The company makes available to its customers a comprehensive orientation and training program complete with forms, instruction guides, videotape, and other learning aids. Wausau maintains (and is supported in this claim by its own and customer experience) that by using its RTW program, customers can realize the following benefits: reduce claim costs, improve employee relations, enhance corporate image, avoid costly litigation, and save premium dollars. In implementing the program, users must apply the following guidelines: make a commitment to the RTW program, develop a RTW action plan, provide training to managers and employees, evaluate and change attitudes toward persons with disabilities where necessary, and express concern for individuals with disabilities. The RTW program has five major elements.

1. Return-to-Work Commitment—The purpose of this commitment is to return workers with work- and non-work-related illnesses and injuries to their preinjury jobs, with the same employer, as early as is medically possible.

2. Preclaim Planning—Preclaim planning calls for implementing the following initiatives:

- Mobilize the company for a strong RTW effort. This requires assigning someone responsibility for returning injured employees to productive roles. This responsibility should be put in writing, and the individual should be given the authority to carry out the mission.

- Communicate RTW goals to everyone in the organization and identify everyone who can contribute.

- Make everyone aware that returning injured employees to work will accomplish the following benefits:
  o Maintain an experienced work force
  o Reduce insurance costs
  o Accelerate the injured employee's recovery
  o Provide a positive image for the company

- o Foster the self-satisfaction that comes from doing something good and something right
- o Enable the injured employee to contribute at some level as opposed to a lengthy absence and no contribution

- Review procedures for managing injuries and provide:
  - o Temporary, modified employment
  - o Written job descriptions for both preinjury and modified jobs
  - o Individual capability information for both preinjury and modified jobs
- Consider ergonomics in the workplace.
- Train employees in first aid.
- Train maintenance employees in proper disposal of blood and other potentially infectious material.
- Demand prompt reporting of all injuries.
- Authorize a physician for every injury that results in time lost.
- Make sure that all employees are aware of RTW policies.
- Maintain ongoing communication with injured employees.
- Negotiate a strong RTW policy with unions where applicable.
- Where jurisdiction permits, set up and maintain a medical panel to determine which physician can best treat a particular injury and which physicians share the RTW philosophy and practice with integrity. Wausau Insurance Companies representatives actually assist their customers in developing and maintaining this panel.

3. Early Management of the Injury

- Immediate response: First aid, and then direct the injured to further medical care. Notify family of injury.
- Same-day response: If hospitalization is required, call insurance company's claim office.
- Contact injured employee following medical care: Be empathetic as well as positive about returning to work.
- Medical guidance: Suggest special doctors and offer to make appointments and provide transportation.
- Investigate the accident: Be positive. Talk to witnesses. Survey the accident scene. Preserve contributing items or causes.

4. Stressing Abilities, Not Disabilities—Benefits of re-employing workers with permanent impairments:

- Lower loss experience and reduce claims costs.

- Enhance corporate image.

- Savings of premium dollars.

- A better work force. U.S. Office of Vocational Rehabilitation surveys show that *disabled workers are more productive* and less likely to experience accidents on the job. The surveys also show that absenteeism and turnover rates are lower among handicapped workers, which results in even higher total productivity of disabled employees.

Facts about employing workers with permanent impairments:

- Accommodating employees with disabilities is generally not expensive.

- Employing workers with disabilities does not affect an employer's workers' compensation premium.

- Treat employees with disabilities like other employees. Let them compete, and do not pamper them.

5. The Supervisor's Role—A supervisor should always respond positively to an employee's first report of injury.

- Take time to manage the injury properly.

- Authorize medical attention immediately.

- Believe the employee. Do not suspect fraud.

- Investigate the accident and record all pertinent information.

A supervisor can play an important role in bringing an injured employee back to work.

- Visit the employee and encourage fellow employees to do the same; balance this item with the employee's right to privacy.

- Keep informed about the employee's progress.

- Reassure the employee that "the team" needs him or her.

A supervisor's attitude can make an employee's RTW last.

- Make the returning employee feel welcome and happy to be back.

- Provide temporary, modified work that has been approved by the employee's physician.

- Explain the duties of the temporary job clearly and emphasize the importance of the temporary job.

- Point out any new safety precautions or old ones that the employee may have forgotten.

6. Back on the Job—Assign appropriate work to prevent reinjury.

- Modify the job according to medical limitations.

- Discuss the importance of modified work with the employee's supervisor.

Create a positive atmosphere. Let the employee ease back into production.

- Adjust production quotas.

- Suggest working half days or returning mid-week.

- Encourage the employee to keep up with prescribed exercises or treatments.

- Explain the necessity and importance of lighter duties to the injured employee's co-workers to reduce peer resentment.

The first day back to work is especially important.

- Meet and welcome the employee back! Explain the employee's new job in general and point out safety hazards or review safety precautions for the previous job. The employee's immediate supervisor should demonstrate or explain in detail the individual's actual duties. Later in the day, check back with the employee. Let the individual know you are interested.

- Report the employee's RTW and subsequent changes in employment status to the insurance carrier.

Wausau's Return-to-Work Policy Statement

To help assure company-wide conformance to the purpose, goals, and spirit of the company's RTW concept, the following policy statement has been prepared.

Return to Work After Illness or Injury Policy

It is the intent of Wausau Insurance Companies to promptly return employees with disabilities to work and to comply with the Americans with Disabilities Act. Whenever possible, disabled employees are returned to their own jobs, to positions of similar pay and status, or to other appropriate positions. Toward that goal, the following is our corporate policy regarding return to work.

Responsibility for managing/monitoring return to work belongs to the first line supervisor and the manager. In accordance with Human Resources policy, individuals are responsible for notifying their manager or supervisor regarding absence from work. When the absence is expected to continue for more than five days, the manager/supervisor provides the employee with form 41-29-1, "Physician's Report," which is completed by the practitioner's office at the request of the employee. The form is returned to Health Services. Where there is no health services nurse, the form is presented to the Human Resources representative.

The responsibility for obtaining the medical information rests with the employee. Determination of eligibility for disability benefits depends upon the company receiving objective medical information regarding the employee's abilities and limitations. The health services nurse should be able to advise when additional reports may be necessary in case of a longer term absence and will determine if and when it is appropriate to contact the practitioner's office directly about those cases. The corporate manager of Health Services is available for consultation when necessary.

In instances when a disability does not appear to be permanent or long-term, the employee should return to work in the original unit. Any work restrictions or limitations stipulated by the physician must be honored and reasonable accommodations made. These restrictions may include, but are not limited to, the length of the work day, ergonomic considerations, etc. Normally these restrictions are short-lived and, following the period of recovery, can be lifted, allowing the employee to return to his/her prior level of job performance.

In dealing with what appear to be long-term or permanent restrictions, the employee is to be retained in the original work unit whenever possible. This will undoubtedly require accommodations such as, but not limited to, modified work schedules, restructuring a job by reallocation of marginal functions, or modifying equipment. It may also be necessary to assign the employee to a different job within the work unit or function. Health Services and/or Human Resources representatives must be consulted when planning accommodations for employees with long-term or permanent restrictions.

If the above efforts are not successful in returning the employee to work in the original unit, the case will be reviewed by Wausau's Disability

Case Review Panel. This Panel is chaired by the Director of Employee Benefits and includes representatives from Human Resources, Corporate Legal, and the individual's management.

The panel will review the case and determine what additional reasonable accommodations must be made. The panel may recommend that the individual be considered totally disabled, returned to work in the original unit, or placed in another unit. If it is recommended that the individual be placed in another unit, Human Resources has the responsibility to identify a position within the capabilities of the individual and to place the employee in that position. All expenses associated with the employee remain with the original unit until the employee is placed in another unit. If problems ensue regarding placement of a disabled employee that cannot be resolved by Human Resources, senior management may be contacted to make an independent review.

Americans with Disabilities Act Policies and Procedures

At a more comprehensive level than its RTW program, the company has a long-standing policy to accommodate employees with disabilities, whether the disability occurred while on the job or was a new hire's pre-existing condition. The following policy statement is designed to demonstrate the company's strong commitment to its accommodation process and to provide managers with guidance on the key implementation issues.

Americans with Disabilities Act Policies and Procedures

Statement of Policy

Wausau Insurance Companies is an equal opportunity employer and makes employment decisions on the basis of qualifications. We want to have the best available persons in every job. Company policy prohibits unlawful discrimination based on race, color, creed, sex, marital status, age, national origin, physical handicap, disability, medical condition, or ancestry or any other consideration made unlawful by federal, state, or local laws. All such discrimination is unlawful.

The company is committed to complying with all applicable laws providing equal employment opportunities to individuals regardless of race, color, creed, sex, marital status, age, national origin, physical handicap, disability, medical condition, or ancestry. This commitment applies to all persons involved in the operations of the company and prohibits unlawful discrimination by any employee of the company, including supervisors and co-workers.

It is the policy of Wausau Insurance Companies to comply with all the relevant and applicable provisions of the Americans with Disabilities Act (ADA). Wausau Insurance Companies will not discriminate against any qualified employee or job applicant with respect to any terms, privileges, or conditions of employment because of a person's physical or mental ability. Wausau Insurance Companies also will make reasonable accommodation wherever necessary for all employees or applicants with disabilities, provided that the individual is otherwise qualified to safely perform the essential duties and assignments connected with the job and provided that any accommodations made do not require significant difficulty or expense.

Wausau Insurance Companies' policy of nondiscrimination applies to all human resources practices, including: hiring, upgrading, transfer, recruitment or recruitment advertising, layoff or termination, compensation of any kind, selection for training, education programs, and company-sponsored social activities.

Wausau Insurance Companies will review all human resource policies and procedures to ensure that job applicants and employees with disabilities are given nondiscriminatory consideration when their job qualifications are assessed. All employment and advancement decisions will be based solely upon the objective determination of each candidate's job qualifications.

Definitions

The ADA defines the term "disability" to mean:

1. A physical or mental impairment that substantially limits one or more of the major life activities of such individual (current disability);

2. A record of such an impairment (past disability); or

3. Being regarded as having such an impairment (perceived disability).

"Physical or mental impairment" is broadly defined to mean:

Any physiological disorder, or condition, cosmetic disfigurement, or anatomical loss affecting one or more of the following body systems: neurological, musculoskeletal, special sense organs, respiratory (including speech organs), cardiovascular, reproductive, digestive, genitourinary, hemic and lymphatic, skin and endocrine; or

Any mental or psychological disorder, such as mental retardation, organic brain syndrome, emotional or mental illness, and specific learning disabilities.

A physical or mental impairment is not a disability under the first part of the definition unless it "substantially limits" one or more "major life activities." Major life activities consist of the following but are not limited to: caring for one's self, performing manual tasks, walking, seeing, hearing, speaking, breathing, learning, working, procreation, and intimate personal relations. Obvious examples of physical or mental impairments may include orthopedic impairments, visual impairments, speech impairments, hearing impairments, cerebral palsy, epilepsy, muscular dystrophy, multiple sclerosis, cancer, heart disease, diabetes, mental retardation, and emotional illness.

"Disability" is defined broadly and is intended to protect individuals with serious disabilities, not minor or temporary impairments.

An individual may have a record of a substantially limiting condition when he/she satisfies any single part of the three-part definition of disability. Thus, someone who previously had, but no longer has, an impairment which substantially limited one or more major life activities may be covered by the act because he or she has a record of an impairment. This category protects individuals such as former cancer patients from discrimination because of their history of being impaired. Those who may have been misclassified in the past as learning disabled are also now protected under the act.

In order to have a "history" of an impairment, the individual must have been able to satisfy Part 1 of the ADA's definition of disability at one point in the past. Also, the person must have a "record" of a disability. Such records include, but are not limited to, education, medical, employment, or other records.

Individuals who are "regarded as" having a covered impairment, but in fact do not, are covered under Part 3 of the definition. There are three ways a person can satisfy this part of the definition:

1. The individual has an impairment which does not substantially limit major life activities but is perceived and treated as if he or she did.

2. The individual has an impairment that substantially limits major life activities only because of the attitudes or beliefs of other people, or

3. The individual may not have a covered impairment or any impairment at all but is nonetheless treated as if he or she did.

Exclusions

Characteristics and conditions excluded may include physical—green eyes, left-handed; mental characteristics—poor judgment, quick temper; external conditions—environmental disadvantages, cultural disadvantages, economic disadvantages, prison record; temporary conditions—cold, flu, broken bone, concussion. Also excluded are exhibitionists, current drug users, pyromaniacs, kleptomaniacs, and voyeurs.

Essential Functions

A qualified individual with a disability is an individual who satisfies the requisite skill, experience, and educational requirements of the position and one who can perform the essential functions of the job with or without a reasonable accommodation.

Essential functions of the job are tasks which bear a fundamental relationship to the job in question. "Essential functions" are job duties or functions which must be performed, even if the manner of performance by an individual with a disability is slightly different than for a nondisabled employee. A function may be essential because the reason the job exists is to perform the function. Consideration can be given to employer's judgment as to what functions are essential and also any written job description.

Reasonable Accommodation

A reasonable accommodation must be an effective accommodation. It must provide an opportunity for a person with a disability to achieve the same level of performance or to enjoy benefits or privileges equal to those of an average similarly situated nondisabled person. The reasonable accommodation obligation applies only to accommodations that reduce barriers to employment related to a person's disability; it does not apply to accommodations that a disabled person may request for some other reason. A reasonable accommodation need not be the best accommodation available, as long as it is effective for the purpose; that is, it gives the person with a disability an equal opportunity to be considered for a job, to perform the essential functions of the job, or to enjoy equal benefits and privileges of the job.

Wausau Insurance Companies will make an accommodation only to the *known* limitations of an otherwise qualified individual with a disability. In general, it is the responsibility of the applicant or employee with a disability to inform Wausau Insurance Companies that an accommodation is needed to participate in the application process, to perform essential job functions, or to receive equal benefits and privileges of employment. Wausau Insurance Companies may request documentation of the individual's functional limitations to support a need for an accommodation.

Reasonable Accommodation Identification Process

An applicant who requires an accommodation in order to perform the essential functions of the job should inform Human Resources. Any employee who requires an accommodation or some adjustment or change to do a job because of the limitations caused by a disability should contact their manager who should immediately contact Human Resources. Human Resources will consult with Home Office Corporate Legal.

The following four steps will take place:

1. Analyze the job. The purpose of the job and the essential functions will be identified and recorded by Human Resources.

2. Consultation with the individual requesting an accommodation will take place to find out his or her specific physical or mental abilities and functions of the job. Barriers to successful job performance will be identified and assessed in how the barriers could be overcome with an accommodation. The individual will also be requested to suggest an accommodation.

3. Identify possible accommodations. If the above consultation does not identify an appropriate accommodation, technical assistance will be sought from outside sources without cost to the individual and recommendations will be documented.

4. Selection of the most appropriate accommodation will take place. If there are several effective accommodations that would provide an equal employment opportunity, consideration will be given to the preference of the individual with a disability and the selection of the accommodation will be chosen that best serves the needs of the individual and Wausau Insurance Companies. Each accommodation request will be decided on a case-by-case basis. Representatives from Human Resources, Corporate Legal, Health Services, and the affected department will serve as the accommodation panel.

Complaint

If an applicant or an employee believes that he or she has been subjected to any form of unlawful discrimination, the individual should provide a written complaint to the Director of Field Human Resources Services or Home Office Human Resources Manager for coordination of the resolution of the complaint. The company will conduct an investigation to identify the barriers that make it difficult for the applicant or employee to have an equal opportunity to perform his or her job. The company will identify possible accommodations, if any, that will help eliminate the limitation. If the accommodation is reasonable and will not impose an undue hardship, the company will make the accommodation.

If the company determines that unlawful discrimination has occurred, effective remedial action will be taken, commensurate with the severity of the offense. Appropriate action will also be taken to deter any future discrimination. Whatever action is taken will be made known to the individual, and the company will take appropriate action to remedy any loss to the individual as a result of the discrimination. Wausau Insurance Companies will not retaliate against an individual for filing a complaint and will not knowingly permit retaliation by management employees and co-workers.

Documentation

Documentation of the reasonable accommodation request and solution is the responsibility of Human Resources. The human resource manager will summarize the steps as listed on the Reasonable Accommodation Checklist. The investigation, resolution, and recording of facts should be completed within a minimum of opinion or judgment. All records pertaining to requests for accommodation or complaints are to be sent to Home Office Corporate Legal.

Confidentiality

Applicants and employees are assured that all information regarding a disability shall be kept completely confidential except that:

- Appropriate supervisors and managers may be informed regarding restrictions on the work or duties of disabled employees and any accommodations that have been made;

- If the condition may require emergency treatment, first-aid and safety personnel may be informed; and

- Government officials investigating compliance with federal laws may be informed.

Employees with management responsibility are advised that they are to treat any such knowledge with confidentiality. A record of any request or complaint will remain confidential and not part of any personnel file.

Reasonable Accommodations at Wausau

Examples of reasonable accommodations covering persons with disabilities at Wausau fall into two categories: those implemented as a result of its RTW program and those that were designed to satisfy the needs of new hires with disabilities.

Return-to-Work Accommodations

- A number of individuals who developed carpel tunnel syndrome were transferred to other positions.

- An executive whose involvement in an automobile accident resulted in limited use of his hands and no use of his lower body was given several accommodations that enabled the company to continue to utilize his managerial talent. These accommodations included sticks in special hand holders which enabled him to operate his computer keyboard, a scanner to enter mail and other printed material into his computer, a speaker phone, desk and doors modified to permit wheelchair access, and special security keys.

- A mental health disability was accommodated for a person in a marketing and sales position through a combination of carving out those parts of the job that the individual could accomplish and part-time work. The end result of this effort was a promotion for the individual.

- Wausau has implemented work-at-home accommodations for temporarily physically disabled employees. Positive results have been achieved using computers, modems, and electronic mail. The success of a work-at-home accommodation requires careful articulation to managers and supervisors regarding the company's belief that most people want to work and that some productivity during early recovery periods is better than none. It also leads to faster recovery and to a more rapid total RTW. In terms of productivity and its RTW program, Wausau takes the long view and treats productivity performance as a time-line effect rather than an instantaneous, inflexible standard. The total positive productivity and financial results of this approach have been significant.

New Hire Accommodations

- Interpreters are provided to assist hearing-impaired persons.

- A typist with an autistic condition produced very high-quality work but was easily distracted and difficult to communicate with. The outside rehabilitation agency with which Wausau worked in finding a position for her also indicated that she was given to bizarre behavior. The accommodation made was simply to have the management team and her supervisor explain the situation to employees with whom she would work. Having been prepared in this way, employees made the situation work.

- Speakers use special microphones so that hearing-impaired persons can hear them through headset amplifiers. TDD telephones are made available for necessary personal phone calls.

- A general "can-do" attitude is prevalent among managers and employees in accommodating persons with disabilities. They refuse to be intimidated by the accommodation process.

- The following accommodations have been provided for employees with multiple sclerosis:
  - o Evacuation plan for fire and tornado
  - o Daily bathroom assistance
  - o Special wheelchair access
  - o Periods of standing with assistance
  - o Availability of a bed with side rails for rest periods
  - o Personal computers and modems provided for work at home
  - o Reserved parking under the building

Wegmans Food Markets, Inc.

28

Wegmans is a private corporation founded in 1916 with the following promise to its customers: "Every Day You Get Our Best." This philosophy, along with other positive beliefs, has enabled the company to grow from a single product cart to the most talked about supermarket in the industry. Today, Wegmans ranks among the 100 largest private companies in the United States. It has 51 food stores and 15 Chase-Pitkin home and garden centers, in excess of $2 billion in annual sales, and more than 23,000 employees. Its new food stores average 90,000 to 125,000 square feet and total warehouse and distribution space is 1,293,000 square feet.

Strategy for Implementing the Provisions of the Americans with Disabilities Act

Wegmans has implemented many programs to accommodate people with disabilities. While accommodations were routinely made prior to the passage of the Americans with Disabilities Act (ADA), several proactive steps were taken when the act was passed.

The Facilities Survey—A proactive facilities survey is used to help assure compliance with ADA criteria and to better serve the company's customers and employees. Each of the 51 store managers completed this survey and implemented the required accommodations. The survey was prepared for Wegmans by the Food Market Institute.

Training—Two training initiatives were introduced to educate the company's managers on the scope and content of the ADA. One of the training programs covers several of the basic criteria of the act, including a description and definition of "disabled," a section covering reasonable accommodation, and what undue hardship means in connection with accommodations. The second training program was prepared by an outside legal firm. In addition to legal issues connected with the ADA, it covers New York State's workers' compensation law and its interaction with the ADA. Each state's workers' compensation law should be referred to in order to assure total compliance.

Job Hardening—In order to assist persons with back injuries and other disabilities return to work, the company initiated a work hardening program.

Education and Communications—Information and education regarding the ADA and its implications for the company was aggressively pursued through national and local seminars, as well as informational sessions for all store managers. District managers are kept abreast of issues connected with the ADA through intercompany communications. Noteworthy actions and accommodations put into effect are communicated to all employees through the company's newsletter.

Accommodations

Wegmans' experience demonstrates that accommodating persons with disabilities enhances employee morale. The following are examples of accommodations made for customers and employees:

- A pharmacy technician who was wheelchair bound was accommodated by installing a ramp in the pharmacy so that he could access medications stored on a raised platform.

- A mobility-impaired person whose job was to clean the bakery at the end of the workday requested assistance in moving a very heavy work table. A simple accommodation was to put casters on the legs of the table.

- A customer with a bad back requested assistance in placing groceries into the store's deep shopping cart. The customer could not bend over to place groceries into the cart without experiencing pain. The store's manager and maintenance man designed a clever but simple solution by installing a portable shelf inside the cart so that the customer could place items into the cart without having to bend over as far.

- The company worked with its vendor in designing a customer checkout counter that was accessible to employees who were wheelchair bound and who worked in that position.

- An employee undergoing kidney dialysis requested a private space to perform her treatment and to heat her dialysis solution. The procedure took one hour every day. A private area was provided.

A key to Wegmans' success in adapting to the requirements of the ADA is its cultural family orientation of listening to, caring about, and responding to the needs of its customers and employees.

CASE STUDIES: REHABILITATION ORGANIZATIONS

Baylor Biomedical Services

29

Baylor Biomedical Services (BBS), located in Dallas, with satellite centers in Houston, Lubbock, and San Antonio, Texas, is dedicated to opening doors and creating opportunities for the disabled. The company's rehabilitation engineers and technicians are highly experienced at matching the needs of the disabled with state-of-the-art technology.

BBS defines rehabilitation engineering as the application of engineering principles and techniques to problems encountered in rehabilitation. Ideally, a group that supplies rehabilitation engineering services should employ degreed engineers with extensive training and experience in medical and rehabilitation settings.

BBS is a biomedical engineering services company with 7 degreed engineers, 4 of whom are registered professional engineers, and 18 technicians. In addition to rehabilitation engineering, BBS installs, modifies, and maintains medical and computer systems ranging from surgical lasers to office computer networks. This wide range of technical experience provides BBS with the ability to quickly find solutions to the many unique challenges encountered in rehabilitation. BBS rehabilitation engineers provide services in the areas of computer access, environmental controls, augmentative communication, seating and positioning, powered mobility, and custom design.

Worksite Accommodation

Title I of the Americans with Disabilities Act covers all aspects of employment, including the application process and hiring, on-the-job training, advancement and wages, benefits, and employer-sponsored social activities. An employer must provide reasonable accommodations for disabled workers, unless that would impose an undue hardship on the employer. This part of the law became effective on July 26, 1992 for companies with 25 or more employees. On July 26, 1994, it became applicable to virtually all companies.

Reasonable accommodation can be accomplished in many ways, often without any technology required. Some situations, however, require a change to the work environment in order to accommodate a worker's disability.

There are an incredible number of potential solutions to the challenges faced by disabled people in the workplace. This is an area where an experienced rehabilitation engineer can be of great benefit in finding a workable solution at a reasonable cost. A rehabilitation engineer, often working in conjunction with an occupational therapist, assesses the abilities of the worker and the demands of the job. Finding ways to bridge the gap where abilities fall short of demands requires extensive knowledge and experience.

It is important to consider the aesthetics of any worksite modification. Many people do not like the "gimmicky" look which may result from a modification. It is important to make changes in a worksite as unobtrusive as possible and also to keep the site accessible to the rest of the work force. Suggestions from the disabled worker should be considered when designing an accommodation. Making the user part of the design team not only makes good sense but helps the user buy into the solution, thus improving the chances for success. Also, the best and least expensive solutions often come from suggestions from the employee.

About 70% of all U.S. jobs are in an office environment. This environment represents one of the greatest opportunities for employing people with disabilities. As offices become more automated, it becomes easier for people with physical disabilities to access the tools necessary to perform their work. Alternative computer access methods is one of BBS's specialties, and they can generally find a suitable method for any computer or terminal.

Many solutions exist for alternative methods of phone control. Speakerphones and voice-controlled phones are two possible solutions.

Computer Access

The power of the personal computer is seen as the "great equalizer" for many disabled individuals. Work produced on a computer by a severely disabled person is indistinguishable from that produced by an able-bodied person. Computers can be used for entertainment, education, and to control devices as diverse as televisions and industrial machines. The ability to access and operate computers can go a long way toward minimizing the handicapping effects of a physical disability. Fortunately, a wide variety of computer access methods have been developed for people who cannot use a standard keyboard.

Adapted keyboards offer a fairly simple solution for many people with physical impairments. Expanded keyboards offer larger keys which require less precision when typing. Small, one-handed keyboards can be operated with very small movements. Keyguards (shields that cover the keyboard with holes over each key) allow the user to rest the typing hand on the keyboard without accidentally pressing keys. A combination of an adapted keyboard, mouth stick, and wrist splints will provide adequate computer access for the majority of physically impaired users. Two examples of the many adapted keyboards available are:

Keytime   A keyboard that can be specially configured to make one-handed input convenient

Comfort   A three-segment keyboard that allows adjustment to the most comfortable position

A variety of other methods are available if an adapted keyboard cannot be used. If the user has good head control, computer access can be achieved with a joystick controlled with the chin. A screen cursor can be controlled with head position and, with the aid of an on-screen keyboard display, text can be entered simply by moving the cursor on the screen with small head movements. Three of the most popular devices are:

HeadMaster   This device uses ultrasonic ranging technology (similar to many autofocus cameras) to move a cursor on the computer screen in response to the user's head movements. The user can select keys from an on-screen keyboard for data entry.

HeadMouse   This device is similar to HeadMaster but uses infrared technology to sense head movements.

Liaison   This system uses a chin-controlled joystick to move a cursor on a separate monitor. It can be used for both keyboard-type data entry as well as mouse control. An advantage of the separate monitor is that no keyboard is overlaid on the application screen. This system is compatible with all application software and provides most environmental control functions such as phone and appliance control.

If head control is not adequate, the computer can be controlled through the use of switches which are adapted to the movements available to the user. Switches can be used to select items from on-screen menus, or a modified form of Morse code can be used for direct entry. Examples of this technology are:

ALTKEY   A low-cost user-configurable system that provides for one- or two-switch input using either an on-screen menu or Morse code methods.

EZ KEYS   The only system available that combines dual word prediction, abbreviation expansion, full keyboard control, and voice output and works with a standard keyboard to run standard software with one finger, a head stick, or a mouth stick, faster and easier than ever.

If the user's utterances are consistent, voice recognition systems may allow access to the computer. The best voice recognition systems on the market are DragonDictate and VoiceTypes. Both use algorithms developed by Dragon Systems and require minimal training. These systems learn how a user speaks and can adapt to unusual accents as well as many speech impediments.

DragonDictate   This system has a standard vocabulary of 25,000 words. The user can add up to 5000 additional words, bringing the total vocabulary to 30,000 words. It requires an 80386 or higher processor running DOS at a clock speed of at least 20 MHz, with 8 Mbyte of RAM recommended.

VoiceTypes   Similar to DragonDictate except that it has a standard vocabulary of 5000 words. Up to 2000 additional words can be added by the user, for a total vocabulary of 7000 words.

Many computer solutions require some specialized technical expertise to assure optimal performance. This can range from proper selection and mounting of access switches to setting up computers with proper interrupt and port codes. The engineering and technical staff at BBS is qualified to integrate multiple technologies into systems that work.

Examples of Worksite Accommodations

BBS engineer Rex Moses described the following examples of rehabilitation engineering services as representative of numerous worksite accommodations recommended by BBS and implemented by its clients.

Case I—A young woman with dwarfism was hired by a hospital to work as a switchboard operator. Her voice was very high-pitched, almost childlike. After she had worked on the switchboard for about a month, the hospital began receiving complaints from physicians and callers asking why a child had been hired to answer the phone. A Texas rehabilitation agency sent the woman to a speech therapist, but that effort was unsuccessful. The hospital then approached BBS to ask if anything could be done to modify her voice to make her sound more professional.

BBS first made digital and analog recordings of her voice and then utilized special software to modify her voice to make her sound more professional. BBS engineers then located a device that would provide real-time modification to her voice and connected it to the hospital's phone and paging systems. The device is called a harmonic digitizer, also referred to as a harmony machine in the entertainment industry. The woman merely speaks into the device using her normal high-pitched voice and the output delivered through the phone or paging system sounds like a professional female voice. The BBS engineers knew that their work was successful when the woman's counselor called the hospital on the day that the system was installed and upon hearing the digitized voice thought that the woman had not yet returned to work. The cost of the entire solution including the device was approximately $2000. As of this writing, the woman is still working at the hospital and is very effective in her job.

Case II—An example of a less technological solution involved a man in his forties who had a history of spasticity and could not use his right hand. His right hip was replaced in 1991 and he also had a knee problem. He needed a wheelchair to cover long distances and used a quad cane to navigate short distances. He was employed as a stock clerk and was responsible for receiving and storing stock, bringing items to the front office, and entering inventory records into a computer.

BBS engineers visited the site to assess working conditions and the man's limitations. One of the tasks he was unable to perform was stocking and loading 80-pound batteries, 18-inch brake drums, 50-pound bags of absorbent, and other large items that he could not lift from storage shelves. The solution to the employee's problem was an electric scooter coupled with a modified trailer. The trailer was modified to be in line with the lower shelves of the storage racks, where the heavy items were stored. With the modified trailer, the employee could slide the heavy items onto the trailer and easily transport them. A basket was attached to the front of the cart so that he could collect small items to be stocked or brought to the front counter. The engineering cost, including modification to the cart, was $1600, and the cost of the cart was $4000. The employee's insurance company paid for the scooter and cart, and the Texas Rehabilitation Commission paid BBS for its work in developing and executing the solution.

Case III—In 1989, an individual with a spinal cord injury came to BBS seeking help in accessing his computer so that he could continue working at the Internal Revenue Service. The solution was a software system called Liaison, used in conjunction with a joystick. The man was able to continue working at the IRS. About a year later, he was involved in an automobile accident and lost what function he had in his arms. He returned to BBS to be reevaluated.

This individual's job required that he speak to customers over the phone while also operating his computer. A partial solution in terms of operating his computer was the use of a speech synthesizer. A complication arose, however, in that while speaking to the customer, it was necessary to cut off the speech to the computer, and while giving voice instructions to the computer, it was desirable to cut off sound to the customer. BBS engineers solved this problem with an "ability switching device" which the man could activate with his arm (he had enough use of his arm to be able to activate the switch). He uses speech synthesis to communicate with his computer at the IRS and is reported to be as productive as his non-disabled peers.

This individual's original difficulties were solved at a cost of $4000, which was paid for by the Texas Rehabilitation Commission. The more recent speech synthesis solution was funded by the IRS at a cost of less than $5000. Typical training in the use of speech synthesis systems requires only five to ten hours.

Case IV—A significant challenge to BBS's staff involved an individual with both cognitive and physical impairments. Her job required accessing a computer and three phone lines. She had to route calls and take phone messages. BBS's solution was a pad with six large buttons, each approximately 3 1/2 inches in diameter. A special key guard was used to prevent her from hitting the wrong button. Three buttons were used to forward calls to a particular phone line; one button took the phone on and off the hook, another button turned a tape recorder on and off so that she could take messages, and a flash button allowed her to forward calls.

BBS has also developed telephone use solutions for single telephone lines using multiline switches activated by infrared controllers.

In BBS's experience, the productivity of disabled employees who receive appropriate accommodations is close to equal that of their peers performing the same work when productivity is measured purely on a unit-per-hour basis. When overall productivity is factored into the equation, persons with disabilities are clearly more productive than their peers. Overall productivity includes absenteeism, turnover, and other factors.

Division of Vocational Rehabilitation Services, State of Florida

30

James M. McHargue,
Rehabilitation Policy Administrator

The vocational rehabilitation movement began as an extension of the Soldier's Rehabilitation Act of 1918. Congress realized that the many soldiers disabled as a result of service in World War I would require retraining if they were to be able to engage in civilian occupations. The success of this effort, coupled with the growing number of industrially injured workers, led to the passage of the Smith-Fess Act of 1920, which launched the civilian vocational rehabilitation program.

Through the ensuing 70 years, new legislation expanded and refined the program, culminating in the Rehabilitation Act of 1992. This law is a complement to the Americans with Disabilities Act of 1990, which is the civil rights act for persons with disabilities.

It is the philosophy of the vocational rehabilitation program that individuals with disabilities have the inherent right to enjoy the financial and emotional independence gained through participation in meaningful work. Given that there are 43 million Americans with disabilities, disability must be viewed as a natural part of the human experience. Because this is one of the most disadvantaged groups in our society, the goals of the nation must include the assurance that individuals with disabilities enjoy full inclusion in all aspects of our culture. The key, of course, is economic self-sufficiency. With it come independence, self-determination, participation in the mainstream, and the ability to contribute.

While these goals are in keeping with America's social values, there is also an economic impact which is not inconsiderable. The cost–benefit ratio of the vocational rehabilitation program has been estimated in various ways, but a generally accepted figure is ten to one; that is, for every dollar spent on the rehabilitation of an individual with a disability, ten dollars are returned through tax payments. That ratio is even greater when entitlement costs such as disability payments and other public support are factored in. For example, suppose an individual receives social security disability income of $600 per month. Assuming this is a catastrophically injured young person who will live a normal life span, the costs associated with just that one individual are substantial. With successful vocational rehabilitation intervention (e.g., retraining, rehabilitation technology, and job placement), disability payments cease and a person once dependent on public support becomes a taxpayer.

The vocational rehabilitation program is a state/federal partnership. Approximately 80% of the funding comes from federal resources and 20% from the states. Each state must adhere to federal legislation governing the program, which ensures a national rehabilitation program with consistent eligibility criteria and service delivery. Eligibility and the types of services provided are discussed in the remainder of this chapter.

Eligibility

Anyone interested in the services provided by the program may apply; however, an individual must be declared eligible by a vocational rehabilitation counselor in order to receive services. Eligibility is based on three criteria, and an individual with a disability must meet all three before receiving services. The criteria are:

1. A documented physical or mental impairment which for that individual constitutes

2. An impediment to employment and

3. The individual must require rehabilitation services in terms of an employment outcome.

Individuals with documented disabilities who are employed at occupations consistent with their skills and abilities would not be eligible for services. Some individuals with impairments do not require rehabilitation services (e.g., someone who needs college training but who has grants or scholarships to cover the cost of tuition and room and board).

Two examples of individuals who are eligible for services, one with a physical and the other with a mental impairment, follow.

> Bob G. is a telephone lineman. While repairing the roof of his home, he slipping on a loose tile and fell. He suffered a spinal cord injury which left him paraplegic. After a work evaluation and other vocational and intellectual assessments, Bob and his counselor deter-

mined that he would be retrained in data entry. Bob was declared eligible for services.

In this case, it is clear that Bob had a severe physical impairment which was an impediment to employment; that is, he could no longer engage in his former occupation and required vocational rehabilitation services to re-enter the labor market.

> Janet B. had been an elementary school teacher for 15 years. Over the course of the past school year, she began exhibiting bizarre behavior both in the classroom and in her interactions with co-workers. She began to dress inappropriately, spoke rapidly and loudly, advised others how to teach, and when rebuked became agitated and hostile. Her behavior continued to deteriorate, and she was placed on medical leave and referred to the local mental health center. Following a psychiatric evaluation, she was diagnosed as having a bipolar disorder and received psychotherapy and medication. As her condition stabilized, she was referred to the vocational rehabilitation program. After several sessions with her counselor, it was decided that she should not return to the stresses of classroom teaching. After being declared eligible for services, a plan was designed for Janet to return to college to become certified in library science and begin a new career as a librarian in a less stressful environment.

The following is an overview of the services provided by the vocational rehabilitation program and some examples of how the program helps individuals with disabilities return to employment.

Physical or Mental Restoration

Some impairments can either be corrected or improved through treatment. In such cases, the program purchases the necessary services from private physicians, psychiatrists, or psychologists. Hospitalization, lab work, x-rays, and medication are some of the additional medical-related costs paid for by the program.

> William H. was referred to the program by his employer. Three years earlier, he had been injured in an automobile accident in which his left leg had been so badly mangled that it had to be amputated above the knee. He wore a prosthesis, but the nature of his job in heavy construction had further damaged his leg to the point where he was having difficulty walking. The situation was further complicated by

an infection in his stump. The vocational rehabilitation program declared him eligible for services and provided corrective surgery, a new and lighter prosthesis, and gait training to learn to use the new prosthesis. William eventually returned to his former job. A rehabilitation engineer was then brought in to evaluate his job tasks and make recommendations for modifications that would reduce the stress on his prosthesis.

Vocational rehabilitation utilizes community-based programs through either a contractual or fee-for-service arrangement. In the case of community hospitals, the program generally pays a per diem rate for individuals who undergo medical, psychiatric, or rehabilitation treatment. The above case study illustrates the use of a general hospital for medical treatment. For psychiatric hospitals, a vocational rehabilitation counselor is available to assist in the vocational aspects of post-discharge planning and community follow-up. The counselor works closely with mental health providers to achieve community reintegration in all areas of adjustment (e.g., independent living, return to work, and resocialization).

Of all the outpatient and inpatient hospital services, perhaps the one that best illustrates the comprehensive nature of rehabilitation is the rehabilitation hospital. These institutions are designed to meet the total needs of individuals who are catastrophically impaired by trauma or disease. They provide expert treatment in all phases of an individual's life affected by severe disability. Major areas of focus are physical and occupational therapy, psychological and sexual adjustment to the effects of disability, self care and independent living skills, medical rehabilitation to the highest functional level possible, and therapeutic recreation and leisure activities.

In some states, vocational rehabilitation services are begun as soon as possible after injury, and in others the program begins after medical rehabilitation has been completed. There are numerous benefits to early intervention, as the following case study illustrates.

Terry J., 24 years old, was employed by a security agency. He attended a local community college and had recently passed the admissions examination to enter the local police academy. While sitting in his car at a stoplight, he was struck by a tractor trailer attempting to turn the corner. He sustained a complete cervical spinal cord injury, which resulted in paralysis of all four extremities. He was stabilized by emergency medical technicians at the scene of the accident and taken to the local regional medical center. Terry and his family were emotionally devastated by the extent of his injury and the permanent nature of his paralysis. After the acute phase of his injury had passed, he was transferred to the local rehabilitation hospital, where he underwent intensive therapy. A vocational rehabilitation counselor was a member of the interdisciplinary team. As part of Terry's program, he recommended a work evaluation to determine transferable skills, vocational aptitude, and occupational interests. A list of possible occupations was drawn up, and the physical demands of each was reviewed by a physical therapist, occupational therapist, and the primary treating physician. After reviewing a labor market survey prepared by the vocational rehabilitation counselor, Terry decided to become a 911 operator. After his discharge from the rehabilitation center some three and a half months later, Terry began on-the-job training. His vocational rehabilitation counselor arranged job site modifications through the program's rehabilitation engineering section. After six months of training, Terry was hired full time and continues to work in his new occupation.

While it is the responsibility of other state agencies to provide psychiatric hospitalization and treatment as well as community support systems, vocational rehabilitation services assist in planning for such post-discharge activities as training, job placement, and transportation. Very often, the stress associated with returning to a former job or starting a new one is a critical juncture for an individual with an emotional disorder and requires close follow-up by a vocational rehabilitation counselor.

Bill W. had been institutionalized for several years with a diagnosis of paranoid schizophrenia. He experienced hallucinations, confusion, and anxiety and did not take his medication as prescribed. Upon discharge from the state hospital, his case was transferred to the local mental health center and he was placed in a halfway house. His condition was stabilized with medication, and he began to improve his independent living skills. He was referred to the vocational rehabilitation program and evaluated for job placement. Unfortunately, the halfway house in which he was living closed due to lack of funding. The vocational rehabilitation counselor was able to secure another residential program and, with the assistance of Bill's mental health case manager, a job in a restaurant. Although Bill's job busing tables was only part time, his dedication to the job (his first in over ten years) earned him additional assignments and increased working hours. His independent living skills continued to improve, as did his sense of self-esteem, which allowed him to move into a supervised apartment setting. While his mental health case manager and vocational rehabilitation counselor continue to follow his progress, Bill's psychological stability and work success indicate that he will soon be an independent and contributing member of society.

Training

One of the primary services provided by the vocational rehabilitation program is training, whether to help an individual with a disability prepare for and enter employment or to retrain an individual when a former occupation is no longer suitable because of a disabling condition. Training is not a random or arbitrary service, but rather is well planned and necessary if an individual is to return to gainful employment. Issues to be considered include:

- Is the individual so severely disabled that only through training can he or she become employed at a level commensurate with his or her ability and motivation?

- Is the training appropriate given the individual's functional limitations?

- Is there a market for the occupation for which the individual will be trained?

Training can run the gamut from technical and highly complex to simple and straightforward, depending on what the individual with a disability requires.

The next three case studies illustrate the three major approaches to training. It should be noted, however, that training varies to the extent that occupations and disabilities vary. The first case is an example of the on-the-job approach to training.

> John L. was a 45-year-old male with a ninth grade education. He was referred to the vocational rehabilitation program because he was unable to retain employment other than heavy manual labor, which he could no longer engage in because of chronic obstructive pulmonary disease. An evaluation also revealed a problem with alcohol, although he was attending Alcoholics Anonymous and his dependence had been in remission for more than a year. Intellectually he functioned at a borderline level, and this cognitive deficit ruled out any academic training. In discussing his vocational interests with his counselor, John was adamant that his employment be out of doors. Because of this request, his functional limitations, and the skills he exhibited in a vocational evaluation, a job as a mason was selected. Because the local vocational school did not have a class in masonry, and John needed income as soon as possible, an on-the-job training situation was sought. The counselor located a contractor who was willing to train John. As with most on-the-job training, the vocational rehabilitation program participated in the cost of the training, which was planned for a three-month period. John would begin at minimum wage, with half paid by the contractor and half by the

vocational rehabilitation program. If the training was successful, John would be hired after the three-month training period, although the contractor was under no obligation to do so. John did succeed and was hired by the company. In the fall, he enrolled in the local vocational/technical school to enhance his skills in masonry and obtain additional training in plumbing.

Although on-the-job training is an excellent approach which has the advantage of possible employment with the company providing the training, public vocational/technical schools provide quality training which is generally state-of-the-art. This resource is utilized so often that vocational rehabilitation counselors are sometimes outstationed at schools. In the event some courses are so highly specialized or the employment market so limited that it is not feasible for vocational/technical schools to offer training in a certain field, the vocational rehabilitation program can purchase it from private or proprietary schools.

Mary R. had led a physically active life until the age of 24 when she was involved in a motorcycle accident during a cross-country trip with her boyfriend. When he lost control of his bike, it careened off a bridge abutment and overturned several times. He was killed and Mary's injuries were so severe that both legs were amputated below the knee. She had worked only sporadically since the accident, and although she had a year of college credit, she had no real vocational goals. Her orthopedic surgeon referred her to the vocational rehabilitation program, primarily for prostheses and gait training. These services were provided, but she also underwent a vocational evaluation and intense counseling for her post-traumatic depression. Based on tests which indicated that she had skills in drawing, design, and mathematics, Mary and her counselor chose drafting as a career goal. Mary was enrolled in the computer-assisted design program at the local vocational/technical school and continued to undergo psychotherapy to deal with her mild depression and sense of loss. She made surprising progress in her training. With her academic success came improved self-esteem, and her depression was treated without medication. She ultimately found employment with an architectural firm. After some job site modifications to make her office accessible, she was considered rehabilitated and her file was closed.

Again, there are many types of training, some of which do not fit neatly into the three broad categories discussed here; however, these three approaches represent the preponderant resources utilized by the vocational rehabilitation program.

Vocational rehabilitation makes extensive use of community colleges and universities when serving individuals with disabilities who are intellectually capable of academic training but whose disabilities are so severe as to preclude many occupational choices. Some schools serve specific disability groups which require specialized environments (e.g., Gallaudet University in Washington and the National Technical Institute for the Deaf in Rochester, New York, provide college training for the hearing impaired). Private schools are sometimes used when a specialized curriculum is required.

> Harry A. was referred to the vocational rehabilitation program during his senior year in high school. When he was 15, he had developed juvenile rheumatoid arthritis. Hip involvement rendered ambulation difficult, and he often used crutches, particularly during periods of inflammation. Otherwise, he was well adjusted, academically sound, and popular with his classmates. After the necessary evaluations were completed, Harry and his counselor decided that with his functional limitations, notably in the area of mobility, and his intellectual ability, college would be the appropriate choice. Because Harry did not know what vocation he would pursue, he attended the local community college before transferring to a university setting. Once enrolled, he decided on a career as a teacher. Although his arthritis worsened somewhat, he continued his course of study without interruption and during his senior year was awarded an academic scholarship. He presently teaches math and science in middle school and is attending school in the summers to obtain a graduate degree in educational administration.

Support Services

Supplemental services available through the vocational rehabilitation program provide support to the major services previously discussed. For example, individuals with disabilities often have difficulty getting to and from their rehabilitation services. The program can meet their transportation needs in a number of ways, such as paying for taxi rides or some form of public transportation. In many states, the program pays for modifications to vehicles to allow individuals to drive with hand controls, transfer from a wheelchair to the driver's seat, or drive from a wheelchair. In order to gain and keep employment, transportation to and from work is always a prime consideration.

In many cases, involvement in a rehabilitation services program creates additional expense for the individual. For example, in order to receive training appropriate to their needs, some people must relocate to another area, which creates living expenses they might not ordinarily incur. In other situations, individuals might need some income during their rehabilitation program if they are to derive its full benefit. A mother who is disabled and has cared for her preschool children at home might enter a training program and suddenly face day-care costs. In such cases, after searching for other public and private means of financial support, the vocational rehabilitation program can provide monthly income or "maintenance" to the individual during the period of rehabilitation. Similar to transportation, maintenance is not a service needed by everyone; however, if a successful rehabilitation outcome is endangered by lack of financial stability, maintenance can be provided. The amount is tailored to individual needs.

Often individuals served by the program opt for self-employment or operating a small business. After training has been completed or small business plans have been thoroughly evaluated, vocational rehabilitation services can assist with the purchase of tools and equipment, obtaining occupational licenses, and in some cases establishing a small business.

A group of therapies provided by the vocational rehabilitation program supplement and enhance other services. For purposes of explanation, they can be divided roughly into the physical therapies and the occupational therapies. In the physical therapies, passive and active exercises, treatment, and orthotics are used to improve range of motion, muscle tone, and stamina. Generally, physical therapy is effective with closed head injury, stroke, arthritis, pulmonary disease, and orthopedic trauma. Speech therapy and cognitive retraining are often used with certain conditions as well.

Occupational therapy teaches individuals good work behavior and job retention skills. While occupational therapy is utilized in hospitals and rehabilitation centers to achieve optimal return of function, there is a major emphasis on personal and work adjustment training. Because many individuals have never worked or have been absent from the workplace for many years, training alone might not be adequate in achieving their vocational goals. Proper dress and hygiene, interpersonal relationships with co-workers and supervisors, adhering to normal working hours, and workplace behaviors all need to be assessed and dealt with appropriately. Even areas tangential to the workplace, such as use of leisure time, money management, and proper nutrition, must be addressed because problems in these areas can directly affect job performance.

> Tommy W. was referred to vocational rehabilitation at the age of 49. When his mother died, his legal guardian brought him to the program for an interview. He was mentally retarded and had spent his life hidden away by his family. During the interview, he avoided eye contact, could not answer questions with complete sentences, and was unable to sign his name. There was some doubt that the program

could render this middle-aged man with multiple work and social disadvantages employable. After a work evaluation was completed, it was decided that work adjustment training would be essential to teach him to be more outgoing and to approach peers and supervisors with confidence. Tommy was placed in a sheltered workshop and underwent intensive adjustment training for almost a year. He was ultimately placed in competitive employment as a custodian for a service organization. He now signs his name, arranges his own transportation, and lives independently. His supervisor describes him as a dedicated worker who is very proud of his status as an employed citizen.

The vocational rehabilitation program provides personal assistance services for both on- and off-the-job support, but the need for assistance must in some way be related to an employment outcome. Examples of personal assistance services for individuals with severe spinal cord injury include dressing, meal preparation, transportation, and programs for individuals with loss of bowel control. Personal assistive services for hearing-impaired individuals might include providing an interpreter and job coaching to teach work skills and workplace behavior.

Rehabilitation technology is the use of engineering principles to address the functional limitations of individuals with disabilities and adapting their work and living environments through the use of mechanical, electrical, and ergonomic approaches. Rehabilitation engineering is relatively new to the rehabilitation profession, but its emergence has allowed for the successful integration of individuals with very severe disabilities into mainstream society. Whether the challenge is transportation, the working environment, or living independently, rehabilitation technology has enabled individuals with major loss of function to adapt in all major life activities. Modification may be simple (e.g., adding a ramp, widening doors to allow wheelchair access, installing hand controls in an automobile) or highly sophisticated, state-of-the-art technology (e.g., a computerized environment that allows an individual with no use of the arms or legs to turn on lights, open and close doors, or program a computer with a mouth stick or voice recognition technology). Those who just a decade ago had little or no chance to live without assistance and very limited employment opportunities are now self-sufficient and working members of society. Through adaptive devices, job modifications, and reengineering the environment, rehabilitation technologies have created opportunities for individuals with disabilities that hold unlimited promise for their future.

Carol J. was injured during her sophomore year in college. While on a sorority outing, she dove head first into a lake, struck a submerged log, and suffered a compression fracture of the cervical region of the spinal cord. The accident left her paralyzed from the neck down. After hospitalization for acute care and rehabilitation, Carol returned to college with the assistance of the vocational rehabilitation program. She used a power wheelchair for mobility and lived in accessible housing with the support of a student who provided personal assistance services. After graduating with a degree in rehabilitation counseling, Carol secured employment with the state rehabilitation agency and was assigned spinal cord and head injury cases. She and her counselor identified the accessibility barriers which had to be addressed in order for her to do her job effectively and independently. A rehabilitation engineer was brought in to assess her work and living environment. Her apartment was fairly accessible and required few modifications; doors were adapted to open electronically and the kitchen stove was equipped with touch pads for easy operation. Her workstation was also modified; her desk was raised to accommodate her wheelchair and a voice-activated computer was installed. With these few modifications, Carol excelled in her profession by combining counseling skill with a genuine empathy for her clients born of personal experience. She is presently enrolled in a graduate program in counseling and has been recognized for her professional success.

Guidance, Counseling, and Placement

Guidance, counseling, and placement are an integral part of every rehabilitation services program. These services are provided by the rehabilitation counselor, and the measure of success is a satisfactorily employed client and an employer who is pleased with the rehabilitated worker. Job placement and follow-up to assure adequate adjustment are the final parts of the rehabilitation process, yet they are planned at the initial interview and permeate the total program. If an individual is not working after all services planned for are delivered, the program is not considered to have been successful.

The relationship between the client and counselor is the touchstone of the rehabilitation process. The program is a joint effort, and each has certain responsibilities. Some individuals require more counseling than others, and counselors are trained to ascertain the level of involvement necessary and the most effective way to provide it. In some cases, just guiding the client through the array of services available is all that is needed, but in other instances, intensive counseling may be required to deal with workplace or personal problems, accept limitations and emphasize positive attributes, recognize and confront dysfunctional behaviors, or teach job seeking and retention skills. The counselor is trained to assess the level of intervention required, choose the appropriate counseling technique, and determine the frequency and duration of sessions necessary to ameliorate the problems identified.

The vocational rehabilitation counselor is also often actively involved in locating and securing employment. The level of that involvement is determined on an individual basis and can range from providing job leads to actually making contacts on behalf of the client. Some individuals require little or no assistance while others need help with building interview skills, preparing resume, and making initial contact with prospective employers. After placement, the counselor maintains contact with the client and the employer for an agreed-upon period of time to ensure that both are satisfied and to determine if any other services or intervention is necessary.

Through post-employment services, the vocational rehabilitation program can remain involved with the client and the employer even after the case has been removed from active status. Additional services can be provided to help a client retain or advance in a job. The availability of post-employment services as well as follow-up after the original placement is a guarantee to the employer that the services will continue to be provided as needed.

> Johnny F. was referred to the vocational rehabilitation program after being discharged from a number of minimum wage jobs. Although he was a high school graduate and had some technical school training in electronics, he exhibited a hostile attitude toward supervision and was confrontive and sarcastic in his dealings with the public. His relationship with his wife was strained because of his increasing periods of unemployment. A review of Johnny's records revealed a borderline personality disorder which was not severe enough to require psychiatric intervention but was certainly interfering with his ability to retain employment. Johnny realized that he needed to change his behavior if he was to achieve some stability in his work and personal life. He and his counselor identified his counterproductive attitudes and behavior and scheduled biweekly counseling sessions to discuss them and to develop coping strategies to channel them into socially and vocationally acceptable behavior. As the counseling relationship began to demonstrate observable progress, his counselor integrated a placement plan into their sessions. A vocational assessment indicated Johnny's continuing interest in electronics. Johnny and his counselor decided that Johnny should pursue employment with the city as an electrician. They completed an application and discussed interview questions, in particular how to handle questions about his spotty work history. Johnny was ultimately hired as a trainee and within a year was promoted.

Special Populations

Although any physical or mental impairment can affect employment and necessitate the services of the vocational rehabilitation program, there are special disability populations which require major programmatic development and activity in order to meet needs that are specific to their disabilities. The following groups are special by virtue of disability, ethnicity, or educational status.

Hearing Impaired

The hearing impaired include those who are deaf or hard of hearing. Surprisingly, this group constitutes 10% of the population. This disability can isolate an individual from the mainstream of society by reducing or eliminating communication. When asked whether deafness or blindness was more disabling, Helen Keller replied that blindness cuts one off from things, but deafness cuts one off from people.

To serve individuals who are hard of hearing or deaf, the program must provide a communication bridge to the hearing world. Solutions ranges from hearing aids and cochlear implants to sign language interpreters. As mentioned earlier, although special schools may be necessary in some cases, many deaf individuals choose the mainstream educational route.

> Sally G. was referred to the vocational rehabilitation program by her special education teacher. She was prelingually deaf (loss of hearing before language development), and tests indicated that she was also mildly mentally retarded. Her rehabilitation program initially consisted of personal adjustment and vocational training through Goodwill Industries and later placement assistance and a sign language interpreter. She was employed by a local mall in custodial work, but had a difficult adjustment initially because she enjoyed spending too much time in the game room. A job coach was brought in to teach her appropriate work behaviors, and she successfully addressed her tendency to become diverted. After a year of excellent work as a custodian, she was promoted to mall courier.

Brain and Spinal Cord Injured

Brain and spinal cord injuries are life-altering disabilities, generally caused by trauma, which require major medical, psychological, and vocational intervention. Although there are many causes of these injuries, the majority are the result of vehicle accidents, falls, diving into unknown waters, gunshot wounds, and various other insults to the brain and spinal cord.

With spinal cord injury, the individual experiences neurological deficit which can include loss of bladder and bowel control, sensory losses, and paralysis at the level of the injury. Depending on the site of injury, paralysis occurs at the cervical, thoracic, or lumbar region of the spinal column and results in loss of use of all four extremities, partial loss of use of the upper extremities, or loss of use of the lower extremities, respectively.

In brain injury, depending on the region of the brain suffering the trauma as well as the severity, the individual experiences behavioral, cognitive, and physical impairment. Sometimes called the "silent epidemic," brain injury affects as many as 500,000 to 750,000 individuals each year. Brain injury can occur at any age, but most occur between the ages of 15 and 24. Because males are more likely to take risks, they are twice as likely as females to be injured.

Motor vehicle accidents are the leading cause of brain injury (most studies indicate 50 to 60%), and alcohol plays a role in over half.* Safety devices such as seat belts, air bags, and helmets (for motorcyclists and bicyclists) can prevent or greatly reduce the severity of brain injury.

Brain injury is not always visible, but the enduring physical, emotional, intellectual, and social changes create an enormous burden for the individual and his or her family and present a formidable challenge to the rehabilitation community.

Developmentally Disabled

Developmental disabilities are conditions that occur during the developmental phase of life. They are categorized into five major diagnoses: mental retardation, epilepsy, autism, cerebral palsy, and spina bifida. Each can vary in severity, but with appropriate rehabilitation services, a large percentage of individuals with these conditions are able to enter the labor market. For example, when placed in work settings appropriate to their skills and aptitudes, mentally retarded individuals have proven to be loyal and hard-working employees. An individual with a seizure disorder can work in most settings if given some minor accommodations such as flexible working hours, modified artificial lighting, and an employer who understands the basic facts about epilepsy.

Emotionally Impaired

The National Institute on Mental Health (NIMH) estimates that over 11 million persons are affected with severe mental illness during their lifetime. In light of this large of number of persons affected, it is important to define what constitutes mental illness. Severe mental illness refers to major disorders such as schizophrenia, bipolar affective disorder, and major depression. NIMH esti-

---

* Statistics courtesy of the National Head Injury Foundation, Florida chapter.

mates the number of persons currently affected at 4.6 million.* When other disorders such as substance abuse, anxiety disorders, and depression are added, the number rises dramatically. Almost 20% of the population, or one out of every five people 18 and older, is affected.

Whether treated on an inpatient or outpatient basis, this group represents a large portion of the vocational rehabilitation caseload. Rehabilitation programs may consist of any number of approaches, including support for treatment, medication, training or retraining, counseling, job placement, and monitoring on-the-job behaviors and adjustment. While many individuals can return to their previous employment, and indeed a large percentage do, the vocational rehabilitation program has had marked success with people who benefit from services tailored to their particular situation and who adjust well in the work setting. Being a productive member of the work force is therapeutic in that it generates a healthy self-concept and a feeling of worth that few other life experiences can provide.

Blind and Visually Impaired

In some states, the blind and general vocational rehabilitation programs are combined, while in others they are separate. Although services are generally the same, the blind program provides additional services which address the unique needs of that population. For example, under primary sponsorship of the Library of Congress, regional libraries provide reading material on tape, in braille, and in large-print format. Another unique program is the independent living center, which teaches skills required to live independently and provides orientation and mobility training.

While blindness and visual impairment occur in all age groups, the majority of individuals affected are over 60.

Students with Disabilities

A new approach to providing vocational rehabilitation services to youths with disabilities has gained momentum and community support during the last decade. Transition from School to Work stresses the intervention of vocational rehabilitation during secondary school. The assumption is that early rehabilitation services will prevent chronic unemployment and the myriad problems that accompany it. It should be noted that the name Transition from School to Work is somewhat of a misnomer in that oftentimes a student will enter post-secondary training such as a vocational school or college prior to entering the world of work.

---

* *Public Health Reports,* Nov.-Dec. 1992, Vol. 107, No. 6.

The Individuals with Disabilities Education Act of 1990 requires transition planning for students with disabilities at age 16, but planning can begin two years earlier. Part of the planning must include identification of what community services the student will need and what agencies will provide them. This act is the perfect complement to the vocational rehabilitation transition program, and the combination of the two enhances the independence and vocational success of the student with a disability.

The Unserved and Underserved

Congress has legislated that the vocational rehabilitation program seek out and, through specially designed programs, provide services to the unserved and underserved. Two such groups which readily come to mind are migrant and seasonal farm workers and American Indians. Programs for the former must address the needs of farm workers, whether the individual with a disability is migrant or year round on one agricultural site. The latter group can receive rehabilitation services either on a reservation or through regular programs.

Rehabilitation professionals serving both groups have found that the use of indigenous counselors, counselor aides, or rehabilitation technicians from these populations can effectively overcome such barriers as language, customs, and lack of trust.

> Vicki R., an American Indian with a disability, was considering being referred for vocational rehabilitation services. Because a core tradition in the American Indian culture is respect for elders, she was concerned that her counselor might be much younger than she and would ask detailed and intimate questions. The Native American rehabilitation technician made a home visit to discuss Vicki's concern and indicated that although she was younger than Vicki, she had experience with situations similar to Vicki's. Vicki agreed to speak with the counselor and found her respectful, knowledgeable, and professional. Over the course of the next year, Vicki successfully completed cosmetology training, passed her state certification, and found employment. The intervention of the Native American technician resolved a cultural issue and cleared the way for a successful rehabilitation.

Benefits to Employers

While the Americans with Disabilities Act requires non-discrimination in the employment practices of all employers with 15 or more workers, it is important to note that hiring individuals with disabilities makes good sense from a business standpoint. The following incentives illustrate that contention.

- *On-the-Job Training*—The vocational rehabilitation program will work with an employer to design an on-the-job training program when it is mutually agreed that this is the best training approach. Once time frame and cost are determined, the vocational rehabilitation program usually shares those costs. In certain cases, a minimum wage exemption can be obtained from the Wage and Hour Division of the U.S. Department of Labor.

- *Access Tax Credits*—Small businesses that qualify can receive tax credits in the amount of 50% of "eligible access expenditures" over $250, not to exceed $10,250 per tax year.

- *Tax Deduction*—A maximum of $15,000 per year can be claimed for the removal of architectural or transportation barriers.

- *Targeted Jobs Tax Credits*—An employer can claim a tax credit for up to 40% of the first year's salary for an individual with a disability who is hired and works for at least 120 hours or is employed for 90 days. (Note: This provision expired at the end of 1994; however advocates, employers, and consumers are urging its renewal by Congress.)

Services Directly Provided by the Vocational Rehabilitation Program

When an individual with a disability has completed an individualized rehabilitation program, the prospective employer is provided with a prescreened applicant who is ready for work. The vocational rehabilitation counselor is available to handle issues or problems that arise after job placement. Even after an individual's file has been removed from active status, post-employment services are available. If an employee needs additional services to retain or advance in his or her occupation, assistance is still available through the vocational rehabilitation program. Resources are available to both employer and employee as needed. The program has been in existence for almost 75 years.

The program will also conduct an accessibility survey for an employer. Moreover, awareness training can be provided if an employer believes that it would be helpful in assuring that employees understand and accept a co-worker with a disability.

As discussed in the beginning of this chapter, the vocational rehabilitation and employment of individuals with disabilities is a good investment by government and its citizens. Employers often ask, "What jobs can people with disabilities do?" The answer, of course, is any job there is. There is the right person for any job opening that exists; it is simply a matter of selectively matching the two. Would you as an employer hire someone in a management position who uses a wheelchair for mobility, someone who has survived a major heart attack, or someone who has a severe back problem and is in constant pain? These disabilities did not prevent three 20th century presidents from serving the nation.

Employers can become partners with the vocational rehabilitation program in assisting one of society's most disadvantaged groups enter the economic and social mainstream. Not only do individuals with disabilities benefit, but so do the employers and America as a whole.

International Center for the Disabled

31

The International Center for the Disabled (ICD) is a freestanding outpatient rehabilitation facility located in New York City. It treats adults with a broad range of functional impairments that are the result of orthopedic, musculoskeletal, neuromuscular, vascular, neurological, and psychogenic dysfunction, including back and joint pain, joint replacement, amputation, stroke, traumatic brain injury, and spinal cord injury.

ICD is an extraordinary rehabilitation organization with a record of over 75 years of service to persons with disabilities. In the last ten years alone, 1500 ICD clients have been placed with employers. However, ICD's activities extend far beyond direct services; the center has always placed a strong emphasis on both research and education and training and provides leadership and direction to the rehabilitation community nationally and internationally.

The center's leading role in rehabilitation is made possible by contributions from foundations, corporations, and individuals.

Overview of ICD Rehabilitation Programs

Vocational Rehabilitation

ICD is proud of its tradition of "working beyond the center's doors," and nowhere is this tradition stronger than in its partnership with the business sector. An integral part of ICD's comprehensive care is its ongoing commitment to vocational rehabilitation. In training persons with disabilities for today's workplace, the center provides extensive vocational services, including evaluation of an individual's strengths, aptitudes, and abilities; work adjustment to prepare clients for training and placement; remedial services to enhance academic potential; training to develop skills for rewarding employment; and placement in appropriate jobs and work environments.

As part of vocational rehabilitation, many clients are tested using the MicroTOWER group vocational evaluation system, developed by ICD and recognized as a world standard. The work samples that clients complete are actual tasks encountered in today's businesses, such as electronics assembly, mechanical assembly, graphics illustration, accounting functions, and clerical and mail room services, to name a few. A client's aptitude profile, together with personal aims and ambitions, are used to select the best training program and career area.

Instruction is offered in such areas as data processing and other technical office skills, paraprofessional functions in human services, and food and custodial services. In the Vocational Improvement Program, disabled individuals develop a positive employee identity and abilities that facilitate increased productivity and the capacity to handle the day-to-day demands of employment. To meet the needs of area employers, ICD's Westchester satellite facility trains clients in high-level office skills and food services.

From the Classroom to the Business World

Many of ICD's younger clients are trying to make their way from the high school classroom to the business world. Frequently they lack basic skills as well as appropriate attitudes and behaviors. These clients enter ICD's transitional work programs, which are designed to help them build the talent, stamina, and commitment needed for successful performance in entry-level jobs.

As part of ICD's continuing outreach to the business community, the Industrial Rehabilitation Center uses an interdisciplinary approach to assess an injured employee's ability to return to the work force through short-term, goal-oriented evaluation/treatment programs. Such factors as general productivity, safety, and interpersonal behavior are considered. A realistic and specific treatment program which simulates actual tasks is set up to progressively increase physical stamina, strength, and productivity.

The Employee Rehabilitation Service (ERS), an important component of the Industrial Rehabilitation Program, operates in partnership with the business sector and its insurance carriers to provide comprehensive case management. Through home visits, consultations with employees and clinicians, and referrals to appropriate sources, ERS is able to help control costs by returning substantial numbers of workers to active employment.

In collaboration with many major corporations, ICD's Business Advisory Committee recommends training programs suitable to the needs of the labor market, arranges internships, and assists in job placement.

ICD's Mentoring Program provides one-to-one partnerships between vocational clients and members of the corporate community. In this innovative alliance, mentors (who are representatives from different areas of the business and cultural worlds) provide guidance and counseling to trainees seeking employment in the clerical field. This highly successful program builds self-esteem while introducing prospective employees to an actual employment setting.

The Direct Care Training Program, a segment of ICD's Human Services Assistant Program, prepares disadvantaged young adults with learning disabilities and other impairments for employment in residential and day-center programs for persons with developmental disabilities. Following a comprehensive skills evaluation, program staff develop an individualized study plan for each student. The curriculum is demanding. Students learn to function as part of an interdisciplinary healthcare team and then complete hands-on internships in organizations such as United Cerebral Palsy, the Association for Children with Retarded Mental Development, Lutheran Family Services, and local nursing homes. ICD's Placement Department guides graduates into full-time employment following completion of this rigorous training program. Project staff assist other agencies in replicating ICD's model.

ICD's Social Services Department provides intake interviews to the Vocational Evaluation Unit in addition to providing counseling to any client who is active in a program. Working with individuals, groups, families, and significant others, the department offers assistance in such areas as benefits applications, home attendant services, and housing as part of an effort to enable individuals faced with disabilities to live and work independently in their communities.

Outpatient Rehabilitation Services

As a full-service diagnostic and treatment center, ICD's Medical Department includes a staff of rehabilitation physicians (physiatrists) who work with patients to enhance their personal functioning and overall well-being. The department is a proven resource for referrals from major healthcare centers and provides access to and guidance through the rehabilitation process.

Preparing tomorrow's physicians necessitates interdisciplinary training in healthcare. Through its Residency-in-Rehabilitation Program, developed in partnership with Columbia-Presbyterian Medical Center, Kingsbrook Medical Center, Mount Sinai Medical Center, New York Hospital-Cornell Medical Center, and St. Vincent's Hospital and Medical Center, ICD trains physicians in a wide range of rehabilitation specialties. As part of the program, residents are offered comprehensive outpatient experience in ICD's medical rehabilitation, behavioral medicine, social services, and vocational departments. At present, no other institution in the New York area offers physicians a program that focuses so directly on vocationally oriented rehabilitation. This emphasis on cooperation in education and practice brings together a rich array of resources and support for both patient and practitioner.

A patient's comprehensive medical evaluation often leads to highly individualized physical therapy services, which can include exercise programs and mobility training, modalities used in the relief of pain and muscle spasm, development of post-discharge home exercise programs, or referrals to community resources. In individual or group sessions, emphasis is placed on goal-directed treatment choices to maximize personal potential.

When appropriate, clients are referred to ICD's Orthotics and Prosthetics Clinic, which prescribes, fits, modifies, and maintains orthotic and prosthetic devices. Physiatrists, physical therapists, and assistive device vendors meet clients to assess their needs and help design customized equipment. ICD offers the necessary physical and occupational therapies to ensure maximum benefit, comfort, and function.

ICD is working in partnership with Memorial Sloan-Kettering Cancer Center to provide outpatient rehabilitation services for cancer patients, using a comprehensive medical, psychological, and vocational approach. Physical and occupational therapy, relaxation techniques, and group or individual counseling may all be part of an individually tailored program.

Over the last decade, one of the most important changes in healthcare has been increased outpatient treatment instead of the traditional lengthy inpatient rehabilitation hospitalization. Recognizing this trend, ICD has developed The Stroke Program, a unique outpatient hospital rehabilitation program for younger stroke survivors with potential for returning to the work force. The program provides intensive case management and the comprehensive services (including physiatry, physical and occupational therapies, speech/language services, psychological therapy, social work services, and rehabilitation nursing) usually available only in an inpatient setting. ICD developed The Stroke Program as a research and demonstration project with support from foundations and a reimbursement plan from the healthcare insurance sector. This collaboration enables ICD to offer a new option in the stroke survivor's continuum of care.

Specific Rehabilitation Programs at ICD

Industrial Rehabilitation Program: Cost-Containment Services for Industry

The Industrial Rehabilitation Program (IRP) helps local industry contain disability costs by successfully returning injured workers to the job as well as bringing workers' compensation cases to closure and providing injury-prevention programs and consultation.

Return-to-Work Program

IRP's interdisciplinary staff, including a physiatrist, physical therapist, occupational therapist, psychologist, social worker, and vocational counselor, works with the injured employee to develop an individual return-to-work plan. One or more of the following services may be used in this process.

Functional Capacity Evaluation—A one-day evaluation that provides objective data about an injured worker's physical capacity and other work-related factors to determine whether a return to work is possible.

Work Hardening Program—To prepare the worker to return to an identified job, IRP staff design a short-term intensive program using real and simulated work activities to increase the worker's strength and productivity and to develop any needed workplace behaviors.

Work Capacity Evaluation—When an injured worker is unable to meet the physical demands of the job, this ten-day assessment of physical capabilities and transferable work skills provides a basis for planning realistic vocational goals.

Educational and Consultation Services

Work Site Analysis—To ensure that the workplace is structured to enable the worker to meet the demands of the job, an occupational therapist assesses the work site and, when appropriate, recommends modifications to enhance the worker's ability to perform the essential job demands and help prevent future injury.

Back Injury Prevention Program—This custom-designed "wellness" program teaches workers how to care for their backs, prevent further back injury, and obtain appropriate treatment when needed.

ADA Audit—An occupational therapist analyzes the work environment to determine whether it complies with ADA requirements and is accessible to individuals with disabilities. When appropriate, recommendations for reasonable accommodations to the work site are made.

The ADD Program: Outpatient Treatment for Alcohol, Drugs, and Disability

The ADD Program is an intensive outpatient 12-step treatment program for chemically dependent men and women with physical disabilities. Guided by a team of chemical dependency experts and rehabilitation specialists, and with support from peers, participants address their substance abuse and the role their disability plays in their addiction. Treatment, which is confidential, respectful, and caring, helps participants abstain from using alcohol and other mood-altering drugs and achieve an improved, healthier lifestyle.

Participants attend the ADD Program during mid-day or late afternoon hours. The complete program is seven to eight months long, depending on the individual treatment plan, and includes three phases:

- *Pretreatment*—A minimum of eight weekly group sessions that help participants identify whether they are ready to give up their use of alcohol and/or drugs and explore their choices about their substance abuse and other aspects of their lives.

- *Intensive Treatment*—Participants who decide to seek treatment begin a six-week intensive group program which meets four times a week for three hours. During this time, participants learn about chemical dependency and its meaning in their lives.

- *Continuing Care*—Attendance in group meetings begins to decrease from four times a week to once a week during the four months of this phase of treatment. Participants now focus on relapse prevention, problem solving, and developing the ongoing behaviors necessary for long-term recovery.

Features of the ADD Program include:

- Thorough assessment
- Individualized treatment plans
- Individual counseling sessions
- Mandatory attendance at 12-step meetings (AA groups meet at ICD twice a week)
- Wheelchair-accessible program site
- Transportation arranged by ICD
- Random alcohol and drug screening
- Referral to on-site medical, vocational, and psychological services, as needed

ICD Education and Training

ICD offers a comprehensive series of training programs related to rehabilitation and the Americans with Disabilities Act. Over 100 seminars are offered between

8:30 a.m. and 10:00 a.m. There is no admission charge; seating is limited, however, and registration is on a first-come, first-served basis.

Seminars are given on subjects such as chemical dependency, subjects persons with disabilities need to know, ADA information for the human resources professional, rehabilitation assessment and other topics of interest to the head injury professional, expediting rehabilitation of the injured worker through successful case management, pain management for AIDS and cancer patients, occupational and physical therapy, behavioral issues in rehabilitation of the injured worker, ethnicity and cultural diversity in rehabilitation, computers as a vocational rehabilitation tool, and cost-effective rehabilitation of the injured worker, to name just a few.

For a complete list of seminars offered, contact ICD at 340 East 24th Street, New York, NY 10010 (phone: 212-679-0100).

ICD Bibliography

Copies of the following items may be obtained by contacting The Publication Office, External Affairs Department, ICD-International Center for the Disabled, 340 East 24th Street, New York, NY 10010-4097.

- Employing Persons with Learning Disabilities: A Handbook for Employers, Trainers and Supervisors

- The ICD Survey of Disabled Americans: Bringing Disabled Americans into the Mainstream

- The ICD Survey II: Employing Disabled Americans

- The ICD Survey III: A Report Card on Special Education

Marriott Foundation for People with Disabilities

32

The Marriott Foundation for People with Disabilities was established in 1989 by the family of J. Willard Marriott, founder of the Marriott Corporation. The mission of the foundation is to foster the employment of young people with disabilities. To achieve this mission, the foundation developed and operates a transition program, "Bridges...From School to Work," which develops paid internships for students in their final year of high school.

In late 1989, the foundation launched the pilot of the Bridges program in Montgomery County, Maryland, headquarters of Marriott Corporation, which in October 1993 split into two companies, Marriott International, Inc. and Host Marriott Corporation. The program was expanded to Chicago and San Francisco in 1990, Washington, D.C. in 1991, Los Angeles in 1992, and San Mateo County, California in 1993. To date, Bridges has placed nearly 1600 students in internships with some 640 employers. The foundation's goal is to replicate the program in a number of cities across the United States.

Richard E. Marriott, chairman of Host Marriott Corporation, serves as chairman of the foundation's board of trustees. The other board members are Dr. I. King Jordan, president of Gallaudet University, and Jay Rochlin, former executive director of the President's Committee on Employment of People with Disabilities.

At each location, the foundation selects an organization to administer and operate the Bridges program. This organization serves as a liaison with the school system, employers, and other participants. TransCen, Inc. administers the program in Montgomery County, Maryland; Washington, D.C.; and Los Angeles, San Francisco, and San Mateo County, California. The University of Illinois at Chicago administers the program in Chicago.

Education, training, and support are central to the success of the Bridges program. To help prepare interns for the workplace, the program provides orientation and training for students and their parents. Managers and supervisors attend seminars on employing people with disabilities, where workplace issues such as supervision, communication, and discipline are addressed. To support the internship, the program employs and trains staff (employer representatives) who help businesses identify internship positions, match student interests and capabilities with job requirements, and provide ongoing support to employers and interns.

The foundation involved a number of nationally recognized consultants in the development of the Bridges program. Milt Wright and Associates, noted for designing training programs for the employment of people with disabilities, assisted in developing Bridges training components. The Virginia Commonwealth University Rehabilitation Research and Training Center, a widely acknowledged leader in supported employment training, conferred regularly on the program. A number of other experts in the fields of disability, education, and employment served on a key advisory committee during program development.

Local Bridges projects are supported in part by grants from the U.S. Department of Education, Rehabilitation Services Administration and the U.S. Department of Labor. The success of the Bridges program (see Exhibit I for statistics on the number of students in the program and number of placements effected) is due in large measure to the extraordinary support of local employers, who provide paid internships in the final year of high school for students with disabilities. Virtually every type of business, from large to small and manufacturing to service, has participated. The Bridges program is a splendid example of a public/private partnership that works. It benefits students with disabilities, local businesses, and communities.

The program has two important purposes: to provide students with job training and work experience that enhance their employment potential and to help local employers gain access to an often overlooked source of employees. The Bridges program provides students with disabilities an opportunity to learn, grow, and succeed through a program that involves employers, schools, and students and their parents.

The role of the employer is to:

- Select managers and supervisors to attend a foundation-sponsored half-day disability awareness training session

- Actively work with program staff to identify and analyze potential paid internship positions

- Interview students referred for internships and make final selection decisions

- Utilize the program's staff to assist company personnel in orienting, training, supervising, monitoring, and evaluating the intern

EXHIBIT I

Bridges...From School to Work
Spring 1990 through March 1995

Students entering project	1911
Placement efforts underway	29
Placements made	1571
% of placements completing internships	83%
% of completions offered ongoing employment	81%
Participants by Disability	
Learning disability	49%
Mental retardation	25%
Emotional/behavioral	14%
Audio impairment	5%
Mobility impairment	2%
Other	4%
Visual impairment	1%
Participants by Gender	
Male	61%
Female	39%
Participants by Race	
Black	51%
White	22%
Hispanic	18%
Asian	7%
Other	2%
Mean hourly wage	$5.20
Mean hours per week	20

The administering organization manages all aspects of the local Bridges program under the direction of the Marriott Foundation for People with Disabilities. This organization hires and supervises employer representatives who:

- Work closely with employers to identify potential internship positions and determine job requirements

- Develop appropriate student internship matches based on analysis of work site/job needs and student interests and abilities

- Assist company personnel in working effectively with the intern
- Provide on-site follow-up support to the employer and student during the internship
- Assist the employer in conducting regular performance appraisals of the intern, including final evaluation at the completion of the internship period

The role of the school system is to:

- Identify and recommend prospective students with disabilities in their final year of high school for internship positions
- Assist students in applying and interviewing for Bridges participation
- Maintain regular contact with employer representatives
- Provide additional support to the intern and his or her family, as needed, and integrate the student's internship experience into the school program

Employment of People with Disabilities: A Sound Business Decision

The Labor Challenge

Regardless of economic fluctuations, one of the greatest challenges facing American businesses today is maintaining a qualified work force. Statistics show that "baby boomers" (people born from 1946 to 1964) are having only about half as many children as their parents did. As a result, the number of 16- to 24-year-olds entering the labor force will continue to fall. The result will be a continuing reduction in the traditional source of job applicants, especially for entry-level positions.

It is clear that employers must rethink the way they have been doing business. Attracting and managing an increasingly diverse work force will be critical to success through the rest of the 1990s and beyond.

An Overlooked Resource: People with Disabilities

Many companies continue to expand their recruitment efforts to target minorities, women, and older workers. However, people with disabilities represent another market which has been largely overlooked. The ongoing shortfalls in other applicant groups as well as the Americans with Disabilities Act mandate for equal job opportunities for people with disabilities mean that employers can no longer afford to overlook this group.

According to the U.S. census, about 10% of the population is considered disabled. A recent Harris Poll indicated that there are currently more than 18 million working-age adults with disabilities in the United States. More than 12 million are unemployed, two-thirds of whom would like to work but do not.

Traditionally, people gain their first job experience while in high school. However, for students with disabilities, these opportunities are often either temporary or non-existent. National studies have shown that well over 50% of the country's 250,000 special education students who leave the educational system annually remain unemployed one year later. Many more are under-employed.

Historical Barriers

Employers have been reluctant to hire workers with disabilities for a number of reasons. Common barriers to employment include:

- Lack of awareness about people with disabilities and how they can contribute

- Lack of awareness about how to hire people with disabilities

- Lack of understanding or knowledge about job accommodations

- Lack of awareness of support services offered by community organizations

- Concerns on the part of co-workers and managers about people with disabilities in the workplace

Benefits

According to many companies that have hired people with disabilities, these individuals generally are motivated, capable, and dependable. A 1987 Harris Poll found that almost 90% of workers with disabilities received "good" or "excellent" performance ratings from their managers. Managers also felt that employees with disabilities did their jobs as well as—or better than—other employees in similar jobs and that these workers were no more difficult to supervise than other employees.

Over 80% of the managers surveyed indicated the average cost of hiring an employee with a disability is less than or equal to that of a non-disabled employee. A recent study sponsored by the federal government found that more than 50% of accommodations cost nothing, while another 30% cost less than $500.

The 1981 "DuPont Survey of Employment of the Handicapped" found that supervisors rank employees with disabilities higher on safety issues than their non-disabled peers. This finding is supported by recent U.S. Department of Labor studies.

Employing people with disabilities need not be a complicated process. Many community agencies stand ready to offer technical assistance. These include local and state vocational rehabilitation organizations which provide assistance with recruiting, screening, hiring, job analysis, training, and job accommodation. The Job Training Partnership Act may also offer wage subsidies while an eligible employee is in training. These programs, in addition to others which offer compensation for the cost of accommodations and protection from workers' compensation claims for pre-existing conditions, are designed to ensure that the needs of the employer are fully met.

Special Recognition Awards to Participating Companies

The Marriott Foundation for People with Disabilities provides special recognition to outstanding companies for their commitment to providing opportunities for young people with disabilities. Each area where the program is administered provides its own awards.

"The success of Bridges in the Washington, D.C. area is due to the tremendous support of local employers, who provide paid internships for students with disabilities in their final year of high school," said Richard E. Marriott, chairman of Host Marriott Corporation and chairman of the Marriott Foundation's board of trustees. Bridges has placed more than 640 students with disabilities with some 280 employers in the Washington area. Approximately 86% of the students completed their internships, 79% of whom were offered continued employment.

The following awards, given in Washington, D.C. on June 2, 1994, demonstrate the accomplishments of the Bridges program. The awards were presented at a dinner held at the JW Marriott Hotel in Washington, D.C. Joining in the presentation were actor James Earl Jones; Franklin L. Smith, superintendent of the District of Columbia Public Schools; and Paul L. Vance, superintendent of Montgomery County Public Schools.

The Chairman's Award, which recognizes an individual who has significantly advanced both the Bridges program and transition opportunities for students with disabilities, was presented to Joy Johnson Brown of Hewlett-Packard Company. A member of the Bridges Business Advisory Council, Ms. Brown has helped increase awareness of the potential of people with disabilities in the workplace. Her efforts reflect the long-standing commitment of Hewlett-Packard Company to providing equal employment opportunity.

Blockbuster Entertainment Corporation was honored with the Leadership Award, which acknowledges advocacy for people with disabilities and exceptional participation in the Bridges program. Widely recognized for promoting diversity in the work force, Blockbuster has placed students in internships that develop skills and provide opportunity for social development, while raising public awareness of the capabilities of people with disabilities.

The Small Business Award recognizes outstanding participation in the Bridges program by a small business. It was presented to Ford's Theatre, which has given young people with disabilities the opportunity to explore employment in the unique environment of the theater, while setting an example for others in the arts community.

The Employer of the Year Award, which recognizes an employer that has demonstrated exemplary involvement in the Bridge program, was presented to Safeway, Inc., a company often cited for respecting and valuing individual differences. Safeway has provided numerous internships for students in its stores throughout the region, and the company's experience and resources have helped strengthen the Bridges program.

In the District of Columbia and Montgomery County, there are nearly 800 special education students preparing to leave the education system. With the passage of the Americans with Disabilities Act, they should no longer be overlooked. While many employers are not prepared to work effectively with these students, Bridges works to close this gap by identifying students' skills, interests, and aptitudes and preparing employers to effectively integrate employees with disabilities into the work force.

MEED Program   33

The MEED (Microcomputer Education for Employment of the Disabled) Program is a non-profit training program that enables unemployed physically disabled adults to become microcomputer or PC applications specialists. Following training, which includes an internship at one of the many companies that support the program, graduates find employment in career-level positions related to business information management.

MEED is located on the downtown (Wolfson) campus of Miami-Dade Community College and the program serves the Dade and Broward communities. It is the first program in the United States designed to provide microcomputer training for disabled persons. Since the program was established, MEED has graduated over 150 students whose average salaries equal $23,000 per year.

Classes begin every six months, and the program takes one year to complete. All students take between 40 and 45 credit hours in completing the program, with all credits applied toward an associate of arts degree. Instructional activities run from 9:00 a.m. to 5:00 p.m. Monday through Friday, thus simulating the physical stresses that students would find in normal full-time work.

Training is free for qualified students. Students may be eligible for support for tuition and program fees from the Department of Education, the Division of Vocational Rehabilitation, Project Independence, workers' compensation, scholarships, or loans.

Support from the Business Advisory Council

Business advisory councils (BACs) can be found in cities throughout the United States. In the case of MEED, senior executives in the data processing, human resources, and public relations departments of major corporations volunteer their expertise to set policy for every aspect of the MEED Program. BAC members help select the students, guide the curriculum, acquire resources, publicize the program, mentor individual students, and develop internship and career positions in local corporations.

BAC members supporting the MEED Program include the following companies: American Bankers Insurance Group, Arthur Andersen & Co., AT&T, Barnett Bank, Burger King Corporation, Coulter Electronics, Evensky & Brown, IBM Corporation, Intercontinental Bank, John Alden Life Insurance, Murray Press, Northern Trust Bank, Southern Bell, Sunbank/Miami N.A., *The Miami Herald,* and many others.

Benefits to Employers

Interviews with both employers of MEED Program graduates and graduates themselves indicate that employers are gaining highly qualified, job-ready microcomputer experts who can increase business productivity and efficiency from the very first day on the job. MEED graduates have proven themselves to be quick learners, self-starters, and strongly motivated, loyal employees. The following comments from executives whose companies employ MEED graduates further support the latter observation:

> "Teaming with MEED helped my company migrate to state-of-the-art electronic publishing."
>
> *President, Murray Press, Inc.*

> "My first MEED intern was so successful, we hired her and set up an ongoing internship position."
>
> *Senior vice president, Intercontinental Bank*

> "The MEED program is a unique business/community college partnership success story."
>
> *Employment recruiter, The Miami Herald*

> "I've hired many new graduates, but the MEED graduate was the first one who was productive from the first day."
>
> *Administrator, Audit Department, Arthur Andersen & Co.*

> "Very few things have impacted me like the MEED Program. My intern is dedicated, skilled, productive and will be a valuable employee."
>
> *Human resources director, Schering Laboratories*

> "Our MEED graduates have made a real contribution right from the start. And they are some of our most able employees."
>
> *Corporate scientist, Coulter Corporation*

In addition to obtaining highly productive and dedicated employees, companies that employ MEED graduates can also benefit from federal and state tax benefits and expense allowances.

Special Features of the MEED Program

A noteworthy attribute of the MEED Program, and one that explains much of its success in developing highly qualified graduates, is the faculty, which is composed of computer industry professionals who are qualified college instructors. These professionals are state-of-the-art practitioners who volunteer to teach MEED students.

MEED's software training is focused. The program provides hands-on experience in word processing, database management, electronic spreadsheets, operating systems, microcomputer accounting and bookkeeping, local area network (LAN) management, and desktop publishing.

Students receive training in career development, including such areas as job readiness, job search strategy, resume and cover letter preparation, interviewing, and job referrals, and are matched with business mentors. In addition, leading business authorities share their knowledge with students in weekly guest lectures. Periodic visits to corporate sites allow students to see PCs and software in action.

Adaptive services are available for those students who require special accommodations. Examples of these services include adaptive software to compensate for disabilities, sign language interpreters, tutors, and notetakers. Enrichment courses in business math and business writing are also provided.

Finally, MEED is able to provide each student with a three-month internship as part of the curriculum. In this way, students gain experience in a supportive business environment. They are able to demonstrate their capabilities and gain valuable experience in adjusting to the workplace.

Overview of the MEED Curriculum

Core Curriculum: Session I
- Introduction to Microcomputers
- Word Processing
- Business Writing
- Guest Lectures, Skills/Field Trips

Core Curriculum: Session II
- Spreadsheets
- Database Management
- Operating Systems
- Guest Lectures/Skills/Field Trips

Core Curriculum: Session III
- Information Systems for Management
- Career Development
- Guest Lectures/Skills/Field Trips

Applications Support Specialist	Technical Support Specialist
• Desktop Publishing	• Database Programming
• Independent Study	• Networking

Session IV	Session IV
• Internships	• Internships

Course Listings

Individual courses and respective credits, all of which may be applied to a two-year associate of arts degree, are as follows:

Introduction to Microcomputer Usage	4 credits
Microcomputer Word Processing	4 credits
Microcomputer Spreadsheet	4 credits
Microcomputer Database Management	4 credits
Business Writing	3 credits
Operating Systems—DOS/Windows	4 credits
Information Systems for Management	4 credits
Microcomputer Desktop Publishing	4 credits
Database Applications Programming	4 credits
Microcomputer Networking	4 credits
Independent Study	3 credits
Cooperative Education Work Experience (Career Development)	3 credits
Cooperative Education Work Experience (Internships)	4 credits

Jobs Held by MEED Graduates

Some of the most recent positions held by graduates of the MEED Program reflect a diversity of responsibilities:

Employer	Job Title
American Bankers Insurance Group	Operator I, technical writer
Applied Solutions Group	Database/Lotus programmer
Arthur Andersen & Co.	Microcomputer coordinator
Baxter Diagnostics	Technician
Bayside Gourmet Distributor	Computer operations manager
Burger King Corporation	Database programmer
Byte Technologies	Technical service manager
Carnival Cruise Line	Sale and sign clerk
Christian Community Service Agency	Support staff
City of Coral Gables	Microcomputer operator
CNS Bank	Letters of credit specialist
Comprehensive Cancer Center	Data control coordinator
Coulter Electronics, Inc.	Computer analyst, Lotus programmer, microcomputer specialist, network administrator, publishing systems specialist
Dade County Medical Examiner's Office	Microcomputer system administrator
Dade County Public Schools	Computer technician
Dade County Special Housing Dept.	Microcomputer specialist
Deloitte and Touche	Computer specialist
Family Counseling Services	Systems manager
First Presbyterian Church	Microcomputer specialist
Fleet Credit Corporation	System programmer
Gaebe & Murphy	System manager
General Analysis Corporation	Sales service engineer
Gould Electronics	Human resources systems technician
Health Council of South Florida	Administrative assistant
Jackson Memorial Hospital	Clerk II
KPMG Peat Marwick	Microcomputer specialist
Medi-Trak, Inc.	Administrative assistant
MEED Program	Assistant administration technician, student recruiter

Employer	Job Title
Miami-Dade Community College	Microcomputer instructor, network administrator
Miami Heart Institute	Computer operator
Miami Rescue Mission	Computer systems manager
North Miami Police Department	Computer operator
Respect of Florida	South Florida representative
Royal Caribbean Cruise Line	Data entry clerk
Silhouette Publishers	Author
Trade Litho, Inc.	Personnel assistant
University of Miami	
Department of Oncology	Senior staff assistant
Department of Psychiatry	Staff associate/accounting
Medical School	Senior staff assistant
Vital Healthcare Corporation	Receptionist/computer support
VMS Realty	Computer operator
WPBT Channel 2	Database analyst

Profile of a MEED Graduate

Andrew Warren, who has quadriplegia, entered the MEED Program in March 1993. He maintained a 3.85 grade point average for the 41 credit hours he earned in the intensive program and graduated in April 1994 with the honor of Outstanding Student. Completion of the Microcomputer Technical Support Specialist and Application Technician certificate programs required a three-month internship, which Andy served at John Alden Life Insurance Company. His is currently working in the data network services department at John Alden.

The following questions and answers are from an interview conducted by Susan Montie, career coordinator at MEED.

What is your current position and what skills are needed for you to meet the job requirements? My current position is network data technician on the help desk. The skills needed are knowledge of WANs and LANs (wide and local area networks) and personal computers and their maintenance.

What accommodations were made for you at work? The accommodations I required were a PC equipped with voice recognition hardware and software and a special telephone that I could answer using an sip-and-puff pneumatic switch. AT&T modified the phone and John Alden purchased the

VoiceType Dragon by IBM and Listen for Windows by Verbex voice recognition software.

How did you help facilitate the accommodations? After having the voice recognition systems installed, it was my responsibility to create the speech commands that would be needed to run the type of software that I was using. This required many hours of writing special files that contained several voice macros for performing the many tasks on John Alden's mainframe.

What are you doing now that will help enhance your job performance and therefore benefit the company? Right now I am creating a speech interface for Windows-based software called Lotus Notes. This is a special database program that allows the help desk staff to receive problem calls and enter the information. A technician will read this database and help the person having trouble with their PC or terminal. When I complete this special interface I, too, will be able to receive calls and provide necessary user support.

Any other comments? Setting up this special workstation was a very challenging and rewarding experience. I think it will show many employers that it is possible for a severely disabled person to perform well in a work environment using this type of modern technology.

The Internship Program

There is no actual or implied obligation that the company providing the internship will hire the trainee. This period is viewed as an important part of the training process and a chance for the company to evaluate the trainee for future employment.

Interns are not paid. The primary focus of the internship is to provide interns with quality work and supervision. To a large extent, the amount and type of supervision is left to the employer's discretion. In general, the employer provides the same type of supervision as would be provided for any entry-level employee. Periodic feedback is given to MEED's career coordinator, and a brief performance evaluation is prepared upon completion of the internship.

The length of the internship is flexible, depending on the objectives and responsibilities of the intern. The intern is basically expected to work the regular established hours of the company, up to a maximum of eight hours a day for three or four days a week. Internship periods can last from 4 to 24 weeks.

Very little paperwork is required of the employer. The MEED career coordinator is responsible for maintaining all records and necessary documentation.

The employer or a designated representative confirms attendance records and participates in evaluating the intern.

The career coordinator and the director of MEED prescreen interns and refer them to host companies based on the needs of both the company and the intern. Employers are encouraged to interview prospective interns.

A Final Word

The MEED Program is a cost-justified approach to training persons with physical disabilities. Graduates of the program are highly productive and motivated to maintain high performance levels. Employers gain pretrained employees with little or no accommodation costs. The community gains self-supporting, tax-paying citizens.

The results of the MEED Program are well documented and very impressive. It serves as a model for other communities, and the concept should be implemented on a national basis.

Physical Ergonomics Rehabilitation Center of Dallas

34

Physical Ergonomics Rehabilitation Center has been selected for inclusion in this book because of its highly professional and successful approach to physical rehabilitation. This rehabilitation organization serves as a model for its genre in working effectively with patients, employers, and physicians.

The center's goal is to provide all parties involved in a worker's recovery with an accurate assessment of the client's physical and functional capabilities and an aggressive rehabilitation program to help the client progress to his or her maximum functional potential quickly and safely. Programs are focused on flexibility exercises, aerobic conditioning, and progressive resistive strength training, as well as functional restoration activities and work simulation, postural stabilization programs, and back education.

The following services are provided at Physical Ergonomics, all of which are available with a prescription from a physician or chiropractor. Protocols for specific injuries to the hands, wrists, knees, and all other extremity joints may be incorporated, as well as programs for back and neck injuries.

Industrial Rehabilitation Program

1. Functional capacity evaluations

2. Physical rehabilitation (therapeutic exercise, kinetic activities, functional activities, aerobic conditioning)—four to eight weeks

3. Work hardening (work simulation, functional training, back/neck care educational programs, case management, job site visits)—four weeks, followed by a final functional capacity evaluation with return-to-work recommendations

Physical Therapy Services

- Therapeutic exercise, kinetic activities, functional activities
- Interferential electrical stimulation
- High-volt EMS/muscle re-education
- Myofascial release techniques (MFR)
- Soft tissue/joint mobilization (cervical, lumbar, and/or extremities)
- Whirlpool
- Traction (cervical and lumbar)
- Moist heat/ice/cold pack
- Ultrasound
- Phonophoresis
- Gait training
- TENS setup and instruction
- Paraffin (hands)
- Splinting (hands and wrists)
- Bracing
  o Hand-molded L5-S1 rigid
  o Lumbar rigid
  o Lumbar neoprene
  o Industrial back support
  o Dynamic seating orthosis
  o All extremities (rigid or neoprene)
  o Cervical lumbar rolls
  o Lumbar support pillows/rolls

Note: Physical therapy protocols specific to all extremity joints are available.

Consultation Services

- Impairment ratings
- Physical medicine evaluation/consult
- Peer review
- Biofeedback
- Neuropsychological evaluations and counseling

Case Study

This case study describes a typical situation in which Physical Ergonomics provided physical therapy, a work hardening program, and a job site analysis in assisting in an employee's return to work.

A woman who worked as a machinist suffered a herniated disc in her lumbar spine (lower back). Despite extensive medical treatment, physical therapy, and surgery, she continued to suffer chronic pain. Physical Ergonomics conducted a functional capacity evaluation and then designed a physical therapy program. The program included flexibility, aerobic, and strengthening exercises and postural stabilization exercises, which teach a patient with a back injury to utilize the trunk muscles to stabilize the spine in order to reduce stress to the injured intervertebral discs and ligaments. The woman made excellent progress and showed physical improvement.

The patient then began a work hardening program. This program moved from the exercise routine to include individual and group counseling, body mechanics techniques, and finally work simulation activities which progressed from two hours per day to eight hours per day over a four- to six-week period.

Upon completing the program, a final functional capacity evaluation was conducted. This evaluation indicated that the patient's abilities were consistent with the activities she indicated were necessary to perform her job. Her employer wanted her to return to work but was concerned about the possibility of reinjury. Physical Ergonomics was asked to conduct a job site analysis to provide an objective, unbiased assessment of what the job tasks required physically and, based on this information, to determine if the patient was ready to return to work.

The job site analysis covered the essential job tasks and constraints and provided a detailed assessment of the requirements of the job. The assessment included recommendations for reasonable accommodations (i.e., a stool with lumbar support at the workstation, an industrial lumbar support belt, and allowance for occasional one-minute stretching and bending breaks to alleviate discomfort) and an evaluation which indicated that the job site analysis and the functional capacity evaluation were compatible and that the patient could, therefore, return to work.

Physio-Control Corporation

35

Physio-Control Corporation is a world leader in the manufacture, sale, and service of defibrillator/monitors and pacemakers. The company was founded in 1955 by renowned cardiovascular surgeon Dr. K. William Edmark, who was determined to reduce the number of sudden deaths related to cardiac surgery. His research in treating the chaotic, abnormal hearth rhythm of ventricular fibrillation with a direct current electric shock led to the development of the first commercial direct current defibrillator. This product soon became a prototype for medical instrumentation used worldwide by hospitals and emergency medical services. A defibrillator delivers an electrical shock to synchronize the heart's random electrical activity so that the heart's natural pacemaker can regain control. Delivery of an electrical shock may or may not successfully resuscitate the patient. Without defibrillation, however, ventricular fibrillation results in death.

In 1968, Physio-Control developed the LIFEPAK® 33 defibrillator/monitor, a battery-powered unit which revolutionized the defibrillator marketplace forever. It gave healthcare providers flexibility of use in and outside of the hospital setting and became the unquestioned standard for emergency paramedic teams nationwide. Its flexibility both in and outside of the hospital setting led to the development of a long line of LIFEPAK defibrillator/monitors.

Since the early 1980s, the company's products have expanded defibrillation capabilities for emergency technicians and first responders delivering lifesaving measures to patients in the field. Today, a trained fire fighter, for example, can use an automatic advisory defibrillator to administer lifesaving shock without having to wait for a paramedic to arrive. Patient monitoring and non-invasive cardiac pacing products have also been developed and refined.

Physio-Control has sales and service offices throughout the world. Listed in the past two editions of *The 100 Best Companies to Work for in America*, the company is known for its innovative work environment. It employs about 1000 people, known as "team members," who enjoy a continuing education system, financial aid for adoption, and a high-tech facility nestled in a rural setting.

A Positive Corporate Culture Toward Diversity

In 1983, Physio-Control embarked on an innovative path toward employing persons with developmental disabilities with a concept and program called supported employment. The key to the successful introduction of this innovative concept was the company's positive cultural orientation toward diversity and the company's employees, who are referred to as team members. A strong team orientation is reflected in the company's belief in each individual's personal integrity and in its support in enabling its people to achieve their individual potential.

Physio-Control's belief in the importance of a diverse work force is reflected in the following statement: "Physio-Control embraced the supported employment program motivated by a sense of civic duty, a belief in the value of diversity, and a desire to help the individual, but there was always an expectation the program would be self-supporting. We realized all these benefits and more. The effort not only swelled our appreciation for others' contributions but also built on each Team Member's sense of team and pride in Physio-Control."

An Innovative Supported Employment Pilot Work Program for Persons with Developmental Disabilities

In 1983, Physio-Control implemented one of the first supported employment programs in the state of Washington as well as the United States. Today, thousands of companies of all sizes have discovered the benefits of recruiting and retaining highly productive and capable employees with disabilities. Beyond the benefits to the participating companies, local communities gain productive, tax-paying citizens.

A representative of Trillium Employment Services, a non-profit employment service, contacted the human resources department at Physio-Control in 1983 to suggest that the company consider participating in a pilot program to put persons with developmental disabilities to work. As the result of a successful research project at the University of Oregon which showed that persons with developmental disabilities could perform complex electronics assembly work, a special state grant was made available to fund the pilot effort.

Before agreeing to participate in the pilot project, Physio-Control managers met with the Trillium representative several times to discuss their concerns and to get a clear picture of what the project would involve. Concerns included how to handle absenteeism, the types of disabilities represented, medical insurance, liabilities, training, and special workstation needs. Once Physio-Control agreed to participate in the pilot project, Trillium took care of outside agency funding and finding appropriate candidates. Initially, two candidates were identified. Their work was analyzed, and special training was provided. In addition, Trillium trained company team members in providing positive support to persons with disabilities. This training was extremely important to the success of the pilot program and to ongoing efforts. By 1986, the company had transcended the pilot program and was committed to continuing to employ persons with Down's syndrome and other developmental disabilities.

The company's innovative efforts were so successful that Physio-Control gained widespread recognition for its work. In March 1986, a company representative was asked to testify before a subcommittee of the U.S. Senate Committee on Labor and Human Resources. Following the presentation by Dave Jay, the company's representative, Senator Lowell Weicker, Jr., chairman of the subcommittee, asked Mr. Jay to respond to the following questions:

1. Do you really think that other employers can do what you have done?

2. What is the extent of involvement between disabled employees and non-disabled employees in your company?

3. Have there been any problems?

Mr. Jay's response clearly indicates that Physio-Control's positive results can be replicated by other organizations, and it outlines the key attributes that led to success. Mr. Jay also outlined potential problems and how to address them.

Since Mr. Jay's presentation to the subcommittee, Physio-Control has found that it can effectively place newly hired disabled team members directly into the mainstream of employees without first placing them in an enclave.

Supported Employment Objectives and Purpose

Supported employment was introduced in the 1980s as a way to promote this largely untapped labor force. Companies initially viewed supported employment as a way to give something back to the community. Participating companies discovered, however, that the benefits of supported employment go far beyond that initial commitment to the community.

Supported employment consultants help companies analyze and restructure work in order to maximize the performance of all employees. In almost every job situation, there are tasks that do not match the specific talents of the worker. These same duties could be challenging and rewarding for other individuals who have rarely been able to participate as productive members of the workplace.

Founded on solid human resource principles, supported employment capitalizes on a broad array of skills and interests. It emphasizes improved listening, team building, and positive reinforcement. Co-workers improve their communication and interpersonal skills, which enhances their ability to work more effectively with a greater variety of people and situations. Supported employment consultants offer ongoing technical assistance and prepare managers for expanded leadership and training roles as a natural extension of the support process. The bottom line is a more effective work force.

Benefits to the workplace are mirrored by the personal benefits to people with disabilities. With the assistance of local supported employment professionals, thousands of companies have been able to offer opportunities to people who otherwise may have never had the chance to work.

The results are dynamic. The new employees gain the full benefits of earning a paycheck, along with independence and the ability to support themselves. They acquire skills, make friends, and broaden their lives. Most importantly, they gain self-respect. The company gains valuable employees and the community gains productive, tax-paying citizens.

A valuable benefit of supported employment is the positive change it creates in the workplace, especially for co-workers. Since supported employment uses everyone's strengths to the fullest, co-workers have the opportunity to participate in different and challenging tasks. Jobs take on added meaning and employees find a new interest in their work.

Co-workers and supervisors find that working side by side with people who communicate, learn, or perform in a different way adds challenge and variety to their jobs. They feel more committed and responsible through reaching out and helping others. As co-workers appreciate and value differences, they flourish. In turn, so do productivity and job satisfaction.

In addition to Physio-Control, other companies in the Puget Sound area that have embraced the supported employment concept include the Boeing Company, First Interstate Bank, and Caravali Coffees. As of September 1993, 1177 adults in Washington State with developmental disabilities were looking for individual supported employment positions and 1637 individuals were employed.*

Task Design, Task Analysis, and Job Analysis

Task design and task analysis are activities performed by supported employment consultants and by co-workers in order to optimize the training, productivity, and quality performance of the disabled employee.

Task design is a process whereby the various parts of a job are identified in

* Source: Lyn McIntyre, Washington Initiative for Supported Employment (WISE).

order to determine (1) the range of skills involved in the task, (2) the sequence of steps within the task, (3) the efficiency of the task as structured, and (4) the supervisor's tolerance for restructuring the task if necessary.

Task analysis is a process whereby a task is broken down into specific steps and the related cues, responses, and criteria for each step are listed.

Job analysis is performed in order to determine the information needed by the consultant and co-workers supporting a disabled employee. In this phase, the consultant is preparing to serve as a job coach and provide direct support to the disabled employee until he or she can function independently.

Supported Employment and Productivity

Physio-Control's results in employing the disabled match the experiences of many other companies. Whether measuring partial or total productivity, disabled employees are at least as productive as non-disabled employees performing the same work.

The first person who entered Physio-Control's supported employment program in 1983 had an initial productivity level of 40%. This increased to 70% after the individual became fully trained and oriented to the job. All subsequent disabled team members achieved a productivity level of over 90%. The absentee rate of the disabled group was actually lower than that of non-disabled team members.

Other Disabled Team Members

Initial efforts to employ the differently abled at Physio-Control focused on the developmentally disabled. After completing the learning curve with that group, the company hired a number of individuals with other disabilities. The following are examples of Physio-Control's differently abled team members:

- Two quadriplegic team members work in the information technology department as computer programmers. Although they are permitted to start work later in the morning, they still work a full eight-hour day five days a week. The only other accommodations provided are mouth wands to operate their computers and telephone answering machines.

- An amputee who uses a wheelchair works in the customer support unit, servicing field personnel. No special accommodations are required.

- A deaf mute works in the manufacturing area and has been with the company for 15 years. No special accommodations are needed.

- A blind team member who has been with the company for 17 years works on the assembly line building recorders composed of 17 parts. He uses a voice-activated calculator to manage his inventory for the assemblies he builds. To enable him to do his work, the company labels his parts in braille, purchased a special computer program to give him access to all inventory data, and purchased special tooling (talking caliper and talking micrometer).

Trillium Employment Services

Trillium is a small, cost-effective, non-profit organization that leverages its limited resources by training clients' in-house staff in how to work with and best utilize the abilities of employees with disabilities. Trillium has been extraordinarily successful in helping companies implement employment programs for persons with developmental disabilities.

In 1991, Trillium won first place in the National Search for Excellence in Rehabilitation competition in the category of community-based work services. At a special luncheon in Washington, D.C., Senator Bob Dole and Jeremiah Milbank, Jr. presented the award to Trillium on behalf of the Dole and J.M. foundations.

Trillium's goal is to build competence within organizations to manage a diverse work force that includes individuals with developmental disabilities. Services to businesses include:

- Assisting management in identifying appropriate jobs to be filled by persons with disabilities

- Providing detailed departmental and job analyses

- Making recommendations on job structuring and job accommodation

- Assisting with recruitment and selection of job candidates

- Training lead personnel and co-workers to support employees with disabilities

- Facilitating on-the-job training for employees with disabilities

- Assisting with job design to ensure quality and optimum productivity

- Developing strategies for performance improvement

Trillium is currently working with many innovative employers, both large and small, including The Boeing Company, Physio-Control, Virginia Mason Medical Center, the Government of King County, and Tower Records.

Professional Courtesy Corporation and Medical Software Development Corporation

36

Robert F. McIntyre, M.D.

The question you should be able to answer after reading this chapter is whether it was Karl Marx or Groucho Marx who said, "Economics is a bitch when you become disabled!" This chapter also provides an 11-year overview of the mission, corporate history and philosophy, achievements, market opportunities, and future goals of Professional Courtesy Corporation (PCC) and Medical Software Development Corporation (MSDC). Both corporations are totally committed to employing or helping disabled physicians and other healthcare colleagues find meaningful employment after a disability. Due to their unique knowledge and perspective, disabled healthcare professionals have many significant and creative contributions to offer society, industry, and especially themselves. PCC and MSDC's corporate vision and mission are to make the path leading to personal and economic dignity an easier objective for the disabled healthcare professional to achieve.

Mission Statement

PCC and its sister firm, MSDC, share a common vision and mission, which are to "assist the disabled physician and other healthcare professionals to regain personal and financial dignity after disability." Disabled physicians and other healthcare professionals are an untapped human resource. When gainfully employed, they can generate significant financial benefits for industry, society, and, most importantly, themselves.

Corporate History and Philosophy

Let's clear up one issue regarding the disabled physician. To quote Dr. Stanley F. Wainapel, "Largely over-looked has been the physician who, because of congenital disease, acquired illness, or trauma, is left with a physical disability such as paralysis, visual loss, or hearing loss."[1] This is in contrast to physicians who are called "impaired" due to mental illness, drug abuse, or alcoholism. Physician disability is not rare and can occur at any stage in one's career. It is estimated that there may be anywhere from 14,000 to 60,000 disabled physicians in the United States. Disabled physicians represent all specialty groups, geographies, medical schools, colleges, and academies. The economic loss to society is indeed profound, since it costs society over $100,000 to train a doctor.

In 1983, while practicing medicine, I personally experienced a disability (i.e., a close head injury) as the result of an auto accident. When I had to use my own occupational-specific non-cancellable disability insurance contract, I experienced firsthand the financial, rehabilitative, and structural inadequacies typical of these contracts. Occupation-specific disability contracts actually hinder the disabled insured from regaining financial/emotional dignity after a disability occurs and keep millions of dollars tied up unnecessarily in the disability reserve for insurance carriers. The bottom line is the increased premiums that policyholders pay for disability insurance coverage and inadequate rehabilitative benefits.

Becoming disabled is not like "winning the lottery" when one has to receive monthly disability benefits from an insurance carrier. Disability actually represents a multi-faceted catastrophe. The disabled are perceived as different mentally, physically, socially, financially, and legally. Without comprehensive assistance, the effects of a disability are devastating and the core foundations of a person's life are shaken. A medical or other professional career can be lost, a family permanently damaged, and the individual destroyed. To quote Charles Soule, president and CEO of Paul Revere Insurance Group and author of a brilliant work called *Disability Income Insurance—The Unique Risk*, "The adage that insurance is a business of delayed rewards and delayed penalties is indeed true in disability income."[2] In their report entitled *Non-Cancellable Disability Insurance—Decision Time 1993,* Conning and Company confirm that the disability insurance industry is now indeed paying the penalty for rehabilitative, financial, and structural inadequacies in their disability policies. According to the report, "The aggregate underwriting loss for the 32 companies studied amounted to 39% of premium in 1992..."[3]

In 1985, I was fortunate to meet the late Thomas McComb, Actuary, who agreed with my observations and assumptions regarding the disability industry.

In 1986, we developed the first universal income replacement policy in the nation to address the rehabilitative, financial, and structural inadequacies in disability policies.

It is also noteworthy that it was Tom McComb who developed the first universal life product in the United States. According to Mr. McComb, it took 15 years for major carriers to copy the market lead of small life companies that brought out universal life products. It has taken PCC 11 years and $500,000 to develop this much needed program for the marketplace. In many ways, the insurance industry is like a dinosaur when it comes to accepting and being able to make progressive economic changes that do not have to increase rates for policyholders.

But change the disability market must! In their 1993 report, Conning and Company state, "We believe that the financial record of this line of business suggests that the non-cancellable product is financially *non-viable.* We believe that companies should strongly consider making fundamental change by moving to guaranteed renewable contracts,"[3] such as PCC had developed back in 1986. Aetna, Equitable, General American, The Hartford, John Hancock, Monarch Life, National Life of Vermont, New England Mutual, Provident Mutual, UNUM, Paul Revere, and others have either withdrawn from the non-cancellable occupation-specific line of business or reduced their exposure significantly.

Contractual changes are probably the easiest problem to fix in the insurance industry. The concept of economic rehabilitation of disabled insureds is another matter, however, as are the resources, philosophy, and in-place networks to implement the concept.

To again quote Charles Soule, "Professional risks, especially dentists and physicians, are causing higher claim costs than assumed in the rates. As individual risks they have lost some of the unique motivational characteristics of the past; that is, they were independent workers, self employed, with high incomes, stature, and scarcity. An oversupply of these professionals earning less income, employed by group practices, under more government regulation have caused changes in behavior at time of claim. How serious a deterioration occurs in professional morbidity will take several years to develop and determine."[2]

While I respect Charles Soule's opinion, I believe the problem squarely rests in:

1. The financial and rehabilitative inflexibility of non-cancellable occupation-specific contracts, which the insurance industry sold to the healthcare profession

2. The lack of investment money and resources that insurers should have long ago committed to develop rehabilitative program expertise and networks for the economic rehabilitation of its disabled insureds

3. The cyclic nature of the disability insurance business itself (i.e., profits will be less than expected during economic recessions and greater than expected during periods of economic growth and high employment)

For example, it takes 9 to 14 years of training to become a physician. Even in the current medical environment, most physicians retain the work ethic developed during their medical training. The key problem actually is overspecialization. When a disability occurs, the physician asks himself or herself: "What can I do now to retain economic dignity and utilize my knowledge base, after all this time I've spent in my specialty? I just don't have any other marketable skills."

In 1992, PCC published *Sample Economic Rehabilitation Options for Disabled Physicians and Dentists.* It is an excellent beginning on how to assist the disabled physician with either practice modification or career transition. Additional employment options have since been developed, through MSDC, with Fortune 100 pharmaceutical firms, for-profit rehabilitation corporations, and other medical software companies.

Corporate Achievements

In 1986, PCC, along with Tom McComb, developed the first equity-building income replacement policy in the nation to feature superior rehabilitation for policyholders. Income replacement, as the name implies, looks at the amount of income lost, instead of the nature and extent of the disability, to calculate how much it will pay. Further, the equity side fund buildup provides a necessary buffer for the unforeseen economic hardships that occur when a disability strikes a professional. Tom McComb designed the side fund so that an "insurable interest" was created to assist disabled policyholders in regaining "long-term" economic rehabilitation. Significant tax-free or tax-deferred benefits can thus be transferred to disabled policyholders when they are finally employed in order to help them financially "catch up" from the "true economic loss" of a disability. In 1987, PCC and its products were endorsed by the American Society of Handicapped Physicians.

In 1992, PCC was also instrumental in helping to found the American Medical Association's Rehabilitation and Relief Fund for disabled and HIV-infected physicians. The American Dental Association has had a relief fund for their disabled dentists since 1910. Organized medicine has only recently recognized a similar need for physicians.

In 1994, MSDC successfully tested the first "no-see physician" program utilizing disabled physicians for a Fortune 100 pharmaceutical firm. A "no-see physician" or "difficult-to-see physician":

1. Does not see pharmaceutical sales representatives

2. Represents a $6 to $8 billion market access problem for each pharmaceutical firm

3. Is valued at $100,000+ per account to the pharmaceutical company

4. Now represents between 15 to 30% of all practicing physicians

The "no-see physician" program is discussed further in the next section.

It is interesting to note that Conning and Company's 1993 report strongly recommends an "aggressive managed care" concept regarding rehabilitation. To quote, "Some insurance companies have started to apply managed care techniques to mental/nervous and other potentially long-term types of claims. These programs emphasize rehabilitation and seem to be yielding some positive results in reducing claim continuance. We feel that further implementation of these techniques would be likely to reduce claim costs."[3] MSDC's "no-see physician" program is far more sophisticated than "aggressive managed care" of rehabilitation as recommended by Conning. MSDC's program has achieved the unique distinction of having the capability to:

1. Employ disabled physicians in large numbers

2. Employ disabled physicians on a cost-effective basis

3. Utilize a disabled physician's knowledge base and medical contacts to financially benefit society, industry, and the disabled physician

This is in contrast to the "hodgepodge" approach to rehabilitation that most rehabilitation managers implement for their respective companies. This approach demonstrates no economy of scale or profitability for the medical industry.

MSDC is currently working with Management Recruiters of Dallas to place disabled physicians in other related healthcare positions. Management Recruiters is the nation's largest executive search firm, with over 570 offices nationally with 2500 search specialists.

Corporate Market Opportunities for Disabled Physicians: Case Example

Problem

According to pharmaceutical industry statistics, the cost to bring a new drug to market is approximately $250 to $300 million. "It is estimated that 6 to 8 billion dollars in sales, or an average of $100,000+ per no-see account, is lost by the failure of pharmaceutical sales representatives (PSRs) to call on or see selective physicians for their respective pharmaceutical companies."[4] "No-see/selective-see physicians" currently make up between 15 to 30% of the 600,000+ physician population and are increasing in number.

The problem is compounded when coupled with the high turnover rate of PSRs, which results in the loss of physician rapport/identification with the pharmaceutical company in managed and non-managed care settings. Recent pharmaceutical company downsizing and mergers have exacerbated the problem. Physicians in managed care settings also face time management and economic issues when seeing PSRs. Therefore, even if a drug is on formulary, pull through of sales is not ensured due to the lack of detailing time allotted to PSRs.

Pilot Test Results

90	"No-see physicians'" names were selected by a major pharmaceutical company from the northeast region
45	"No-see physicians" met face to face with the pharmaceutical company's PSRs after the disabled physician set an appointment
50%	Telemarketing success rate was experienced with the physician-to-physician approach
68	Additional physicians who were not on the original list became accessible
113	Is the upper range of possible new accounts that resulted from the pilot project

Bottom Line

Projected financial results from the pilot project may range from 4.5 million to 11 million at $100,000 per "no-see" account within a 12- to 24-month time frame. These projections are based on feedback from the regional pharmaceutical sales manager. The manager also noted that numerous PSRs reported anecdotal meetings with "no-see physicians" that lasted 60 to 90 minutes as compared to the usual 3 to 5 minutes.

Why the "No-See" Test Pilot Project Was Successful for the Pharmaceutical Company

A disabled physician can reach/access "no-see physicians" because:

1. He or she is a peer.

2. The physician's office staff is trained to respect calls from physician colleagues and allow access without hesitation.

3. The disabled physician is economically motivated. American Medical Association statistics show a 40 to 50% drop in earning power for those disabled physicians who are able to continue practicing medicine.

4. Disabled physicians are ultimately effective, beyond reproach, and
   - Establish credibility through depth of knowledge and shared experience
   - Build and maintain relationships through shared experiences and goals
   - Exercise influence based on credibility and relationships

5. Disabled physicians are not used by competitors.

Additional Opportunities Utilizing Disabled Physicians

Future potential areas of interest to a pharmaceutical company in utilizing disabled physicians include, but are not limited to, the following:

- Market research
- Clinical consultations/investigations
- Formulary committee influence
- Public education
- Direct detailing
- Payor side consultations
- HMO, PPO, and IPA consultations
- Consultant panels
- Medical symposia
- Major medical meetings
- Regulatory affairs
- Disease management

Future Corporate Goals

PCC is in the final phase of formalizing an agreement to market its equity-building income replacement policy with an A+-rated carrier in 1995. PCC will also establish and manage, in the near future, a portion of policyholders' side fund buildup. The entity will be called The Health Professional Venture Capital

Fund, or simply The Fund, and will create an "insurable interest" in the long-term economic rehabilitation of the disabled insured. Simply put, The Fund will allow the policyholder to share in the risk and major financial benefits of developing long-term economic rehabilitation options. The logic behind The Fund is as follows:

1. In a 1994 article in *National Underwriter,* Charles Soule, president and CEO of the Paul Revere Insurance Group, said, "Moving to the future, I expect to see a product design that's less capital intensive by allowing the policyholder to share more of the risk with the Company."[5] As stated earlier, it is not cheap to develop cutting edge rehabilitation programs that allow a disabled policyholder to hopefully become financially whole again after disability. It has been an 11-year and $500,000 effort for PCC.

2. Insurance is one of the most important legal ways to create wealth. If there were ever a time, reason, or need for creativity, it is definitely the period of time when one is trying to recover from the economic effects of a disability. The disabled policyholder suffers an "economic gap in earnings" when disability strikes him or her. The longer the disability persists, the larger the gap grows for the individual, and as it now stands, it is unlikely that lost earnings will ever be recaptured over time. As a case in point, the disabled cannot make contributions to fund a pension plan for retirement or even save for a child's education. Since disability income replaces 40 to 80% of income after the elimination period, it becomes clear how the "gap in earnings" grows. There are, of course, the potentially high costs of medical expenses, career retraining, and just daily living.

3. Much has been written in the insurance literature about how formerly highly motivated individuals lose their motivation to return to work once they start collecting on a disability claim. Many individuals on disability claim are depressed that they cannot do their life's work and feel they have failed their families and themselves. Many report that it is difficult to "pull out" of their depressed state and that their insurance carriers add to the problem rather than help. This situation is readily understandable. How can insurance carriers expect the disabled policyholder to "go off claim" when carriers have not developed or invested in (equity-building income replacement) policies and rehabilitation networks? By taking PCC's approach, the disabled policyholder would be allowed to first "catch up" economically from a disability and then re-establish his or her earnings before "going off claim."

   Also, the truth of the matter is that it is the harsh economics of disability that kills most people's motivation. For example, if the disabled worker is able to return to his or her former employment, government taxation of earnings on an annual basis adds even greater economic stress to an already stressed individual and family. Consider the impact of taxation on an individual who is attempting economic rehabilitation because she or he has to find a new career or business opportunity. It is totally inappropriate for the government to harshly tax a disabled worker/entrepreneur before he or she has had a chance to "catch up" from the economics of disability. To quote an old adage, it is a "penny-wise and pound-foolish" governmental policy.

4. It is vital that the true economic cost and impact of a disability be quantified in order to calculate "how much money" it will take to actually "catch-up" the policyholder after maximum medical improvement or recovery from a disability, assuming, of course, that a state of overinsurance does not exist.

5. The policyholder is sharing in the risk of developing long-term economic rehabilitation options, should he or she become disabled and need them. The policyholder has an "insurable interest" in his or her economic rehabilitation by agreement. Because of an "insurable interest" in rehabilitation, significant tax-free or tax-deferred benefits can be transferred to the disabled insured when employed by The Fund. Employment through The Fund is optional. If a policyholder never becomes disabled, then side fund buildup will supplement his or her pension plan.

6. People would not be buying an equity-building income replacement plan as an investment medium, but rather would be buying it for protection and long-term economic rehabilitation. Protection of earned income and the ability to regain earning power after a disability is what the program is all about. "If the policyholder desires to withdraw accumulated side funds *prior* to a disability, then under the well established tax doctrine of constructive receipt, the policyholder would have to give up something of substantial value, i.e., his/her equity building income replacement policy."[6]

7. The insurance carrier will experience a significant *decrease* in the disability reserve through the successful economic rehabilitation activity of The Fund. For example, in the example of the "no-see physician" program, a disabled physician can add between $25 to $50 million to the top line of a major pharmaceutical corporation per year. Creative compensation packages with industry can be negotiated for the disabled policyholder through The Fund, if so desired. Mature and medical

growth companies need the knowledge, contacts, and services of a disabled physician candidate pool. The present-day value of a disabled physician's network of medical contacts helps to *insure* successful economic rehabilitation.

Bibliography

1. Wainapel, Stanley F. "The Physically Disabled Physician," *JAMA*. June 5, 1987, Volume 257.

2. Soule, Charles E. *Disability Income Insurance, The Unique Risk*. Business One Irwin, Burr Ridge, Illinois.

3. Conning and Company. *Non-Cancellable Disability Insurance—Decision Time 1993*. Conning and Company, 1993.

4. Lefkowitz, David. *The Myth of the No-See Physician*. Sales Management.

5. Cox, Brian. "Paul Revere Acts to Limit Exposure in Doctors Mkt," *National Underwriter*. November 1994.

6. McComb, Thomas M. "The Great Hog Slaughter," *Best's Review*. February 1988.

Managing AIDS in the Workplace: An Overview for Managers

37

Based on recent estimates from the Centers for Disease Control, more than two-thirds of companies that employ 2500 persons and nearly one in ten companies with fewer than 500 employees have already had an employee with HIV (human immunodeficiency virus, the virus that causes AIDS) infection or AIDS.

AIDS has generated more individual lawsuits across a broad range of health issues than any single disease in American legal history. We can anticipate that the rate of individual lawsuits will accelerate as the number of cases of HIV infection and AIDS accelerates. The magnitude of the issue is daunting. Already, over 100,000 people in the United States have died from AIDS—more than were killed in the Vietnam and Korean wars combined. Federal health officials estimate that over one million persons in America are infected with HIV.

For those companies that have not prepared their managers and employees, the AIDS issue can result in significant legal, healthcare, and productivity costs. All of the literature on this subject and the experience of those companies that have taken a proactive approach in dealing with AIDS point to the need for developing business policies and educational programs for the work force. Strategies, policies, communication programs, and resources to assist management in developing an AIDS program specific to an individual organizational culture are presented in this chapter.

Federal Law

Under the Americans with Disabilities Act (ADA), an employer may not refuse to hire a qualified applicant because the applicant has HIV infection or AIDS. Unless it can be demonstrated that it would impose an "undue hardship" on the business, the ADA requires an employer to make reasonable accommodations

347

that enable an infected employee to perform essential job functions. Research indicates that the vast majority of accommodations made in HIV/AIDS-related cases involve very little expense and that "undue hardship" is very difficult to demonstrate.

An employer must ensure that an HIV/AIDS-infected person is not subject to discrimination in hiring, job assignments, performance appraisals, termination, and other terms and conditions of employment because of his or her condition.

What Management Can Do

The following article presents a concise and effective approach for companies that have no policy or strategy for dealing with AIDS in their organizations. It is reprinted with permission from the Sexuality Information and Education Council of the United States (SIECUS).

AIDS in the Workplace

Laurel A. Pickering, M.P.H., C.H.E.S.
Associate Director, New York Business Group on Health

In a variety of ways, the American workplace is vulnerable to the consequences of the HIV/AIDS epidemic. Persons aged 15–44, who are at greatest risk for contracting HIV, make up over 50 percent of the U.S. work force, and they spend about one-third of each workday in the workplace. Also, the most sexually active segment of the U.S. population is in the work force. Research by the New York Business Group on Health shows that employers are the most credible source of health information to employees. Nevertheless, well into the epidemic's second decade, HIV/AIDS in the workplace—and ignorance about it—still fosters discrimination, anxiety, and discomfort among employers and employees. Many companies have responded to the epidemic by creating HIV/AIDS policies, training managers and supervisors, or developing educational programs for their employees. Many more, however, have upheld the prevailing view among employers that HIV/AIDS does not affect them.

Next Steps for Companies That Have Not Yet Addressed HIV/AIDS

Companies that have not yet addressed HIV/AIDS should develop an AIDS policy, offer training for managers and supervisors, and provide employees with information to dispel fears and ignorance.

HIV/AIDS Policy—An HIV/AIDS policy outlines a course of action for an organization to follow when an employee has HIV/AIDS. Such a policy should emphasize flexibility and should cover the following:

- *Time Off*—Employees with HIV/AIDS require time off for physicians' visits and illnesses. These needs many vary, and the employer is not expected to pay for all this time. Flexible sick leave and flexible scheduling are important.

- *Job Accommodation*—The 1990 Americans with Disabilities Act includes HIV infection in the definition of disability and requires employers to make "reasonable accommodations." Employers should review each case for job adjustments or reassignments that may help the employee function in the job. This may include permitting the employee to work at home, providing more breaks, arranging job sharing, using labor-saving equipment, or transferring the employee to a position that is less labor-intensive.

- *Confidentiality*—Just as with other medical information, the diagnosis of HIV infection must be kept confidential by the employer. The HIV/AIDS policy should contain a statement regarding confidentiality.

- *Provisions for Caregivers*—Employees who are caregivers of people with AIDS require similar compassion and flexible arrangements.

- *Medical Overview*—Employers may also want to include basic information about how HIV is—and is not—transmitted.

Management Training—Managers and supervisors must be trained to deal effectively with employees who are HIV-infected. It is essential that managers and supervisors be prepared to execute the company's policy and address the effects of an infected worker's presence on productivity and morale of coworkers. Managers who have experienced HIV/AIDS in the workplace have said that it demands much more than what is usually taught in a seminar or training program. When faced with "real people doing real work in real organizations," managers are often unprepared. As a result, businesses often call upon organizations such as the Gay Men's Health Crisis in New York City to provide one-on-one counseling for managers who are having problems dealing with an infected employee and coworkers. Although this approach may not be as cost-effective as training managers in a group, it is often a necessary tool.

Educational Efforts—Various educational strategies may be used in the workplace, ranging from distributing informational materials to providing a comprehensive program. Organizations can disseminate information in newsletters, on bulletin boards, in pay envelopes, or in libraries. Comprehensive programs can include a video presentation, a discussion led by a health expert, and backup counseling and referral. Companies often engage an outside organization (such as the American Red Cross) to conduct an on-site program. These programs can be one-time or ongoing.

Next Steps for Companies That Have Already Addressed HIV/AIDS

If an organization has already addressed AIDS in the workplace, through either policy development, manager and supervisor training, or education, it must continue to do so. This is important for two main reasons. First, organizations are constantly hiring new employees, whose levels of knowledge regarding HIV/AIDS may vary. Second, since the AIDS epidemic is many years old, the media have covered it extensively, and AIDS and other health organizations have aggressively distributed the HIV prevention message, many people assume that by now, knowledge of the facts about AIDS is universal. Yet, this is not true, and employers must be careful not to make this assumption. Employees who do not know the basic facts about AIDS may be afraid to express concern, show their ignorance, or ask questions. For those who do have an understanding of AIDS, their fears may override knowledge. Therefore, the employer must continually provide a venue that is safe and encouraging for employees to have their concerns addressed and questions answered.

Activities and Resources

Community HIV/AIDS organizations can help meet the need of employers in their area by providing HIV/AIDS education programs for employees, managers, and supervisors. By contacting area employers, local HIV/AIDS organizations can determine whether the issue has been addressed and offer assistance in providing education. Meanwhile, businesses should call their local HIV/AIDS organizations to get more information on how to educate their employees in order to prevent any disruption in the workplace and facilitate the dissemination of this important public health message.

The U.S. Centers for Disease Control and Prevention (CDC) has developed an initiative known as Business Responds to AIDS (BRTA), whose goal is to encourage HIV/AIDS education in the workplace. One of the cornerstones of the program is a partnership between business and labor, as represented by corporate executive officers and presidents of union and trade associations, respectively. An integral component of BRTA is a resource service housed at the National AIDS Clearinghouse. Experts at the resource service are available to provide materials, community referrals, and other technical assistance. Kits for labor leaders and for managers with information on developing workplace policies, implementing employee education programs, and additional resources are available through this service. The resource service has been shown to facilitate the implementation of HIV/AIDS education programs, by either improving their comprehensiveness or actually "getting them off the ground."

The National Leadership Coalition on AIDS (NLCOA), an alliance of nearly 200 major corporations, labor unions, and other organizations, provides leadership in guiding the workplace response to HIV/AIDS. NLCOA's conferences, publications, and resource center have been a source of information for many employers. One of the Coalition's recent publications focuses on an aspect of HIV/AIDS that employers are beginning to address: accommodation. Now that HIV/AIDS is covered under the Americans with Disabilities Act, employers need to look for ways to keep their infected employees working as long as possible.

Conclusion

The next steps in HIV/AIDS prevention education in the workplace are very much like the first steps. The many companies that have not yet addressed HIV/AIDS must take the first steps to introduce the issue to their employees. Companies that have dealt with this issue must continue to relay the HIV/AIDS prevention message. An infected employee can be very costly to an employer. These costs can be measurable, such as loss in productivity or increase in health insurance costs, or not so measurable, such as declining morale and increased fear and discomfort among employees. Most important, since there is no cure or preventive vaccine, education and the adoption of behaviors that reduce the likelihood of transmission are the best defense against HIV/AIDS. The workplace is an optimal setting for the communication of the HIV prevention message. Using it as such will benefit both employers and society as the fight to prevent the spread of HIV/AIDS continues.

Reasonable Accommodations for People with HIV/AIDS

Most business managers are by now aware that the ADA requires employers with more than 15 employees to provide "reasonable accommodations" for their employees with disabilities, including HIV infection and AIDS. What many do not know, however, is how to go about effectively shaping a workplace accommodation for an employee living with HIV.

Accommodating an employee with AIDS or HIV infection is a process of ongoing negotiation between employee and manager. Because the manifestations of HIV vary in different people, accommodation is not a one-time alteration of a job description or physical structure. As the manifestations of illness becomes more frequent, both the employee and managers are challenged to work together to determine alternative means of accomplishing work assignments.

Shifts and adjustments are inevitable. Business plans and schedules are more realistic and effective when they include backup strategies that anticipate the need for and application of resources—human, financial, and otherwise—as circumstances unexpectedly change.

The crucial moment is deciding when and how to get started in designing your "best effort" response to HIV disease. The most common—and costly— mistake is to defer that decision until an employee walks into your office and says, "I have AIDS. What are we going to do?"

What are the desired outcomes and expected benefits of responding to AIDS compassionately and fully? For HIV-infected employees, there is some relief and reassurance in simply knowing that one's employer and co-workers are well prepared to understand the disease and to be allies in responding to a grievous burden. For many, there is some reprieve from the loneliness and anxiety of trying to manage forbidding but no less real bottom-line questions.

For co-workers, there is greater confidence in their employer, knowing that managers are prepared to pursue a course of action in the best interest of all parties—the infected employee, affected co-workers, and management. That translates into increased employee morale and confidence in how co-workers might fare should they confront such a critical condition in their own lives.

For shop stewards and labor leaders, there is the knowledge and reassurance that AIDS need not become an issue for disagreement requiring arbitration. The disease can be an opportunity to work together to design favorable outcomes.

For management and executives, there are opportunities to provide leadership within the company and to set constructive examples in the community. Setting goals that reflect and embody the highest standards of the company helps to inspire greater commitment among staff and generate awareness among other businesses of the positive role the business sector can and should play in this epidemic.

For everyone affected, there is inevitable grief and loss. Unfortunately, an infected person can only stave off death for so long. But for friends, co-workers, and family, there is the reward of knowing that everybody involved tried to do their best to work together to resolve one of the most painful and costly health conditions confronting humankind.

The National Leadership Coalition on Aids conducted a study of companies that had formal policies and accommodation strategies for dealing with employees who have HIV/AIDS. Participants in the study included Bank of America; Chubb Group of Insurance Companies; Digital Equipment Corporation; Foote, Cone & Belding Guiness Import Company; Hemophilia Health Services; Levi

Strauss & Co.; Loblaw Companies Limited; *The New York Times*; and Polaroid Corporation. The following is a sample list of accommodations generated from the study:*

Job modifications
* Becoming a part-time employee while training another employee to do the job (job sharing)
* Changing from a commission basis to a salary for compensation
* Changing to a less stressful job
* Providing a flexible work schedule
* According time off for health-related appointments
* Working at home
* Converting from an employee to a consultant
* Providing greater structure for the job

Individual support
* Assuring the employee that she or he will not lose her or his job
* Assuring the employee that she or he will not lose or have reduced health insurance coverage
* Respecting the employee's wishes about confidentiality
* Assisting the employee and/or family with benefit claim forms

Utilization of benefits
* Disability income when working part time
* Short-term disability leave
* Long-term disability leave
* An advance on a life insurance policy
* Prompt notification of continuing health benefits when discontinuing employment

The work environment
* Providing counseling and related services through an employee assistance program
* Assigning an individual in human resources to be the HIV/AIDS point person responsible for facilitating the reasonable accommodation negotiation and acting as a resource for both managers and employees
* Providing support groups for co-workers
* Developing, if appropriate, an "information sharing" system so that co-workers can be informed of an employee's condition when she or he is on sick leave and can develop visitation schedules

---

* Reprinted with permission from "Accommodating Employees with HIV Infection and Aids: Case Studies of Employer Assistance," The National Leadership Coalition on Aids.

- Providing, if appropriate, ongoing educational seminars and information
- Participation of corporate leaders in the response to HIV/AIDS
- Providing support groups for caregivers to persons with HIV/AIDS

The coalition's study also presented the following lessons managers learned about providing accommodations to people with HIV/AIDS:*

Advice to Managers from Employees with HIV/AIDS
- Listen to the employee.
- Don't lower your expectations of an employee because she or he tells you that she or he has HIV/AIDS.
- Negotiate reasonable accommodations with the employee; don't dictate.
- Don't treat people with HIV/AIDS differently just because they have HIV/AIDS.

Lessons Managers Learned About Providing Accommodations to People with HIV/AIDS
- Create an open and supportive atmosphere.
- Honor the employee's request for confidentiality.
- Set clear job performance expectations and a monitoring schedule.
- Hold employees accountable for their work.
- Use the resources and support structures available—both within the company and outside the company.
- Employees with HIV/AIDS may identify themselves through the employee assistance program where they confront their HIV status when seeking treatment for alcohol and/or drug abuse.
- An accommodation is an investment which pays off in increased effort and productivity by the employee.
- A positive response to an employee with HIV/AIDS increases the morale, productivity, and loyalty of other employees.

Business Policy for HIV/AIDS

Because the number of people living with HIV disease is increasing dramatically and across a broad social spectrum, managers in all functional areas can expect to have to deal with issues related to AIDS. Thousands of people in the United States continue to work effectively while being HIV infected. Infected individuals may, in fact, work for many years before their job performance suffers. Given proper corporate guidance on this issue, managers can have a positive

---

* Reprinted with permission from "Accommodating Employees with HIV Infection and Aids: Case Studies of Employer Assistance," The National Leadership Coalition on Aids.

impact on the productivity and quality of life of those who are infected as well as their families and co-workers. The purpose of this section is to provide management with typical policy statements that have been formulated by several leading organizations. The following policy statement was developed by Alamo Rent A Car, Inc. It is given to all managers and supervisors. The approach taken by Alamo in developing its policy statement is to include all life-threatening illnesses within the scope of the statement.

Alamo Rent A Car, Inc.

Subject: Life-Threatening Illnesses
Effective Date: July 1, 1989

Directive to Managers and Supervisors

Alamo recognizes that family members with life-threatening illnesses, including cancer, heart disease, acquired immune deficiency syndrome (AIDS), etc., may wish to continue to engage in as many of their normal pursuits as their condition allows, including work. As long as these family members are able to meet acceptable performance standards and the medical evidence indicates that their conditions are not a threat to themselves or others, you should be sensitive to their condition and ensure that they are treated consistently with other family members.

You should follow the guidelines outlined below when dealing with situations involving family members with life-threatening illnesses.

- Keep in mind that a family member's health condition is personal and confidential, and take precautions to protect information regarding a family member's health condition.

- Contact Family Wellness for guidance in handling family members with terminal illnesses or a specific life-threatening illness, or for guidance in managing a situation that involves a family member with a life-threatening illness.

- Contact Family Wellness if there is any concern about the possible contagious nature of a family member's illness. They will coordinate with Risk Management when necessary.

- Contact Family Wellness to determine if a statement should be obtained from the family member's attending physician that continued presence at work will pose no threat to the family member or co-workers. Alamo reserves the right to require an examination by a medical doctor selected by the company.

- If warranted, make reasonable accommodation for family members with life-threatening illnesses consistent with the business needs of the department or rental facility.

- Make a reasonable attempt to transfer family members with life-threatening illnesses who request a transfer and are experiencing undue emotional stress.

- Be sensitive and responsive to co-workers' concerns. Family member education can be arranged through Family Wellness.

- Be sensitive to the fact that continued employment for a family member with a life-threatening illness may sometimes be therapeutically important in the remission or recovery process, or may help to prolong that family member's life.

- Advise family members who are known to have a life-threatening illness that consultation on benefits, to assist them in effectively managing their situation, is available through Family Wellness.

- Encourage family members with a life-threatening illness to seek assistance from established community support groups. Information on these can be requested from Family Wellness.

The National Leadership Coalition on AIDS publishes a pamphlet entitled "Sample Policies," which includes both life-threatening and HIV/AIDS-specific approaches to policy statements. Companies that use a life-threatening approach in their policy statements include Bank of America, Cowles Media Company, DAKA International, Northwestern Mutual Life Insurance Company, and Syntex (U.S.A.) Inc. Policy statements from Bank of America and Northwestern Mutual Life Insurance Company are provided as examples.

Bank of America

Assisting Employees with Life-Threatening Illnesses

The company recognizes that employees with life-threatening illnesses—including but not limited to cancer, heart disease, and AIDS—may wish to continue to engage in as many of their normal pursuits as their condition allows, including work. As long as these employees are able to meet acceptable performance standards, and medical evidence indicates that their conditions are not a threat to themselves or others, managers should be sensitive to their conditions and ensure that they are treated consistently with other employees. At the same time, the company seeks to provide a safe work environment for all employees and customers. Therefore, precautions should be taken to ensure that an employee's condition does not present a health and/or safety threat to other employees or customers.

Consistent with this concern for employees with life-threatening illnesses, the company offers the following range of resources available through your Human Resources representative:

- Management and employee education and information on terminal illness and specific life-threatening illnesses.

- Referral to agencies and organizations that offer supportive services to employees and dependents directly or indirectly affected by life-threatening illnesses.

- Benefits consultation to assist employees in effectively managing health, leave, and other benefits.

Guidelines to Help You Deal with a Situation

When dealing with situations involving employees with life-threatening illnesses, managers should:

- Remember that an employee's health condition is personal, should be treated as confidential, and reasonable precautions should be taken to protect information regarding an employee's health condition.

- Contact your Human Resources representative if you believe that you or other employees need information about terminal illness, or a specific life-threatening illness, or if you need further guidance in managing a situation that involves an employee with a life-threatening illness.

- Contact your Human Resources representative if you have any concern about the possible contagious nature of an employee's illness.

- Contact your Human Resources representative to determine if a statement should be obtained from the employee's attending physician that continued presence at work will pose no threat to the employee, co-workers, or customers. The company reserves the right to require an examination by a medical doctor appointed by the company.

- If warranted, make reasonable accommodation, consistent with the business needs of the unit, for employees with life-threatening illnesses.

- Make a reasonable attempt upon request to transfer employees who have life-threatening illnesses and are experiencing undue emotional stress.

- Be sensitive and responsive to co-workers' concerns, and emphasize employee education available through your Human Resources representative.

- Give no special consideration beyond normal transfer requests to employees who feel threatened by a co-worker's life-threatening illness.

- Be sensitive to the fact that continued employment for an employee with a life-threatening illness may sometimes be therapeutically important in the remission or recovery process, or may help to prolong that employee's life.

- Encourage employees to seek assistance from established community support groups for medical treatment and counseling services. Information on these can be requested through a Human Resources representative or Corporate Health Program #3666.

Northwestern Mutual Life Insurance Company

Policy: Communicable Diseases and/or Life-Threatening Illnesses

Northwestern Mutual recognizes that employees with life-threatening illnesses, including but not limited to AIDS, may wish to continue to engage in as many of their normal pursuits as their condition allows, including work. As long as these employees are able to meet acceptable performance standards, and medical evidence indicates that their conditions are not a threat to themselves or others, managers should be sensitive to their conditions and needs and ensure that they are treated consistently with other employees.

At the same time, Northwestern Mutual is committed to all employees to provide a safe work environment. Every precaution will be taken to ensure that the health and/or safety of Northwestern Mutual employees and guests is not threatened.

The Employee Relations Division and Health Clinic of the Human Resources Department shall be resources for management and employee education, referral to agencies and organizations which offer supportive services for life-threatening illnesses, and benefit consultation to assist employees and their managers in effectively managing health, leave, and other benefits.

Procedure

Upon learning that an employee has contracted a communicable disease or a life-threatening illness, contact the Employee Relations Division or Health Clinic of the Human Resources Department. Further:

- Managers should remember that an employee's health condition is personal and confidential. Northwestern is always careful to keep medical information about its employees confidential and managers should also take reasonable precautions to protect information regarding an employee's health condition.

- Manager's should be sensitive to the fact that continued employment for an employee with a life-threatening illness may sometimes be therapeutically important in the remission or recovery process, or may help to prolong that employee's life. If able to work, provide the employee with usual work assignments. The Health Clinic will determine if a statement is needed from the employee's attending physician that continued presence at work will pose no threat to the employee or co-workers.

- If warranted, reasonable accommodation for employees with life-threatening illnesses, consistent with the business needs of the division, should be made. Reasonable attempts shall be made to transfer employees with life-threatening illnesses who request a transfer and are experiencing undue emotional stress.

- Managers should keep open and candid communication with the individual including forthright discussions on such matters as personal hygiene/hand washing.

- If the employee is unable to work, he/she will be eligible for disability leave on the same basis as for any other disability.

- To control medical and group Disability Income costs, hospice and home care will be encouraged.

- Employees should be encouraged to seek assistance from established community support groups for medical treatment and counseling services. Information on these can be requested through Employee Relations or the Health Clinic.

- Education and/or counseling (e.g., bereavement) will be provided as appropriate for co-workers.

Organizations with an HIV/AIDS-specific approach in developing their policy statements include AFL-CIO, Franklin County Children Services, Harbor Sweets, National Association of Manufacturers, the Principle Financial Group, RJR Nabisco, San Francisco AIDS Foundation, and Wells Fargo Bank. Policy statements developed at the Principal Financial Group and RJR Nabisco, Inc. are provided as examples

---

The Principal Financial Group

Subject: Handling AIDS Situations

Company Policy—This document explains the approach and procedure to be used when dealing with someone afflicted with Acquired Immune Deficiency Syndrome (AIDS). It summarizes guidelines published by the National Center for Disease Control about AIDS in the workplace. These guidelines emphasize the fact that AIDS is not transmitted through casual contact such as that which occurs in the workplace. Also, this procedure tries to incorporate the moral, psychological, and legal aspects of the topic.

Considerations—Below are some points to remember when dealing with someone who has AIDS.

1. As a manager, you have a moral obligation to respect the individual's need for confidentiality, and to treat the person with the same personal consideration as others who have severe health problems.

2. Psychological needs of affected individuals will vary. Obviously, they experience fear for their health and their life. They probably experience a loss of some social contacts and, if not properly handled, could perceive themselves as being outcasts and isolated from society. We want to help these individuals as much as possible by referring them to the proper resources in the community and by creating an assuring situation as their employer.

3. Legal considerations are intertwined with the others. The confidentiality issue can become a legal issue if not handled properly. The way in which the employee is treated from the work standpoint is a legal issue.

AIDS victims must be treated the same as others who contract major diseases or illnesses. Sometimes, employers tend to perceive that such persons are disabled when they really aren't.

If this is the case and they are forced out of the workplace (either by discharge or forced disability), there can be some serious legal implications for the employer. Such individuals are typically protected from these actions either through the Federal Rehabilitation Act of 1973 or through state statutes. In both legal structures, even the perception that a person is disabled can allow that individual protection against discrimination.

Procedure—Below is the procedure recommended if an employee tells you he or she has AIDS:

1. Put the person at ease by telling him or her you're glad he or she felt free to discuss it with you.

2. Assure the person his or her job isn't in jeopardy as long as the work can be done. If the person becomes unable to do the job, the company's sick leave and disability plan will take over.

3. Advise the person to see his or her general physician, if he or she hasn't done so already, since the physician can counsel the person further. Tell the person a doctor may advise him or her about who else should be told about the situation, based on the contact the person has had with others.

4. Counsel the employee that, unless the doctor advises otherwise, there is no need to inform fellow workers with whom he or she has had only casual contact.

5. Assure the person you will keep the information confidential. The only people you will tell are those who have a need to know. This includes Dr. Haessler, the medical director, and Don Keown, the Human Resources officer, both of whom the person may feel free to contact.

Questions?   It is hoped you won't need this information, but that it will be helpful if you do. It is important that all such situations are handled consistently. If you have any questions, or need help with such a situation, contact Human Resources.

RJR Nabisco Management Statement on AIDS

RJR Nabisco treats AIDS and HIV infection as disabilities in accordance with our policy on Equal Employment Opportunity (EEO) and the requirements of the Americans with Disabilities Act of 1990 and the Rehabilitation Act of 1973. In addition to the provisions of the company's EEO policy on non-discrimination and reasonable accommodation for disability, the following guidelines are intended to assist managers in maintaining a work environment that is responsive to the workplace issues created by AIDS and HIV infection and the concerns of employees who may request management assistance:

- RJR Nabisco recognizes that a supportive and caring response from managers and coworkers is an important factor in maintaining the quality of life for an employee with AIDS or HIV infection. Managers should be sensitive to the special needs of employees and assist them by demonstrating personal support, referring them to counseling services and arranging for benefits counseling as necessary. Studies show that the support of others in the workplace can be therapeutic for the employee with AIDS or HIV infection and may help to prolong the employee's life.

- AIDS does not present a risk to the health or safety of coworkers or customers. On the basis of current medical and scientific evidence, RJR Nabisco recognizes that AIDS is a life-threatening illness that is not transmitted through casual personal contact under normal working conditions.

- Coworkers will be expected to continue working relationships with any employee who has AIDS or HIV infection. Managers are encouraged to contact the Personnel Department for assistance in providing employees with general information and information about AIDS and HIV infection. Any employee who is unduly concerned about contracting AIDS may be further assisted through individual counseling.

- An employee's health condition is private and confidential. An employee with AIDS or HIV infection is under no obligation to disclose his or her condition to a manager or any other employee of RJR Nabisco. Managers are expected to take careful precautions to protect the confidentiality of information regarding any employee's health condition, including an employee with AIDS or HIV infection.

- An employee with AIDS or HIV infection is expected to meet the same performance requirements applicable to other employees, with reasonable accommodation if necessary. If an employee becomes disabled from performing the work involved, managers will make reasonable accommodation, as with any other employee with a disability, to enable the employee to meet established performance criteria. Reasonable accommodation may include, but is not limited to, flexible or part-time work schedules, leave of absence, work restructuring or job reassignment.

RJR Nabisco is following the progress of medical research on AIDS and HIV infection. If any significant developments occur, these guidelines will be modified accordingly. Any questions concerning AIDS related issues should be directed to Personnel and Administration.

Access
Technologies

38

The access technologies described in this chapter can play a significant role in enabling persons with disabilities to be employed in many different job functions that were previously unavailable to them. Several of the technologies listed enhance the productivity and quality of work being performed by employees with disabilities.

Dr. Gregg C. Vanderheiden, who works out of the Trace R&D Center at the University of Wisconsin, defines accessibility as follows:

> Accessibility refers to the ability of products and environments to be used by people. In this particular context, accessibility is used to refer to the ability of standard application software to be accessed and used by people with disabilities. Although the way people access the software may vary, a program is accessible to an individual if the individual is able to use it to carry out all of the same functions and to achieve the same results as individuals with similar skills and training who do not have a disability.

The flexibility of current personal computers has led to a proliferation of enhancements or add-ons which may be used to customize and streamline personal computer use. Examples of common add-ons are modem cards, mouse input devices, and memory-resident software such as desktop organizers, calculators, and notepads. Certain add-ons are of particular benefit to users with disabilities; these include speech synthesizers, speech recognition devices, and software for screen enlargement, screen review, and keystroke control, among other hardware and software items. For users with disabilities, the provision of appropriate add-ons improves access to information resources; in some cases, the add-ons enable an individual to independently complete tasks that previously could not be performed without assistance due to the disabling condition.

outSPOKEN for Windows

Berkeley Systems, developer of the original outSPOKEN for the Macintosh (1989), has announced the release of outSPOKEN for Windows. This state-of-the-art screen reader converts Microsoft Windows® graphics and text to a full speech and audio interface for blind, visually impaired, or learning disabled computer users. outSPOKEN for Windows is a powerful and flexible screen reader that is able to read all windows, menus, and dialog boxes. It can operate in any video mode or color scheme and is able to read any font style, regardless of where it appears on the screen. outSPOKEN is easy to turn on and off and does not modify the Windows interface, which makes it ideal for use on computers shared with non-outSPOKEN users.

outSPOKEN uses the Windows mouse pointer as a screen review cursor and provides a simple and intuitive keyboard-driven pointer navigation system which allows the user to review even the most complex window layouts with ease. Furthermore, outSPOKEN is able to track and announce all changes of highlighting and focus, permitting seamless use of built-in Windows commands. A wide array of special features and adjustable feedback settings allow the outSPOKEN user to immediately begin working with most standard Windows applications.

outSPOKEN supports over 30 speech synthesizers and a variety of DOS screen readers. This makes it quite likely that outSPOKEN will work with most current hardware and software. Documentation is easy to use, and technical support is extremely responsive to the needs of users.

Reading and Navigation—The outSPOKEN user reads the screen with a set of powerful pointer navigation commands which are issued from the keyboard. As the pointer moves, outSPOKEN speaks the line, word, character, or graphic that corresponds to the location of the pointer. To provide continuity, outSPOKEN restricts reading to the current window, yet makes it easy to move the pointer between windows on the screen. outSPOKEN allows the user to navigate smoothly through complex dialog boxes as well as plain text documents. Its sophisticated understanding of layout and structure allows the user to easily read through list boxes, group boxes, and other graphically grouped controls. This advanced reviewing capability is not available in any other Windows screen reader.

DOS Screen Readers—outSPOKEN is a Windows application. This means that it runs from inside Microsoft Windows. Naturally, it can still read DOS sessions that are opened within Windows. In addition, it supports a large number of DOS screen readers, which enables the outSPOKEN user to read Windows with outSPOKEN while using a DOS screen reader for work with DOS applications.

Supported Hardware—outSPOKEN works with over 30 speech synthesizers including Accent, Artic, Audapter, Braille'n Speak, DECtalk, DoubleTalk, Echo, KeyNote, SoundingBoard, and many more. outSPOKEN is extremely flexible in its handling of input and output; it allows communication with a wide variety of I/O devices, including braille output and speech input. For a current list of supported hardware, contact Berkeley Systems or an outSPOKEN dealer.

Support and Documentation—Berkeley Systems is well-known for its responsive product support and excellent documentation. With the purchase of outSPOKEN for Windows comes unlimited free telephone technical support. Documentation can be followed by users of all levels of ability and is provided on disk, on cassette, in braille, and in print. Each copy of outSPOKEN includes unique tactile diagrams illustrating Microsoft Windows concepts and situations. The look and feel of these Braille diagrams makes them particularly valuable to beginning Windows users; sighted and non-sighted users are able to use the same training materials and communicate in similar terms about the Microsoft Windows environment. This makes outSPOKEN ideal for use on shared computers in an office, public school, or library or at home.

For more information or a demo version of outSPOKEN for Windows, contact: Berkeley Systems, Inc., 2095 Rose Street, Berkeley, CA 94709 (voice: 510-540-5535 ext. 716).

JAWS

JAWS (Job Access With Speech) is a powerful software application program from Henter-Joyce, experts in access technology. Designed to work with a voice synthesizer, JAWS is loaded with features which improve the productivity level of visually impaired employees and the learning ability of blind students. By streamlining keyboard functions, automating commands, and eliminating repetition, JAWS allows the operator to learn faster and easier than ever before. JAWS is based upon an entirely new approach to talking computers—designing software with the priorities of the blind user in mind. Yet the sighted trainer or supervisor has not been forgotten, as JAWS offers both audible and visual flexibility.

Why is JAWS so different? Some of its key features are: (1) dual cursor design, which eliminates the need for "review" mode; (2) built-in autospeak macro keys that make decisions and read the screen automatically; (3) both audible and visible Lotus™-style pop-up menu system; (4) logically designed speech pad which can be operated with one hand; (5) windows for selective screen reading; (6) screen enhancements which recognize monochrome or color automatically; (7) numerous voice configurations; and (8) special "help" mode which makes learning the keyboard quick and easy.

JAWS is being used by employees with disabilities in the following job categories:

- Programmers
- Reservationists
- Customer service representatives
- Operators
- Farmers
- Ministers
- Lawyers
- Rehabilitation counselors
- Computer trainers

For further information, contact: Henter-Joyce, Inc., 10901-C Roosevelt Boulevard Suite 1200, St. Petersburg, FL 33716 (phone: 813-576-5658, U.S. toll free: 800-336-5658, fax: 813-577-0099).

inLARGE 2.0

inLARGE 2.0 is software for the Macintosh that gives people with low vision full access to all mainstream software. Without requiring additional equipment, inLARGE magnifies everything on the screen. As the user types or moves the mouse, the view follows the cursor. inLarge includes the following features:

Macintosh Compatibility—inLARGE works smoothly with System 7 and with both color and black-and-white Macintosh monitors.

Screen Motion Options—Users can choose from "push" mode (magnified area only changes when cursor is moved to an edge of the screen), "continuous" mode (magnified area changes whenever cursor is moved), and "centered" mode (cursor stays fixed at the center of the screen).

Scanning—In scanning mode, users can scan text automatically. Speed, direction, and line height can be customized from the keyboard.

Control Panel Interface—inLARGE can be accessed through a control panel document. All commands can also be performed from the keyboard.

Magnification—inLARGE magnifies from 2 to 16 times. The user can easily adjust the rate of magnification.

Reverse Video—Screen inversion (white letters appear on a black background) works independently of magnification. On color monitors, colors remain true when inversion mode is used.

Crosshair Cursor—The crosshair cursor, for those who prefer to see the cursor as an intersection of two full-screen lines, has customizable width.

Horizontal and Vertical Magnification—For those who find wide letters or tall letters easier to read, inLARGE permits the horizontal and vertical rates of magnification to be defined independently.

Magnifying Glass and Blanking—The size of the "magnifying glass" can be defined by the user, from a small portion of the screen up to the full screen. Unmagnified portions can be blanked out, so that only the magnified area is shown.

Minimum System Requirements—Macintosh Plus or better with 1 MB of RAM, running System 6.05 or later. inLARGE requires 100K of floppy disk or hard disk space.

Cost—$195.00 per single copy. Contact Berkeley Systems for information on discounts, multiple copies, educational institutions, and dealers.

For more information, contact: Berkeley Systems, Inc., 2095 Rose Street, Berkeley, CA 94709 (phone: 510-540-5535 ext. 716, fax: 510-849-9426, TTY: 510-540-0709).

TeleSensory

Closed-circuit television (CCTV) systems offered by TeleSensory come in several monitor sizes and magnification capabilities.

Basic Description—People who have macular degeneration, cataracts, diabetic retinopathy, glaucoma, detached retina, or retinitis pigmentosa may be missing out on the world of print. Over 12 million people have some degree of visual impairment, but there is help!

TeleSensory's innovative CCTVs magnify reading, writing, and other materials up to 60 times the original size. Almost anyone who has some vision can benefit from TeleSensory's family of visual aids. CCTVs have helped over

80,000 people successfully undertake activities they thought were no longer possible.

TeleSensory's CCTVs were designed for professionals, students, and home use. In the office, activities such as reading memos, writing reports, and balancing ledger accounts are accomplished with ease. In the classroom, a student can use the same textbooks, handouts, and library materials that other students use. At home, writing letters, reading newspapers, and pursuing hobbies are all possible again with a video magnifier.

How It Works—Place any book, magazine, or letter on the viewing table. The table glides vertically and horizontally, allowing the text to be viewed. The camera then produces the magnified image on the screen. Controls are conveniently located on the front panel and easy to identify. Users can control magnification, brightness, and contrast to suit individual reading and writing needs.

For information, contact: TeleSensory, 455 N. Bernardo Avenue, P.O. Box 7455, Mountain View, CA 94039-7455 (phone: 415-960-0920, telex: 278838 TSI UR, fax: 415-969-9064, 800-227-8418).

Miniature Electronic Visual Aid

Portability that Succeed—TeleSensory's latest addition to low-vision technology is MEVA (Miniature Electronic Visual Aid). Weighing less than eight pounds, MEVA is the portable member of TeleSensory's family of video magnifiers for reading and writing. The MEVA system includes a hand-held camera, a four-inch flat screen CRT monitor, and magnification lenses. The complete system is carried in an attractive shoulder strap softpack case. Whether used in class, at the office, or while traveling, MEVA allows hours of battery-powered use.

Four different magnification lenses permit a user to select a comfortable reading level of three, four, five, or eight times normal image size when viewed on the four-inch monitor. The high-quality image is displayed in black letters on white background or white letters on black background, depending on personal preference. Users can also switch between digital and analog display mode. MEVA's new digital mode provides enhanced contrast by making dark tones darker while leaving whites bright.

MEVA's camera unit can be connected to TeleSensory's screen magnification monitors.

For information, contact: TeleSensory, 455 N. Bernardo Avenue, P.O. Box 7455, Mountain View, CA 94039-7455 (phone: 415-960-0920, telex: 278838 TSI UR, fax: 415-969-9064, 800-227-8418).

Computer Magnification Systems by TeleSensory

Having limited vision no longer means limited access to computers or video images. TeleSensory's magnification systems allow a person with low vision to magnify computer screens and print documents while easily navigating around a screen and manipulating text or graphics.

For hundreds of tasks—from word processing, to spreadsheet calculations, to electronic mail, to terminal emulation—TeleSensory's large-print computer systems take the lead in providing solutions that work on the job, at school, and at home.

Vista®—TeleSensory's family of powerful color text and graphics magnification (up to 16 times) systems for IBM PC and PS/2 computers and compatibles. Vista is the only screen enlarging system that is completely mouse-controlled. The mouse can be used to stretch an image taller, wider, or both. Users can choose among three distinctive type fonts. With the mouse, automatic scrolling and location of cursor tracking are at one's fingertips. A locator view shows the normal screen with the portion to be magnified in inverse video.

Lynx—Brings video power to Vista by importing video images onto the computer screen in black and white or full color.

Large-Print Display Processor (DP)—The hardware-based solution for users of IBM or Apple computers. DP creates sharp, smooth characters with no software conflicts.

For information, contact: TeleSensory, 455 N. Bernardo Avenue, P.O. Box 7455, Mountain View, CA 94039-7455 (phone: 415-960-0920, telex: 278838 TSI UR, fax: 415-969-9064, 800-227-8418).

MultiVoice

MultiVoice is a voice synthesis product based on Digital's DECtalk™ technology. It can be used by people with communication, learning, and vision disabilities. The technology offers highly intelligible speech, featuring a range of built-in voices—adult male, adult female, and child. It also provides the ability to customize and modify these voices.

MultiVoice is lightweight, portable, and battery powered. It can be used with most computers available on the market today.

MultiVoice is sold and supported directly by the Institute on Applied Technology, Children's Hospital, Boston.

For more information, call or write: Institute on Applied Technology,

Children's Hospital, Fegan Plaza, 300 Longwood Avenue, Boston, MA 02115 (phone: 615-735-6486).

An Open Book: A Reading Machine by Arkenstone

A reading machine is an electronic appliance that scans a printed page and, through an internal synthesized voice, reads the printed material back to the user. A good reading machine is compact, easy to use, and versatile, with a pleasant, tactile surface and a clear voice that uses lifelike intonations.

You don't need to be an electronic whiz to use it. A good reading machine lets you read now or save the scanned material and read it later, building a library of your favorite books.

Arkenstone has created just such a tool. It is called An Open Book, because it is as easy to use as sitting down and opening a book.

Arkenstone's dynamic reading tool is easy to use and can scan most pages with an accuracy of 99% or better. It needs no extra apparatus or cables. All you need is an electrical outlet and something to read.

An Open Book is perfect for home, office, or school. It has memory capability to hold thousands of pages in its internal library. An Open Book can be inexpensively upgraded into a personal computer.

An Open Book is

- *A scanner*—It "sees" the page.

- *A reading machine*—It records, translates, and saves the scanned words into text, to be read back now or later.

- *A pleasant, tactile keypad*—It has easy to remember and use controls.

- *A voice synthesizer*—It reads the scanned page back in a choice of nine different voices.

For information, contact: Arkenstone, 1390 Borregas Avenue, Sunnyvale, CA 94089 (phone: 800-444-4443 (U.S. and Canada), fax: 408-745-6739, TDD: 800-833-2753).

Words+

Words+ is a company dedicated to improving the quality of life for people with disabilities. From the beginning, its goal has been "unlocking the person"—by providing the highest quality communication and computer access systems available.

In 1980, Lucy Evans was experiencing difficulty communicating because of ALS (Lou Gehrig's disease). Walt and Ginger Woltosz, founders of Words+, Inc., were both employed in the aerospace industry—Walt, with two master's degrees, as an engineering manager in a rocket motor company, and Ginger, with a degree in business, as an administrative assistant. Lucy Evans was Ginger's mother.

Unable to locate anything commercially available to help Lucy communicate, they decided to try making their own system based on an early Radio Shack personal computer with 16K of memory and a cassette tape drive. Lucy patiently tried the strategies and switches that they devised for several months until she lost her battle with ALS in October of 1980.

With encouragement from rehabilitation professionals, Walt and Ginger continued work on the system and decided to make a business out of it. Words+, Inc. was incorporated in 1981.

Their first commercially available augmentative communication system based on a personal computer was sold in October 1981 to Stanford Children's Hospital. Since that time, Words+ has been the industry leader in innovations:

- 1983—The first battery-powered portable PC-based augmentative communication system with speech output.

- 1986—The first commercially available augmentative communication system capable of using a mouse or trackball; Talking Screen™, the first portable pictographic communication system with a dynamic graphic display, and the first system with adaptive word prediction.

- 1985–88—ACES (Augmentative Communication Evaluation System).

- 1987—The first software voice synthesis, and the first keyboard emulators with speech output.

- 1989—The only keyboard emulator systems with dual word prediction and other advanced features.

- 1990—Instant Phrases™, which provides access to hundreds of thousands of stored phrases/sentences.

- 1992—System 2000™ with every major language strategy, both digitized and synthesized speech in a portable unit; VocaLite™ voice synthesizer; MessageMate™, a small hand-held unit that allows easy recording and playback of short messages; and U-Control™, a low-cost, comprehensive environmental control system.

- 1993—The first color dynamic display system in Talking Screen 4.0; Finger-Foniks, the first one-pound communicator that can say anything and includes both synthesized and recorded speech; Simplicity, the first wheelchair mount that can be lowered without swinging through an arc away from the chair.

- 1994–95—With EZ Keys for Windows and Talking Screen for Windows software, the exciting world of Windows can provide even greater freedom to persons who use AAC and alternative computer access. Windows not only provides the graphical user interface that Macintosh users have long praised, but with Windows comes support for the absolute latest in state-of-the-art technologies for personal computers.

Such exciting new functions as multimedia, for example, can provide both audio and full-motion video on an AAC device. Select a symbol in Talking Screen for Windows and see excerpts from a CD-ROM encyclopedia showing President Kennedy as he gave his "We choose to go to the moon" speech. See and hear a space shuttle launch; watch and listen to the astronauts as they float a banana across the inside of the space shuttle in zero gravity. The possibilities are nearly endless!

EZ Keys for Windows users will find a combination communication/computer access system unequaled in its ease of learning and ease of use, speed of communication, and numerous additional functions, both built-in and accessible through thousands of other Windows programs. Gone are the memory problems from the days of DOS. Users can even run several programs at once and jump from one to the other while EZ Keys for Windows remains active in all of them.

Words+ continues to be at the cutting edge of the state-of-the-art in augmentative communication and computer access. Its policy of free software upgrades for life means that software stays up to date.

From world-renowned astrophysicist Dr. Stephen Hawking to preschool children, the success of Words+ users is both an inspiration and a testimony to the effectiveness of its systems. Words+ helps in the process of "unlocking the person" and in providing a substantial improvement in the quality of its users' daily lives.

Its new products reflect the fact that Words+ listens to what users want—friendly, menu-driven systems with on-line help; solid products that keep on working in the punishing environments that augmentative communications system often experience; high-quality voice output; fair prices; a friendly voice on the telephone when customers have a question or a problem; and an understanding of what users are dealing with from day to day, because they've been there.

For information, contact: Words+, 40015 Sierra Highway, Building B-145, Palmdale, CA 93550 (phone: 800-869-8521).

Viewpoint VGA

HumanWare, Inc. manufactures the Viewpoint VGA, a hand-held camera with computer access (CCA). It provides a convenient, economical system that can combine, on one screen, an enlarged image of reading materials or handwriting with a magnified computer display.

Viewpoint VGA offers three models, each of which incorporates a unique hand-held CCD camera. Users can also choose a screen type and size to suit their individual visual needs.

Individuals who need to access a computer in their job, studies, or leisure pursuits can choose one of the computer-compatible models of the Viewpoint VGA and integrate all their large-print information on one display screen.

To magnify handwriting, a Handwriting Stand can be added to any Viewpoint VGA system.

Viewpoint VGA is a truly elegant solution to large-print access needs, yet it takes up no more room than a personal computer. In fact, those who already have a computer with a VGA display screen can create a complete large-print workstation simply by adding the Viewpoint VGA control unit and camera.

Reading with the Viewpoint VGA is a very simple process. Just switch on the system, place the camera on the reading material (the camera is instantly in focus), select a suitable magnification with the push-button controls, and start reading.

The Viewpoint VGA uses a revolutionary CCD camera that fits comfortably in a user's hand and can be rolled over any printed or handwritten text to produce an enlarged image on the display screen.

Magnification ranges from 8 to 32 times. The appropriate size is selected electronically with the touch of a button. Perfect focus is maintained at each magnification setting.

For information, contact: HumanWare, Inc., 6245 King Road, Loomis, CA 95650 (phone: 800-722-3393).

Microsystems Software, Inc.

Microsystems offers several adaptive access software systems for the sight-impaired and physically disabled individual.

MAGic—Magnifies text or graphics instantly and smoothly. The basic package enlarges up to two times. The Deluxe version offers magnification of text up to 12 times and Windows magnification up to 8 times. The Deluxe version also offers smooth fonts, eight-direction smooth panning, and screen locator.

HandiWORD—Word prediction software that provides abbreviation expansion and macro capabilities to increase computer input rates and lower fatigue for persons with limited keyboarding ability. HandiWORD learns the user's vocabulary and presents options in order of frequency used. The user simply chooses from the list when the desired word or expansion is displayed, and HandiWORD completes the entry. The Deluxe version provides foreign language translation dictionaries to/from English for French, Spanish, German, and Italian.

HandiKEY—Provides an input alternative for those who cannot use a keyboard. Using an external switch device (e.g., mouse, head mouse, foot switch, trackball, sip-and-puff), the user selects information or commands from on-screen matrices. Delivered with a comprehensive set of matrices, the user can completely modify each cell and enter up to 2000 characters. The Deluxe version adds the ability to support speech output with standard voice synthesizer equipment.

HandiCODE—Provides extensive PC input and control using Morse code with single, dual, or triple switches. Input speeds are governed only by the user's ability. Powerful macro capabilities allow for extensive abbreviation expansion. HandiCODE supports both text- and graphics-based programs and can be used for speech output. The Deluxe version adds the complete HandiWORD software.

HandiCHAT—Gives voice to words on the computer screen so that people with speech impairments can more readily communicate. It works with most industry standard text-to-speech synthesizers to vocalize any text in the "chat window" or any line, sentence, or screen displayed. The Deluxe version adds a predefined phrase window with 1300 commonly used statements.

HandiPHONE—Provides hands-free access to standard phone systems. Access is through devices such as voice recognition products, switches, trackball, mouse, or joystick. Microsystems' PopDIAL software holds up to 10,000 names and 30,000 phone numbers so users can dial, receive calls, and access voice mail systems, paging, call transfer, call waiting, and other popular services. The complete system includes a specially modified modem, a hands-free speakerphone or headset, and cables.

HandiSHIFT—Makes executing multiple-key keyboard commands easy by using a single finger or device. It includes two-key and three-key combinations such as "Ctrl-C" and "Ctrl-Alt-Del." The user can choose between "shift-the-next-character" or between two forms of "shift-lock."

SeeBEEP—Turns a PC's audible beep into a visual screen display to aid people with hearing impairments. This tiny utility alerts the user to errors, messages, or other events typically reported by an audible sound.

TEAM—Lets the user take full command of his or her home or work environment. The Transparent Environment Access Module (TEAM) can activate alarms, appliances, lights, televisions, and relays via computer from within any PC application. The user can design a control system to meet individual needs. All connections to devices are wireless and easy to install using X-10 modules or infrared controllers.

ADAPTA-LAN—Delivers all the HandiWARE and MAGic adapted access software to users on a local area network. This package brings all of the Deluxe versions to users in one easy solution. ADAPTA-LAN supports most LAN operating systems and meets government-mandated ADA requirements at an affordable, low cost.

Demonstration Software—A free demonstration version of each software product is available on disk or directly from Microsystems' own bulletin board system (508-875-8009). In addition, low-cost packages with demonstration versions of all software, manuals, and hardware can be ordered. A complete evaluation package also is available.

For a complete catalog or to find a local dealer, contact Microsystems Software, Inc., 600 Worcester Road, Framingham, MA 01701 (phone: 508-879-9000 or 800-828-2600, fax: 508-879-1069).

The Eyegaze System

The Eyegaze System allows people with physical disabilities to operate a computer with their eyes. By looking at control keys displayed on a computer monitor, they can synthesize speech, control their environment (lights, appliances, television, etc.), type, operate a telephone, and run computer software.

A specialized video camera mounted below the computer monitor observes one of the user's eyes. Sophisticated image-processing software in the computer continually analyzes the video image of the eye and determines where on the computer screen the user is looking. Nothing is attached to the user's head or body.

With the *Typewriter* program, the user types by looking at keys on visual keyboards. Four keyboard configurations, from simple to complex, are available. Typed text appears on the screen above the keyboard display. The user may also "speak" or print what he or she has typed.

The *Telephone* program allows the user to place and receive calls. Frequently used numbers are stored in a telephone "book." Non-verbal users can access the speech synthesizer to talk on the phone.

The *Phrases* program, in conjunction with a speech synthesizer, provides quick communications for non-verbal users. Looking at a key causes a preprogrammed message to be spoken. The system accommodates up to 126 frequently used phrases.

For information, contact: LC Technologies, Inc., 9455 Silver King Court, Fairfax, VA 22031 (phone: 800-733-5284 or 703-385-7133, fax: 703-385-7137).

DynaVox and DynaWrite

DynaVox is an augmentative communication aid for the voice-impaired individual. Using this equipment, the individual can compose messages (displayed on a small screen) and save, reload, and re-edit them as needed. Finished compositions can then be displayed or spoken at a user-controlled pace or output to a printer for hard copy.

For information, contact: Sentient Systems Technology, Inc., 2100 Wharton Street, Pittsburgh, PA 15203.

Direct Computer Access by Pointer Systems

Pointer Systems presents some of the most powerful tools available to help people with a variety of motor impairments use computers and communicate. Pointer Systems' products provide full direct access to the vast majority of mainstream computer hardware and software currently in use. In addition, they are affordable and easy to use, even for those unfamiliar with computers. The products enable people to "type" without using the keyboard. Users select "keys" from an on-screen keyboard image. Products are easily adjusted to meet the needs of the individual user.

With Pointer Systems' products, people with cerebral palsy, multiple sclerosis, ALS, and other neuromuscular impairments, as well as amputees, quadriplegics, and those with high-level spinal cord injuries and impairments resulting from a stroke, can access IBM and compatible personal computers and Macintosh and Apple IIGS computers. These individuals now have the power to perform any of the following functions with independence:

- Use the same computers and software as the able-bodied population

- Write and print letters, school papers, and other documents

- Qualify for jobs in data entry, bookkeeping, etc. which require use of a computer
- Dial the phone or dial into computer bulletin boards
- Control lights, heat, or appliances at home
- The non-vocal can use their computers to speak for them

Pointer Systems uses several technologies and systems to achieve computer access for the disabled. One example is its FreeWheel system which offers optical head-pointing computer access for persons with physical disabilities. The FreeWheel System, for the IBM and compatible personal computers, is designed for people who have good head movement and control. An infrared optical pointer provides cursor control, which in turn provides access to all keyboard functions.

Wearing only a lightweight reflector, the user "types" using only small movements of the head, without being physically "tethered" to the hardware for maximum independence.

For information, contact: Pointer Systems, Inc., One Mill Street, Burlington, VT 05401 (phone: 802-658-3260).

HeadMaster Plus

HeadMaster Plus from Prentke Romich Company provides computer access to individuals who cannot use their hands but have good head control. This equipment works with Macintosh or IBM computers without special adapters.

The HeadMaster Plus uses the operator's head movements to exactly imitate a desktop mouse. The head movements are captured by ultrasound imaging and converted to electrical signals identical to those produced by a normal mouse. Since the unit connects to the computer's regular mouse port, the computer operates as if a normal mouse were attached.

For further information, contact the computer access department at: Prentke Romich Company, 1022 Heyl Road, Wooster, OH 44691 (phone: 800-262-1984, fax: 216-263-4829).

Conference-Mate

The Conference-Mate Infrared Listening System is a technically advanced assistive listening device. Designed and developed to provide a "barrier-free" business environment for the hearing impaired, the Conference-Mate Infrared

Listening System offers one solution for satisfying the requirements set forth by the recently enacted Americans with Disabilities Act.

High-Tech, Yet User Friendly—The heart of the system is the revolutionary Conference-Mate tabletop microphone/transmitter. Housed within an attractive hardwood enclosure, measuring only five and one half inches in diameter and three inches high, it is a patented ultra-sensitive, omni-directional microphone system and infrared transmitter. Placed in the center of a conference table, desk, or other hard surface, the device equalizes the sound level of each speaker's voice and transmits a crystal clear signal by way of safe, invisible infrared light to each listener's wireless headset.

The Conference-Mate Infrared Listening System utilizes the world's lightest wireless audio headset. Weighing only 1.4 ounces, including the small rechargeable battery, the headset is so physically comfortable and natural sounding that the wearer will virtually forget that it is there. Featuring excellent sound quality, each headset can be adjusted by way of a built-in volume control to a level best suited for each individual listener. The performance of the headset, as well as the overall system, is in no way hampered by the virtually limitless number of headsets that can be used with one tabletop unit.

For information, contact: Conference-Mate Systems, 466 Kinderkamack Road, Oradell, NJ 07649 (phone: 201-967-5500, fax: 201-967-9078).

ABLEDATA

ABLEDATA is an extensive and dynamic database that lists information on assistive technology available both commercially and non-commercially from domestic and international manufacturers and distributors.

The field of assistive and rehabilitation technology holds much promise for people with disabilities. It is one of many keys that can unlock the doors to a life of greater independence for people with disabilities. However, assistive technology is nothing but another unfulfilled promise unless current, usable information on existing assistive devices and services is made available to any and all information seekers.

ABLEDATA is a mechanism through which this promise can be fulfilled. It is an information system that enables persons with disabilities to identify and locate the devices that will assist them in living a more independent life at home, work, school, or in the pursuit of leisure activities. ABLEDATA is a resource for practitioners, researchers, engineers, and advocates in the rehabilitation field. It is a means of communicating information between manufacturers, developers, and vendors of assistive technology and the consumers of such technology.

ABLEDATA is a meeting point of current assistive technology, future developments, and ever-present consumer needs.

ABLEDATA is available to all information seekers regardless of race, creed, age, gender, and type or severity of disability. ABLEDATA search information is available in large print or braille, on tape or diskette, and in Spanish on request.

For information, contact: ABLEDATA, Silver Spring Centre, 8455 Colesville Road, Suite 935, Silver Spring, MD 20910-3319 (phone: 800-227-0216).

APPENDICES

Resources

I

"Steps to Success: A Blueprint for Employing Individuals with Disabilities," developed by the Industry-Labor Council, National Center for Disability Services, Albertson, New York, provides an extensive list of resources in the following areas:

- Accessibility
  - General
  - Surveys/consultants

- Alternative dispute resolution

- Council of State Administrators of Vocational Rehabilitation

- Disability management/return to work

- Disability-specific organizations

- Federal enforcement agencies
  - Americans with Disabilities Act
  - The Rehabilitation Act of 1973
  - Vietnam-Era Veterans' Readjustment Assistance Act of 1974

- Job analysis

- Labor–management cooperation

- Magazines targeted to persons with disabilities

- Medical examinations

- Reasonable accommodation
  - Alternative testing formats
  - Braille
  - Captioning
  - General
  - Sign language interpreters

- Recruitment
- Tax credits and deductions
- Telecommunications relay services
- Training
  - Accessibility
  - General or disability specific
  - Interviewing
  - Packaged programs

ADA in Action: Supervisor's Guide

II

Courtesy Commonwealth Edison Company

Commitment to the Americans with Disabilities Act

On July 26, 1992, the Americans with Disabilities Act (ADA) becomes law. Commonwealth Edison's goal is to actively support the intent and spirit of this law. Our long-standing commitment to hiring and promoting qualified, talented, capable individuals, including those with disabilities, is consistent with the ADA. This commitment is also consistent with the Restatement of Equal Employment Opportunity Policy, our Collective Bargaining Agreements and our tradition of being a responsible corporate citizen. We recognize the value to the Company of providing employment opportunities, premises and services that are accessible to all customers, applicants and employees, including those with disabilities. All of our employees are expected to understand and act in accord with this commitment.

James J. O'Connor
Chairman

Commonwealth Edison has a long-standing tradition of providing equal opportunity and reasonable accommodation for individuals with disabilities.

The Americans with Disabilities Act of 1990 (ADA) established formal guidelines for employing disabled individuals. With the potential of affecting nearly 43 million disabled Americans, this Act represents one of the most significant changes in the federal regulation of private sector employers since the Civil Rights Act of 1964.

The ADA's goal is "to provide a clear and comprehensive national mandate for the elimination of discrimination against individuals with disabilities." Title I of the ADA, which is specific to employment, is effective on July 26, 1992.

To you—supervisors and managers at Commonwealth Edison—the ADA represents not only a chance to refine existing efforts to provide equal opportunity and reasonable accommodations, but a challenge to make our workplace approachable to all.

This booklet has been created specifically for your reference. It offers basic information about the ADA and outlines specific actions that Commonwealth Edison has already taken to comply with the ADA.

- *ADA Overview* explains the key terms you should know and summarizes the highlights of Title I of the Act.

- *Making It Work* gives you information on how you can be more aware of your actions when interviewing or working with people with disabilities.

- *Reasonable Accommodation Process* reviews the ADA's guidelines for reasonable accommodation and the procedure that Commonwealth Edison is using to meet those standards.

To test your understanding of the ADA, take the following quiz; then review the answers at the end of this booklet.

You can direct questions about this booklet or the Act itself to your local Human Resources office.

ADA Awareness Quiz

Circle True or False

True   False   1. Pre-offer medical examinations are permitted under the ADA.

True   False   2. When conducting job-related interviews, it is appropriate to question a candidate about his/her disability since this may affect his/her ability to do the job.

True   False   3. A Human Resources Representative/Test Administrator is required to provide an accommodation for the testing process if he/she knows beforehand that an individual has a disability that impairs sensory, manual or speaking skills.

True   False   4. An employer is always obliged to accommodate an employee or applicant once a disability is known.

True   False   5. When talking to a person using a wheelchair, you should try not to use common expressions such as "Let's sit down" and "Walk this way."

True   **False**   6. Accommodation always means having to make expensive structural changes to facilities or work sites.

True   **False**   7. Persons with a disability are better employees than persons who are not disabled.

True   **False**   8. When adequately trained and properly placed, persons with a disability are just as safe on the job as any other group of workers.

Check all that apply

9. Which of the following could be considered a "disability" under the ADA?

- ❑ (a) muscular dystrophy
- ❑ (b) epilepsy (controlled by medication)
- ❑ (c) cosmetic disfigurement
- ❑ (d) emotional illness
- ❑ (e) pregnancy
- ❑ (f) drug addiction
- ❑ (g) speech and hearing impediments
- ❑ (h) HIV infection
- ❑ (i) old age
- ❑ (j) exhibitionism
- ❑ (k) broken limb

10. Which of the following are evidence that a particular activity is an essential job function?

- ❑ (a) the employer's judgment
- ❑ (b) written job descriptions
- ❑ (c) terms of a collective bargaining agreement
- ❑ (d) marginal functions that are incidental to the performance of the fundamental job functions
- ❑ (e) because I say so
- ❑ (f) consequences of not performing the task
- ❑ (g) amount of time spent performing the function
- ❑ (h) past work experience of incumbents in similar jobs

ADA Overview

ADA at-a-Glance

Who is protected by Title I of the ADA? A qualified individual with a disability is:

- an individual with a disability who meets the skill, experience, education and other job-related requirements of a position held or desired, and who, with or without reasonable accommodation, can perform the essential functions of a job.

Who is a person with a disability? The ADA definition of an individual with a disability is very specific. A person with a "disability" is an individual who:

- has a physical or mental impairment that substantially limits one or more of his/her major life activities
- has a record of such an impairment, or
- is regarded as having such an impairment.

What are the essential functions of a job? Job functions are essential if:

- employees in the position are actually required to perform the function
- removing that function would fundamentally change the job, or
- the position exists to perform the function.

What is a reasonable accommodation? Reasonable accommodation is a critical component of the ADA's assurance of nondiscrimination. Reasonable accommodation is any change in the work environment or in the way things are usually done that results in an equal employment opportunity for an individual with a disability that does not create an undue hardship on the employer.
Accommodations may include:

- making facilities readily accessible to and usable by an individual with a disability
- restructuring a job by re-allocating or redistributing marginal job functions
- altering when or how an essential job function is performed
- offering part-time or modified work schedules
- obtaining or modifying equipment or devices
- modifying examinations, training materials or policies
- providing qualified readers or interpreters

- reassigning the individual to a vacant position
- permitting use of accrued paid leave or unpaid leave for necessary treatments
- providing reserved parking for a person with a mobility impairment
- allowing an employee to provide equipment or devices that an employer is not required to provide.

A reasonable accommodation must always consider two unique factors:

- the specific abilities and functional limitations of a particular applicant or employee with a disability, and
- the specific functional requirements of a particular job.

Americans with Disabilities Act of 1990 (ADA) Title I—Employment

Effective Date

Federal law effective July 26, 1992.

General Purpose

Title I (Employment) prohibits a "covered entity from discriminating against a qualified individual with a disability in regard to job application procedures, hiring, advancement, discharge, compensation, job training and other terms, conditions and privileges of employment."

A "covered entity" is defined as an employer, employment agency, labor organization or joint labor management committee.

Employers Affected

The law applies to entities employing 25 or more employees as of July 26, 1992, and 15 or more employees as of July 26, 1994. The Act prohibits discrimination against disabled individuals in the following areas: employment, public services, public accommodations and telecommunications.

Definition of Disability—A person is considered disabled if he or she meets one of three tests: 1) a physical or mental impairment that substantially limits one or more major life activities, 2) a record of such an impairment, or 3) is regarded as having such an impairment.

Physical or Mental Impairments—Physical impairments include:

- physiological disorder or condition

- anatomical loss affecting one or more of the following body systems: neurological, musculoskeletal, special sense organs including speech organs, respiratory, cardiovascular, reproductive, digestive, genitourinary, hemic or lymphatic, skin and endocrine.

Mental impairments include:

- mental retardation
- organic brain syndrome
- emotional or mental illness
- specific learning disabilities.

Also included are conditions, diseases or infections such as: orthopedic, visual, speech and hearing impairments, cerebral palsy, epilepsy, muscular dystrophy, multiple sclerosis, infection with the Human Immunodeficiency Virus, cancer, heart disease, diabetes, drug addiction and alcoholism.

The term disability *does not* include: homosexuality, bisexuality, transvestism, pedophilia, transsexualism, exhibitionism, voyeurism, compulsive gambling, kleptomania or pyromania. The term also does not include gender identity disorders, current psychoactive substance use disorders, induced organic mental disorders, any other sexual behavior disorders and current illegal drug use.

Substantially Limits—A person is considered disabled when the condition, manner or duration of an individuals' important life activities are significantly restricted compared to the average person in the general population.

Major Life Activities—They may include:

- caring for one's self
- performing manual tasks
- walking
- seeing
- hearing
- breathing
- learning
- working.

This list is not exhaustive.

Drug and Alcohol Rules—For purposes of this Act, a qualified individual is not covered if he or she currently engages in the illegal use of drugs or is under the influence of alcohol.

However, an individual is covered under this Act if:

- the individual has successfully completed a supervised drug rehabilitation program and no longer uses illegal drugs, or has otherwise been rehabilitated and no longer uses illegal drugs, or
- the individual is participating in a supervised rehabilitation program and no longer uses illegal drugs, or
- is erroneously regarded as using illegal drugs or under the influence of alcohol.

An individual who is a recovered alcoholic or who has successfully completed a supervised rehabilitation program is also covered under the Act as a person with a disability.

Discrimination Prohibited Under Title I of the ADA

1. Discriminating on the basis of a disability by employers with respect to all terms, conditions and privileges of employment.

2. Limiting, segregating or classifying a job applicant or employee in a way that adversely affects the opportunities or status of such person because of his or her disability.

3. Participating in a contractual agreement or other arrangements or relationships that would subject an employer's qualified applicant or employee with a disability to the discrimination prohibited by this title. (This applies to employment or referral agencies, labor unions, any organization providing fringe benefits to the covered entity or an organization providing training or apprenticeship programs.)

4. Utilizing standards, criteria or methods of administration that have the effect of discrimination on the basis of a disability or that perpetuate the discrimination of others who are subject to common administrative control.

5. Excluding or otherwise denying equal jobs or benefits to a qualified individual because of the known disability of a person with whom the qualified individual is known to have a relationship or association.

6. Using qualification standards, employment tests or other selection criteria that screen out or tend to screen out an individual with a disability or a class of individuals with disabilities—unless the standard, test or criteria as used by the entity is shown to be job-related and consistent with business necessity.

7. Failing to select and administer tests concerning employment in the most effective manner to ensure that such tests accurately reflect the skills, aptitude or other factors, rather than reflecting the impaired sensory, manual or speaking skills of an employee or applicant (except where such skills are the factors that these tests purport to measure).

8. Not making reasonable accommodations to the *known* physical or mental limitations of an otherwise qualified individual with a disability who is an applicant or employee, unless the employer can show that the accommodation will pose an *undue hardship* on the operation of the employer's business.

9. Denying employment opportunities to a job applicant or employee who is an otherwise qualified individual with a disability, if such denial is based on the need of a covered entity to make reasonable accommodation to the *known* impairments of the employee or applicant.

Reasonable Accommodation—A reasonable accommodation should be made on a *case-by-case* basis. Accommodations may include:

- making existing facilities used by employees readily accessible to and usable by individuals with disabilities
- restructuring a job (applies to non-essential functions of a job)
- offering part-time or modified schedules
- reassigning an individual to a vacant position (does not apply to applicants)
- acquiring or modifying equipment or devices
- appropriately adjusting or modifying examinations, training materials or policies
- providing qualified readers and interpreters.

This list is not exhaustive.

Essential Functions—A qualified individual with a disability is one who, with or without reasonable accommodation, can perform the essential functions of the job.

The term "essential functions" applies to primary job duties that are intrinsic to the position the individual holds or desires. The term does not include the *marginal* functions that are incidental to the performance of primary job functions.

A job function may be considered essential for several reasons including, but not limited to, the following: a) it is essential because it is the reason the position exists, b) there is a limited number of employees among whom the job function can be distributed, and c) this function is highly specialized and the incumbent holds the position because of his/her expertise in performing that job function.

Evidence of whether or not a job function is essential includes the employer's judgment, written job descriptions prepared before ads or interviews, the amount of time spent performing the function, the consequences of not requiring the function to be performed, terms of a collective bargaining agreement and past and current work experiences of incumbents in similar jobs.

Undue Hardship—An action that requires significant difficulty or expense when considering a reasonable accommodation is considered an "undue hardship." Factors to consider when determining if an accommodation would pose an undue hardship are:

- nature and cost of needed accommodation
- site factors: financial resources, number of persons employed, effect on expenses and resources
- the overall financial resources of the covered entity, overall size, number of employees, and number, type and location of facilities, and
- the relationship between the site and overall covered entity

Pre- and Post-Employment Inquiries and Medical Examinations

1. Pre-Offer—The ADA prohibits pre-offer employment inquiries regarding whether an individual has any disabilities that will inhibit his/her performance of the job. The employer may ask about the person's ability to perform job-related functions.

2. Post-Offer, Pre-Employment—An employer may conduct a medical examination after an offer of employment has been made, but before employment begins. An employer may condition an offer to commence employment on the results of the examination provided that:

- All entering employees in the same job category are subjected to the same examination process.
- Information regarding the medical condition is collected and maintained on separate forms and in separate medical files and is treated as a confidential record except that: 1) supervisors and managers may be informed regarding necessary restrictions on the work or duties of the employee and necessary accommodations, 2) first aid and safety personnel may be informed, as appropriate, if the disability might require

emergency treatment, or 3) government officials investigating compliance with the Act are provided relevant information on request.

A drug test is not considered a medical exam, but must meet the same standards as other post-offer, pre-employment medical exams.

3. Post-Offer, Post-Employment—An employer cannot require a medical examination from—or make inquiries of—an incumbent employee regarding the existence of a disability or the severity of a disability, unless the examination or inquiry is shown to be job-related and consistent with business necessity.

An employer may conduct voluntary medical examinations including voluntary recording of medical history as part of an employee health program available to all employees at the work sites. The results of the examinations can be used only in accordance with the provisions of the Act.

The ADA does not automatically pre-empt medical standards or safety regulations established by federal laws or regulations. It does not pre-empt state or local laws or regulations that are consistent with the ADA and are designed to protect the health and safety of others from individuals who pose a direct threat that cannot be eliminated by reasonable accommodation.

Insurance

An employer cannot discriminate on the basis of a disability by failing to provide health insurance coverage equal to that offered to individuals without disabilities. Individuals with disabilities must have equal access to the coverage that the employer provides to all employees. Pre-existing condition clauses are not prohibited provided they are not used as a "subterfuge to evade the purposes of the ADA." Employer policies may also limit coverage for certain procedures or treatments, or limit the types of drugs or procedures covered. Any limitations, however, must be applied equally to all employees.

Enforcement

The ADA will be enforced by the Equal Employment Opportunity Commission (EEOC).

Remedies

An ADA case may be tried before a jury. The jury may award any or all of the following: the position sought, back pay, retroactive seniority, compensatory ("pain and suffering") and punitive damages, attorneys' fees, costs and other relief that the jury decides is appropriate. In some instances, front pay or orders that affirmative action programs be implemented may be awarded.

Other Applicable Laws

Federal, State and Local Laws—The ADA does not pre-empt local and state laws that are equal or greater in coverage.

Federal—The Rehabilitation Act of 1973 requires that all federal contractors of $2,500 or more not discriminate against qualified individuals with handicaps. The Rehabilitation Act uses the term "individuals with handicaps." It defines that term as any person who:

- has a physical or mental impairment which substantially limits one or more of such person's major life activities
- has a record of such impairment, or
- is regarded as having an impairment.

This is essentially the same definition used by the ADA in defining an individual with a disability. While employers must provide reasonable accommodation, they may exclude persons who cannot perform the essential functions of the job.

City of Chicago—The Chicago Human Rights Ordinance covers any employers employing one or more employees. The Chicago Commission on Human Relations is the regulatory agency that enforces the Ordinance.

The Ordinance prohibits any employer from directly or indirectly discriminating against any individual in hiring, classification, grading, discharge, discipline, compensation or other terms or conditions of employment because of the individual's race, color, sex, age, religion, disability, national origin, ancestry, sexual orientation, marital status, parental status, military discharge status or source of income. No employment agency may directly or indirectly discriminate against any individual in classification, processing, referral or recommendation for employment because of the individual's race, color, sex, age, religion, disability, marital status, national origin, ancestry, sexual orientation, parental status, military discharge status or source of income.

The prohibitions contained in this paragraph do not apply to the hiring or selecting between individuals for bona fide occupational qualifications.

Illinois—The Illinois Human Rights Act covers employers with 15 or more employees and is enforced by the Illinois Department of Human Rights. Under the Interpretive Rule of the Illinois Human Rights Commission that regulates the Act, "determinable physical or mental characteristics exclude transitory and insubstantial conditions that are not significantly debilitating or disfiguring." In its discussion of alcohol and drug abuse, the Rules state that behavior such as absenteeism, poor quality or quantity of production, or disruptiveness that fails to meet acceptable standards *is presumptively* related to the ability to perform. A complaint must be filed within 180 days of the alleged discriminatory act.

Indiana—The Indiana Civil Rights Law covers employers with six or more employees. The law is silent on issues such as reasonable accommodation and drug and alcohol addiction. Section 22-9-1-13 states that employers are not required to modify any physical barriers or administrative procedures to accommodate a handicapped person.

Sources of Materials

- Americans with Disabilities Act of 1990 (Text)
- Illinois Human Rights Act of 1980
- The Rehabilitation Act of 1973
- Chicago Human Rights Ordinance—1990
- The E.E.O.C.'s Regulations 29 CFR Parts 1602, 1627, 1630
- E.E.O.C. Technical Assistance Manual

Making It Work

Interviewing People with Disabilities

The interview process gives you the opportunity to evaluate a candidate's skills, knowledge and abilities as they relate to a particular job. As with all candidates, conduct each interview with a person who has a disability in a way that focuses on experience, abilities, knowledge and achievements. Your first goal is to determine whether a candidate is able to perform the essential functions of the job—with or without reasonable accommodation.

The interview process also gives the candidate an opportunity to describe his or her qualifications. Be sure to keep communication open so that the exchange of information can flow. For more information on interviewing, consult appropriate Targeted Selection Interviewing guidelines.

It is not uncommon for interviewers to be uncomfortable interviewing an applicant with a disability. This discomfort can stem from a lack of contact with people with disabilities or a general sense of uneasiness because you are uncertain how to act in their presence. Use the following as a guide when interviewing an applicant with a disability.

Remember, an employer may ask questions to determine whether an applicant can perform specific job functions. The questions should focus on the applicant's *ability* to perform the job, not on a disability.

Do This

- Do explain clearly and accurately the job's essential functions.
- Do ask questions about the applicant's ability to perform job-related functions.

    ### Examples:

    "Can you operate a drill press?"

    "Can you push a mail cart?"

    "Can you lift 150 pound?"

    "This job requires a chauffeur's license. Do you have one?"

- Do ask the candidate about job-elated experience and training.
- Do ask all questions in a straightforward, matter-of-fact manner.
- Do look at the applicant directly when addressing them. Deliberately averting your gaze is impolite and can be uncomfortable.
- Do speak directly to the applicant, even if the applicant is accompanied by a helper.
- A sign language interpreter should sit next to you so that the hearing-impaired person can shift his face back and forth from the interpreter to you easily.
- Do relax while listening. Your ear will adjust more quickly to the sound of the applicant's speech.
- Be aware of where wheelchair ramps and restrooms are located so you can refer to them if necessary.
- Involve the candidate with a disability in the appropriate and relevant issues affecting his or her employment so the individual can make in-formed suggestions and decisions.
- You may ask the candidate how he or she would perform the specific duties that are essential to a particular job. Be sure to phrase your questions in terms of performance of duties, not in terms of the candidate's limitations.

    Example: You are interviewing a candidate with a visual impairment for a position that requires reading reports and analyzing their contents about 80 percent of the time. Explain this essential function of the job and ask the individual if he or she can perform that function.

    Ask: "How would you read these reports and analyze them?"

    Do not ask: "You probably wouldn't be able to read these reports, would you?"

Example: You are interviewing a candidate who uses a wheelchair for a position that requires traveling to various system locations. After you explain this essential function of the job, ask the individual if he or she is available to travel.

> *Ask:* "The job will require that you travel weekly to various company locations. How do you feel about that? Will you be able and available to go to company sites?"

> *Do not ask:* "Since you use a wheelchair, you probably wouldn't be able to travel, would you?"

- If the candidate volunteers that he or she could perform the job's essential functions if provided with an accommodation, you may then discuss possible devices, equipment or other recommendations that may assist the applicant in performing the job.

Don't Do This

- You can refuse to hire an individual who currently uses illegal drugs. You cannot refuse to hire someone who has successfully completed a drug rehabilitation program and who is no longer using drugs.

- You cannot refuse to hire an applicant with a disability because the person presents a slightly increased risk of harm to himself or others.

- You cannot deny an otherwise qualified applicant a position based on speculation that he or she won't be able to perform the job in the future, or because by hiring him or her, your workers' compensation or health insurance costs may increase.

- You may not ask a disabled applicant about his or her history of workers' compensation claims at the pre-offer stage.

- You cannot require an applicant to take a medical exam before making a job offer. However, after a job offer is made, you may ask an applicant to take a medical exam if everyone who will be working in that job category will be required to do so as well.

- Do not ask if the candidate has a valid driver's license if this is not an essential function of the job.

- Do not ask a candidate with a disability how he or she will get to work.

- Do not ask a candidate how often an approved leave for treatment would be required.

- Do not ask the applicant about any visible physical characteristics, such as scars, burns or missing limbs.

- Do not tell the applicant that you admire his or her courage. Do not express sympathy for him or her.
- Do not avoid certain questions because you assume that the applicant is sensitive or fragile.
- If a candidate volunteers information about a family member or significant other with a disability, treat this information confidentially. Do not ask questions about the other person's health needs.

Never Ask

- Are you a diabetic?
- Have you ever had a heart attack?
- How long have you been like that?
- Were you born blind?
- Will you ever be able to walk again?
- Have you ever been hospitalized? If so, for what condition?
- Have you ever been treated by a psychiatrist or psychologist? If so, for what condition?
- Is there any health-related reason why you may not be able to perform the job for which you are applying?
- Have you had a major illness in the last five years?
- How many days were you absent from work because of illness last year?

Etiquette for Working with People with Disabilities

Appropriate etiquette is important. Using common sense, courtesy and sensitivity, etiquette allows each of us to show dignity and respect for others. Here are a few examples of how we can let individuals with disabilities know we recognize and respect their desire to control their physical surroundings and their lives. These examples apply to customers and co-workers alike.

- Relax. Be yourself and act naturally. If you are unsure about how to act or communicate with an individual who has a disability, feel free to ask the person what you should do.
- When greeting an individual with a disability, shake whatever the person offers—a hand, prosthesis, hook or elbow.
- When greeting an individual with a vision impairment, always identify yourself and introduce anyone else who might be with you. When talking in a group, announce the name of the person to whom you are speaking. Speak in a normal tone of voice.

- After greeting an individual who uses a wheelchair, sit down so that the person won't have to strain to look up and make eye contact.
- To make it easier for an individual with a hearing impairment to read your lips, face the person, keep your hands away from your mouth and speak normally. It's not necessary for you to over-enunciate.
- When talking with an individual with a speech impairment, ask short questions that require short answers or a nod of the head.
- Don't pretend to understand a response if you don't. Rephrase your questions or comments, or ask the person to repeat what you do not understand.
- Do not be distracted if an individual with an obvious vision impairment does not make eye contact.
- Never lean on a person's wheelchair. The chair is part of the body space that belongs to the person who uses it.
- Never patronize individuals using wheelchairs by patting them on the head or shoulder.
- Don't shout when talking with a person with a hearing impairment. Shouting distorts sounds accepted through hearing aids and inhibits lip reading. If you are having difficulty communicating, try exchanging written notes.
- Listen attentively when you're talking to a person with a speech impairment. Be patient. Don't try to speak for the person who has speech difficulty. Repeat what you do not understand.
- Don't assume that a person with a disability needs or wants assistance.
- Offer assistance in a dignified manner with sensitivity and respect. For example: "How may I help you?" When a more formal offer is appropriate, you could ask: "I hope I don't offend you, but may I be of any assistance?"
- If your offer is accepted, don't assume you know what needs to be done. Ask for—and listen to—instructions.
- Be aware that your offer to help may be declined. If it is, honor the person's wish and do not insist.
- Allow a person with a visual impairment to take your arm, at or about the elbow, enabling you to guide the person.
- Do not play with or pet a guide dog or other service animal because it distracts it from its main responsibility.
- Offer to carry or hold packages. You could ask, for example: "May I help you with your packages?"

- When offering to hang a coat or umbrella, do not offer to hang a cane or crutches, unless the individual requests you to do so.

Appropriate Terms and Expressions

The words and expressions in the left column show respect for people with disabilities. Compare these positive words to their negative counterparts in the right column. By incorporating positive words into our everyday vocabulary, we help shape a positive and constructive attitude toward disabilities. It is as important to stop using inappropriate expressions as it is to begin using appropriate ones.

Appropriate Terms and Expressions	Inappropriate Terms and Expressions
Deaf	Deaf mute, deaf and dumb
Developmentally disabled	Defective
Differently able	Handicapped, afflicted
Hearing impaired	Deaf mute
Mentally retarded	Retard
Mentally/emotionally disabled	Crazy, insane
Mobility impaired	Maimed
Multi-disabled	Invalid, deformed
Nondisabled	Normal
Paralyzed, paralysis	Gimp, crip, cripple, lame, paralytic
Persons with cerebral palsy	Cerebral-palsied
Persons with disabilities, disabled	Poor unfortunate victims, handicapped
Persons with paraplegia	Cripple, withered
Seizure	Spastic, spaz, stricken
Wheelchair user, uses a wheelchair	Confined to a wheelchair, wheelchair
Blind, visually impaired	bound, in a wheelchair

The Reasonable Accommodation Process

The ADA requires that qualified individuals with disabilities be reasonably accommodated to help them perform the jobs they are seeking or currently hold—as long as such accommodations do not impose "undue hardship" on the employer. Making a reasonable accommodation means making a change in the usual way of doing things so that a qualified person with a disability can participate. A reasonable accommodation does not require the employer to do the most expensive or difficult thing to assist the individual with a disability.

Reasonable accommodation can fall into any of the following three categories:

- ensuring equal opportunity in the application process
- enabling a qualified individual with a disability to perform the essential functions of the job
- enabling an employee to enjoy equal benefits and privileges of employment.

The ADA does not require employers to hire unqualified individuals with disabilities. Also, employers are free to select the most qualified applicant available. For example, if two people apply for a job as a typist and fast typing skills are necessary for successful job performance, the employer may hire the applicant with the higher typing speed, whether or not that individual has a disability.

Additionally, the ADA does not require an employer to hire an individual who poses a direct threat (i.e., a significant risk) to the health and safety of himself/herself or others if that risk cannot be lowered to an acceptable level by reasonable accommodation. However, an employer should not simply assume that a threat exists. The employer must establish, through objective medically supportable methods, that there is a significant, specific current risk that substantial harm could occur in the work place.

There are two main components associated with the Company's efforts to provide reasonable accommodations for employees with disabilities. The elements of the first activity are summarized in the "Guide to Identifying Essential Functions." Numerous Company departments worked together to specify what job duties are "essential functions" for specific positions. By definition, the term "essential functions" refers to the fundamental job duties of a position.

The elements of the second activity are described in the "Reasonable Accommodation Procedure." Managers, Supervisors and Human Resources personnel should familiarize themselves with the content of this form since it will be used to document employment decisions as they relate to making reasonable accommodations. As a guide to completion of the form, we have included a flowchart that takes you step-by-step through the process.

Guide to Identifying Essential Functions

The first step in qualifying an individual for a job is to see if they have met the necessary prerequisites, such as education, work experience, training skills, licenses, certificates and other job-related requirements (e.g., communications skills or ability to learn).

The second step is to determine if the individual can perform the essential functions of the job with or without an accommodation.

Ways to identify whether a function could be considered essential:

- first consider whether employees in the position are actually required to perform the function
- then consider whether removing that function would fundamentally change the job.

Reasons why a function could be considered essential:

- the position exists to perform the function
- there are a limited number of other employees available to perform the function, or among whom the function can be distributed
- a function is highly specialized and the person in the position is hired for his or her special expertise or ability to perform it.

Evidence to be considered in determining if a function is essential:

- the employer's judgment
- preparations before advertising or interviewing:
  - job descriptions (Labor Relations, Compensation Programs)
  - job dimensions (Employment Programs)
  - physical demands analysis (Medical, Employment Programs)
- amount of time spent performing the job task
- consequences of not requiring a person in this job to perform the job task
- terms of a collective bargaining agreement
- actual work performed by incumbents and people previously in the job
- other relevant factors:
  - how the organization chooses to do its work (i.e., team structure)
  - the nature of the work operation (e.g., assembly line—one task per individual vs. many tasks per individual).

Reasonable Accommodation Procedure

❑ Employee   ❑ Applicant

Name_____   Location _____

Job Title _____   Department _____

Completed by _____   Date _____

I. Analyze job.

Look at the particular job involved and determine its purpose and essential functions.

II. Consult with the individual with the disability and with medical to find out specific limitations as they relate to the essential functions of the job.

What does the individual indicate as his or her disability?

_____

_____

What essential function(s) is the individual unable to perform without reasonable accommodations?

_____

_____

III. Identify potential accommodations and assess how <u>effective it is for the individual</u>: "Effective for the individual means that the accommodation gives the individual an equally effective opportunity to apply for a job, perform essential job functions or enjoy equal benefits."

What accommodation does the individual suggest?

_____

_____

Is it effective?   ❑ yes ❑ no   If not, why?_____

Is it reasonable? ❑ yes ❑ no   If not, why?_____

Other accommodations identified:

	Effective		Reasonable	
_____	❑ yes	❑ no	❑ yes	❑ no
_____	❑ yes	❑ no	❑ yes	❑ no
_____	❑ yes	❑ no	❑ yes	❑ no
_____	❑ yes	❑ no	❑ yes	❑ no
_____	❑ yes	❑ no	❑ yes	❑ no

IV. Select the most appropriate accommodation.

Which reasonable accommodation best serves the needs of the individual and of the Company?_____

_____

_____

Why? _____

_____

_____

Date accommodation implemented _____

Cost $ _____

Function _____

If no reasonable accommodation is possible, check the reason for this decision.

❑ unduly costly

❑ substantial

❑ extensive

❑ disruptive

❑ would fundamentally alter nature/operation of business

Explain _____

_____

_____

Approved _____   Date _____

      Human Resources

_____   Date _____

      Line Supervision

_____   Date _____

      Employment Programs

Copy to: Employment Programs, Employee Personnel File
You may attach any relevant information that explains the above.

Procedure Flowchart

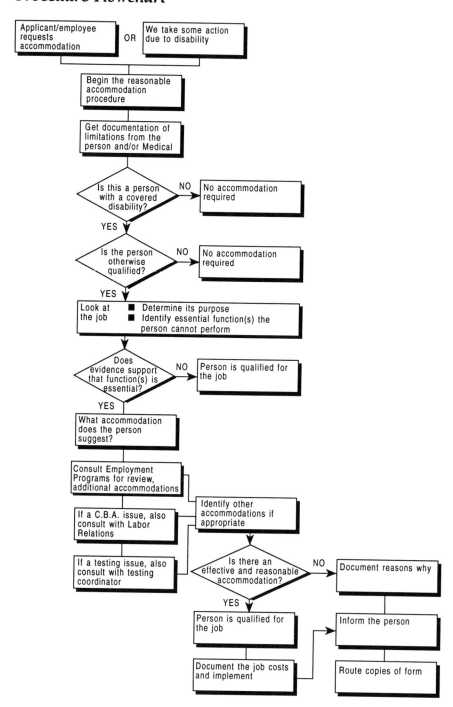

ADA Awareness Quiz Answers

1. Pre-offer medical examinations are permitted under the ADA.

False. An employer may not require a job applicant to take a medical examination, to respond to medical inquiries or to provide information about workers' compensation claims before the employer makes a job offer.

2. When conducting job-related interviews, it is appropriate to question a candidate about his/her disability since this may affect his/her ability to do the job.

False. The ADA prohibits any pre-employment inquiries about a disability. The employer may, however, ask questions about the ability to perform specific job functions and may, with certain limitations, ask an individual with a disability to describe or demonstrate how he/she would perform these functions.

3. A Human Resources Representative/Test Administrator is required to provide an accommodation for the testing process if he/she knows beforehand that an individual has a disability that impairs sensory, manual or speaking skills.

True. The ADA requires that tests be given to people who have impaired sensory, speaking or manual skills in a manner that does not require the use of the impaired skill, unless the test is designed to measure that skill. (Sensory skills include the abilities to hear, see and to process information.) Generally, an employer is only required to provide an accommodation of a test if the employer knows before administering a test that an accommodation will be needed.

4. An employer is always obliged to accommodate an employee or applicant once a disability is known.

False. An employer must reasonably accommodate the known physical or mental limitations of a qualified applicant or employee with a disability, unless the employer can show the accommodation would impose an undue hardship on the business.

5. When talking to a person using a wheelchair, you should try not to use common expressions such as "Let's sit down" and "Walk this way."

False. Common expressions are not puns unless you make them so.

6. Accommodation always means having to make expensive structural changes to facilities or work sites.

False. Among the numerous low- or no-cost accommodations are the following:

- restructure job duties to allow the worker to alternate sitting and standing
- use a job coach to supplement training and supervision
- allow a worker to return to work on a gradual basis.

7. Persons with disabilities are better employees than persons who are not disabled.

False. As workers, persons with a disability are no better or worse than other workers. Pre-screening by a vocational rehabilitation agency does provide employers with qualified, motivated applicants. This may account for the perception that workers with disabilities are better employees.

8. When adequately trained and properly placed, persons with disabilities are just as safe on the job as any other group of workers.

True. When the physical and cognitive demands of a job are well understood and appropriately matched with the skills and abilities of workers with disabilities, they are no more likely to have an on-the-job injury than a person who is not disabled.

9. Which of the following could be considered a "disability" under the ADA?

Condition	Covered ADA Disability	Rationale
(a) Muscular Dystrophy	Yes	It is a physical impairment.
(b) Epilepsy (controlled by medication)	Yes	A person's impairment is determined without regard to any medication or assistive device used.
(c) Cosmetic Disfigurement	Yes	It is a physical impairment if it is considered so by the employer or if the condition affects one of the major body systems (e.g., muscular, circulatory, sensory).
(d) Emotional Illness	Yes	It is a mental impairment.
(e) Pregnancy	No	It is not a covered disability because it is not an impairment—it is a physical condition that is not the result of a physiological disorder; and it is not substantially limiting because it is temporary.

Condition	Covered ADA Disability	Rationale
(f) Drug Addiction	Yes	It is a physical or mental impairment. A person who is currently using drugs illegally is not protected by the ADA.
(g) Speech and Hearing Impediments	Yes	It is a physical impairment.
(h) HIV Infection	Yes	It is a physical impairment.
(i) Old Age	No	It is a physical condition that is not the result of a physiological disorder.
(j) Exhibitionism	No	It is a sexual/behavioral disorder.
(k) Broken Limb	No	A broken leg that heals *normally* would be considered a temporary impairment.

10. Which of the following are evidence that a particular activity is an essential job function?

Evidence of whether or not a job function is essential includes:

(a)   the employer's judgment

(b)   written job descriptions prepared before ads are placed or interviews are performed

(c)   terms of a collective bargaining agreement

(f)   the amount of time spent performing the function, consequences of not requiring the function to be performed and past work experiences of incumbents in similar jobs.

The term "essential functions" does not include:

(d)   the marginal functions that are incidental to the performance of the fundamental job functions

(e)   the individual supervisor's desires, if not based on fact.

References

Commonwealth Edison Company Affirmative Action Plan for Handicapped Individuals

Accommodating Disabilities Business Management Guide
Commerce Clearing House

Americans with Disabilities Act of 1990
EEOC Technical Assistance Manual

Communicating with Employees and Managers About ADA
Bank of America

Compliance Guide to the Americans with Disabilities Act
The Employment Policy Foundation and the Equal Employment Advisory Council
(EEAC)

Sidley & Austin

The Job Accommodation Handbook
RPM Press, Inc.

Disability Awareness Information

1. Windmills

Windmills is a sensitivity training program designed to help participants examine their own attitudes, fears, and biases toward people with disabilities in the workplace. The material includes various booklets and brochures which address employment and reasonable accommodations for persons with disabilities. (Published by the California Governor's Committee for Employment of Disabled Persons, P.O. Box 826880, MIC 41, Sacramento, CA 94280-0001.)

2. Opportunity 2000—Creative Affirmative Action Studies for a Changing Workforce

This book was developed as a project funded by the U.S. Department of Labor. Chapter 3, entitled "Disabled Workers," provides good information on this population group in the U.S. work force. (Available at local bookstores.)

3. AIDS and the Law: A Basic Guide for the Nonlawyer

This book provides a layman's understanding of the legal issues relating to HIV disease. It is designed to help the businessperson understand the legal rights of persons who have AIDS and thereby avoid infringement on those rights as well as potential legal expense. (Published by Hemisphere Publishing Corp., Washington, D.C., ISBN 1-56032-219-5.)

4. Library Search of the Periodical Literature

For articles on the subject of disabled workers and the Americans with Disabilities Act, many local libraries offer access to University Microfilms, Inc. databases. Title, author, journal/magazine, subject covered, and an abstract of each article are provided.

5. Job Accommodation Network (JAN)

JAN, a service of the President's Committee on Employment of People with Disabilities, is a free consulting service that provides up-to-date information on worker accommodation devices and systems. (Telephone: 1-800-232-9675.)

6. Centers for Disease Control (CDC), National AIDS Clearinghouse

The CDC publishes a comprehensive "Manager's Kit" on AIDS. The kit contains booklets on workplace policy and employee education, plus an extensive list of resources. This very professionally developed package is designed specifically for business and is a must for every business library. (Address: P.O. Box 6003, Rockville, MD 20849-6003. Telephone: 1-800-458-5231.)

7. The General Services Administration Information Resources Management Service

The General Services Administration publishes a softcover handbook entitled "Managing End User Computing for Users with Disabilities," prepared by the Clearinghouse on Computer Accommodation of the Information Resources Management Service, General Services Administration. The handbook provides guidance to federal managers and other personnel who are unfamiliar with the application of computer and related information technology to accommodate users with disabilities and provide for their effective access to information resources. Issues reviewed represent lessons learned by agencies and General Services Administration's Clearinghouse on Computer Accommodation. The handbook offers a wealth of information for private industry. (Address: Washington, D.C. Telephone: 202-501-4906 V/TDD.)

8. The U.S. Equal Employment Opportunity Commission (EEOC)

The EEOC publishes an "Americans with Disabilities Act Technical Assistance Manual (Title I)." The manual is designed to explain the basic employment non-discrimination requirements of the Americans with Disabilities Act. The first three chapters provide an overview of Title I legal requirements and discuss in detail the basic requirement not to discriminate against a "qualified individual with a disability," including the requirement for reasonable accommodation. The remaining chapters apply these legal requirements to specific employment practices and activities. (Address: Superintendent of Documents, P.O. Box 371954, Pittsburgh, PA 15250-7954.)

INDEX

413